MASTERPLOTS
FIFTEEN-VOLUME
COMBINED EDITION

Volume Nine
Mari-Nati

MASTERPLOTS

15-Volume Combined Edition

FIFTEEN HUNDRED AND TEN

Plot-Stories and Essay-Reviews

from the

WORLD'S FINE LITERATURE

Edited by

FRANK N. MAGILL

Story Editor

DAYTON KOHLER

VOLUME NINE — MARI-NATI

SALEM PRESS
INCORPORATED
NEW YORK

This work also appears under the title of
MASTERPIECES OF WORLD LITERATURE IN DIGEST FORM

MARIA CHAPDELAINE

Type of work: Novel
Author: Louis Hémon (1880-1913)
Type of plot: Regional romance
Time of plot: Early twentieth century
Locale: Northern Quebec
First published: 1916

Principal characters:

MARIA CHAPDELAINE, a French-Canadian farm girl
SAMUEL CHAPDELAINE, her father
MRS. CHAPDELAINE, her mother
FRANÇOIS PARADIS, a trapper
EUTROPE GAGNON, a farmer-pioneer
LORENZO SURPRENANT, a factory worker

Critique:

This novel is, in part, autobiographical. Hémon, born, reared, and educated in France, emigrated to the Canadian Lake St. John country in 1912. There he worked as a laborer for eight dollars a month on a farm near Péribonka, the village which is named in *Maria Chapdelaine* and which forms part of the background of the novel. On a neighboring farm lived a young woman, Eva Bouchard, who became the heroine of Hémon's novel. Maria Chapdelaine's parents were modeled on Samuel Bedard and his wife, the owners of the farm on which Hémon was employed. The novel had astounding success during the early 1920's, although the author, killed by a train shortly after posting the manuscript, did not live to see that success. As a result of the popularity of this novel, a search was made of Hémon's manuscripts and four other volumes were published.

The Story:

Maria Chapdelaine was a French-Canadian girl whose family lived in the northern part of Quebec province near Lake St. John, a country to which spring came very late in the year and the winters, always severe, came too soon. Maria's father, Samuel Chapdelaine, had moved his family several times to new locations in the north country. Each time he hoped to get away from neighbors and civiliza-

tion, for he was a man who took great delight in the hard work of clearing land from the wilderness but disliked to farm that land after it had been won.

When she was in her late teens, Maria Chapdelaine was sent to spend part of one winter with relatives in town. Her father met her on her return to Péribonka, the settlement nearest to the farm, and they stayed in the village overnight in order to attend church before leaving for their home in the wilderness. At church they met François Paradis, a young man who had lived near the Chapdelaines in another location some years before. Young François Paradis instantly fell in love with Maria and promised to visit the family on his way into the back country to trade for furs with the Indians.

The following summer was one of hard work for the entire Chapdelaine family. The women, including Maria, had their part in putting away food for the winter and taking care of the men's needs as they reclaimed farmland from the forest by cutting away the trees and underbrush and removing the stumps that were left. The first break in the difficult and tedious work came near the end of July, when the blueberries ripened. At that time everyone stopped work to go on a berrypicking expedition.

The night before the berrypicking,

François Paradis arrived at the Chapdelaine cabin. The next day he and Maria wandered off from the rest of the berrypickers. After they had filled their large pails with berries, they sat down to rest. François, in an offhand manner that betrayed the emotion he felt, asked Maria to marry him the following year. He told her that he would be back to visit her once again before going off into the woods to act as foreman of a logging crew during the winter.

The summer passed with all the hard work attendant on carving a farm from the Canadian forests. Before long the winds of winter began to blow, and soon afterward deep snow fell. François Paradis went to the logging camps, as did many of the men, including the two oldest brothers of Maria Chapdelaine.

In the meantime two other suitors for Maria's hand presented themselves. Eutrope Gagnon was a hardworking young man who, like Maria's father, was trying to hew a farm from the wilderness. The other, Lorenzo Surprenant, was a young French-Canadian who had emigrated to the United States to work in a factory. The first of the suitors said very little, knowing he had small chance against François Paradis. The second talked a great deal about the easier life in cities of the United States far to the south. Maria barely listened to his wily talk.

Shortly after Christmas, word came of the tragic death of François Paradis. Leaving the lumber camp to visit Maria and her family during the holidays, he had arrived at a railroad line only to learn that trains were not running. He then set out on foot across barren wastes and forests to reach the Chapdelaine farmstead, but he had lost his way and died of exposure. Maria was greatly saddened by his death, even though their engagement had been only between themselves and no word had been given to her parents or the parish priest. Because of her grief, her father was forced to take her to the village to get advice from the priest. After talking to him, Maria seemed outwardly composed.

The following summer was a bad one for the district, including the Chapdelaine family. Spring came late, drought occurred during the summer, and the snows of winter came several weeks early. Everyone, including Maria, began to wonder if life were worth the struggle against the elements in northern Quebec.

During the second winter, Gagnon and Surprenant still spoke to Maria about marriage, and she, apathetically, listened to them. Gagnon said much less than the other suitor, for he knew that if Maria married him she would merely exchange the hard life on her father's farm for a similar life on his farm. But Surprenant spoke glowingly of life in the Massachusetts city in which he worked and told how much easier urban life in a warmer climate was than rural life in the far north. Maria heard him patiently and with some interest, for the northern wilderness which had swallowed François Paradis had become an enemy to her.

At Christmas time Surprenant made a special trip north to see Maria and to tell her once more how much happier she could be. Almost, but not quite, Maria made up her mind to accept his offer of marriage and leave the wilderness. For Gagnon she had few words; she felt that there was little he had to offer.

Soon after Christmas, Maria's mother fell ill, and nothing the family could do for her seemed to help. At last Samuel Chapdelaine decided to brave the wintry storms to get a doctor. He was successful in reaching the settlement, but when the doctor arrived and examined Mrs. Chapdelaine, he could find nothing to help her, and he advised that they send for the priest. While Chapdelaine went for the priest, the rest of the family decided to call in a skillful bonesetter in whom they had great faith. He, like the doctor, told them he knew of nothing to help the ailing woman. The priest finally arrived and administered the last rites of the Church to Mrs. Chapdelaine, who died soon afterward.

Sitting up with the corpse, to keep her father company during the long hours of night, Maria listened to her father's stories of the aid her mother had given him during his long struggle to carve first one farm and then another from the wilderness. Maria, listening avidly, finally resolved that she, like her mother, could stand the hardships of wilderness life.

When Eutrope Gagnon again spoke of marriage, telling her how he could work in the lumber camps for a winter to earn the money needed to set up housekeeping, Maria agreed that she would wait and marry him when he returned.

MARIA MAGDALENA

Type of work: Drama
Author: Friedrich Hebbel (1813-1863)
Type of plot: Domestic realism
Time of plot: Nineteenth century
Locale: Germany
First presented: 1844

Principal characters:
ANTHONY, a cabinetmaker
ANTHONY'S WIFE
CLARA, his daughter
KARL, his son
LEONARD, Clara's fiancé
THE SECRETARY, a second suitor for Clara's hand

Critique:

Friedrich Hebbel was a playwright and literary critic who has only in recent years been recognized for his important place in the literature of his country. Of his literary work, his dramas are the most important, and this play is generally considered one of his best. In his plays, as in Shakespeare's, we find the tragedy of man as an individual. The consequences that befall his characters are a result of the incurable defects in humans, rather than the results of evils in an entire society. In *Maria Magdalena*, however, we find the tragedy of the individual fused with a new type of realism that was new to all literature of the time and especially the drama. There is an abundance of the details of everyday life in a lower middle-class German household under older family traditions of Germanic culture. The play anticipates the later realism of Ibsen.

The Story:

After a long illness, from which she was not expected to recover, Anthony's wife, a woman in her fifties, felt that she had been given another chance to make herself worthy of heaven. To show her gratitude for another chance, she dressed herself in her wedding gown, which was also to be her shroud, and went to church the first Sunday morning she was able.

Before she went, she and her daughter Clara had a heart-to-heart talk, during which the mother disclosed her fears about her son Karl, who spent too much time drinking and playing, and not enough time working steadily. The mother felt that his attitudes and his conduct were her fault, but still she refused to believe he was really a bad young man.

The mother and Clara also discussed Clara's fiancé, a young clerk named Leonard, who had only a little money and very poor prospects. The mother told Clara that she hoped the girl could find a better man. Shortly after the mother left for church, Leonard came to see Clara and explained that he had not seen her for two weeks for a particular reason. During that time he had been attentive to the mayor's daughter in an effort to get himself a job as clerk for the city.

Leonard also accused her of being in love with another man, even though a very short time before Clara had given herself to Leonard in order to prove her love. After they had straightened out the situation, Leonard told Clara he had come to ask her father for her hand in marriage. Clara assured him that they must soon be married, unless her sin were to show. Even so, she had some misgivings about him when she learned of the chicanery he had executed in securing his position as town clerk.

Her father, when he learned of the proposed marriage and Leonard's prospects, seemed agreeable to the marriage. Then the young man, knowing that old Anthony had a large sum of money out at interest, brought up the question of a dowry. He was surprised to learn, however, that Anthony had called in his money and paid it to help an old man who had befriended him in his youth. When the man had died, Anthony refused to collect from the widow and put the dead man's note in his casket. Leonard began to think that, pregnancy or no, Clara was not a desirable wife for him.

At that time the mother came home from church and told of having seen a newly prepared grave at the churchyard, a grave the sexton dug as an extra, in case it were needed while he was on a holiday. Old Anthony viewed it as an evil omen. Then the talk turned to a jewel robbery at the home of a rich merchant in town. Anthony recalled that his worthless son Karl had done some work at the house on the day of the robbery. Hardly had he said so when bailiffs knocked at the door and demanded permission to search the house for the stolen goods. The shock was so great that the mother swooned and died. Leonard, who was already none too eager to marry Clara, seized upon the charge as an excuse to break his betrothal to the girl.

As the days passed Anthony's house was a place of wretchedness. All evidence seemed to point to Karl's guilt in the matter of the theft, even though the jewels were not discovered in the house. And Anthony began to suspect that Clara had strayed from the paths of virtue. He told her that he wished he had the courage to kill himself, now that everyone in the town was sneering at him for rearing such terrible children. Clara, not wanting to be the cause of her father's death, decided to commit suicide before her father could do away with himself. One day, while Anthony was away visiting a deaf old woodcutter who had not heard of his family's disgrace, the rich merchant appeared at the house with word that Karl was not guilty, that the jewels had been discovered in his own home, where the merchant's own mad wife had hidden them.

Clara, pleased to learn that Karl had been exonerated, believed also that something would occur to make her life right again. Her belief seemed to come true when a childhood sweetheart called to tell her that he still loved her and wished to marry her. Even after Clara told him of her fall from virtue, he said he loved her and would make her his wife. But he also swore that he would arrange a duel with Leonard and seek to kill the man who had seduced Clara. Since the man had a good job as a secretary, Clara knew that her father would be glad to see her married to him. After the secretary left, however, all Clara's doubts again assailed her, and she once more began to think of suicide.

At last Clara decided to go to see Leonard, whom she found planning to fulfill his ambitions by marrying the mayor's daughter. Clara confronted him with the letter he had written her on the day of her mother's death, a letter telling her that he found it impossible to unite himself with the sister of a thief. Even though her brother had been cleared of the charges, Leonard still did not want to marry her, for he knew that a marriage with the mayor's daughter held greater prospects for him. When Clara told him of her father's plans for suicide, Leonard said the old man thought too well of life to take his own. Even though Clara told him she herself contemplated death, he shrugged off her threat, telling her she was not the first woman to be faced with the prospect of producing an illegitimate child. While they spoke, a boy entered with a challenge from the secretary in love with Clara. After Leonard had again refused to marry her, Clara left.

Shortly after her departure the secretary appeared with a pair of pistols, and forced Leonard to leave with him. As they went to fight a duel, Clara, at home, met her brother, who told her of his plans to go to sea. He asked Clara to get him something to eat. She complied and then went to the well, ostensibly to get some fresh water, but actually to drown herself. While she was gone, Anthony returned from his visit with the woodcutter. Soon afterward the secretary, mortally wounded from the duel, staggered to the door. He told how Leonard had been killed and asked old Anthony to forgive the girl. Just as Anthony began to realize that he had been too harsh with Clara, the neighbors came to tell that she had drowned in the well. The secretary pointed out to Anthony that his own weakness and pride had caused him to talk of suicide and thus send his daughter to her death, lest her sin be a reflection on her father. All old Anthony could say was that he no longer understood the world.

MARIANNE

Type of work: Novel
Author: Pierre Carlet de Chamblain de Marivaux (1688-1763)
Type of plot: Novel of manners
Time of plot: Late seventeenth century
Locale: France
First published: 1731-1741

Principal characters:

MARIANNE, COUNTESS OF ———, a virtuous orphan
M. DE CLIMAL, Marianne's benefactor and Mme. de Valville's brother
M. DE VALVILLE, affianced to Marianne
MME. DE VALVILLE, his mother
MLLE. VARTHON, loved by Valville
MLLE. DE TERVIRE, now a nun

Critique:

In his own day, the author of *Marianne: or, The Life of Countess ———* was considerably more famous as a playwright than novelist. During his busy career he wrote some thirty to forty very popular and successful plays, and his three best-known dramas, *Le Jeu de l'amour et du hasard* (1730), *Les Legs* (1736), and *Les Fausses confidences* (1737), are still kept in the repertoires of French dramatic companies. Many critics have asserted that Marivaux was the founder of modern "drawing room" comedy; and others maintain that he was among the first to introduce recognizable features of the modern psychological novel to French prose. His two most significant novels are *Marianne* and *Le Paysan parvenu* (1735), both left incomplete. Both were written in the first person, and each concerned the fortunes of the major character. Like Le Sage, his contemporary, Marivaux created episodic plots and was fully as much interested in moral tales, philosophizing, and analysis as he was in the story itself. In *Marianne,* centered about everyday situations and ordinary people, Marivaux pictured life in France with careful detail. Moreover, the style that he used is still remarkable for its subtleties, its precise but unusual and mannered diction, and its refinement of phrase; in this respect he ranks high among eighteenth-century writers of prose. These qualities make *Marianne* a leisurely-paced but interesting story of an extraordinary woman, enlivened by amiable irony and modest gaiety and charm.

The Story:

The writer, shortly after he rented a country house near Rennes, came upon a manuscript in several notebooks containing the story of a lady, presented in her own handwriting. At the request of his friends the author agreed to edit and publish her account.

Marianne, for this was the name the lady in the autobiography gave herself, was a countess, about fifty years of age at the time she was writing. She explained that she was describing her past because her dear friend had entreated her to tell the full story of her life.

While still an infant, Marianne had been orphaned in an attack by brigands on the coach in which she and her parents were traveling. Since she was the only survivor of this brutal encounter on the highroad, her identity was unknown. Passersby rescued the child and put her in the care of the sister of the local priest. Marianne remained the ward of that kind person until she was fifteen years old. At that time she accompanied her foster mother on a visit to Paris.

Misfortune came to her almost immediately. An epidemic broke out, and all those intimately concerned with Marianne's welfare were fatally stricken. Soon another benefactor appeared, M. de Climal, who offered to aid her out of charitable piety. Marianne was by this time a beautiful young woman, and Climal showed his fondness by buying her expensive clothing and arranging for her lodging with a widowed shopkeeper, Mme. Dutour. Marianne objected strongly to the bourgeois atmosphere of her new home, but her circumstances gave her no other choice. For a religious holiday, she dressed in her finery and strolled about the city after church. The young blades ogled her; one, in particular, was especially attracted to her and she to him, although no words passed between them. Bemused by the encounter, Marianne stepped into the path of a moving carriage and was knocked down.

Her unknown admirer, who was M. de Valville, came immediately to her assistance. At the time neither learned the other's identity, for M. de Climal arrived and jealously insisted on taking his charge home. Beside himself, Climal declared his undying love and offered to set Marianne up in an apartment. Proudly refusing this hypocritical proposal and also his protection, she went to a nearby convent to live. Meanwhile, Valville set about to learn her name and whereabouts. Successful in his search, he arrived at the convent soon after Marianne had acquired a loving benefactress who turned out to be the mother of Valville. Upon the disclosure of their mutual attraction, Mme. de Valville agreed that her son and Marianne could well be in love, but she counseled delay in the affair. In the meantime Climal had succumbed to a fatal illness; as an act of repentance, he bequeathed one-third of his estate to Marianne. The remainder was to go to his nephew, Valville.

As soon as Valville's noble and influential relatives found out about Marianne's dubious parentage and her brief stay with a shopkeeper, they took steps to stop the marriage. In an elaborate abduction scheme, they succeeded in luring Marianne away from the convent. Then she was told that she had two choices: to become a nun or marry a young man they had provided. In the hope of gaining time, she agreed to talk with the prospective bridegroom. Her decision was, however, that she would wed no one but Valville, and she so informed her captors. At that moment, Mme. de Valville and her son caught up with the plot and arrived to defend Marianne. At last the relatives, convinced of Marianne's strength of character, nobility, and worthiness, withdrew their objections to the marriage of Valville and Marianne.

Accordingly, plans for the wedding were made and within a few weeks Marianne was to leave the convent and become a bride. Then a chance call upon friends brought a Mlle. Varthon to the attention of Valville. During a brief illness when Marianne was confined, Valville became infatuated with Mlle. Varthon, who promptly told Marianne of her love for the young man. Deeply grieved by her son's infidelity, Mme. de Valville assured Marianne of her own love and affection, which she continued to shower upon the unfortunate girl until death ended her acts of kindness a short time later. Once more Marianne was alone in the world.

To take Marianne's mind off her misfortunes and to give her a perspective on the curious happenings that befall human beings, a nun who had become very friendly with her suggested that she tell Marianne the story of her own life. Depressed and lonely, Marianne agreed to listen to her account.

The nun, the daughter of M. de Tervire and Mlle. de Tresle, had learned early in life that her father was dead. Sometime later her mother married a grand seigneur of the court, and the young girl was left to the care of a farmer. Although her mother sent money for her support and promised again and again to bring her daughter to live with her in Paris, the invitation was constantly delayed. When she was seventeen years of age, Mlle. de Tervire was sought in marriage by Baron de Sercour. An unscrupulous trick by the baron's heir disgraced the bride-to-be, however, and the marriage never took place. Mme. de Dursan then became the young girl's foster mother. She willed her estate to Mlle. de Tervire, but an estranged son turned up as Mme. de Dursan was dying and the will was changed. When relatives of Mme. de Dursan refused to give the girl her one-third of the property, as had been promised, she decided to go to Paris.

On the stagecoach, she met a Mme. Darcire. Ultimately Mlle. de Tervire discovered that Mme. Darcire knew her mother well. From a lawyer, they learned that Mme. la Marquise, the girl's mother, had been persuaded to turn her estates over to her son. He in turn took all the property and abandoned his mother to poverty. Furious at this turn of events, for the marquise was very ill, Mlle. de Tervire went to her sister-in-law and demanded that her half-brother take proper care of their parent.

(Here the story of Marianne breaks off, for Marivaux never completed his novel. He left Marianne alone and jilted, and the nun still had not ended her life story. In a concluding section, added in 1766 by Marie-Jeanne Riccoboni, Marianne finally married Valville after years of tribulation and learned also that she was of noble birth. The nun's story was terminated with the recounting of a disastrous love affair and her ultimate decision to take the veil.)

MARIUS THE EPICUREAN

Type of work: Novel
Author: Walter Pater (1839-1894)
Type of plot: Philosophical romance
Time of plot: Second century
Locale: The Roman Empire
First published: 1885

Principal characters:

MARIUS, a young Roman of pagan tradition
FLAVIAN, a close friend of Marius at school
CORNELIUS, a Roman army officer and friend of Marius
MARCUS AURELIUS, Philosopher-emperor of Rome
CECILIA, a friend of Cornelius and a Christian leader

Critique:

Pater's novel was an answer to those who had misunderstood his views on art and philosophy. The novel is, in great part, a fictional rendering of Pater's own struggle for a philosophical position, and the personality of Marius is a reflection of the author himself. The volume is also an appreciation of the culture of the second century of the Christian era in Roman Italy. Pater's careful study of the environment, while sharply criticized by historians of fact, has caught the spirit of the times and the people. No one who has not some familiarity with the writers of the time, and before, can read with signal success the intellectual adventures and development of the young Roman who is the central figure of the book; the work is, to some extent, a veritable patchwork of ideas and even quotations from the classical authors who would be the basis of knowledge for a young Roman studying seriously in the reign of Marcus Aurelius.

The Story:

Marius was a young Roman whose family had for many years lived on an estate in northern Italy. On that estate, Whitenights, Marius had grown to adolescence in an atmosphere of pagan piety and rural simplicity. The family led a relatively simple life because Marius' grandfather had squandered much of the family fortune. In that atmosphere of his childhood Marius found a great joy in worshiping the household gods and in overseeing the work on the estate. His life one of contemplation rather than one of activity, his idealism and religiosity were almost morbid in their extreme.

While still in his teens, young Marius was taken to a temple of Aesculapius in the Etrurian hills for the cure of a childhood disease. There the quiet, fresh atmosphere of the place, as well as the teachings of Galen, the great Roman physician, gave him a new outlook on life. Upon his return home, Marius found his mother's health failing. She died shortly afterward, and the effect of her passing on Marius was to turn him into a skeptic, a young man who questioned all aspects of life as they presented themselves to him.

Soon afterward relatives sent young Marius to Pisa, where he attended school. While there, he conceived the idea of becoming a poet of the intellectual school. His inclination in that direction was stimulated by his friendship with a young boy named Flavian, a schoolmate. Flavian, three years older than Marius, had great influence over the younger boy. The two read all of the literature and philosophy they could find. Among the works they pored over was the *Metamorphoses* of Apuleius, the ornate style of which was a source of great joy to Marius.

But the studies in literature and philosophy which the two young men planned were short-lived, for Flavian became sick after an excursion he and Marius made; he died soon after of a plague brought back to Italy by the armies of Marcus Aurelius, who had just returned from a campaign into the eastern reaches of the Empire. After Flavian's death Marius, needing an intellectual crutch to carry him through the agony of seeing his young friend die, was attracted to the study of mysticism. But at last he put aside the desire to turn to Oriental mystic lore and turned to early Greek philosophers to find, if he could, some answer to his problems in their writings and thought.

One of the first writers he studied was Heraclitus, who taught him to limit his labors, lest he lose everything by trying to master all knowledge at once. From Heraclitus he turned to the teachings of Aristippus of Cyrene, founder of the Epicurean school. From his study of Cyrenaic philosophy Marius came to the conclusion that knowledge was limited to experiences received through the senses, and he thought therefore that he owed it to himself to have many sensuous experiences in order to reach the highest possible point of wisdom.

The idea appealed to Marius because of the immensely practical ethics that the whole concept implied. Life as the primary end of life was the code which Marius found himself professing; it was, of course, an antimetaphysical metaphysic. Through it Marius hoped to find, by means of cultural knowledge, the secret of the present in the everchanging universe, that he might discover all of the subtle realizations implied in each moment of life. Like epicureans of that time and since, Marius found there were those who misinterpreted his credo and believed that he sought pleasure as an end in itself; yet hedonism, the search for pleasure as the purpose of life, was farthest from his mind. Such a life would have been too gross for one of Marius' pietistic background.

During his search for an answer to life, Marius had turned from poetry to prose, for he felt that his nature and his studies had fitted him better for the latter.

About the time that his epicureanism became crystallized in his mind, Marius felt some pangs of regret that his emotional life seemed to have become stunted. He wondered why it was that he felt more inclined to research of the mind than to normal human emotions. He could not feel the necessity of pursuing feminine company and did not regret that he had not found it a matter of urgency that he acquire a wife. Love, in the ordinary sense of the word, did not seem to be a part of his makeup.

At a time when that problem was disturbing him, he had a summons to Rome which interrupted his worries. He was sent for to become secretary and editor to Emperor Marcus Aurelius, a prolific writer and a patron of the arts and philosophy. He had been working for some time on a memoir and a series of disconnected meditations which he wished someone to put into edited form. That task was assigned to Marius.

On the way to Rome, Marius met a young officer of the army named Cornelius, an officer of the famed Twelfth Legion, who was returning to Rome after service in the farther reaches of northern Europe. Under the tutelage of Cornelius, Marius quickly made himself at home in the city. Fortunately, Marius' family had a house in Rome, although it had not been used in many years. To the young epicurean, Rome was a wonderful place in which to live and for several years Marius was happy there. Experiences of the richest nature were his, for he moved, thanks to his family background and the emperor's patronage, in the best of circles.

There was, however, something which Marius could not fathom. His friend Cornelius seemed much happier than he. Since Cornelius was not a simple materialistic person, Marius could not understand why his friend was so much happier. One day, as they were returning from a trip away from Rome, Cornelius took Marius into a rich home on the Appian Way. It was the residence of the widow of Cecilius, and the Cecilia who was its mistress was a Christian, as was Cornelius. From that moment Marius began to comprehend something of the new religion that was making converts in the Empire. He found a strange kind of happiness in attending mass in the home of Cecilia, and he noticed too that he felt a strange attraction to Cecilia herself.

Some months later, when Cornelius and Marius were once again away from Rome, the small town in which they had stopped was shaken by an earthquake. After the first tremors of the quake had passed, Cornelius, accompanied by Marius, joined a group of Christians who were publicly thanking the Deity for their escape from death. The pagans of the town, fearing that the Christians had been the cause of the earthquake, assaulted them. Marius and Cornelius, because of their rank, were arrested and sent to Rome. On the way their captors learned that one of them was not a Christian. In order to save his friend, Marius said that the non-Christian was Cornelius, who was then set free. Marius himself became violently ill before he and his guards reached Rome. He was left behind to die, but some villagers, who were also Christians, found him and nursed him. He died with Christian prayers in his ears.

MARKET HARBOROUGH

Type of work: Novel
Author: George J. Whyte-Melville (1821-1878)
Type of plot: Sporting romance
Time of plot: Nineteenth century
Locale: England
First published: 1861

Principal characters:
JOHN STANDISH SAWYER, country gentleman and ardent fox hunter
ISAAC, Sawyer's groom and horse handler
THE HONORABLE CRASHER, Sawyer's friend and hunting companion
CECILIA DOVE, with whom Sawyer falls in love
PARSON DOVE, Cecilia's fox-hunting father
TIPTOP, The Honorable Crasher's groom and horse handler

Critique:

Whyte-Melville was an ardent hunter and a recognized authority on fox hunting in England. *Market Harborough,* like other sporting novels he wrote, is therefore regarded as an authentic account of that sport. Yet the twentieth-century reader, accustomed to naturalistic fiction, will not find here the realism of fact to which he is accustomed; there is very little specific information, as compared to what one would expect in a novel by Dreiser or Norris. *Market Harborough* was, however, Whyte-Melville's most popular novel. From a literary point of view, the novel is simply a series of hunting episodes fastened together by the presence of a single character. An interesting sidelight is that the author used his literary earnings to aid charity.

The Story:

John Standish Sawyer, a hard-riding, fox-hunting country gentleman whose farm lay not far from London, decided one fall afternoon that he had too little and too poor hunting in his own country. He also wished to show himself off as a horseman and hunter among a better class of hunters than those in his own vicinity. That evening he sat in his study alone, being a bachelor, and tried to decide, with the help of numerous glasses of brandy and water, what hunting community he would visit during the remainder of the season. He finally decided that he would go to Market Harborough, which had a good season and good at-

tendance.

The following morning Mr. Sawyer walked to a neighboring farm to buy himself a new horse for hunting, since he had only two hunters in his stable. At the neighboring farm, whose owner was more a horse-trader than an agriculturist, Sawyer found a beautiful roan that was just what he wanted. Returning to his own farm, The Grange, Sawyer went out to the stables and informed old Isaac, the groom, that he was to bring the new horse home and then prepare to take the inmates of the stable by railway to Market Harborough. Isaac, knowing his master, did not argue, although he did not quite approve of the journey.

Two days later Isaac and the horses arrived at Market Harborough, where Sawyer joined them after traveling down to London to outfit himself with new, stylish boots and riding clothes. On the train from London to Market Harborough, Sawyer met a tired-seeming young gentleman, also an ardent fox hunter, named the Honorable Crasher. At the time, neither made much of an impression on the other, even though, from Sawyer's position, the Honorable Crasher was quite a fashionable figure.

The first morning after Sawyer's arrival at Market Harborough was a very foggy one. Nevertheless, Sawyer had his groom prepare one of his hunters and joined a group of hunters, one of whom was the Honorable Crasher. When the fog refused to break, the two new friends were invited to lunch with the parson of the neighborhood, Mr. Dove, who was also an ardent hunter. The luncheon was a pleasant one, especially for Sawyer, who was much taken with Cecilia Dove, the parson's pretty young daughter, a girl greatly devoted to fox hunting. The girl, finding Sawyer to be a pleasant chap with a respectable estate, was also quite taken with him.

Several weeks went by swiftly. Sawyer proved himself to be as good as or better than the other riders at Market Harborough. In addition, there were plenty of foxes to be hunted, most of which gave the hounds and the hunters a lengthy and swift chase. Sawyer's new horse, the roan, proved as good as he had expected. Sawyer found himself thrown into the company of some gay bachelors who enjoyed life to the utmost and respected him. In addition, he saw quite a bit of pretty Cecilia Dove, who was as captivated with Sawyer as he was with her.

Word went around one day that a steeplechase was being planned as a main event of the hunting season. The fox hunters of Sawyer's group at first scoffed at the idea, since there would be no fox, but at last they fell in with the plan; the event would provide an opportunity to show off horse and rider, to make a reputation, and to win some money by riding and betting. Sawyer, who really had no horse good enough for the race, kept very quiet with respect to the event; privately, he wanted to enter it.

Old Isaac, Sawyer's groom, knowing his master wanted to get in the race, hit upon a plan that involved a new horse. In Sawyer's stable there was a fine-looking bay which ate well, never got sick, but was a poor hunter. It was this animal that Isaac planned to palm off on the Honorable Crasher. To that end he dropped mysterious hints to Tiptop, the Honorable Crasher's groom. Tiptop fell for the bait and suggested to Isaac that the bay race with one of the Honorable Crasher's horses to see which was the faster.

Early one morning the two met. before sunup, to try out the two horses. The race was to be for a half mile. The two grooms raced and Isaac's horse, even though it was covered with a flowing sheet, won by several lengths. Little did Tiptop realize that Isaac had taken out another horse under the sheet and had won the race illegally, from a very strict moralist's standpoint. Isaac hurried to Sawyer and told his master that he was sure that the Honorable Crasher would ask to buy the unwanted bay.

Isaac was right. That very morning the worthless horse was sold for a tremendous price. When the Honorable Crasher and his groom tried to get speed out of the horse in training him for the steeplechase, however, he could scarcely run. The new owner and his groom were mystified, but Isaac and Sawyer did not breathe a hint of what had happened. With the money from the sale of the worthless bay, Sawyer bought a fine, fast hunter, with which he hoped to win the steeplechase. In honor of Cecilia Dove, of whom he was growing fonder each day, he named the horse Wood-Pigeon.

Before the steeplechase was run, a ball was given by the racing set at Market Harborough. Sawyer, dressed as neatly and dandyishly as a tailor could turn him out, attended in order to dance with Cecilia. She was very coquettish during the evening, however, and by acting warm and cool by turns she angered Sawyer, who finally left the ball. Such treatment was just what the coquette needed to make her realize that she loved Sawyer very much.

The day of the great steeplechase arrived. Six horsemen, all gentlemen, were entered, including Sawyer on Wood-Pigeon. Sawyer, in honor of his love, wore a plum-colored silk shirt, plum being Cecilia's favorite color. It was Sawyer's first steeplechase, but he was a fine horseman on a fine horse, and well coached on the nature of the course by Isaac the groom, who had ridden over it on a reconnaissance run.

Sawyer did not win. In fact, he took an ugly fall near the end of the course, although up to that time he had ridden a fine race. In the fall he suffered a broken collarbone. Cecilia, watching the race, decided then and there that she would marry Sawyer, who had proved himself a courageous gentleman. During his convalescence the engagement was announced, and not long afterward Sawyer and Cecilia Dove were married. Sawyer's new wife succeeded in stopping his hunting; he even sold his horses in the flush of married bliss. But one day a friend saw him reading a book about hunting and guessed that before long he would be back with the hounds again.

MARMION

Type of work: Poem
Author: Sir Walter Scott (1771-1832)
Type of plot: Semihistorical romance
Time of plot: Early sixteenth century
Locale: The Scottish Border
First published: 1808

Principal characters:
LORD MARMION, an English knight
RALPH DE WILTON, wronged by Marmion, disguised as a palmer
CLARE FITZ-CLARE, loved by de Wilton
CONSTANCE DE BEVERLEY, betrayed by Marmion
ARCHIBALD DOUGLAS, Earl of Angus

Critique:

Ranking with *The Lay of the Last Minstrel* and *The Lady of the Lake* as one of Scott's best-known dramatic poems, *Marmion* lacks some of the perfection of detail that marks the other two. It was hurriedly written and published, and its effects are often melodramatic. In this poem Scott did not do the careful revising that was his usual custom. He detracted from the unity of his story by writing for each canto an introduction which has little bearing on the action or the mood. These introductions, addressed to various of Scott's friends, dealt with his daily activities and thoughts. But in spite of its faults, *Marmion* has the lyrical beauty and the flow of brisk and exciting action which we associate with Scott's metrical romances.

The Story:

Wherever Lord Marmion went, he was welcomed and honored as a brave and valiant knight. The English king had sent him to the Scottish court to try to persuade that country's king to end armed raids throughout the Border country. Marmion asked a Scottish lord to furnish him a guide, someone peaceful appearing, and since there was no one else available the lord sent a palmer, a holy man who had made many pilgrimages to religious shrines.

At the same time an abbess, accompanied by several nuns, was making a sea voyage to Cuthbert Isle to hold an inquisition over two prisoners of the Church.

One of the young nuns aboard, still a novice, was Clare Fitz-Clare, a lovely young girl who entered the abbey after her lover, dishonored, was believed dead. One of the accused was Constance de Beverley, a nun who had broken her vows and run away from the convent. Before she was put to death, Constance told the abbess and her other accusers the story of her fall from grace.

Her betrayer had been Lord Marmion. Believing his protestations of love for her, she had escaped from the convent and followed him for three years as his page. Then Marmion met lovely Clare Fitz-Clare, and because she was an heiress of great wealth he abandoned Constance to seek Clare for his bride. The king promised him that he should have Clare, but she loved another knight, Ralph de Wilton. Marmion forged papers which offered false proof that Wilton was not true to the king. The two knights fought a duel, and Wilton was left for dead. Constance, soon to die, gave the papers proving the forgery to the abbess and implored her to get the papers to the king in order to save Clare from a hateful marriage. Although the girl had entered a convent rather than marry Marmion, the king would force the marriage if Clare were found, for Marmion was a great favorite at court. Even though her judges pitied her, Constance was put to a horrible death after she had told her story.

Marmion continued on his way to the court. Guilty thoughts of Constance worried him; he had been responsible for her capture by the Church. But he soothed his conscience with the belief that she would not be severely punished. One night as they stayed at an inn a young boy sang a ballad about the soul's disquiet of every man who would betray a maid. At the end of the song Marmion thought he heard the tolling of a death bell. When the knight mentioned the tolling sound he heard, the palmer spoke his first words, saying that it was the toll of death for a friend. That night Marmion, unable to sleep, went out into the dark to ride. There he was attacked by what seemed a devil, for the man had the face of Wilton, long dead. The strangest part was that Marmion's mysterious adversary could have killed him, but instead sheathed his sword and rode off into the night.

As Marmion and his men rode through the Border country, they noticed everywhere huge numbers of armed clansmen readying for battle. On their arrival at the Scottish court, Marmion could not persuade King James to halt preparations for battle. The Scots, claiming that the English had wronged them, demanded vengeance. Courtesy required that Marmion be given safe conduct during his mission, however, and so the king put him in the care of Archibald Douglas, one of the most powerful of all the lords of Scotland. Douglas also was charged with the care of the abbess and her nuns, who had been taken captive by the Scots, for they were to be returned safely to their convent. But the abbess feared for Clare's safety if Marmion should learn that she was among the party of nuns. To save Clare from a forced and hated union, the holy woman gave the papers proving Marmion's forgery to the palmer and begged him to deliver them to the English king.

Marmion, learning the girl's identity, secured an order directing him to take Clare to her home, with Douglas for an escort. Separated from the abbess, Clare feared for her safety with Marmion, but he planned not to press his suit until she had been returned to her kinsmen, who would be dominated by the king. Mar-

mion and Clare were quartered in Tantallon Castle, owned by Archibald Douglas, Earl of Angus, to await the impending battle between English and Scottish troops.

Clare, lonely and afraid, walked out onto the battlements of the castle. There she met a young knight who proved to be de Wilton. From his lips Clare heard his story. He had not been mortally wounded in his combat with Marmion, but had been healed and cared for by one of his servants. The loyal servant asked one boon for saving his life, that should de Wilton's deadliest enemy fall beneath his sword that enemy should be spared. The young knight wandered far, his name scorned by all who once loved him because he was now branded as a traitor. At last he disguised himself so well that no one recognized in the lowly palmer the once-proud knight. It was de Wilton who had so frightened Marmion during his midnight ride, but he had kept his promise to his old servant and spared the life of the man who had ruined him. The young man had told Douglas his story, which was confirmed by the papers given him by the abbess. That night Douglas restored de Wilton to his knightly honors, and the next day de Wilton would join the English troops.

Marmion, unable to resist the spectacle of troops drawn up for battle, defied Douglas and rode off to join the fight. Having learned from one of his company the palmer's true identity and fearing that he would lose Clare, he took the girl to a place of safety behind the English lines. When the battle began, Marmion was mortally wounded. Clare, pitying the man she hated, tended him gently. Before he died, Marmion learned of the death of Constance and repented all his sins.

The English defeated the Scots in that bloody battle on Flodden Field. De Wilton was everywhere in the thick of the fight ing. After the battle, his lands and his titles were returned to him and Clare was given to him with the king's blessing. The proud name of de Wilton was known again through the land. Marmion, as he   deserved, lay in an unmarked grave.

MARRIAGE À LA MODE

Type of work: Drama
Author: John Dryden (1631-1700)
Type of plot: Comedy of manners
Time of plot: Seventeenth century
Locale: Sicily
First presented: 1673

Principal characters:
RHODOPHIL, captain of the king's guards
DORALICE, his wife
PALAMEDE, a courtier
MELANTHA, his betrothed
POLYDAMAS, King of Sicily
PALMYRA, his daughter
LEONIDAS, the true prince

Critique:

Marriage à la Mode is a curious mixture of heroic tragedy and comedy of manners. One plot concerns the seventeenth-century playful attitude toward married love; another, court intrigue and romance. Since the two plots are only superficially connected, one cannot escape the impression that Dryden was more interested in the popular success of the play than in its artistic unity. Skillful characterization, especially in the comic plot, has saved the play from oblivion.

The Story:

Palamede, a courtier who had just returned to Sicily after an absence of five years, overheard Doralice singing a song which justified inconstancy in marriage. Smitten by her great beauty, Palamede promptly declared his love. Doralice's announcement that she was married did not abate Palamede's ardor; instead, the news prompted him to confess that he himself was to be married in three days. The two resolved to meet again. Having been informed that Rhodophil, her husband, was approaching, Doralice abruptly departed.

Rhodophil welcomed Palamede back to court and sympathized with him over the approaching marriage. He complained that he himself had found no joy in marriage after the first six months. Palamede advised him to take a mistress, a remedy

which Rhodophil said he was already trying to effect. He had found a woman whom he desired, but her obsession with court society had prevented her from keeping her assignations. The conversation ended with the approach of Argaleon, the king's favorite, who brought a message summoning Rhodophil to the king.

Amalthea, sister to Argaleon, discussed with a court lady the reason for the king's visit to so remote a section of Sicily. King Polydamas was searching for his son. Many years before, when Polydamas usurped the throne, the former king's wife had fled with an infant son. To Polydamas' amazement his pregnant wife, Eudoxia, fled with the queen. No news had been heard of them until recently, when Polydamas was led to believe that his wife had died but that their child still lived.

Polydamas ordered brought before him a fisherman in company with a youth and a maid whom the fisherman claimed were his children but who looked too noble to be a peasant's offspring. The fisherman turned out to be Hermogenes, who had fled with Eudoxia and the queen. Under threat of torture, Hermogenes asserted that the queen, her son, and Eudoxia had died, but that Polydamas' son still lived and was, in fact

Leonidas, the youth who accompanied him. Hermogenes insisted, however, that the girl Palmyra was his own daughter. The king accepted Leonidas as his son and decreed that Palmyra should live at court so as not to be separated from her foster brother.

Later, Palamede presented himself to Melantha, the woman his father had ordered him to marry. Much to his regret, he found Melantha to be just such an affected lady as Rhodophil had described as his mistress. Indeed, Palamede soon learned that Melantha was Rhodophil's mistress—at least in name—and that Doralice was Rhodophil's wife. The confusion was compounded when Rhodophil learned that his mistress was to be Palamede's wife.

Meanwhile royal affairs were also entangled. Polydamas ordered Leonidas to marry Amalthea. When Leonidas refused, Polydamas threatened banishment but was temporarily dissuaded by Amalthea from carrying out his intentions. In private, Leonidas swore to Palmyra that he would wed none but her. When spies informed the king that Leonidas loved a commoner, Polydamas ordered Palmyra to be set adrift in a boat. Hermogenes saved her from this fate by producing evidence that she, not Leonidas, was the king's child. Although Polydamas offered to confer nobility on Leonidas, the youth chose to live in poverty with Hermogenes.

In the meantime Palamede had arranged an assignation with Doralice, and Rhodophil with Melantha, both at the same time, in the same place. At the tryst, when each couple discovered the other, all four parties fabricated excuses which each pretended to believe, so that Palamede left with his intended, and Rhodophil with his wife.

Amalthea informed Leonidas that her brother, Argaleon, had arranged to marry Palmyra and to have Leonidas banished. Although Amalthea loved Leonidas, she agreed to help him see Palmyra by taking him to the masquerade that evening.

There Leonidas arranged an assignation with Palmyra at Hermogenes' house, not, however, without being recognized by Argaleon.

Both Doralice and Melantha planned to attend a masquerade dressed as boys, but they got only as far as an eating house where they exchanged insults, much to the delight of their lovers, who hugged and kissed them at each unflattering remark. The game was ended by a message summoning Rhodophil to the king. The two "boys" were left to fend for themselves.

At Hermogenes' house Eubulus, a former governor who had helped Eudoxia in her escape, informed Palmyra that Leonidas was in reality Theagenes, the son of the late king. Leonidas told Palmyra of a plan to unseat the king, her father, and made her a prisoner when she opposed the plan. But before the conspiracy could be carried out, Polydamas arrived with his guards and seized the rebels.

Palamede received news that his father expected him to marry Melantha at once; therefore he solicited the advice of Philotis, her maid, concerning the best means to woo the lady. Philotis supplied him with a list of French words, of which the lady was inordinately fond. Won by these words, Melantha accepted Palamede as her suitor and they agreed to marry. Following this development Palamede and Rhodophil pledged to respect each other's wife, and Rhodophil and Doralice were reconciled.

Affairs in the royal household ended just as happily for most of those concerned. Suspecting that Leonidas was the true heir to the throne, Argaleon advised the young man's immediate execution, advice which Polydamas decided to follow in spite of Palmyra's pleas for mercy. The sentence would have been carried out had not Amalthea revealed Leonidas' true identity, whereupon Rhodophil and Palamede fought successfully to free the prince. The new king forgave Polydamas and asked for Palmyra's hand in marriage, a request gratefully granted. Having rejected Leonidas' offer of clemency, Argaleon was sentenced to life imprisonment. Amalthea, still in love with Leonidas, declared her intention to spend her life in prayer and mourning.

THE MARRIAGE OF FIGARO

Type of work: Drama
Author: Pierre Augustin Caron de Beaumarchais (1732-1799)
Type of plot: Romantic comedy
Time of plot: Eighteenth century
Locale: Spain
First presented: 1784

Principal characters:

FIGARO, a bridegroom-to-be
COUNT ALMAVIVA, his master
COUNTESS ALMAVIVA, his master's wife
DR. BARTHOLO, former guardian of the countess
SUZANNE, lady in waiting to the countess
MARCELINE, the housekeeper
CHÉRUBIN, a page

Critique:

Continuing the merry tale of the little barber of Seville, Beaumarchais takes Figaro through more intrigues and adventures in *The Marriage of Figaro*, or to use the complete title of the drama, *The Follies of the Day of the Marriage of Figaro*. Again the shrewd and clever barber matches wits with those who would suppress him. The story is pure romance, for the lovers must overcome many obstacles planted by their more powerful enemies. But the high good humor and clever wit of Figaro are a match for all. Beaumarchais was the first of many dramatists to use the comic style of this play. Although the style was often copied by other writers of his day, it was never surpassed.

The Story:

Three years after Figaro, the clever barber, had helped Count Almaviva steal his loved one from her guardian, Dr. Bartholo, the count tired of his lovely wife. Instead, he desired Suzanne, the countess' lady in waiting, who was betrothed to Figaro. The count, in fact, desired almost every beautiful girl he saw, but Suzanne in particular stirred his passions. His plan was to send Figaro as a messenger to France so Figaro would be out of the way and not interfere with the count's pursuit of the lovely Suzanne. Figaro knew of the count's plot and swore to prevent it. He was especially incensed because it was he who had aided the count to win his countess only a short time before.

Figaro had trouble from still another source. Marceline, the housekeeper, had his note for some money she had lent him. The note agreed that Figaro would pay her the money or else marry her. Marceline wanted only to get married; any husband would do. Because Figaro was the only man over whom she held power, he was the likeliest prospect. Figaro was young and Marceline old, but her desires were nonetheless strong. She had an ally in Dr. Bartholo, who was still seeking revenge on the count and Figaro for outwitting him.

The count had a page, Chérubin, an amorous young lad in love with all women. The countess was his special desire, and when the count learned of his passion, he banished the page from the castle after ordering him to join the count's regiment. But Figaro had other plans for the page. His plot was to dress the page in Suzanne's clothing and send him to keep a tryst with the nobleman. Figaro believed that the count would appear so ridiculous when it was learned he had been tricked that he would no longer try to outwit Figaro. Figaro also sent the count an anonymous letter saying that the countess had a lover. When the count burst into his wife's chambers, he found no one but Suzanne. The page, who had been in the chamber a few minutes before, jumped out a window. Figaro was delighted when the count was forced to beg his wife's pardon for his unfounded suspicions.

Figaro did not get a chance to send the page to keep a tryst with the count; the countess and Suzanne, meanwhile, were plotting to foil the count's plan to have Suzanne for his own. He had told Suzanne that he would not permit her to marry Figaro unless she met him at a pavilion on a certain night. She consented to meet him only after she and the countess had made plans to outwit him.

Before the time appointed for the tryst Marceline took to court her case against Figaro. Since he wanted to harm Figaro, the count himself presided at the hearing. He ruled that Figaro must either pay Marceline the money he owed her or else marry her, according to the terms of the note. After the sentence had been pronounced, however, Marceline discovered that Figaro was her son by Dr. Bartholo. She said that this relationship was the reason for the love which had made her want to marry Figaro. Marceline and Dr. Bartholo were then married, but Dr. Bartholo was not happy to have his worst enemy for his son.

The countess and Suzanne, carrying out their plan, exchanged clothing in preparation for fooling the count. Figaro, who had not been told of the plot, heard that Suzanne was to meet the count and hid himself in the pavilion to observe her treachery. Dr. Bartholo and Marceline accompanied him. The countess, disguised as Suzanne, met the count and permitted him to woo her. The count, protesting his love for her, compared her with the countess, to the detriment of his wife. Figaro, angered by what he believed was Suzanne's duplicity and thinking that the woman in the countess' clothing was his mistress, also eavesdropping, asked the countess for her favor. Suzanne, revealing her true identity, slapped him soundly for trying to be unfaithful to her. Figaro was happy in the knowledge that Suzanne had not been false to him and that the count had betrayed himself to his wife.

After a confusing scene, during which the chagrined count did not know which way to turn, the situation was untangled. After some persuasion the count won back the favor of his wife, but with no choice except to give his consent to the marriage between Suzanne and Figaro. At the same time Chérubin, who it seemed would forever plague the count, was matched with a maid who had long loved him. Dr. Bartholo and Marceline joined in good wishes for all the happy couples. Both the count and the countess gave heavy purses to Figaro and his bride. Figaro thought himself far removed from the humble barber he had once been. He was now blessed with a mother, a father, a fortune, and a beautiful wife.

MARSE CHAN

Type of work: Short story
Author: Thomas Nelson Page (1853-1922)
Type of plot: Regional romance
Time of plot: Civil War period
Locale: Virginia
First published: 1887

Principal characters:
SAM, Marse Chan's Negro servant
MARSE CHAN, a young Virginian
ANNE CHAMBERLIN, his sweetheart

Critique:

"Marse Chan," from *In Ole Virginia*, is typical of much local color writing in its use of dialect and a regional setting. It is an idealized narrative of Old Virginia, highly romanticized, but emotional in its appeal. Its author was a diplomat as well as a novelist, and served as U. S. ambassador to Italy during World War I.

The Story:

When the baby was born, there was a great ceremony on the Channing plantation. Mr. Channing brought out the baby and let colored Sam hold him. Then he told the young Negro boy that he was to be the baby's body servant from that day on.

When Marse Chan, as Sam called him, grew up and went to school, he carried Anne Chamberlin's books and they were very close friends. The two neighboring families hoped that the friendship would result in a marriage to unite the two families. One day, when the river rose suddenly and Anne was in danger from the high water, Marse Chan waded in and carried her to safety. Mr. Channing was so pleased that he gave his son a pony.

The friendship between the two families was broken soon afterward. When Mr. Channing declared himself a candidate for Congress, Colonel Chamberlin was nominated to oppose him. Mr. Channing lost the election, and from that day on there was enmity between the families.

One day Colonel Chamberlin announced that he intended to sell some of his slaves. Mr. Channing wanted to buy Maria because her husband was one of his own slaves, but the colonel asked far too much for her. Learning of Mr. Channing's intention, the colonel sent someone to bid against him at the auction, but Mr. Channing was successful in buying Maria. Then followed a series of lawsuits between the families.

In the meantime Marse Chan had been going to college. During vacations, in spite of family opposition, his romance with Anne flourished. One day a barn on the Channing plantation caught fire. Old Mr. Channing, in an effort to release the trapped animals, went into the burning structure. He was so badly burned that he lost the use of his eyes. A short time later Colonel Chamberlin and Marse Chan became involved in a public debate on secession. Marse Chan, in the crowd's opinion, was the victor, and he was lustily cheered. The colonel was so angry that he challenged Marse Chan to a duel. Marse Chan fired over the colonel's head and said that he was making a present of him to his family. The colonel was furious.

When the war broke out, Marse Chan was called up for service. He sent a note to Anne and the night before he left he met her in the garden of her home. In reply to his pleadings, she told him that she did not love him. The next day Marse Chan went off to fight for the South. He was accompanied by Sam, his servant since birth. While at the front, Marse Chan met a fellow soldier who spoke disrespectfully of Colonel Chamberlin. The two men had a fight and Sam promptly wrote to his wife Judy to tell her about it. Judy just as promptly informed Anne of the incident. At last Colonel Chamberlin, aware that Anne was suffering and that she really loved Marse Chan, told her to attempt a reconciliation. Accordingly, Anne wrote to Marse Chan that she still loved him. Marse Chan read the letter again and again with great pleasure.

He was killed in battle the next day. Sam took his body back to his home and his family. Then Sam hurried over to the Chamberlin estate because he felt sure that was what Marse Chan would have wanted him to do. After he had told his story, Anne set out with him for the Channing home. Mrs. Channing, who had found Anne's letter in one of Marse Chan's pockets, was on the porch to greet her. They fell into each other's arms and the feud between the families was over. From that day on Anne lived with the Channings and took care of old Mr. Channing and his wife as long as they lived. After the old Channings died Anne went to work in a military hospital. Shortly before the fall of Richmond she became ill with a fever and died. She was buried next to Marse Chan in the Channing graveyard.

Sam, the servant, lived on. Whenever anyone came along the path and saw him with the dog that constantly followed him, he would tell the passerby about Marse Chan. The dog had been Marse Chan's dog; they were the ones, according to Sam, who remembered Marse Chan best.

MARTIN CHUZZLEWIT

Type of work: Novel
Author: Charles Dickens (1812-1870)
Type of plot: Sentimental-mystery romance
Time of plot: Nineteenth century
Locale: England and America
First published: 1843-1844

Principal characters:

MARTIN CHUZZLEWIT, a selfish old man
MARTIN CHUZZLEWIT, his grandson
MARY GRAHAM, old Martin's ward
ANTHONY CHUZZLEWIT, old Martin's brother
JONAS CHUZZLEWIT, his son
MR. PECKSNIFF, a hypocrite
CHARITY, and
MERCY, his daughters
TOM PINCH, young Martin's friend
RUTH PINCH, his sister
MARK TAPLEY, another friend of young Martin
MRS. SARAH GAMP, a bibulous cockney

Critique:

Martin Chuzzlewit is a novel complicated in plot but rich in characterization and Dickensian humor. In addition, this book contains the writer's most outrageous caricatures, in those scenes dealing with young Martin Chuzzlewit's experiences in America. Dickens himself had been disappointed in the United States, and his account of the land and its people is far from flattering. The pictures of rude frontier life fade, however, beside his portraits of Mr. Pecksniff, the arch-hypocrite, and the cockney vitality of Mrs. Gamp, perhaps the author's best humorous character.

The Story:

Selfishness was the quality which set the Chuzzlewits apart from all other men, and the two aged brothers, Martin and Anthony, were not lacking in that strong family trait. From his cradle Jonas Chuzzlewit, Anthony's son, had been taught to think only of money and gain, so that in his eagerness to possess his father's wealth he often grew impatient for the old man to die. Elderly Martin Chuzzlewit suspected the world of having designs on his fortune, with the result that his distrust and lack of generosity turned his grandson, his namesake, into a model of selfishness and obstinacy.

Perhaps old Martin's heart was not as hard as it seemed, for he had taken into his house as his companion and ward an orphan named Mary Graham. Although he told her that she would have a comfortable home as long as he lived but that she could expect nothing at his death, his secret desire was that love might grow between her and his grandson. But when young Martin told him that he had already chosen Mary for his own, he was displeased, afraid that the young couple were acting in their own interests. A disagreement followed, and the old man harshly turned his grandson loose in the world.

Thrown upon his own resources, young Martin decided to become an architect. In a little Wiltshire village, not far from Salisbury, lived Mr. Pecksniff, architect and land surveyor, whose practice it was to train two or three pupils in return for a large premium and exorbitant charges for board and lodging. Mr. Pecksniff thought highly of himself as a moral man, and he had a copybook maxim to quote for every occasion. Although he and Mr. Chuzzlewit were cousins, there had been bad feeling between them in the past. But Mr. Pecksniff saw in Martin a possible suitor for one of his daughters, and he accepted him as a student without payment of the customary fee.

Mr. Pecksniff had never been known to build anything, a fact which took nothing away from his reputation for cleverness. With him lived his two affected daughters, Charity and Mercy, as hypocritical and mean-spirited as their father. His assistant was a former pupil named Tom Pinch, a meek, prematurely aged draftsman who looked upon Mr. Pecksniff as a tower of knowledge.

Arriving in Wiltshire, young Martin took the place of John Westlock in Mr. Pecksniff's establishment. Westlock had never been a favorite in the household; his contempt for Mr. Pecksniff was as great as his regard for honest, loyal Tom Pinch. At first Martin treated Tom in a patronizing manner. Tom, accustomed to the snubs and ridicule of Charity and Mercy, returned Martin's slights with simple good-will, and before long the two became close friends.

One day Mr. Pecksniff and his daughters departed suddenly for London, summoned there by Mr. Chuzzlewit. The old man called on them at Mrs. Todgers' shabbily genteel rooming house and accused Martin of deceiving the worthy man who sheltered him. Mr. Pecksniff was pained and shocked to learn that Mr. Chuzzlewit had disowned his grandson, but he was cheered when the visitor hinted at present good-will and future expectations if the architect would send the young man away at once.

Although Mr. Chuzzlewit's proposal was treacherous and his language insulting, Mr. Pecksniff agreed eagerly enough to the conditions imposed. Returning to Wiltshire, he virtuously announced that Martin had ill-treated the best and noblest of men and taken advantage of his own unsuspecting nature. His humble roof, he declared, could never shelter so base an ingrate and impostor.

Homeless once more, Martin made his way to London in hopes of finding employment. As the weeks passed, his small store of money dwindled steadily. At last, when he had nothing left to pawn, he decided to try his fortunes in America. A twenty-pound note in a letter from an unknown sender gave him the wherewithal for his passage. With him on his adventure went Mark Tapley, hostler of the Blue Dragon Inn in Wiltshire, a jolly fellow with a desire to see the world. Martin could not leave London, however, without seeing Mary Graham. He read her a letter he had written to Tom Pinch, in which he asked his friend to show her kindness if the two should ever meet, and he arranged to write to Mary in care of Tom.

As passengers in the steerage Martin and Mark had a miserable voyage to New York. Martin did not care much for the bumptious, tobacco-chewing Americans he met, but he was excited by accounts of the fortunes to be made out West. Taken in by a group of land promoters, he wrote to Mary telling her of his bright prospects.

Old Anthony Chuzzlewit died suddenly in the presence of his son, Mr. Pecksniff, and a faithful clerk, Chuffey. Mrs. Sarah Gamp was called in to prepare the body for burial. She was a fat, middle-aged cockney woman with a fondness for the bottle and the habit of quoting endlessly from the sayings of Mrs. 'Arris, a friend whom no other of her acquaintances had ever seen. Jonas Chuzzlewit was disturbed by Chuffey's conduct at the funeral. Mrs. Gamp declared that Jonas bore himself in a manner that was filial and fitting.

After the burial Jonas went with Mr. Pecksniff to Wiltshire, for his cautious inquiries had revealed that Mr. Pecksniff was prepared to make a handsome settlement on his daughters when they married, and Jonas was ready to court one or the other. A short time later old Martin Chuzzlewit and Mary Graham arrived to take rooms at the Blue Dragon Inn in the village. There Tom Pinch met Mary and in his humble manner fell deeply in love with her. Only his friendship for Martin kept him from declaring himself.

Mr. Pecksniff had hoped that Jonas would marry Charity, his older daughter, but Mercy was the suitor's choice, much to her sister's dismay. After the ceremony Mr. and Mrs. Jonas Chuzzlewit returned to London, where, before long, he began to treat his bride with ill-humor and brutality. Having some business to transact at the office of the Anglo-Bengalee Disinterested Loan and Life Insurance Company, he discovered that Mr. Montague, the president, was in reality Montague Tigg, a flashy speculator whom Jonas had previously known as an associate of his rascally cousin, Chevy Slyme. Lured by the promise of huge profits, Jonas was persuaded to invest in the company and become a director. Tigg, however, had little trust for his new partner. He told Nadgett, his investigator, to learn whatever he could about Jonas.

Jonas had a guilty secret. Before his father's death he had obtained some poison from a debt-ridden young doctor and had mixed it with old Anthony's medicine. Actually, his father had not taken the dose, but the circumstances, known also to Chuffey, the clerk, would have incriminated Jonas had they been revealed. This secret, uncovered by Nadgett, gave Tigg a hold over his partner.

In Wiltshire, old Martin Chuzzlewit's condition grew worse. When the invalid's mind seemed to fail, Mr. Pecksniff saw his own opportunity to get control of his kinsman's fortune. Hoping to make his position doubly secure, he planned to marry Mary Graham. But Mary found his wooing distasteful. At last she told Tom Pinch about his employer's unwelcome attentions, and Tom, for the first time, realized that Mr. Pecksniff was a hypocrite and a villain. Having overheard the conversation, Mr. Pecksniff discharged Tom after telling Mr. Chuzzlewit that the young man had made advances to Mary.

Tom went to London to see his sister Ruth. Finding her unhappily employed as governess, he took her with him to hired lodgings and asked John Westlock, his old friend, to help him in finding work. Before Westlock could go to his assistance, however, an unknown patron hired Tom to catalogue a library.

In America, meanwhile, young Martin and Mark fared badly. They had bought land in Eden, but on their arrival they found nothing more than a huddle of rude cabins in a swamp. Martin fell ill with fever. When he recovered, Mark became sick. While he nursed his friend, Martin had time to realize the faults of his character and the true reason for the failure of his hopes. More than a year passed before the travelers were able to return to England.

John Westlock had also become interested in Jonas Chuzzlewit. He had befriended Lewsome, the young doctor from whom Jonas had secured the poison, and from Mrs. Gamp, who nursed the physician through an illness, he learned additional details to make him suspect the son's guilt in old Anthony's death.

While old Martin seemed in his dotage, his grandson and Mark went to Mr. Pecksniff's house, where Mr. Chuzzlewit was staying. Martin tried to end the misunderstanding between them, but Mr. Pecksniff broke in to say that the grandfather knew the young man for a villain, a deceiver who would not be allowed to wrong the sick old man as long as Mr. Pecksniff lived. Old Martin said nothing. Young Martin and Mark went to London. There they found Tom Pinch and Ruth and heard from John Westlock his suspicions of Jonas Chuzzlewit.

Jonas became desperate when Tigg forced him into a scheme to defraud Mr. Pecksniff. On their journey into Wiltshire, Jonas made plans for disposing of the man he hated and feared. After Mr. Pecksniff had agreed to invest his money in the company, Jonas returned to London, leaving Tigg to handle the transfer of securities. That night, disguised as a workman, he went secretly to the village and assaulted Tigg, who was walking back to his room at the inn. Leaving the body in a wood, he took a coach to London and arrived there at daybreak. But Nadgett, ever on watch, had seen Jonas leave and return, and he followed the murderer when he tried to dispose of the clothing he had worn on his journey.

Old Martin Chuzzlewit. miraculously restored in body and mind, arrived unexpectedly in London for the purpose of righting many wrongs and turning the tables on hypocritical Mr. Pecksniff. Having heard Westlock's story, he went with him to confront Jonas with their suspicions. A few minutes later police officers, led by Nadgett, appeared to arrest Jonas for Tigg's murder. Trapped, the wretched man took the rest of the poison he had obtained from Lewsome.

The next day old Martin met with all concerned. It was he who had hired Tom Pinch, and it was he who now confessed that he had tested his grandson and Mary and found them worthy. When Mr. Peck-sniff entered and attempted to shake the hand of his venerable friend, the stern old man struck him to the floor with a cane.

The passing years brought happiness to the deserving. Young Martin and Mary were married, followed a short time later by Westlock and Ruth Pinch. Mark Tapley won the mistress of the Blue Dragon Inn. Old Martin, out of pity, befriended Mercy Chuzzlewit. He himself rejoiced in the happiness of his faithful friends. But there was no joy for Mr. Pecksniff. When news of Tigg's murder had reached the city, another partner in that shady enterprise had run away with the company funds. Mr. Pecksniff, ruined, became a drunken old man who wrote begging letters to Martin and Tom and who had little comfort from Charity, the shrewish companion of his later years.

THE MASTER BUILDER

Type of work: Drama
Author: Henrik Ibsen (1828-1906)
Type of plot: Psychological realism
Time of plot: Nineteenth century
Locale: Norway
First presented: 1892

Principal characters:
HALVARD SOLNESS, the master builder
ALINE, his wife
DOCTOR HERDAL, his physician
KNUT BROVIK, in Solness' employ
RAGNAR BROVIK, his son
KAIA FOSLI, Solness' bookkeeper
HILDA WANGEL, Solness' inspiration

Critique:

The Master Builder belongs to a series of dramas which were a departure from the earlier types written by Ibsen. In this play the bitter satire of the social dramas is not present; instead, the play is mysterious, symbolic, lyrical. Ibsen here deals with the human soul and its struggle to rise above its own desires. The idea had been in Ibsen's mind for many years before he actually wrote the play, which is one of the most original of his works.

The Story:

Halvard Solness had risen to his high position as a master builder because of a fire which had destroyed the ancestral estate of his wife's family. On the site he had built new homes which won him fame and assured success in his profession. The fire had given him his chance, but he made his own opportunities, too, by crushing all who got in his way.

Knut Brovik, employed by Solness, had once been a successful architect, but Solness had crushed him and then used him as he had many others. Ragnar, Brovik's son, was a draftsman in Solness' office, and it was Brovik's only wish that before his own death his son should have a chance to design something of lasting value. Although Ragnar had drawn plans for a villa which Solness did not wish to bother with, the builder would not give him permission to take the assignment. Ragnar was engaged to Kaia Fosli, Solness' bookkeeper, and he could not

marry her until he had established himself. Ragnar did not know that Kaia had come under the spell of the master, as had so many other young girls. Solness pretended to Kaia that he could not help Ragnar because that would mean losing her; in reality he needed Ragnar's brain and talent and could not risk having the young man as a competitor.

Solness' physician, Dr. Herdal, and his wife feared that the builder was going mad. He spent much time in retrospection and also seemed to have morbid fears that the younger generation was going to ruin him.

But not all of the younger generation frightened Solness. When Hilda Wangel appeared at his home, he was at once drawn to her. He had met Hilda ten years before when he had hung the traditional wreath atop the weather vane on a church he had built. She had been a child at the time. Now she told him that he had called her his princess and had promised to come for her in ten years and carry her off to build her a kingdom. Since he had not kept his promise, she had come to him. Solness, who could not remember the incident, decided that he must have wished it to happen and thus made it come to pass. This, he believed, was another example of his power over people, and it frightened him.

When Hilda asked to see all he had built, especially the high church towers, he told her that he no longer built churches and would never build one again. Now he built homes for mothers and fathers and children. He was building a home for himself and his wife, and on it he was building a high tower. He did not know why he was putting the high tower on the house, but something seemed to be forcing him. Hilda insisted that he complete the tower, for it seemed to her that the tower would have great meaning for her and for him.

Hilda told Solness that his need of her was the kingdom he had promised her and that she would stay near him. She wanted to know why he built nothing but homes, and he told her of the fire that had given him his chance. At the time of the fire, he and his wife had twin baby boys. Although all had been saved from the fire, the babies died soon afterward from the effects of the fevered milk of their mother. Solness knew that his position and his fame were based on the tragedy of the fire and on his wife's heart-rending loss, but he believed also that he had willed the fire in order to have his chance. Whatever he willed happened, and afterward he had to pay somehow the horrible price for his almost unconscious desires. And so he built homes for others, never able to have a real home himself. He was near madness because his success was based on his and his wife's sorrow.

Solness seemed to have power over human beings as well as events. Brovik was one man who served him, his son Ragnar another. Solness, afraid of Ragnar's younger generation, believed that it would crush him as he had crushed others.

Hilda, begging him to give Ragnar and the other young people a chance, said that he would not be crushed if he himself opened the door to them. She told him that his near-madness was caused by a feeble conscience, that he must overcome this weakness and make his conscience robust, as was hers. She persuaded him to give Ragnar the assignment the young man wanted. She wished Solness to stand completely alone and yet be the master. As final proof of his greatness, she begged Solness to lay the traditional wreath on the high tower of his new home and she scoffed at a builder who could not climb as high as he could build.

Hilda alone wanted Solness to climb the tower, and only she believed that he would do so. Once she had seen him standing on a church tower, and his magnificence had thrilled her. She must have the thrill again. On that other day she had heard a song in the sky as the master builder shouted into the heavens, but it was not until now that she learned what he had shouted. He told her that as he had stood at the top of the church he had known why God had made the fire that destroyed his wife's estate. It was to make Solness a great builder. a true artist building more and more churches to honor God. God wanted him to have no children, no real home, so that he could give all his time to building churches. But Solness had defied God that day. He had shouted his decision to build no more churches, only homes for mothers and fathers and their children.

But God had taken His revenge. There was little happiness in the homes Solness built. From now on he would build only castles in the air, with Hilda to help him. He asked Hilda to believe in him, to have faith in him. Hilda, however, demanded proof. She must see him standing again, clear and free, on the top of the tower. Then his conscience would be freed and he would still be the master builder. He would give her the kingdom he had promised.

Even though his wife and others pleaded with him not to make the ascent, Solness was guided by Hilda's desire. As he climbed higher and higher, she heard a song in the air and thrilled to its crashing music. But when he reached the top of the tower, he seemed to be struggling with an invisible being. He toppled and fell to the ground, lifeless. Then Hilda heard music in the sky. Her master builder had given her her kingdom.

THE MASTER OF BALLANTRAE

Type of work: Novel
Author: Robert Louis Stevenson (1850-1894)
Type of plot: Adventure romance
Time of plot: Mid-eighteenth century
Locale: Scotland, India, France, America
First published: 1889

Principal characters:

JAMES DURRIE, Master of Ballantrae
HENRY DURRIE, James' brother
ALISON GRAEME, Henry's wife
MR. MACKELLAR, factor of Durrisdeer
SECUNDRA DASS, James' servant

Critique:

The Master of Ballantrae: A Winter's Tale is considered by many to be Stevenson's best novel, although it probably is not as well known as Treasure Island or Kidnapped. The story is engrossing, moves with commendable speed, and generally does not seem incredible. However, the novel is lacking in background detail, the author's chief aim, apparently, being a delineation of character.

The Story:

When the Stuart Pretender landed in Scotland in 1745, to assert his right to the throne of England by force of arms if necessary, the Durries of Durrisdeer decided to steer a middle course. One son would fight for the exiled Stuart, the other would bide at home in loyalty to King George. James, Master of Ballantrae and his father's heir, won the toss of a coin and elected to join the Stuart cause. The younger son, Henry, stayed at Durrisdeer. By this means it was hoped by their shrewd old father that either way the struggle went, the family estate would remain intact.

Soon after came word of the defeat of the Scottish forces at Culloden and the news of James' death. Henry became the Master of Ballantrae. In 1748, he married Alison Graeme, who had been betrothed to James. But even after a daughter and a son had been born to them, their marriage was overshadowed by the spirit of the former Master of Ballantrae. James had been the favorite son. Old Lord Durrisdeer had denied

him nothing, and Alison had loved him. This feeling led to domestic difficulties, and later the village gossips idolized James and accused Henry of selling out the Stuart cause.

Colonel Francis Burke, an Irishman, came into this strained situation and announced that he and James had escaped together from the field at Culloden. The old lord was exceedingly happy with this news; Henry felt frustrated; Alison seemed pleased. Burke's mission was to get money from the estate to take to James, who was living in France. Henry arranged to send him money by Burke.

Burke described his association with James and their adventures after leaving Scotland. The ship on which they escaped was boarded by pirates, and James and Burke were taken aboard the pirate ship. The pirates, under the leadership of Teach, their captain, were a drunken, incompetent, ignorant lot.

James bided his time, and when the ship put in for repairs, he escaped with Burke and several members of the crew, after robbing the store chest of money and treasure Teach had accumulated. With their spoils James and Burke eventually arrived in New York, where they met Chew, an Indian trader. They took off with him into the wilderness. When Chew died, they were left without a guide. James and Burke quarreled and separated. James buried the treasure he had and set off through the wilderness for Fort St. Frederick. When he arrived at the fort, he again met Burke, who welcomed him as a long-lost brother and paid his fare to France.

In France, James served in the French army and became a man of consequence at the French court because of his adeptness at politics, his unscrupulousness, and the money from his inheritance in Scotland. His demands finally put the estate in financial difficulties, for over a period of seven years he demanded and obtained a sum amounting to more than eight thousand pounds. Because he practiced strict economy to provide funds for his brother, Henry acquired a reputation as a miser and was upbraided by his wife. Then in 1756 Alison learned the true state of affairs from Mackellar, Henry's factor.

After that matters ran more smoothly in the household until James returned suddenly from France aboard a smuggler's lugger. His father was overjoyed to see his favorite son, who during his stay at Ballantrae was known as Mr. Bally. James' hatred for Henry was known only to Henry and Mackellar. In the presence of the household James seemed to be on the friendliest terms with his brother, but when no one was around he goaded Henry by subtle innuendoes and insinuations. Henry bore this state of affairs as best he could because James, even in exile, was the true Master of Ballantrae. As a further torment for his patient brother, James paid marked attention to Alison, and it really seemed she preferred his company to Henry's.

Matters came to a head one night when James casually mentioned to Henry that there never was a woman who did not prefer him when Henry was around. When this assertion was made, there was no one present but Mackellar, Henry, and James. Henry struck James and hot words quickly led to drawn swords. The brothers ordered Mackellar to carry candles into the garden. They went outside, Mackellar remonstrating all the while, but he could not stop the duel. The air was so still that the light of the candles did not waver as the brothers crossed swords. From the onset Henry became the aggressor, and it was not long before James realized he stood to lose the fight. He then resorted to trickery. As Henry lunged, James seized his brother's blade in his left hand. Henry saved himself from James' stroke by leaping to one side, and James, slipping to one knee from the force of his lunge, impaled himself on Henry's sword. Mackellar ran to the fallen James and declared him dead.

Henry seemed stupified and made off toward the house at a stumbling pace. Mackellar took it upon himself to tell Alison and the old lord what had happened. The four decided that the first thing to do was to remove James' corpse. But when they arrived at the scene of the duel, the body had disappeared. They decided that smugglers, attracted by the light of the candles in the shrubbery, had found the body and taken it away, and their belief was confirmed by blood stains they found on the boat landing the next morning. Mr. Bally was reported in the neighborhood to have left Durrisdeer as suddenly as he had arrived.

As the affair turned out, James had been found alive but seriously wounded. He was taken aboard a smuggler's ship, and when he recovered he went to India. After he made a fortune there, he returned once more to Scotland in the company of an Indian named Secundra Dass.

They arrived at Durrisdeer early one morning. That night Henry with his wife and two children left the house secretly and took the next ship to New York. James, having learned of Henry's plans through the eavesdropping of Secundra Dass, sailed for New York three weeks later, and Mackellar, hoping to help his master, went with James and his servant. When they arrived in New York, Mackellar was pleased to learn that Henry had already taken precautions to forestall any claims which James might make.

When James' allowance from his brother proved insufficient for him to live in the style he desired, he set up shop as a tailor, and Secundra Dass employed himself as a goldsmith. Hatred for James gradually became an obsession with Henry. He reveled in the fact that after many years of humiliation and distress he had his wicked brother in his power.

To recoup his fortunes, James made plans to recover the treasure which he had previously hidden in the wilderness. He asked Henry to lend him the money to outfit an expedition, but Henry refused. Mackellar, although he hated James, could not bear to see a Durrie treated in such a haughty manner; therefore, he sent to Scotland for his own savings to assist James. But Henry had plans of his own, and he conspired with a man of unsavory reputation to guide James into the wilderness and there kill him. Again Secundra Dass overheard a chance conversation and warned his master of danger. Then James sickened and died. He was buried, and his guide returned to report his death to Henry.

Henry, however, believed his brother James to be in league with the devil, with the ability to die and return to life seemingly at will. With Mackellar and a small party, he set out for James' grave. They arrived one moonlit night in time to see Secundra Dass in the act of exhuming James' body and they gathered around to see what would happen. After digging through the frozen earth for a short distance, Secundra Dass removed his master's body from the shallow grave. Then the Indian began strange ministrations over the corpse. The moon was setting. The watchers imagined that in the pale light they saw the dead man's eyelids flutter. When the eyes opened and James looked full into his brother's face, Henry fell to the ground. He died before Mackellar could reach his side.

But the Indian trick of swallowing the tongue to give the appearance of death would not work in the cold American climate, and Secundra Dass failed to bring James completely to life. James, the Master of Ballantrae, and his brother were united in death in the wilderness of America.

MASTRO-DON GESUALDO

Type of work: Novel
Author: Giovanni Verga (1840-1922)
Type of plot: Social chronicle
Time of plot: First half of the nineteenth century
Locale: San Giovanni, Sicily
First published: 1889

Principal characters:

GESUALDO MOTTA, an ambitious peasant
DONNA BIANCA TRAO, one of the poor gentry
DON DIEGO TRAO, and
DON FERDINANDO TRAO, her brothers
NUNZIO MOTTA, Gesualdo's father
SANTO MOTTA, Gesualdo's brother
SPERANZA MOTTA, Gesualdo's sister
FORTUNATO BURGIO, her husband
BARONESS RUBIERA
BARON NINÌ RUBIERA, her son, Bianca Trao's cousin
BARON ZACCO, one of the Trao relatives
DONNA SARINA (or CIRMENA), a poor aunt of the Trao family
DONNA MARIANNA SGANCI, a rich aunt
DIODATA, Gesualdo's servant girl
NANI L'ORBO, a peasant, Gesualdo's servant
CANON-PRIEST LUPI
CORRADO LA GURNA, Donna Cirmena's nephew

Critique:

Giovanni Verga, author of the short story, "Cavalleria Rusticana," which was used as the libretto for Mascagni's opera, is generally regarded as the finest Italian novelist since Manzoni. *Mastro-don Gesualdo* is the second in an unfinished triology, the first being *I Malavoglia* (1881), translated as *The House by the Medlar Tree.* The series, titled *I Vinti* (*The Defeated*), was to have included a third novel, about the Sicilian aristocracy, titled *La Duchessa di Leyra. Mastro-don Gesualdo* is a naturalistic study of the rise and fall of an ambitious Sicilian peasant. His efforts to elevate himself place Mastro-don (workman-gentleman) Gesualdo between two worlds—the peasantry and the gentry—and his marriage to one of the Trao family, who are of the gentry, only widens the gap between him and the others on either side.

The Story:

Shortly after sunrise the bells of San Giovanni began ringing. There was a fire in the Trao house, and the village awakened to answer the summons. Through the smoke the villagers saw the frantic faces of Don Ferdinando and Don Diego, and a voice called out that there were thieves in the house as well. At the same time Don Diego called for his sister, Bianca, who was somewhere in the burning building. Mastro-don Gesualdo appeared, showing great concern about his own house nearby, and other Mottas, including Gesualdo's brother Santo and his sister Speranza, came running both to witness the spectacle and to protect their own property.

Don Diego discovered, to his dismay, that the stranger in the house was not a thief but his sister's lover, the young Baron Ninì Rubiera. After the fire had been extinguished, Don Diego went to the baron's mother, the Baroness Rubiera, one of the Trao relatives, and meekly requested that Ninì marry Bianca.

MASTRO-DON GESUALDO by Giovanni Verga. Translated by D. H. Lawrence. By permission of the publishers, The Viking Press, Inc. Copyright, 1923, by Thomas Seltzer. Copyright, 1951, by Frieda Lawrence.

The baroness refused. Any girl who married her son, she declared, must come prepared with a large dowry. Since Bianca's brothers were poor, though proud of their family heritage, there was no hope of convincing the baroness to change her mind. Consequently, after great persuasion, they agreed to allow Bianca to.marry Gesualdo Motta, a peasant who by his cleverness in business and industry had managed to make himself a rich landowner. Gesualdo had for some time been happy with Diodata, a servant girl, as his mistress, but now hě hoped to elevate himself socially by marrying one of the gentry.

The gentry were aroused to anger by the news that Gesualdo intended to bid for the communal lands at the auction for the taxes on land which had been in the hands of Baron Zacco, another of the Trao relatives. They commented that wealth, not family, was what counted in Sicily. When Mastro-don Gesualdo hesitantly attended a gathering at the Sganci house he was welcomed into the house but put off to one side, even though it was known he was to marry Bianca. Bianca, heartbroken, talked to the young Baron Ninì about his mother's plan to marry him to Fifì Margarone, one of the daughters of Don Filippo Margarone, the political leader in the village. Knowing that his mother's mind was made up, the young man finally managed to escape from Bianca.

Mastro-don Gesualdo continued to work with his laborers, fulfilling contracts to build walls, roads, and bridges. As he sweated with the men and supervised their work, he thought of his father's complaints about losing his position as the head of the family. The elder Motta, Nunzio, had even taken on contracts, using his son's money, in order to reëstablish himself as master of his house; but his ventures had been unsuccessful. Nevertheless, Nunzio continued to criticize his son's enterprises and to make things difficult for him.

Gesualdo, returning home from work, always found faithful Diodata, who greeted him humbly and made him comfortable. When he told her of his plan to marry Bianca Trao, she replied that he was the master; it was apparent, however, that she would never be happy without him. When she was finally married off to another servant, Nani l'Orbo, the children she bore him had been fathered by Gesualdo. Nani took advantage of his position to force Gesualdo to support him with money and property.

A major blow to Gesualdo's fortunes came when a bridge he was building under contract to the town collapsed. His father complained that the failure was Gesualdo's fault, and the villagers who were jealous of Gesualdo's wealth exulted over his misfortune. Only Diodata, who had not yet married Nani l'Orbo, was sympathetic.

Despite the objections of her brothers, Don Diego and Don Ferdinando, Bianca persisted in going ahead with the plan to marry Gesualdo. The brothers finally agreed, only because it was hopeless to forbid her. Bianca knew that she would never marry Baron Ninì Rubiera, and she hoped that by marrying a rich man she could ease the burden on her brothers.

When the wedding was held in the old house of the La Gurna family, which Gesualdo had leased, only Donna Cirmena came to represent the Trao family. When Gesualdo was alone with Bianca he was afraid to touch her, and they talked to each other apprehensively, as if they could never overcome the distance between them.

At the tax auction of the communal lands an effort was made to convince Mastro-don Gesualdo that for the sake of harmony between the Motta and the Trao families he should divide the land with Baron Zacco and the Baroness Rubiera. When Gesualdo refused, Don Filippo Margarone pretended that there was no guarantee that Gesualdo would be able to pay the bid with his own money. For the time being the auction was called off. The Trao family attempted to put pressure on Bianca to dissuade her husband from bidding on the communal lands, but she refused to take part. In the meantime the canon-priest Lupi tried to ingratiate himself with Gesualdo by criticizing the business tactics of the Trao family and by warning Gesualdo that an effort was being made to stir the laborers to revolt against him. Gesualdo began to realize that his money was not bringing him the satisfaction he had hoped for and which he had always associated with wealth.

An uprising of the peasants was quelled by the nobility with military aid. During the trouble Gesualdo sought shelter with Nani l'Orbo, who took advantage of the moment to demand land from Gesualdo as payment for harboring him and for having married Diodata. Until peace was restored Gesualdo was in danger from both the laborers and the police. One result of the disturbance was that Baron Zacco allied himself with Gesualdo, for the peasants were angry at anyone who had anything to do with the communal lands.

When news came that Don Diego was dying, Bianca hurried to the house where her brothers lived. Her arrival caused a great disturbance among the relatives, and matters were further complicated when Bianca fell into a faint because her child was about to be born. In the midst of the uproar Don Ferdinando walked about talking of documents which he claimed proved that the Traos were entitled to royal lands.

Although Baron Nini Rubiera was engaged to be married to Donna Fifi Margarone, he became infatuated with an actress, Signora Aglae, and sent a note to her, composed by Ciolla, a local troublemaker who had stirred up the peasants to revolt. The note was intercepted by Master Titta, the barber, who gave it to Fifi, and as a result of that disclosure the engagement was ended. The young baron's mother was furious with him— not so much because of the scandal as because Baron Nini had gone deeply into debt with Gesualdo in order to entertain the actress.

Bianca's child was christened Isabella. There were rumors that since the child arrived seven months after the marriage and since she looked so much like a Trao, it was possible that Mastro-don Gesualdo was not the father.

Baron Nini, finally becoming disgusted with Signora Aglae, returned home to a furious scene with his mother. The baroness accused him of trying to impoverish them all by his dealings with Gesualdo, and in her frenzy she suffered a stroke and became paralyzed. After his mother's stroke Baron Nini found himself hopelessly entangled by his debts to Gesualdo. In desperation he married a rich widow, Madame Giuseppina Alosi, but even that was not enough to save him. He then tried to get help from Bianca. Although she was affected by his presence, she refused to yield to his appeal.

At school Isabella suffered from taunts that she was a peasant's daughter, and in defense she finally called herself a Trao. Gesualdo allowed the change of name because he loved her more than his own pride.

When a cholera epidemic threatened San Giovanni, Gesualdo brought Isabella home from college; and he then moved his family to Mangalavite. But Don Ferdinando, Nunzio, Speranza, and Burgio chose to stay. At the last moment Donna Cirmena joined the Gesualdo Motta group, bringing with her Corrado La Gurna, who had been orphaned in a cholera epidemic.

At Mangalavite, Isabella fell in love with Corrado, but Gesualdo finally put an end to the romance by sending Isabella to a convent and by putting out an order for the arrest of Corrado. Later he signed a marriage contract, giving his daughter to the Duke di Leyra, a high-living lord who promptly exhausted Isabella's dowry and used up whatever other resources he could get from Gesualdo.

From then on Mastro-don Gesualdo's downfall was rapid. His father had died of fever and the Motta relatives, quarreling over the inheritance, demanded that Gesualdo divide his property among them. His wife being ill with consumption, the servants left for fear of catching the disease. When the laborers revolted again, Gesualdo hardly paid attention to them, for by that time Bianca was dying and his own life was losing its meaning.

After Bianca's death Gesualdo was hurried from place to place to hide him from the rebelling mob. His lands and houses were raided and sacked. At last, wearying of turncoat friends like Baron Zacco, Gesualdo allowed himself to be controlled by his relatives. He lay in bed with a cancerous disease while his son-in-law, the duke, exercised the power of attorney he had wrested from Gesualdo in order to despoil more of his property. One by one his lands disappeared into the hands of others. When he made a last appeal to his daughter to use some of the remaining money for those to whom he owed much, she looked at him from a distance; she was a Trao and he a Motta. After his death the servants, knowing little of his life, commented enviously that Gesualdo must have been born lucky since he died in fine linen like a prince.

MAX HAVELAAR

Type of work: Novel
Author: Multatuli (Eduard Douwes Dekker, 1820-1887)
Type of plot: Political satire
Time of plot: 1857
Locale: Java
First published: 1860

Principal characters:
MAX HAVELAAR, a conscientious Dutch colonial administrator
BATAVUS DRYSTUBBLE, a Dutch coffee broker of Amsterdam
MR. VERBRUGGE, an administrator subordinate to Max Havelaar
RADHEN ADHIPATTI KARTA NATTA NEGARA, the native regent of Lebak,
    Havelaar's district
SHAWLMAN, a schoolmate of Batavus Drystubble and a writer
MR. SLIMERING, Havelaar's superior officer

Critique:

Like his hero in *Max Havelaar*, Eduard Douwes Dekker was an administrator in the Dutch East Indies. As the Resident of Bantam, in Java, he had seen at first hand the scandalous situation which existed there and he devoted himself in later life to the reform of the Dutch government's treatment of the Javanese and the inhabitants of other colonies in the East Indies. Within the novel itself Dekker compared his work to Harriet Beecher Stowe's *Uncle Tom's Cabin*, but in recent years critics have tended to believe that Dekker really wrote *Max Havelaar* as a satire on colonial maladministration of all kinds, governmental blundering, and the smugness and hypocrisy of middle-class Europeans. *Max Havelaar* is but one of Dekker's writings devoted to satire against these things; a drama, a series of fictional love letters, and a string of articles and pamphlets follow the same vein.

The Story:

Batavus Drystubble, a self-proud coffee broker of Amsterdam, was accosted one day on the street by a former schoolmate who had obviously fallen on evil times. The Shawlman, as Drystubble called him, pressed his prosperous former schoolfellow to look over a bundle of manuscripts, in hopes that Drystubble might be willing to help him have some of them published. Drystubble, thinking he might have a book written about the coffee trade, turned over the manuscripts to a clerk in his firm to edit. The clerk agreed to make a book of the materials, after securing a promise from his employer not to censor the results before publication. Out of the bundle of manuscripts came the story of Max Havelaar, a Dutch administrator in Java, in the Dutch East Indies.

Max Havelaar was an idealist who believed in justice for everyone, even the poor Javanese who labored in the fields. When he arrived at Rangkas-Betoong to take over the post of Assistant Resident of Lebak, a section of the residency of Bantam, in Java, he found the situation much worse than he had anticipated, for the Dutch administrators, despite their oath to protect the poor and lowly, had acquiesced in the robbery and mistreatment of the native Javanese by the Javanese nobility, through whom the Dutch ruled the island. The Adhipatti of Lebak was a relatively poor man because his region did not produce many of the exports that the Dutch wanted. In order to keep up appearances befitting his rank and to support a large and rapacious family, the Adhipatti extorted goods, materials, and services from the people, who felt helpless because of the treatment they would suffer from the native chief if they complained to the Dutch officials.

Being a man who loved a good fight for justice's sake, Max Havelaar was glad he had been assigned to Lebak. In his opening speech to the Adhipatti and the lesser chiefs he declared that justice must be done, and he began trying to influence the Adhipatti by advancing him tax money in hopes that the chief would be less exacting on his people. Suggestions and help were of little use, however, for the same evil practices continued. The people, learning that Havelaar wished to see justice done, stole to his home under cover of darkness to lodge their complaints and give the assistant resident information. Havelaar rode many miles to redress complaints. He also gave an example to the chiefs by refusing to use more native labor than the law allowed, even to letting the grounds of the residency go largely untended and revert to jungle. He realized what he was fighting against, for he was a man in his middle thirties who had spent seventeen years in the Dutch colonial service.

His faithful adherent in his battle against injustice was his wife Tine, who was devoted to her husband and knew he was in the right. Of less help was Verbrugge, the controller serving under Havelaar. He knew the Javanese were being exploited, but he hated to risk his job and career, with their concomitant security, by fighting against the tide of complacency of Dutch officialdom. Verbrugge realized that Havelaar's superiors were interested only in keeping peace, in submitting reports that bespoke prosperity, and in providing wealth for the homeland—regardless of what happened to the Javanese.

One example was the story of Saïdyah, the son of a small Javanese rice farmer. One by one the father's possessions were taken from him by extortion, even the buffalo that had faced a tiger to save the boy's life. Finally Saïdyah's father ran away to escape punishment for failing to pay his taxes, and Saïdyah himself left his home village to seek work in Batavia,

vowing to his beloved that he would return in three years' time to marry her. When he returned as he had promised, however, he found that she and her family had been forced to flee and had joined rebellious Javanese on another island. Saïdyah finally found his beloved, but only after she had been killed and mutilated by Dutch troops. Saïdyah himself, overcome with grief, rushed upon the troops and was impaled on their bayonets.

As time went on, Havelaar realized he could expect but little help from Mr. Slimering, the Resident of Bantam and his immediate superior. Yet Havelaar hoped optimistically that some support would be forthcoming from that quarter. Havelaar learned that his predecessor had probably been poisoned because he had sought to stop the exploitation of the population by the native chiefs. Havelaar learned this from his predecessor's native wife, who still lived at the official residence.

Having finally gained what he deemed sufficient information against the Adhipatti, Max Havelaar lodged an official protest with Mr. Slimering. He requested that the Adhipatti and his subordinate chiefs be taken into custody and removed from Rangkas-Betoong, lest their presence intimidate the people and prevent their giving testimony of the abuses. Instead of acceding to any part of the request, Mr. Slimering came to Havelaar's district, denounced Havelaar's actions, and even gave money to the Adhipatti. Havelaar, hoping to find support higher up in the administration, appealed to the Governor-General, saying that unless he received some support to eradicate the injustices he had found he would have to resign after seventeen years of faithful service to the colonial administration.

(At this point in the mss. was inserted a section supposedly written by Batavus Drystubble, who expressed the views of a complacent Dutch businessman in the homeland. Drystubble said that he had been royally entertained by retired colonial officials who assured him that the charges made in Shawlman's manuscripts were groundless. Drystubble added, too, that he felt as a religious man that the heathen Javanese were given their just deserts for not being Christians and that the Dutch were profiting at the expense of the Javanese because the former were decent, God-fearing, and obedient Christian people who deserved divine favor.)

After waiting a month, Max Havelaar learned that he had been relieved of his post in Lebak; he was ordered to another part of Java. This official action he could not accept, knowing that he would have the same fight all over again, a losing battle, in a new assignment. He left Lebak after his successor arrived and went to Batavia to lay his case personally before the Governor-General. That worthy man, too busy to see him, put off Havelaar with one pretext after another. On the eve of the Governor-General's departure for Holland, Havelaar wrote an angry letter as a last hope. That stinging letter did no good; the Governor-General sailed for home, leaving Havelaar poor and forsaken.

(At the end of the novel Multatuli stepped in to break off the story and speak in his own voice, dismissing the clerk from Drystubble's office and Shawlman, who as fictional characters had been writing the novel. Multatuli, after expressing his loathing of the hypocritical, money-grabbing Drystubble, went on to say that he wished to leave an heirloom for Havelaar's children and to bring his appeals to the public. The author said that he knew his book was not well written, but all that mattered was that people learn how the Javanese were being mistreated, thirty millions of them, in the name of King William of the Netherlands.)

THE MAXIMS

Type of work: Epigrams and aphorisms
Author: François, Duc de La Rochefoucauld (1613-1680)
First published: 1665-1678

La Rochefoucauld described his *Maxims* (*Reflections or Moral Maxims*) as a "portrait of the human heart." He wrote in the preface to the first edition that these reflections on human conduct would probably offend many persons because the aphorisms were "full of truths" that would be unacceptable to human pride. Ironically, he wrote that the reader should suppose himself to be the sole exception to the truth revealed and should avoid the tendency to have his opinion influenced by *amour-propre,* or self-love, which would prejudice his mind against the maxims.

The reference to self-love, the basic concern for self by which the value of any action, person, or thing is presumed to be judged, is characteristic of La Rochefoucauld. Critics generally describe this great French writer as a cynic and take as evidence his maxims in which he attributes to self-love the central role in human conduct. But a mere cynic is one who hopes for a better world than the one in which he finds himself; he constantly compares what could be and what ought to be with what is—and the disparity makes him bitter. Consequently, everything the cynic says is a statement of the truth as he sees it; and as he sees it, it is worthy only of a sneer. La Rochefoucauld, on the other hand, takes self-love to be an undeniable fact of human existence, and he does not hope for anything better. Consequently, his view of the world is that of a man amused to see the difference between what men conceive themselves to be and what they are; his delight is in a witty revelation of the facts of life. Throughout the *Maxims,* as in the refreshing self-portrait with which the collection begins, La Rochefoucauld reveals an intelligent sense of humor which takes the sneer out of what critics sometimes choose to call his cynicism.

"My normal expression is somewhat bitter and haughty," he writes in his initial "Portrait"; his expression "makes most people think me supercilious, though I am not the least so really." He goes on to describe himself as "inclined to melancholy" but not from temperament alone: "it is due to . . . many other causes." He calls himself an intellectual who delights in the conversation of cultured persons, in reading, in virtue, and in friendship. His passions are moderate and under control. He is neither ambitious nor afraid of death. He has given up "light amours" and wonders why so many men waste their time paying "pretty compliments." The portrait concludes with the assurance that were he ever to love, he would love with the strong passion that is a sign of noble character; however, he doubts that his knowledge of the value of strong passion will ever "quit my head to find a dwelling in my heart."

The first maxim is important as a summary statement of La Rochefoucauld's central conviction: "So-called virtue is often merely a compound of varied activities and interests, which good fortune or our own assiduity enables us to display to advantage; so it is not always courage that makes the hero, nor modesty the chaste woman."

And with the second, the author names the concern that is essential to the human heart: *"Amour-propre* is the archflatterer."

In many of the maxims La Rochefoucauld expresses his conviction that virtue is the accidental result of an exercise of the passions; acts undertaken passionately to satisfy the demands of a pervasive self-concern are interpreted in other ways, as signs of nobility of character. Thus he writes that "Illustrious deeds, of dazzling brilliance, are represented by politicians as the outcome of great aims, whereas they are usually the result of caprice or passion" (7). Similarly, "The clemency of princes is often nothing more than a political artifice designed to secure the goodwill of their subjects" (15). And, "Such clemency, though hailed as a virtue, is the product sometimes of vanity, sometimes of indolence, not infrequently of timidity, and generally of all three combined" (16).

One way of expressing La Rochefoucauld's philosophy is by saying that, to him, virtue is usually passion misunderstood. A man does something because his own irresistible self-love drives him to it; the world observes the power of his act and mistakes it for the grandeur of courageous virtue.

Not all of the maxims develop this theme, however. Many of the author's comments are both wry and true, and in their pithiness deserve the prominent place so many persons give to the unread sign, "Think." Thus, "The desire to appear clever often prevents our being so" (199); "We all have enough strength to bear the misfortunes of others" (19); "Flattery would do us no harm if we did not flatter ourselves" (152); and "There is no fool so troublesome as a fool with brains" (451).

There is a positive strain to some of the maxims, an appeal to the honesty by which men may lessen the damage their self-love does. Whenever a man finds it possible to recognize another's worth and to do so sincerely, whenever a man knows his own limitations and acknowledges them, whenever a man admits that his show of virtue is often an empty show— there is hope for him. The author respects such honesty, and it is apparent that the *Maxims* are confessional as well as didactic.

La Rochefoucauld found through his own experience certain truths which writers of all ages have expressed in various ways and which gain power through repetition. In several maxims he develops the idea that it is doing a man an injury to be so much concerned about his welfare that he finds himself burdened with the necessity of being grateful. He recognizes that we tend to be free with advice to others, but not eager to accept it for ourselves. We admit certain shortcomings, such as a poor memory, in order to hide others, such as a lack of intelligence.

La Rochefoucauld's psychology is that of the sophisticated courtier. He was too much aware of his own disguises ever to have acquired the knowledge that would have led to a more objective and more scientific psychology. His psychology, like his philosophy, if not that of the man in the street, was at least that of the man at court—clever enough to see behind the masks of those who traveled in high society, but not tolerant enough of possibilities to be willing to admit that what he called "honest" men were more common than he supposed. When his psychology has the strong ring of truth, it is more by accident than discernment; and when it is false, he seems embittered to distortion—hence the charge of "cynicism."

Nevertheless, certain maxims do define something of the human character: "To disclaim admiration is to desire it in double measure" (149); "We easily forget our faults when they are known only to ourselves" (196); "Excessive eagerness to discharge an obligation is a form of ingratitude" (226); and "If we were faultless ourselves, we should take less pleasure in commenting on the faults of others" (31).

Behind the revealing wit of La Rochefoucauld there is the murmur of an injured man. Who can discern the falsity of others better than a man who believes himself betrayed, who finds himself timid, who longs for recognition and gratitude and receives not enough of either? And who, finally, is scornful of grand passion who has not become bored with his own cleverness and isolation and longs to be transformed, even at the expense of becoming a fool? La Rochefoucauld reveals himself when he reveals the desperate *amour-propre* which moves all men.

THE MAYOR OF CASTERBRIDGE

Type of work: Novel
Author: Thomas Hardy (1840-1928)
Type of plot: Psychological realism
Time of plot: Nineteenth century
Locale: "Wessex," England
First published: 1886

Principal characters:
MICHAEL HENCHARD, the mayor of Casterbridge
SUSAN HENCHARD-NEWSON, his abandoned wife
ELIZABETH-JANE NEWSON, his stepdaughter
RICHARD NEWSON, a sailor
DONALD FARFRAE, a grain merchant
LUCETTA LE SUEUR, loved by Henchard, later Farfrae's wife

Critique:

Despite contrived events, the plot of *The Mayor of Casterbridge* works out well. Descriptions of the Wessex countryside are excellent. Hardy's simple country people are realistic and sometimes funny, if not always sympathetic. The modern reader is likely to question the melodramatic and spectacular opening scenes of the novel, in spite of Hardy's insistence that such occurrences did take place in rural districts during the last century. The plot illustrates Hardy's belief that "in fiction it is not improbabilities of incident but improbabilities of character that matter."

The Story:

One late summer afternoon, early in the nineteenth century, a young farm couple with their baby arrived on foot at the village of Weydon-Priors. A fair was in progress. The couple, tired and dusty, entered a refreshment tent where the husband proceeded to get so drunk that he offered his wife and child for sale. A sailor strange to the village bought the wife, Susan, and the child, Elizabeth-Jane, for five guineas. The young woman tore off her wedding ring and threw it in her drunken husband's face; then, carrying her child, she followed the sailor out of the tent.

When he awoke sober the next morning, Michael Henchard, the young farmer, realized what he had done. After taking an oath not to touch liquor for

twenty years, he searched many months for his wife and child. In a western seaport he was told that three persons answering the description he gave had emigrated a short time before. He gave up his search and wandered on until he came to the town of Casterbridge. There he stayed to seek his fortune.

Richard Newson, the sailor, convinced Susan Henchard that she had no moral obligations to the husband who had sold her and her child. He married her and moved with his new family to Canada. Later they returned to England. Susan, meanwhile, had learned of the illegality of her marriage to Newson, but before she could make a positive move Newson was lost at sea. Susan and Elizabeth-Jane, now eighteen and attractive, returned to Weydon-Priors. There they heard that Henchard had gone to Casterbridge.

Henchard, in the intervening period, had become a prosperous grain merchant and the mayor of Casterbridge. When the women arrived in the town they heard that Henchard had sold some bad grain to bakers and restitution was expected. Donald Farfrae, a young Scots corn expert who was passing through Casterbridge, heard of Henchard's predicament and told him a method for partially restoring the grain. Farfrae so impressed Henchard and the people of the town that they prevailed on him to remain. Farfrae became Henchard's manager.

2286

At the meeting of Susan and Hench-ard, it was decided Susan and her daughter would take lodgings and Henchard would pay court to Susan. Henchard, trusting young Farfrae, told the Scot of his philandering with a young woman named Lucetta Le Sueur, from Jersey. He asked Farfrae to meet Lucetta and keep her from coming to Casterbridge.

Henchard and Susan were married. Elizabeth-Jane developed into a beautiful young woman for whom Donald Farfrae had a growing attraction. Henchard wanted Elizabeth-Jane to take his name, but Susan refused his request, much to his mystification. He noticed that Elizabeth-Jane did not possess any of his personal traits.

Bad feeling came between Henchard and Farfrae over Henchard's harsh treatment of a simple-minded employee. Farfrae had succeeded Henchard in popularity in Casterbridge. The complete break came when a country dance sponsored by Farfrae drew all the populace, leaving Henchard's dance unattended. Farfrae, anticipating his dismissal, set up his own establishment but refused to take any of Henchard's business away from him. Henchard, antagonized, would not allow Elizabeth-Jane and Farfrae to see each other.

Henchard received a letter from Lucetta saying she would pass through Casterbridge to pick up her love letters. When Lucetta failed to keep the appointment, Henchard put the letters in his safe. Susan fell sick and wrote a letter for Henchard to open on the day Elizabeth-Jane was married. Soon afterward she died and Henchard told the girl that he was her real father. Looking for some documents to corroborate his story, he found the letter his wife had left in his keeping for Elizabeth-Jane. Henchard, unable to resist, read Susan's letter and learned that Elizabeth-Jane was really the daughter of Newson and Susan, his own daughter having died in infancy. His wife's reluctance to have the girl take his name was now clear, and Hench-ard's attitude toward Elizabeth-Jane became distant and cold.

One day Elizabeth-Jane met a strange woman at the village graveyard. The woman was Lucetta Templeman, formerly Lucetta Le Sueur, who had inherited property in Casterbridge from a rich aunt named Templeman. She took Elizabeth-Jane into her employ to make it convenient for Henchard, her old lover, to call on her.

Young Farfrae came to see Elizabeth-Jane, who was away at the time. He and Miss Templeman were immediately attracted to each other, and Lucetta refused to see Henchard after meeting Farfrae. Elizabeth-Jane overheard Henchard berate Lucetta under his breath for refusing to admit him to her house; she was made further uncomfortable when she saw that Farfrae had succumbed to Lucetta's charms. Henchard was now determined to ruin Farfrae. Advised by a weather prophet that the weather would be bad during the harvest, he bought grain heavily. When the weather stayed fair, Henchard was almost ruined by low grain prices. Farfrae bought cheap. The weather turned bad late in the harvest, and prices went up. Farfrae became wealthy.

In the meantime, Farfrae continued his courtship of Lucetta. Henchard, jealous, threatened to expose Lucetta's past unless she married him. Lucetta agreed. But an old woman disclosed to the village that Henchard was the man who had sold his wife and child years before. Lucetta, ashamed, left town. On the day of her return, Henchard rescued her and Elizabeth-Jane from an enraged bull. He asked Lucetta to give evidence to a creditor of their engagement. Lucetta confessed that in her absence she and Farfrae had been married. Henchard, utterly frustrated, again threatened to expose her. Elizabeth-Jane, upon learning of the marriage, left Lucetta's service.

The news that Henchard had sold his wife and child spread through the village. His creditors closed in, and he became a recluse. He and Elizabeth-Jane were reconciled during his illness. Upon his recovery he hired out to Farfrae as a common laborer.

Henchard's oath having expired, he began to drink heavily. Farfrae planned to set up Henchard and Elizabeth-Jane in a small seed shop, but the project did not materialize because of a misunderstanding. Farfrae became mayor of Casterbridge despite the desire of Lucetta to leave the village.

Jopp, a former employee of Henchard, blackmailed his way into the employ of Farfrae through Lucetta, whose past he knew, because he had lived in Jersey before he came to Casterbridge. Henchard, finally taking pity on Lucetta, gave Jopp the love letters to return to her. Before delivering them, Jopp read the letters aloud in an inn.

Royalty visited Casterbridge. Henchard, wishing to retain his old stature in the village, forced himself among the receiving dignitaries, but Farfrae pushed him aside. Later, Henchard got Farfrae at his mercy, during a fight in a warehouse loft, but the younger man shamed Henchard by telling him to go ahead and kill him.

The townspeople, excited over the letters they had heard read, devised a mummery employing effigies of Henchard and Lucetta riding back to back on a donkey. Farfrae's friends arranged to have him absent from the village during the mummers' parade, but Lucetta saw it and was prostrated. She died of a miscarriage that night.

Richard Newson, not lost after all, came to Casterbridge in search of Susan and Elizabeth-Jane. He met Henchard, who sent him away with the information that both Susan and Elizabeth-Jane were dead.

Elizabeth-Jane went to live with Henchard in his poverty. They opened a seed shop and began to prosper in a modest way. Farfrae, to the misery of the lonely Henchard, began to pay court to Elizabeth-Jane, and they planned to marry soon. Newson returned, obviously knowing he had been duped. Henchard left town but returned for the marriage festivities, bringing with him a goldfinch as a wedding present. When he saw that Newson had completely replaced him as Elizabeth-Jane's father, he went sadly away. Newson, restless, departed for the sea again, after Farfrae and his daughter were settled. Henchard pined away and died, ironically enough, in the secret care of the simple-minded old man whom he had once tyrannized.

THE MAYOR OF ZALAMEA

Type of work: Drama
Author: Pedro Calderón de la Barca (1600-1681)
Type of plot: Romantic tragedy
Time of plot: Sixteenth century
Locale: Zalamea, Spain
First presented: c. 1640

Principal characters:
PHILIP II, King of Spain
DON LOPE DE FIGUEROA, commander of a Spanish regiment
DON ALVARO DE ATAIDE, a captain
PEDRO CRESPO, a farmer of Zalamea
JUAN, his son
ISABEL, his daughter
REBOLLEDO, a soldier
CHISPA, his mistress

Critique:

The Mayor of Zalamea constitutes Calderón's finished and in many ways original reworking of a play by his illustrious predecessor, Lope de Vega. Calderón, who was himself a soldier, delineates in this play the military life of seventeenth-century Spain. He also portrays with sympathy the proud, independent, and canny farmer of the provinces. There are hints of two subplots in the prominence given to several secondary characters at the beginning of the play, but these subplots never fully develop.

The Story:

As the troops of Don Lope de Figueroa approached the village of Zalamea, old campaigner Rebolledo grumbled in true veteran fashion about the hardships of the march. Quite ready to stop and relax in the village, Rebolledo predicted that the mayor of the village would bribe the officers to march the regiment through and beyond the little community. When he was taken to task by his fellows for this unsoldierly talk, Rebolledo declared that he was mainly concerned for the welfare of his mistress, Chispa, who accompanied the troops. Chispa retorted that although she was a woman she could endure the march as well as any man. To cheer up the men, she broke into a marching song.

Chispa's song was barely finished when the column reached Zalamea. It was an-

nounced that the troops would be billeted in the village to await the imminent arrival of their commander, Don Lope. The captain of the column was pleased to learn that he would be billeted in the home of a proud farmer whose daughter was reputed to be the beauty of the neighborhood.

At the same time that the troops entered Zalamea, a down-at-heels squire, Don Mendo, accompanied by his servant, Nuño—the pair bore a marked resemblance to Don Quixote and Sancho Panzo—came to the village also. Don Mendo sought the favors of Isabel, the daughter of the proud farmer, Pedro Crespo. Isabel banged together the shutters of her window when Don Mendo greeted her in foolishly extravagant terms. Crespo and his son Juan found the presence of Don Mendo highly objectionable.

When the sergeant announced to Crespo that the captain, Don Alvaro de Ataide, would be quartered in Crespo's house, the farmer graciously accepted this imposition; Juan, however, was displeased and suggested to his father that he purchase a patent of gentility so that he might avoid having to billet troops in his home. Crespo declared that as long as he was not of gentle blood he could see no point, even though he was rich, in assuming gentility.

Isabel and her cousin Ines, having learned of the presence of the troops,

2289

went to the attic of the house, where they would remain as long as the soldiers were in the town.

On the captain's arrival, the sergeant searched the house but was unable to find Isabel. However, he reported that a servant told him the girl was in the attic and would stay there until the troops departed. The captain planned to win Isabel by any means.

Rebolledo asked the captain for the privilege of officially conducting gambling among the soldiers. The captain granted the privilege in return for Rebolledo's help in his plan to discover Isabel. The captain and Rebolledo then pretended to fight; Rebolledo, feigning great fright, fled, followed by the captain, up the stairs to the attic. Isabel admitted him to her retreat and in pleading to the captain for his life she presented such a charming aspect to the young officer that he was completely smitten.

The clamor of the pretended fight drew Crespo home. He and Juan, with swords drawn, raced upstairs to the attic. Juan sensed the trick and hinted as much, but Crespo, impressed by the captain's courtesy, was duped. Insulted by Juan's innuendoes, the captain was about to come to blows with Juan when Don Lope, the regimental commander, entered. When he demanded an explanation of the scene, the captain said that Rebolledo's insubordination had been the cause. Rebolledo, in denial, explained that the disturbance had been intended to discover Crespo's daughter. Don Lope ordered the captain to change his quarters and the troops to remain in their billets; he himself chose to stay in Crespo's house.

Crespo, jealous of his honor, declared that he would give up all of his worldly goods in submission to the will of the king, but that he would destroy the man who would jeopardize his good name.

The captain, stricken with desire for Isabel, courted her under her window; she remained disdainful. Don Mendo, hearing what had happened, armed himself and set out to meet the captain on the field of honor. Meanwhile the captain had prevailed upon Rebolledo to assist him further in his suit. Rebolledo, reconciled, suggested that Isabel could be overcome with song.

At Crespo's, the proud farmer, mollified by Don Lope's seeming gentility, invited the commander to sup in the garden. Don Lope, wounded in the leg in the Flemish wars, so that he was in constant pain, played upon his infirmity in order to arouse Crespo's pity. When he requested the company of Isabel at supper, Crespo readily assented, assuring Don Lope that he would be proud to have his daughter wait on such a fine gentleman. After Isabel had joined Don Lope, the sound of a guitar and a vocal serenade came from the street outside. Those in the garden were so disturbed by the serenade that the supper came abruptly to an end.

Outside, armed Don Mendo could barely refrain from attacking the captain and his followers, but as long as Isabel did not appear in her window he did not attack. As Chispa sang a particularly vulgar song, Crespo and Don Lope, swords drawn, fell upon the serenaders and scattered them. In the fray, Don Lope belabored Don Mendo, who had somehow become involved. A short time later the captain reappeared with soldiers in an official capacity to maintain the peace. Don Lope commended the captain and assured him that the trouble was of no moment. Since dawn was approaching, Don Lope told the captain to order the regiment out of Zalamea.

The next day, the troops having left, the captain expressed his determination to stay and make a last attempt to enjoy Isabel's favors. Further encouraged by the news that Juan had decided to become a soldier and that he would leave that day with Don Lope, he ordered Rebolledo to accompany him and the sergeant on his mission. Chispa declared that she would go along, disguised as a man.

Toward sundown, Don Lope said his

farewell to Crespo and gave Isabel a diamond brooch. Crespo gave fatherly advice to Juan. As father and daughter watched Don Lope and Juan gallop away, Isabel observed that this was the day for the election of municipal officers. Suddenly the captain and his followers came upon them. The captain seized Isabel; the sergeant and Rebolledo seized Crespo.

Later that night, in the forest near Zalamea, distracted Isabel came upon her father tied to a tree. She told how Juan had come upon the scene of her violation and had fought the captain. Frightened, she had run away from the fight. Crespo, comforting Isabel, vowed revenge. As the old man and his daughter started home, they encountered the town notary, who announced that Crespo had been elected mayor. He added that the wounded captain was in the village.

In Zalamea, Crespo confronted the captain in private. He suggested that the captain, having disgraced the family honor, take Isabel as his wife, but the captain, not fearing a provincial mayor, scoffed at Crespo's request. Crespo then ordered his officers to place the captain and his followers in jail to await the judgment of the king, who was approaching Zalamea.

Returning to his house, Crespo found Juan prepared to take Isabel's life, to wipe out the disgrace she had innocently brought on her family. Crespo, sternly just, ordered his officers to take Juan to jail for having fought his superior officer, the captain.

Don Lope, on the highway, was informed that the captain had been jailed by the mayor of Zalamea. He returned to the village, went to Crespo, and, unaware that Crespo had been elected mayor, declared that he would thrash the town official for arresting one of the king's officers. Crespo revealed that he was the mayor and that he fully intended to see the captain hanged. Don Lope ordered the regiment to return to the public square of Zalamea.

The soldiers having returned, a pitched battle between them and the townspeople of Zalamea seemed imminent when King Philip II entered the village with his entourage. Don Lope explained the situation to the king, and Crespo showed his majesty depositions taken from the captain's associates. The king agreed that the captain's crime was vile; he declared, however, that Crespo had authority neither to judge nor to punish an officer of the king. When Crespo revealed that the captain had already been garroted in his cell and that no one knew who had strangled him, the king, unable to deny that Zalamea had meted out true justice upon the captain, appointed Crespo perpetual mayor of the village.

Crespo, after declaring that Isabel would take the veil of a nun, released Rebolledo, Chispa, and Juan from jail, and returned Juan to the charge of his military mentor, Don Lope.

MEASURE FOR MEASURE

Type of work: Drama
Author: William Shakespeare (1564-1616)
Type of plot: Tragi-comedy
Time of plot: Sixteenth century
Locale: Vienna
First presented: c. 1603

Principal characters:
VINCENTIO, Duke of Vienna
ANGELO, the Lord Deputy
ESCALUS, an ancient counselor
CLAUDIO, a young gentleman
LUCIO, his friend
ISABELLA, Claudio's sister
MARIANA, Angelo's former sweetheart
JULIET, Claudio's fiancée

Critique:

This often-overlooked play by Shakespeare is probably his most contemporary offering, since its theme is sociological. Dealing with political and governmental affairs, it reveals, more than any other of his works, Shakespeare's real attitude toward the society of his day. One of the so-called "dark" comedies, it presents the thesis that honesty and common sense are the basis of good government. A remarkable feature of the play is the deep psychological probing of its chief figure, Angelo.

The Story:

The growing political and moral corruption of Vienna were a great worry to its kindly, temperate ruler, Duke Vincentio. Knowing that he himself was as much to blame for the troubles as anyone because he had been lax in the enforcement of existing laws, the duke tried to devise a scheme whereby the old discipline of civic authority could be successfully revived.

Fearing that reforms instituted by himself might seem too harsh for his people to accept without protest, he decided to appoint a deputy governor and to leave the country for a while. Angelo, a respected and intelligent city official, seemed just the man for the job. The duke turned over the affairs of Vienna to Angelo for a temporary length of time and appointed Escalus, a trustworthy old official, second in command. The duke then pretended to leave for Poland, but actually he disguised himself in the habit of a friar and returned to the city to watch the outcome of Angelo's reforms.

Angelo's first act was to imprison Claudio, a young nobleman who had gotten his betrothed, Juliet, with child. Under an old statute, now revived, Claudio's offense was punishable by death. The young man was paraded through the streets in disgrace and finally sent to prison. At his request, Lucio, a rakish friend, went to the nunnery where Isabella, Claudio's sister, was a young novice about to take her vows. Through his messenger, Claudio asked Isabella to plead with the new governor for his release. At the same time Escalus, who had known Claudio's father well, begged Angelo not to execute the young man. But the new deputy remained firm in carrying out the duties of his office, and Claudio's well-wishers held little hope for their friend's release.

The duke, disguised as a friar, visited Juliet and learned that the punishment of her lover was extremely unfair, even under the ancient statutes. The young couple had been very much in love, and been formally engaged, and would have been married, except for the fact that Juliet's dowry had become a matter of legal dispute. There was no question of seduction in the case at all.

Isabella, going before Angelo to plead her brother's cause, met with little success at first, even though she had been thoroughly coached by the wily Lucio. Nevertheless, the cold heart of Angelo was somewhat touched by Isabella's beauty, and by the time of the second interview he had become so passionately aroused as to forget his reputation for saintly behavior. After telling Isabella frankly that she could obtain her brother's release only by yielding herself to his lustful desires, Angelo threatened Claudio's death otherwise.

Shocked at these words from the deputy, Isabella asserted that she would expose him in public. Angelo, amused, asked who would believe her story. At her wit's end, Isabella rushed to the prison where she told Claudio of Angelo's disgraceful proposition. When he first heard the deputy's proposal, Claudio was also revolted by the idea, but as images of death continued to terrify him he finally begged Isabella to placate Angelo and give herself to him. Isabella, horrified by her brother's cowardly attitude, lashed out at him with a scornful speech, but was interrupted by the duke in his disguise as a friar. Having overheard much of the conversation, he drew Isabella aside from her brother and confided that it would still be possible for her to save Claudio without shaming herself.

The friar told Isabella that, five years before, Angelo had been betrothed to Mariana, a high-born lady. The marriage had not taken place, however, because Mariana's brother, with her dowry, had been lost at sea. Angelo had consequently broken off his vows and hinted at supposed dishonor in the poor young woman. The friar suggested to Isabella that she plan the requested rendezvous with Angelo in a dark and quiet place, and then let Mariana act as her substitute. Angelo would be satisfied, Claudio released, Isabella still chaste, and Mariana provided with the means to force Angelo into marriage.

Everything went as arranged, with Mariana taking Isabella's place at the as-signation, but cowardly Angelo, fearing public exposure, broke his promise to release Claudio and ordered the young man's execution. Once again the good friar intervened. He persuaded the provost to hide Claudio and then to announce his death by sending Angelo the head of another prisoner who had died of natural causes.

On the day before the execution a crowd gathered outside the prison and discussed the coming events. One of the group was Lucio, who accosted the disguised duke as he wandered down the street. Very furtively Lucio told the friar that nothing like Claudio's execution would have taken place if the duke had been ruler. Lucio went on confidentially to say that the duke cared as much for the ladies as any other man and also drank in private. In fact, said Lucio, the duke bedded about as much as any man in Vienna. Amused, the friar protested against this gossip, but Lucio angrily asserted that every word was true.

To arouse Isabella so that she would publicly accuse Angelo of wrong-doing, the duke allowed her to believe that Claudio was dead. Then the duke sent letters to the deputy informing him that the royal party would arrive on the following day at the gates of Vienna and would expect a welcoming party there. Also, the command ordered that anyone who had had grievances against the government while the duke was absent should be allowed to make public pronouncement of them at that time and place.

Angelo grew nervous upon receipt of these papers from the duke. The next day, however, he organized a great crowd and a celebration of welcome at the gates of the city. In the middle of the crowd were Isabella and Mariana, heavily veiled. At the proper time the two women stepped forward to denounce Angelo. Isabella called him a traitor and virgin-violator; Mariana claimed that he would not admit her as his wife. The duke, pretending to be angry at these tirades against his deputy, ordered the women to prison and asked that someone apprehend the rascally

2293

friar who had often been seen in their company.

Then the duke went to his palace and quickly changed to his disguise as a friar. Appearing before the crowd at the gates, he criticized the government of Vienna severely. Escalus, horrified at the fanatical comments of the friar, ordered his arrest and was seconded by Lucio, who maintained that the friar had told him only the day before that the duke was a drunkard and a frequenter of bawdy houses. At last, to display his own bravado, Lucio tore away the friar's hood. When the friar stood revealed as Duke Vincentio, the crowd fell back in amazement.

Angelo, realizing that his crimes would now be exposed, asked simply to be put to death without trial. The duke ordered him first to marry Mariana. After telling Mariana that Angelo's goods, legally hers, would secure her a better husband, the duke was surprised when she entreated for Angelo's pardon. Finally, because Isabella also pleaded for Angelo's freedom, the duke relented. He did, however, send Lucio to prison. Claudio was released and married to Juliet. The duke himself asked Isabella for her hand.

MEDEA

Type of work: Drama
Author: Euripides (480-406 B.C.)
Type of plot: Classical tragedy
Time of plot: Remote antiquity
Locale: Corinth
First presented: 431 B.C.

Principal characters:
MEDEA, a sorceress
JASON, her lover
CREON, King of Corinth
GLAUCE, daughter of Creon
AEGEUS, King of Athens

Critique:

Medea is justly one of the best known of Greek tragedies, for although it was written more than two thousand years ago it has meaning and significance today. Jason and Medea are purely human and even without the intervention of supernatural agencies, tragedy is implicit in their characters. Their story is a perennial caution against excess of emotion and a stern warning against bitter vengeance.

The Story:

When Medea discovered that Jason had deserted her and married Glauce, the daughter of Creon, she vowed a terrible vengeance. Her nurse, although she loved Medea, recognized that a frightful threat now hung over Corinth, for she knew that Medea would not let the insult pass without some dreadful revenge. She feared especially for Medea's two sons, since the sorceress included her children in the hatred which she now felt for their father.

Her resentment increased still further when Creon, hearing of her vow, ordered her and her children to be banished from Corinth. Slyly, with a plan already in mind, Medea persuaded him to allow her just one day longer to prepare herself and her children for the journey. She had already decided the nature of her revenge; the one problem that remained was a place of refuge afterward. Then Aegeus, King of Athens and a long-time friend of Medea, appeared in Corinth on his way home from a journey. Sympathetic with her because of Jason's brutal desertion, he offered her a place of refuge from her enemies in his own kingdom. In this manner Medea assured herself of a refuge, even after Aegeus should learn of the deeds she intended to commit in Corinth.

When the Corinthian women came to visit her, Medea told them of her plan, but only after swearing them to absolute secrecy. At first she had considered killing Jason, his princess, and Creon, and then fleeing with her children. But after she had considered, she felt that revenge would be sweeter should Jason live to suffer long afterward. Nothing could be more painful than to grow old without a lover, without children, and without friends, and so Medea planned to kill the king, his daughter, and her own children.

She called Jason to her and pretended that she forgave him for what he had done, recognizing at last the justice and foresight he had shown in marrying Glauce. She begged his forgiveness for her earlier rage, and asked that she be allowed to send her children with gifts for the new bride, as a sign of her repentance. Jason was completely deceived by her supposed change of heart, and expressed his pleasure at the belated wisdom she was showing.

Medea drew out a magnificent robe and a fillet of gold, presents of her grandfather, Helios, the sun god, but before she entrusted them to her children she smeared them with a deadly drug. Shortly afterward, a messenger came to Medea and told her to flee. One part of her plan had succeeded. After Jason and the children had left, Glauce had dressed herself in her wonderful robe and walked through the palace. But as the warmth and moisture of her body came in contact with the drug, the fillet and gown clung to her body and seared her flesh. She tried frantically to tear them from her, but the garments only wrapped more tightly around her, and she died in a screaming agony of flames. When Creon rushed in and saw his daughter writhing on the floor, he attempted to lift her, but was himself contaminated by the poison. His death was as agonized as hers had been.

Meanwhile the children had returned to Medea. As she looked at them and felt their arms around her, she was torn between her love for them and her hatred of Jason; between her desire for revenge and the commands of her mother-instinct. But the barbarian part of her nature—Medea being not a Greek, but a barbarian from Colchis—triumphed. After reveling in the messenger's account of the deaths of Creon and his daughter, she entered her house with the children and barred the door. While the Corinthian women stood helplessly outside, they listened to the shrieks of the children as Medea killed them with a sword. Jason appeared, frantically eager to take his children away lest they be killed by Creon's followers for having brought the dreadful gifts. When he learned Medea had killed his children, he was almost insane with grief. As he hammered furiously on the barred doors of the house, Medea suddenly appeared above, holding the bodies of her dead children, and drawn in a chariot which Helios, the sun god, had sent her. Jason alternately cursed her and pleaded with her for one last sight of his children as Medea taunted him with the loneliness and grief to which he was doomed. She told him that her own sorrow would be great, but it was compensated for by the sweetness of her revenge.

The chariot, drawn by winged dragons, carried her first to the mountain of the goddess Hera. There she buried her children. Then she journeyed to Athens, where she would spend the remainder of her days feeding on the gall and wormwood of her terrible grief and revenge.

MEDITATIONS

Type of work: Philosophical discourse
Author: Marcus Aurelius (121-180)
First transcribed: c. 167-180

Although the Greek philosopher Zeno is generally given the credit for creating the school of philosophy called Stoicism, its greatest fame arises from the popularity and widespread influence of the utterances of two later figures: Epictetus, a slave, and Marcus Aurelius, Emperor of Rome. Of the two, Marcus Aurelius, born just four years before the death of Epictetus in 125, has probably achieved the greater fame; and this fame results almost entirely from his *Meditations,* one of the most famous philosophical books in the world.

For the average reader, however, there is a disturbing characteristic in the work, which is obscure and often seemingly unrelated; there are passages which suggest that the book has come down to us in a disorganized, even careless, form. One widely accepted cause that has been suggested for this difficulty is the possible intention of Marcus that his writings should be read by no one else, that these recorded thoughts were intended only for their author. It is certain that the *Meditations* was written during the period between Marcus' accession to the imperial rank in 161 and his death in 180; it is equally certain that the various books were indited during rigorous military campaigns and trying political crises. Although these facts explain in part the irregularity of the book, other scholars feel that there is clear evidence of the emperor's design to publish at least parts of the work.

If this is so, and if Marcus did not merely keep a private journal, then the reason for the present form of the *Meditations* probably lies in errors and misunderstandings by copyists and later editors of the text. In either event, the reader finds in this book two generally different styles side by side: a nearly casual, sometimes aphoristic, way of writing, and a more literary, more carefully planned, technique. Throughout the twelve books that make up the whole there are passages that read like admonitions addressed by the author to himself; in contrast to these are sections that sound as if Marcus were offering philosophical advice to the Romans or to all mankind in general.

Despite these irregularities, and in spite of the absence of an organized system of thought, a careful reading reveals that the emperor presents to the world some of the sagest suggestions for leading the good life and some of the most effective expressions of the tenets of later Stoicism to be found anywhere.

To say, however, that Marcus Aurelius can be given credit for profound original thinking is going too far. Like many great contemplative books, the *Meditations* was not written in a vacuum. It rephrases and reinterprets much of that which is usually considered the best of ancient Greek and Roman philosophy. The author acknowledges his debt to his teachers and his wise forbears; his quotations from, and references to, the leading thinkers of his and earlier times prove his wide reading and careful study—his injunction to throw aside one's books and to live one's philosophy notwithstanding.

Perhaps the fact that Marcus did live by his philosophy, one that was tested by almost continually difficult circumstances, is one of the chief charms of his book. There is very little in the *Meditations* that the emperor probably did not find occasion to think of in relation to his own life. Much of practical philosophic value can be found here. His advice at the opening of Book II, for instance, to begin each day with the thought that one will meet during that day men who are arrogant, envious, and deceitful, but to remember that these men are so because of their ignorance of the good and the

2297

right, is surely a sound practical application of the Platonic idea that evil is only the absence of knowledge.

Many readers have found the *Meditations* their surest guide·to living by Stoic principles. Although happiness must surely come by the pursuit of Stoic virtue, duty is the greatest good in the Stoic view. The word *duty* appears rarely in the book, but the emperor's conviction that a man must face squarely his responsibilities is implicit in almost every paragraph. Often a note of Roman sternness appears, as in the beginning of paragraph 5 of Book II:

> Every moment think steadily as a Roman and a man to do what thou hast in hand with perfect and simple dignity, and feeling of affection, and freedom, and justice; and to give thyself relief from all other thoughts.

To achieve true virtue, the emperor says, one must live in accord with nature; that is, with both kinds of nature, the nature of man and the nature of the universe. The book departs from a commonly held view of the philosopher as an isolated dreamer in its insistence that a man must live wisely with his fellow men; he should not be a hermit. Since a man partakes of the same divinity, in his soul, with other men, he must live and work with them; certainly such is the divine intention, and this, then, is one's social duty. The duty one has to the universe is to perceive the informing intelligence that pervades and guides it. Here Marcus is close to pantheism.

With this foundation in mind, the reader can easily understand the emperor's notion of evil as something that cannot harm or disturb the great plan of the universe; it is simply ignorance and harms only the doer. Thus, no man can be harmed by a force outside himself; only he can do himself real injury. The advice of the *Meditations*, along with that of other Stoic writings, is to accept calmly what cannot be avoided and to perform to the best of one's ability the duties of a human being in a world of humans.

Since we cannot understand the workings of the great force that rules the universe, it is our part simply to do what we can in our own sphere.

Though he believes the world to be divinely guided, Marcus has no illusions about life. Therefore, he scorns fears of death. Life is full of trouble and hardship, and no one should be sorry to leave it. In Paragraph 14 of Book II the author says that however long or short a person's life, he loses at death only the present moment because he does not possess the past and the future; further, since the progress of time is simply a revolution, and all things have been and will be the same, a man loses nothing by an early death. This passage displays something of the occasional coldness of the emperor's thought, but it is one of many sections devoted to the consolation of men for the hard facts of existence.

Regardless of the varied character of the writing and the thinking in these paragraphs, it is clear that a reasonably consistent philosophy inspired them. Certainly the statement that a man rarely comes to grief from not knowing what is in another man's soul, that true misery results from not understanding what lies within oneself, is of a piece with the rest of the book.

Some readers have found in Marcus Aurelius a basically Christian spirit, and they believe that the *Meditations* adumbrates in many passages later religious writings. Considerable doubt exists as to his feeling about the Christians or to the extent of his responsibility for their persecution during his reign; but there is little question that a great deal of his thinking is closely allied with that of later spiritual leaders. The book is often compared with other philosophic works of consolation, such as Pascal's *Pensées* and the *Confessions* of Saint Augustine.

Beyond doubt, the readership and influence of this book by perhaps the greatest pagan ruler who ever lived is as·wide as those of any other work of its kind, and far greater than those of most.

MEEK HERITAGE

Type of work: Novel
Author: Frans Eemil Sillanpää (1888-   )
Type of plot: Impressionistic realism
Time of plot: 1857-1917
Locale: Finland
First published: 1919

Principal characters:
JUSSI TOIVOLA, a mild peasant
RINA, his wife
BENJAMIN, his father
KALLE, Rina's son

Critique:

Meek Heritage conveys the atmosphere of a brooding folk epic. Jussi, the protagonist, symbolizes the lower-class Finn who is jostled and led by fate. The harsh climate, the grubbing toil, the cruel class cleavages are his natural lot. Even the birth and death cycles are indifferent to him. His redeeming virtue is his ability to work hard under direction. Over the whole novel lies a tone of melancholy. The style is discursive and penetrating. Sillanpää was awarded the Nobel prize for literature in 1939.

The Story:

Benjamin was an old man who had already buried two wives. His overtures to Maja, the servant girl, were matter-of-fact, but somehow Maja saw in this tobacco-dribbling tyrant an opportunity for improvement. She had borne one child out of wedlock and she longed for position. When they were married, the parson was at some pains to refer to Maja as a maidservant.

As she awaited Jussi's birth, she thought that now she might be like other farm wives. Benjamin drank far too much and quarreled incessantly. The night her labor started, he went to drink with Ollila, a neighbor. Maja was left with only Lovisa, the cupper-woman, to look after her. Lovisa was sharp-tongued but competent; before Maja came to the farm as mistress, she herself had enjoyed Benjamin's favors. In fact, when Benjamin stumbled home long after his son was born, he called for Lovisa.

While Jussi was little, he stayed in his cradle fretting at the lice. As he grew older, he drank coffee sometimes. He early learned to avoid his father, who for fun would poke plug tobacco into his protesting mouth. He played with poorer children on top of Pig Hill and was initiated into many mysteries. He looked forward to his confirmation, for he believed it was the dividing line between childhood and man's estate.

A period of drought seriously impaired the family fortunes. Maja was no longer afraid of Benjamin. Too old and weak to beat her, he continued to drink with Ollila and to borrow money from him. When things got too bad, he took his deeds to Ollila and returned bearing food and money. The sheriff came to take possession of Benjamin's farm the night the old man died. Maja and Jussi set out for her brother's farm on foot. Maja left Jussi at Tuorila with her reluctant brother while she looked for work; she, too, died soon afterward.

While he lived with his uncle, Jussi was confused. For one thing, the house was so big and clean. And he was neither servant nor family. Although he received many orders, he understood few of them. He would have liked to run errands for his aunt, but he could never find things. He finally became a herdsman, a job he could do fairly well.

MEEK HERITAGE by Frans Eemil Sillanpää. Translated by Alexander Matson. By permission of the publishers, Alfred A. Knopf, Inc. Copyright, 1938, by Alfred A. Knopf, Inc.

After his first confirmation Jussi was disappointed because people still treated him like a child. Little by little, however, his uncle gave him more responsibility. One fall evening he was sent to round up crofters for the harvest. Luckily, he found most of them at a harvest celebration. At the merriment Jussi was treated like everyone else: he was given ale to drink and he danced with a boy his age. Later he was in a group that escorted Manda, a farm girl, back to Tuorila. The men made so much noise trying to follow Manda up to her loft that they awoke Jussi's uncle. The master came with a stick and beat the revelers.

Tuorila prospered and the family decided to invite the gentry to a social gathering. Jussi had the job of looking after the horses and carriages. A comrade, Gustav Toivola, loosened the wheel nuts on the guests' rigs. Jussi's uncle blamed him for the accidents and cast him out. Jussi found a temporary home at Toivola with Gustav's parents.

At Toivola, Jussi was not exactly welcome, but he stayed on, helping where he could. A kind of liberation came with the arrival of the timber cutters. The foreman, Keinonen, hired Jussi and helped him keep his wages away from the Toivola family. When the timber cutters left, Jussi went with them. For years, working on the lakes and shores, he earned a little money but not enough to put anything by. Sometimes, although he was too shy to pursue women, he went on sprees with the other men.

After a time the logging slacked off. The best Jussi could do was to go back to his native countryside and take a job as farmhand at Pirjola. Rina, the maid, slept on the other side of the fireplace. She was a slack girl and loose-natured. Jussi often thought of going over to her bed, but he lacked the courage. One Sunday in July, however, he drank some liquor he had bought and slept in Rina's bed. She was willing enough, for she was pregnant and it would be better if her child had a father.

Jussi and Rina were given an old cabin in the swamp. Although they were not regular crofters, for they had no contract, they could raise what they wished on an acre of ground allowed them. Jussi worked for his rent when the master of Pirjola needed him. Rina's first child was born soon afterward. From the beginning Kalle did not seem to belong to the family. Then Jussi's children, Hilda and Ville, came, and much later Lempi and Marti. Once Jussi was prosperous enough to have a horse and a cow, but after the horse died he never had enough money to buy another. Rina, not a good manager, often sold the bread Jussi brought home.

Kalle, always a strange child, hit Ville with a rail and paralyzed his younger half-brother. Medicine for Ville took all Jussi's money until the child died. Kalle was sent away to work as soon as he was big enough. Hilda, a quiet girl, went into service in a distant town. She drowned herself when only the son of the house was at home. Rina, always tired from farm work and weak after the birth of her last child, died of a mysterious feminine complaint.

As he grew old and bald, Jussi's teeth crumbled. Working less and less, he spent more time in the village. Lempi and Marti brought themselves up as best they could. Only on sufferance did Jussi keep his land. Kalle, now a cab driver in the city, sent home newspapers which Jussi had someone read to him. The unrest caused by the war resulted in changes. The working day was now only twelve hours instead of sixteen, and there was agitation for more reforms. Because he had become garrulous, Jussi gained a reputation for frank speaking. When the Socialists began to rule that section of Finland, he was even a member of a delegation.

During the strikes the Socialists posted armed guards and requisitioned what they needed from the farms. Jussi was made a sentry at Paitula and given a rifle. Everyone else knew the strike was ending, but Jussi stayed on, faithful to his assignment. When Paitula was looted, the fleeing Socialists killed a landowner. At last suspecting something, Jussi threw down his rifle and went home.

Government officials came to the farm for Jussi. In the house they found only the two crying children, but in the barn they captured the cowering Jussi. There was a trial which Jussi did not understand very well, and the judge was in a hurry to restore order. Jussi was one of fourteen led out to an open grave and shot.

MELMOTH THE WANDERER

Type of work: Novel
Author: Charles Robert Maturin (1782-1824)
Type of plot: Gothic romance
Time of plot: Early nineteenth century
Locale: Ireland
First published: 1820

Principal characters:
JOHN MELMOTH, a young Irishman
MELMOTH THE WANDERER, young Melmoth's ill-starred ancestor
ALONZO MONCADA, a Spaniard shipwrecked in Ireland
YOUNG MELMOTH'S UNCLE

Critique:

Maturin's novel has been called by many literary scholars the greatest of the novels of terror so popular in English fiction during the early years of the nineteenth century. In addition, other writers have admired and have been influenced by *Melmoth the Wanderer*, partly because of the striking qualities of the plot and partly because of the theme of the never-ending life which it describes. Balzac wrote a sequel to Maturin's novel entitled *Melmoth Reconciled*. Among the admirers of the novel were Edgar Allan Poe, Dante Gabriel Rossetti, and Baudelaire. Oscar Wilde, after his disgrace in the 1890's, took for himself the name of Sebastian Melmoth, which combined the idea of the wanderer with that of the arrow-pierced saint. Interestingly enough, Maturin, in his preface, said that he was ashamed of appearing as a novelist but that his profession as a clergyman did not pay him enough to avoid such shameful activities as writing novels.

The Story

In the autumn of 1816, John Melmoth, a student at Trinity College, Dublin, left his school to visit an uncle, his only surviving relative, who was dying. Melmoth's uncle was particularly glad to see his young nephew, for the old man was fearfully afraid of something which he had not revealed to anyone else. The uncle died, leaving all his money and property to John Melmoth. At the end of the will was a note telling John Melmoth to destroy the hidden portrait of an earlier John

Melmoth, a painting dated 1646, and a packet of letters to be found in a secret drawer.

The day after his uncle's death young John Melmoth made inquiries to learn whether his uncle had been a man of superstitious nature. He was told that the uncle was not a superstitious man, but that in recent months he had insisted that a strange man appeared and disappeared about the manor house.

Young Melmoth destroyed the portrait, as the will requested, but opened the packet of manuscript, which contained a strange story about the man whose portrait he had destroyed. The document, telling how the original John Melmoth had been seen many times after his reported death in Germany, had been written by an Englishman named Stanton, who had actually met Melmoth the Wanderer in Spain. The Wanderer, apparently angered by Stanton's curiosity, had prophesied that Stanton would be confined in Bedlam, even though he was sane. The prediction having come true, the Wanderer appeared to Stanton in his misery and promised the miserable man his freedom if he would sell his soul to the devil. Stanton refused, and the Wanderer disappeared. Stanton wrote down his experiences and left the manuscript with the Melmoth family when he visited Ireland in order to discover more about the man who had tempted him.

After reading the manuscript, young Melmoth went to bed. That night he, too, saw the Wanderer. His strange ancestor paid the young man a visit and as proof

2302

of his appearance left a bruise on John Melmoth's wrist.

The next night a ship was wrecked on the Irish coast not far from the Melmoth estate. When young Melmoth and his retainers went to help rescue the sailors, Melmoth saw the Wanderer high on a rock overlooking the ruined ship and heard him laugh derisively. Young Melmoth tried to ascend the rock but fell into the sea, from which he was rescued by Alonzo Moncada, a Spaniard who escaped from the doomed ship. Young Melmoth and the Spaniard returned to the manor house. A few days later the Spaniard disclosed that he, too, knew the Wanderer.

Moncada told young Melmoth a series of stories about the activities of the Wanderer in Spain. The first story was about the Spaniard himself, who was an exile from his country, even though he was descended from a noble family. Moncada, having been born out of wedlock, could not inherit the ducal title of his ancestors. As a means of getting him out of the way, lest his presence tarnish the proud name of his house, his family had destined him for a monastery. Moncada did not want to be a monk, but his wishes in the matter were ignored by his family, including his own mother.

After a few years Moncada's brother had a change of heart and tried to secure the monk's release from his vows and thereby called down the hatred of the Church upon both Alonzo and himself. Failing to secure a release legally, the brother then arranged for Moncada's escape. Monastery officials, learning of the scheme, had the brother killed and denounced Moncada to the Inquisition. While he lay in prison, Moncada was visited by Melmoth the Wanderer, who tempted him to secure release by selling his soul to Satan. Moncada refused; he escaped later when the prison of the Inquisition burned.

Moncada found refuge with an old Jewish doctor who had become interested in the history of the Wanderer. From the Jew Moncada learned the story of still another person whom the Wanderer had tempted.

The Jew told how Don Francisco di Aliaga, a Spanish nobleman, had lost his daughter in a shipwreck while she was still little more than a baby. The child and her nurse had been cast upon an unknown and uninhabited island. The nurse died, but the baby grew up alone on the island, to become a beautiful girl. To her the Wanderer appeared on several occasions, each time tempting her to sell her soul to Satan in order to gain knowledge of the world. Strangely enough, the girl and the Wanderer fell in love. She refused to marry him, however, under any auspices but those of the Church.

Soon afterward the girl was found and returned to her family in Spain. There the Wanderer saw her again. Their love being still great, they were, unknown to anyone, married in what was actually a Satanic ceremony. Meanwhile the Wanderer, conscience-stricken by fears that he would bring sorrow to the one he loved, had appeared to Don Aliaga and warned him, by stories of the Wanderer's Satanic activities, of dangers surrounding the girl.

The Wanderer told Don Aliaga of the temptation of a father whose children were starving, and of a young woman, during the reign of Charles II of England, who had been tempted in order to have the man she loved. In both cases, however, those tempted had refused to pay the price of damnation in return for earthly happiness. Don Aliaga recognized the meaning of these tales, but pressing business affairs kept him from acting at once.

When Don Aliaga finally returned to his home, he brought with him the young man he had selected to be his daughter's husband. Unknown to all, however, the girl was about to give birth to a child by the Wanderer. When the Wanderer appeared to claim her at a masked ball, her connection with the accursed guest was revealed and she was turned over to the Inquisition. Shortly after giving birth to her child she died, her dying words the wish that 'she, and the Wanderer too, would enter Heaven.

Such was the tale the Jewish doctor told

to Alonzo Moncada, who was escaping from Spain when he was shipwrecked on the Irish coast. The tale ending, the Wanderer suddenly appeared in the room with them. He told his horrified listeners that he had returned to his ancestral home to end his earthly wanderings. His fate had been to roam the earth for one hundred and fifty years after his death, under a terrible command to win souls for the devil. Everyone he had tempted, however, had refused to exchange earthly happiness for eternal damnation.

The Wanderer then asked that he be left alone to meet his destiny. A short time later young Melmoth and the Spaniard heard strange voices and horrible noises in the room where they had left the Wanderer. The next morning the room was empty. The only sign of the Wanderer was a scarf caught on a bush at the place where he had plunged or had been thrown into the sea.

THE MEMBER OF THE WEDDING

Type of work: Novel
Author: Carson McCullers (1917-   )
Type of plot: Impressionistic realism
Time of plot: 1945
Locale: Georgia
First published: 1946

Principal characters:

BERENICE SADIE BROWN, colored cook in the Addams household
FRANKIE ADDAMS, a twelve-year-old girl
MR. ADDAMS, her father
JARVIS, her brother, a corporal in the army
JOHN HENRY WEST, her cousin
JANICE EVANS, fiancée of Jarvis
HONEY CAMDEN BROWN, Berenice's foster brother
A SOLDIER

Critique:

All of Carson McCullers' fiction turns on the theme of loneliness and longing as the inescapable condition of man. In *The Member of the Wedding* the issues of the larger world are reflected in the experiences of the twelve-year-old girl trapped in the confusion of her own adolescence. The novel tells the story of several decisive days in the life of Frankie Addams, and much of the meaning of her plight is made clear in her random talk with Berenice Sadie Brown and John Henry West as the three sit around the table in the kitchen of the Addams house. Frankie seizes upon her soldier brother's approaching wedding to will herself into the social community, only to discover that the bride and groom must by necessity reject her and that she must learn to fend for herself. In the story of Frankie Addams the writer has reduced the total idea of moral isolation to a fable of simple outlines and a few eloquently dramatic scenes, set against a background of adolescent mood and discovery familiar to us all. It is easy enough to understand why this novel has also been a success in dramatic form. The play of the same name, written by Mrs. McCullers, is a sympathetic study of inward conflicts. It received both the

Donaldson Award and the New York Drama Critics Prize in 1950.

The Story:

In the summer of her twelfth year Frankie Addams felt that she had become an unjoined person. She was a lanky girl with a crew haircut and skinned elbows. Some of the older girls she had played with the year before had a neighborhood club and there were parties with boys on Saturday nights, but Frankie was not a member. That summer she got herself into so much trouble that at last she just stayed home with John Henry West, her little cousin, and Berenice Sadie Brown, the colored cook. Through long, hot afternoons they would sit in the dingy, sad Addams kitchen and play cards or talk until their words sounded strange, with little meaning.

Berenice Sadie Brown was short and black and the only mother Frankie had ever known, her own mother having died when she was born. The cook had been married four times and during one of her marriages she had lost an eye while fighting with a worthless husband. Now she owned a blue glass eye which always interested John Henry West. He was six and wore gold-rimmed glasses. Sometimes Frankie grew tired of him and sent him home. Sometimes she begged him to stay all night. Everything seemed so mixed up that she seldom knew what she did want.

Then, on the last Friday in August, something happened which made life wonderful once more. Her brother Jarvis, a soldier home from Alaska, had come to dinner with Janice Evans, a girl who lived at Winter Hill. They were to be married there on Sunday, and Frankie and her father were going to the wedding. After dinner Janice and Jarvis returned to Winter Hill. Mr. Addams went downtown to his jewelry store. Later, while she sat playing cards with Berenice and John Henry, Frankie thought of her brother and his bride. Winter Hill became all mixed up in her mind with snow and icy glaciers in Alaska.

Jarvis and Janice had brought Frankie a doll, but she had no time for dolls any more. John Henry could have it. She wished her hair were not so short; she looked like one of the freaks from the Chattahoochee Exposition. Suddenly angry, she chased John Henry home. When Berenice teased her, saying that she was jealous of the wedding, Frankie declared that she was going to Winter Hill and never coming back. For a minute she wanted to throw a kitchen knife at the black cook. Instead, she hurled it at the stairway door.

Berenice went out with Honey Camden Brown, her foster brother, and T. T. Williams, her beau. Because Honey was not quite right in the head, Berenice was always trying to keep him out of trouble. T. T. owned a colored restaurant. Frankie did not know that the cook's pity for the unhappy, motherless girl kept her from marrying T. T.

Left alone, Frankie wandered around the block to the house where John Henry lived with Aunt Pet and Uncle Eustace. Somewhere close by a horn began to play a blues tune. Frankie felt so sad and lonely that she wanted to do something she had never done before. She thought again of Jarvis and Janice. She was going to be a member of the wedding; after the ceremony the three of them would go away together. She was not plain Frankie Addams any longer. She would call herself F. Jasmine Addams, and she would never feel lonely or afraid again.

The next morning, with Mr. Addams' grunted permission, Frankie went downtown to buy a new dress and shoes. On the way she found herself telling everyone she met about the wedding. That was how she happened to go into the Blue Moon, a cheap café where she knew children were not allowed. But F. Jasmine Addams was no longer a child, and so she went in to tell the Portuguese proprietor about the wedding. The only other person in the café was a red-headed soldier from a nearby army post. Frankie scarcely noticed him at the time, but she remembered him later when she saw him on the street. By that time he was drunk and trying to buy an organ-grinder's monkey. The soldier bought Frankie a beer and asked her to meet him that night at the Blue Moon.

When Frankie finally arrived home, she learned that Berenice and John Henry were also to attend the wedding. An aged kinsman of the Wests had died and Aunt Pet and Uncle Eustace were going to the funeral at Opelika. Berenice, dismayed when she saw the orange silk evening dress, the silver hair ribbon, and the silver slippers Frankie had bought to wear at the wedding, tried, without much success, to alter the dress for the gawky young girl. Afterward they began to talk about the dead people they had known. Berenice told about Ludie Freeman, the first husband she had truly loved. The story of Ludie and the three other husbands made them all feel lonesome and sad. Berenice held the two children on her knees as she tried to explain to them the simple wisdom life had taught her. They began to sing spirituals in the half-dark of the dingy kitchen.

2306

Frankie did meet the soldier that night. First she went with John Henry to Big Mama's house and had her palm read. Afterward she told John Henry to go on home; she did not want him to know she was meeting someone at the Blue Moon. The soldier bought two drinks. Frankie was afraid to taste hers. He asked her to go up to his room. Frightened when he tried to pull her down beside him on the bed, she picked up a glass pitcher and hit him over the head. Then she climbed down the fire escape and ran all the way home. She was glad to get into bed with no one but John Henry by her side.

The wedding next day turned into a nightmare for Frankie. Everything was lovely until the time came for the bride and groom to leave. When they carried their bags out to the car, she ran to get her own suitcase. Then they told her, as kindly as possible, that they were going away alone. She grasped the steering wheel and wept until someone dragged her away. Riding home on the bus, she cried all the way. Berenice promised her a bridge party with grown-up refreshments as soon as school opened, but Frankie knew that she would never be happy again. That night she tried to run away. Not knowing where else to go, she went to the Blue Moon. There a policeman found her and sent for her father.

But by November Frankie had almost forgotten the wedding. Other things had happened. John Henry had died of meningitis. Honey Camden Brown, drug-crazed, had tried to hold up a drugstore and was in jail. Mary Littlejohn had become her best, real friend. She and her father were leaving the old house and going to live with Aunt Pet and Uncle Eustace in a new suburb. Berenice, waiting to see the last of the furniture taken away, was sad, for she knew that Frankie would depend on her no longer. Frankie —she wanted to be called Frances—was thirteen.

MEMOIRS

Type of work: Autobiography
Author: Giovanni Jacopo Casanova de Seingalt (1725-1798)
Time: 1725-1773
Locale: Europe and the Near East
First published: 1826-1838

Principal personages:
CASANOVA, the narrator
TERESA, an actress who became the traveling companion of Casanova
for a time
C. C., a young Venetian woman who loved Casanova
MADAME LA MARQUISE D'URFÉ, an aged French noblewoman duped by
Casanova
THÉRÈSE TRENTI, also called Thérèse Imer and Madame Cornelys, an
actress, adventuress, and mother of one of Casanova's illegitimate chil-
dren
M. DE BRAGADIN, a Venetian senator and Casanova's benefactor

In his *Memoirs* (*Mémoires écrits par lui-même*), Casanova, who took for himself the additional name of Seingalt, set forth his amazing life of adventures as he remembered them in his old age. Not everything in his reminiscences tallies with discoverable historical fact, either because the writer's memory was faulty in his old age or because he colored the truth for the sake of a better story. In his autobiography Casanova reveals himself as a man ruled by pleasure, passion, and a delicate sense of revenge. He was superficial, amoral, proud, and sometimes extremely foolish. As he tells the story, he was also a brave man. He faced poverty, ill fortune, imprisonment, and even possible death with fortitude. The only situation before which he quailed was marriage, a state which would have put an end to his unconventional way of life. Although Italian was his mother tongue, he wrote his *Memoirs* in French. In the work there is perhaps less philosophizing than one might expect from an old man. Casanova seems generally to have thought his life a full and generous one, over which there was little need to ponder or grieve because of past follies or mistakes.

Casanova was the oldest child of Gaëtan Joseph Jacques Casanova and his wife Zanetta, the beautiful daughter of a Venetian shoemaker. When a child, he was left with his maternal grandmother while his parents continued their careers on the stage. Rather strangely, Casanova could remember nothing of his life before he was eight years old. His earliest recollection was of a terrible nosebleed from which he suffered and for which his grandmother took him to see an old woman who performed a strange cure, apparently by witchcraft, for his malady.

At his father's death Casanova, one of three children, was taken in hand by the Abbé Grimani, who placed the boy in a strict school. Though he hated his studies, he was precocious by nature and at the age of sixteen he became a Doctor of Law. Returned to Venice, he was befriended by M. de Malipiero, a retired senator. While visiting in Paséan, Casanova met a young girl named Lucy, whom he admired and respected. When he revisited the town again a few months later, he learned that the girl had eloped with another. Disappointed and resentful, he decided that he might as well make love to women instead of treating them with devotion and respect.

At seventeen Casanova entered a seminary, from which he was shortly expelled. Later he fell in with a Franciscan friar named Brother Stephano, with whom he had several adventures. On one occasion he was presented to Pope Benedict XIV, who treated him kindly. For a time Casanova stayed in the household of Cardinal Acquaviva, but an adventure with a girl put the police on his trail and he went to Constantinople, where he had several amorous adventures. On the way to Turkey he met Teresa, an actress who had disguised herself as a boy. The young woman left her family and went with Casanova to become his mistress for a time. Soon afterward Casanova assumed the dress of a military officer. In Constantinople a noble Turk, pleased with the young Venetian, offered him a fortune and his daughter's hand in marriage if Casanova would only become a Moslem. On his return to Europe, Casanova stopped at Corfu, where he actually became an officer. Not entirely happy in military service, he left it before long and returned to Venice.

With his fortunes at a low ebb, Casanova took up the profession of a fiddler at the Theater of Saint Samuel. One day he had the opportunity to befriend M. de Bragadin, a Venetian senator, when the old man was suddenly taken ill. The senator, a wealthy man, took Casanova into his home and treated him as his son. He and two of his wealthy friends were soon convinced that Casanova had occult powers. Realizing their gullibility, Casanova hoaxed the old men into marrying off for him a young girl with whom he had had a very interesting affair.

Casanova then left Venice and traveled to Milan and Cesena. In the latter place he met a woman named Henriette, who abandoned her lover to accompany Casanova to Parma. She turned out to be a noblewoman who soon had to return to her family. During a period of reform which followed this adventure, Casanova became a Freemason and later went to Paris. After various adventures, including one in which he passed himself off as a doctor, he went to Dresden. There a tragi-comedy he had written had some success on the stage. On his return to Venice he met C. C., a beautiful heiress with whom he fell in love. He was overjoyed to find his love reciprocated. Her family did not approve of the match, however, partly because of the girl's youth, and she was placed in a convent.

One day when he visited the convent Casanova impressed one of the nuns, a very beautiful and worldly woman. The nun, M. M., arranged through her lover for an affair with Casanova. During many months of 1753 they met outside the convent and had a very happy time, until the woman's lover, M. de Bernis, the French ambassador to Venice, returned to Paris. Soon afterward M. M. and C. C. learned that they loved the same man; much to Casanova's anger and discomfiture, they changed places one night.

As his affair with M. M. was drawing to a close, Casanova was arrested by the state Inquisition, which confined him in the notorious prison known as The Leads because of his supposed heresy and his dabbling in black magic. After some months in the prison, Casanova found a bolt from which he made a combination tool and weapon. He was almost ready to escape when a change in cells brought his plan to light. He started all over again, with accomplices inside the prison, and eventually made a daring escape with a man named Balbi; the two escaped by making a daring passage over the roofs of the prison itself. Casanova succeeded in making his way from Venice to Munich, but his companion was captured and returned to The Leads.

From Germany, Casanova went to Paris, arriving there in January, 1757, shortly after Damiens had attempted to assassinate King Louis XV. While in Paris, Casanova raised several million francs for the crown by means of a lottery and thus came into favor in court circles. He met Madame la Marquise d'Urfé, a wealthy and elderly noblewoman fascinated by the occult arts. Becoming the old woman's companion in experiments in magic and alchemy, he was able to fleece her of a great deal of money.

On a trip to Amsterdam, Casanova again met Thérèse Trenti, whom he had known some years before as Thérèse Imer. Now an actress, she was the mother of Casanova's daughter and of a son by another father. Casanova took the boy back to Paris and put him in the care of Madame d'Urfé. In Paris he also helped out Mlle. X. V. C., who had become pregnant and feared her family's wrath. For his pains he fell afoul of the police, although he himself was innocent of any wrongdoing.

After he had cleared himself he traveled to Holland and then to Germany, having many adventures in love on the way and making some money, most of it by gambling. In Cologne he had an amusing affair with the wife of the burgomaster. From there he went to Würtemburg, where he was cheated and robbed by three army officers who then betrayed their victim to the police and charged him with unlawful gambling. With the help of two pretty women Casanova made his escape and went to Zurich, Switzerland. At Zurich he had several pleasant affairs, including one with a pretty French widow named Dubois, who served as his housekeeper. In the summer of 1760 Casanova went to Geneva to visit Voltaire, whom he found a charming man but too much addicted to republicanism for Casanova's taste.

From his visit to Voltaire, Casanova went to Aix-en-Savoie, where he had an interesting experience with a nun who much resembled his M. M. Having become pregnant, the nun had arranged to leave her convent with a supposed illness that could be treated by the waters at Aix. He helped her through her confinement and then returned her to her order.

Casanova went on to Rome, where he was received by the Pope, who promised to help him obtain a pardon from the Venetian authorities. Nothing came of the promise, but the pontiff did bestow the Cross of the Order of the Golden Spur on Casanova.

Leaving Rome, Casanova visited Bologna, Modena, Parma, Turin, and Chambéry. At Chambéry he arranged for a banquet with the second M. M., whom he had sent back to her convent. Finally back in Paris, Casanova found Madame d'Urfé hopeful of being reborn as a male child through certain occult rites. Casanova, seeing the woman was set in her ideas, promised to help her. Much of his time for almost two years was spent in occult pursuits which enabled the adventurer to make himself a small fortune at the noblewoman's expense.

In Milan the adventurer tried to have an affair with a Spanish countess who retaliated by trying to take his life with magic. Casanova had greater success with the Countess Clementina at the chateau of San Angelo, where he was the guest of Count Ambrose. He won the countess' love and then, as usual, proceeded to leave her. He always had adventures and affairs, but his next great exploits took place in England. He went to London, where he found Thérèse Trenti, who now called herself Madame Cornelys, and her children an unhappy domestic combination. To relieve his boredom and gloom he advertised for a woman to rent an apartment in his house. Pauline, a Portuguese noblewoman who had taken refuge in England, answered the advertisement. Casanova and Pauline had an affair which lasted until she was compelled to return to her homeland. After Pauline's departure, Casanova met Miss Charpillon, an adventuress who proved more than a match for him, even driving him to contemplate suicide. After this disaster, Casanova often lived a seedy and wretched existence as he drifted about Europe from Russia to Spain. At the time of writing his *Memoirs,* in 1773, he was still waiting to receive from the Venetian authorities the pardon which would allow him to return to the city and republic he loved.

THE MEMOIRS OF A CAVALIER

Type of work: Novel
Author: Daniel Defoe (1660-1731)
Type of plot: Adventure romance
Time of plot: 1630-1648
Locale: England and the Continent
First published: 1720

Principal characters:
>THE CAVALIER, the unidentified second son of a landed family in England
>CAPTAIN FIELDING, the Cavalier's friend and traveling companion
>SIR JOHN HEPBURN, the Cavalier's friend in the Swedish army
>GUSTAVUS ADOLPHUS, King of Sweden and Protestant champion in the Thirty Years' War
>CHARLES I, King of England, served by the Cavalier in the English Civil War

Critique:

The year 1720 was an eventful one in the career of Daniel Defoe, for in that year he published three works: *The Memoirs of a Cavalier, Captain Singleton,* and his *Serious Reflections of Robinson Crusoe.* Like the other book-length narratives by Defoe, *The Memoirs of a Cavalier* did not originally carry the author's name, a circumstance apparently intended to lend an air of authenticity to his realistic work. Over the years attempts have been made to prove that Defoe merely edited the memoirs of some real person, but scholars are now in agreement that this book, along with others by Defoe, was his own creation and that he probably had no specific person in mind as the original for his fictional narrator-protagonist. One interesting feature of the novel is that its hero is a member of the upper class, while the usual Defoe hero is taken from the middle or lower classes, groups that Defoe knew at first hand, as he did not know the life of the upper class. The Cavalier who narrates the story is similar to other Defoe creations in that, uninterested in religion as a young man, he is worldly and materialistic. Also noteworthy is the fact that Defoe, a Protestant himself and a Dissenter from Anglicanism, glorifies the Protestant side in the Thirty Years' War but has little to say for the English Protestants who rebelled against the monarchy and the Anglican Church during the

1640's.

The Story:

The Cavalier was the son of a landed gentleman in the county of Salop, born, according to his own report, in 1608. As a child he was taught by good tutors; as a young man he was sent to Oxford University, where he spent three years deciding that he was not interested either in continuing academic life or entering one of the professions—law, the Church, or medicine. His father hoped the young man, who was his favorite son, would settle down near his home. He even agreed to settle an estate worth two thousand pounds per year upon the young man, but the Cavalier, much as he loved his father and appreciated the offer, decided, with his father's permission, to travel on the Continent.

In 1630 the Cavalier crossed the Channel and began his adventures in life. With him went a college friend named Fielding. Because of his martial bearing the friend had been nicknamed the "Captain," and the name stuck to him. After some minor adventures on the road, the Cavalier and his friend arrived in Paris. Their stay in that city was cut short when the Cavalier killed a man in a swordfight and the two friends left the city hurriedly to escape the authorities. They journeyed to Italy and traveled there for some time, returning later to France to observe how

Cardinal Richelieu was administering that country for his king. Again the two Englishmen found themselves in trouble from which they were extricated by the Queen Mother, who gave them a pass that enabled them to travel on to see the fighting between the French forces and those of the Duke of Savoy. Unimpressed in Italy by the antiquities of Rome and by the Italian people, who seemed much degenerated from their Roman ancestors, the Cavalier and his friend traveled northward into central Europe, arriving in Vienna in 1631 and then going on into Bavaria. In Germany they had a chance to see the fighting between the Protestant Germans, led by the Elector-Duke of Saxony, and the Catholic forces headed by Emperor Ferdinand. One of the dreadful experiences the two Englishmen had was to observe the end of the siege of Magdeburg. The fall of that city was marked by terrible looting, rape, and murder; the city itself was almost completely destroyed, and the population reduced to a mere handful from an original population of more than 25,000 souls.

After the fall of Magdeburg to the Catholic forces, the Cavalier and Fielding journeyed on until they encountered the invading army of Gustavus Adolphus, King of Sweden, who had joined the Protestant Germans against Emperor Ferdinand. The Cavalier was quite impressed with the Swedish army and the person of the Swedish king, to whom he was introduced by Colonel Hepburn, a friend of the Cavalier's father who had taken service in the Swedish army. Fielding joined the Swedish forces, as did the Cavalier himself after a time, serving first as a gentleman volunteer and later as a commissioned officer. The, Cavalier distinguished himself many times in the Swedish service. His father raised a regiment of cavalry and, with the consent of the English king, sent it to Gustavus Adolphus, who made the Cavalier its colonel. In addition to his service as a commander, the Cavalier also became a special attendant to the king and sometimes his emissary. Captured by the Im-

perial forces shortly before the Battle of Lützen, in which Gustavus Adolphus lost his life, the Cavalier was allowed to continue his travels after he had given his parole.

In 1635, the Cavalier found himself in Holland, where he observed the Dutch army under its famous commander, Prince Maurice, opposing the forces of Spain. Later in the same year the Cavalier returned to England, where he rested for some months until he was called from his inactivity by Charles I, who asked the Cavalier to enter his service in the campaign against the Scots. Serving as a gentleman volunteer rather than as a commissioned officer, he found the campaigns against the Scots little to his liking, inasmuch as there was little real action, only minor skirmishes, and the war was over religious dissent, a cause in which the Cavalier could see little reason.

At the outbreak of the English Civil War the Cavalier had little feeling about war from a moral standpoint. He considered himself a professional soldier who did his duty honorably, not worrying particularly about the causes of war or the countryside that was devastated or the injuries done to its populace. As the war continued, however, he saw that England, as a country was losing, whether victory fell to King Charles or to the Parliamentary forces which opposed the monarchy.

When the Civil War broke out in 1642, the Cavalier was still serving Charles I in the Scottish campaigns. He continued to follow the monarch, even though he recognized that the king was ill-prepared to battle for his throne. Rather than take a commission, the Cavalier still fought as a gentleman volunteer in the royal troop of guards. Later, when his father was injured, the Cavalier took the command of the royalist force his father had recruited.

Fighting in many of the minor battles of the Civil War, the Cavalier saw most of the action as the armies marched and countermarched, sometimes to do battle, sometimes to escape it. During the great battle at Edgehill, however, the Cavalier realized that he had a greater stake in the war than the interests of a professional soldier. From that time on he wished that an honorable peace could be arranged between King Charles and Parliament.

During his years of campaigning for the monarchy the Cavalier had many adventures, but he was fortunate to escape with no serious injury. Even a dangerous mission as a disguised spy turned out well. One effect of the war which angered the Cavalier was the activity of the Scots against King Charles. The Cavalier thought that the Scots had no call to make war on the monarch, who had acceded to all their demands, even to abolishing the episcopacy in favor of the Scots' native Presbyterianism.

Toward the end of the war the Cavalier's father was taken prisoner by Parliamentary forces. The Cavalier offered to take his father's place, but his father was able to buy his freedom by giving his parole and paying four thousand pounds. A short time later the Cavalier was cut off from the royal army. He and a group of companions managed to escape, making their way by sea to Cornwall, where they joined Lord Hopton's forces. When the king surrendered to the Scots, who later turned him over to the Parliament, Lord Hopton's troops also surrendered. The Cavalier, like other royalists, was given the choice of leaving the country or peaceably going home. The Cavalier returned to his home, content that he had served his king, his country, and his honor as best he could. Having given his parole that he would take no further part in the war, he retired from active life.

MEMOIRS OF A FOX-HUNTING MAN

Type of work: Novel
Author: Siegfried Sassoon (1886-   )
Type of plot: Social chronicle
Time of plot: 1895-1916
Locale: England and France
First published: 1929

Principal characters:
   GEORGE SHERSTON, the fox-hunting man
   AUNT EVELYN, with whom he lived
   TOM DIXON, Aunt Evelyn's groom
   DENIS MILDEN, George's friend and master at Ringwell, later at Packlestone
   STEPHEN COLWOOD, George's schoolmate and friend
   MR. PENNETT, George's trustee,
   DICK TILTWOOD, George's friend in the army

Critique:

Memoirs of a Fox-Hunting Man is the scarcely concealed autobiography of the author. The tone of the book is nostalgic. The passages concerning cricket and the more technical passages about fox hunting are somewhat tedious, but for the most part this sensitive record of a young man's quiet, well-ordered life in pre-war England is interesting and illuminating. The class distinctions may be difficult for an American reader to understand, but Sassoon indicates that later in life he himself came to be more liberal in his feeling about people of lower social ranks.

The Story:

George Sherston was orphaned so early that he could not remember when he had not lived with his Aunt Evelyn at Butley. At the age of nine he became the possessor of a pony, bought at the urgent request of Aunt Evelyn's groom, Tom Dixon. Aunt Evelyn would not let George go to school until he was twelve, and his early training was given him by an incompetent tutor, Mr. Star. Dixon, however, taught him to ride, and this training he valued more highly than anything Mr. Star taught him. Because George's early life was often lonely, he welcomed the diversion of riding.

At last Dixon thought George was ready to see some fox hunting. Since there was no hunting in the Sherston neighborhood, they had to ride some nine miles to the Dumborough Hunt, where George was thrilled by the color and excitement of the chase. He saw a boy of about his own age who carried himself well and was obviously one to be imitated. The next Friday at a dance George saw the boy again and was pleased that the boy, Denis Milden, remembered seeing him at the hunt.

After his first year in school at Ballboro' George was happy to be back at Aunt Evelyn's. Dixon met him at the station with the word that he had secured a place for George on the village cricket team, which would play next day at the Flower Show Match. George had played good cricket at school, but he did not know how he would show up facing players of long experience. The next day, learning that he was to be last at bat, he spent the afternoon trying to forget his nervousness. Once in the game, he suddenly gained confidence and brought his side the victory.

George's trustee and guardian, Mr. Pennett, was disturbed when his ward quit Cambridge without a degree. George settled down with Aunt Evelyn at Butley. He played some cricket and some golf. He ordered a great many books from London. Dixon began to revive George's interest in hunting, but Mr.

Pennett would not give George the full amount of his annual income and so George could not afford the kind of horse he wanted. Dixon, however, soon found a suitable horse within the limits of George's budget, a hunter named Harkaway. The season was well on, and George was out only three days. Later in the spring he attended the Ringwell Hunt Point-to-Point Races, where Stephen Colwood, a friend whom he had known at Ballboro', won the Heavy-Weight Race.

The following autumn George made one of his rare trips to London. There he heard a concert by Fritz Kreisler and bought some clothes suitable for a fox-hunting man. His first hunting was with the Potford Hunt, an experience he found much more exciting than that he had known with the Dumborough. He also went down to Sussex to stay with Stephen at his father's rectory. While visiting Stephen, George bought another horse, Cockbird, in defiance of Mr. Pennett. When he returned to Butley with his new horse, his Aunt Evelyn, realizing that he could not afford the hunter, sold one of her rings and gave George the money for Christmas.

Cockbird was more than a satisfactory horse. Riding him with the Ringwell Hounds, George qualified for the Colonel's Cup Race. One of his competitors was riding a horse owned by Nigel Croplady, a noisy young braggart liked by very few people. Another competitor was his friend Stephen. During the race Stephen was forced to drop back, but he encouraged George so much that George came in to win. As the afternoon came to a close, someone drew his attention to the new master of the Ringwell Hounds. It was Denis Milden.

That summer George played in a number of cricket matches. Stephen, now in the artillery, spent a weekend at Butley. As autumn drew on, George became impatient for the hunting season to begin. Stephen, now stationed near his home, asked George to spend some time at the rectory and ride with the Ring-

well Hounds. Nothing could have pleased George more, for he was a great admirer of Denis. The two became good friends, and George sometimes stayed at the kennels with Denis. Denis proved to be an excellent master, skillful in the hunt and careful and patient with his hounds.

Early in the following season, however, Denis resigned to become master of the Packlestone Hunt, and he insisted that George go up to the Midlands with him. To ride with the Packlestone Hounds would be an expense George knew he could not afford, but he went for the first season. He was always embarrassed, for he knew that his new friends were unaware of his economic limitations. The year was 1914.

War was declared. George, aware of his incompetency as a soldier, had turned down two opportunities to be an officer, and was serving in the army as a cavalryman. To have to salute Nigel Croplady made him feel silly. One day the horse George was riding threw him, and he broke his arm. Two months later he was sent home to allow his arm to heal. One afternoon he went to see his neighbor, Captain Huxtable, and asked that he be recommended for a commission in the infantry. The commission came through. George proceeded to his new camp. There he made friends with Dick Tiltwood, a pleasant young man not long out of school.

They crossed the Channel together and were assigned to a battalion coming back from the front for a rest. Dick and George spent many hours sightseeing and talking and reading. George took Dick out riding frequently. They would pretend they were fox hunting. George, assigned to headquarters, felt rather shaken when Dick was sent to the trenches without him. Word reached George that Stephen had been killed. Dixon, who was also in service and who wanted to be transferred to George's company, died of pneumonia. Then when George learned that Dick had died of a throat wound, he asked to be transferred to the trenches. There he served bravely, always angry at the war which had taken away his best friends.

MEMOIRS OF A MIDGET

Type of work: Novel
Author: Walter de la Mare (1873-1956)
Type of plot: Fantasy
Time of plot: Late nineteenth century
Locale: England
First published: 1921

Principal characters:
　　MISS M., a midget
　　MRS. BOWATER, her landlady
　　FANNY BOWATER, Mrs. Bowater's daughter
　　MRS. MONNERIE, Miss M.'s patroness
　　MR. ANON, a dwarf

Critique:

Memoirs of a Midget is a highly original novel which mingles poetry and social criticism. Exquisitely written, it has an unfailing charm and interest. Remarkable is the careful and exact use of the proper perspective throughout the thoughtfully executed work. Nor can the reader fail to note the veiled criticisms of society which the author puts into the mouth of tiny Miss M.

The Story:

Miss M., a perfectly-formed midget, was born to normal parents and in pleasant surroundings. Until her eighteenth year she was brought up in seclusion. Then her mother died, followed shortly thereafter by her father, and tiny Miss M. was left alone in the world. Her godmother offered to take her in, but the girl, having inherited a modest fortune, decided to take lodgings instead. She made her first humiliating excursion in public when she moved to her new home.

Her lodgings were in the home of Mrs. Bowater, a stern woman, who nevertheless had a great affection for her small roomer. At Mrs. Bowater's Miss M. met Fanny, the daughter of her landlady. A teacher in a girls' school, Fanny was both charming and clever. Because of the friendship between the two, the midget became involved in the love affair of Fanny Bowater and the curate, an affair which ended with the curate's suicide when Fanny rejected his suit.

After a time Miss M. began to go out in society. She became the friend of Lady Pollacke, whose friendship she was never to lose. At their home she met the wealthy Mrs. Monnerie, the youngest daughter of Lord B. Mrs. Monnerie took such a fancy to the tiny girl that she invited her for a vacation at Lyme Regis, a fashionable watering place in Dorsetshire.

Before she left on her vacation Miss M. accidentally met a new friend, Mr. Anon, a deformed and hunchbacked creature only a few inches taller than Miss M. Miss M., unaware of the ways of the world, introduced Mr. Anon to Mrs. Bowater, who approved of him in a grudging way. They saw each other frequently, and Miss M. once solicited his aid when she wanted to secure money for Fanny while she was away at Lyme Regis. Soon after they returned from their holiday, Mrs. Monnerie invited Midgetina, as she called Miss M., to visit at her elaborate town house in London.

Miss M. accepted the invitation and became another prized possession Mrs. Monnerie could exhibit to her guests. In London she met the niece and nephew of her patroness. Percy Maudlen was a languid, ill-mannered youth whom the small girl disliked. Susan Monnerie was a pleasant person of whom Miss M. became very fond. After a visit of six weeks, Miss M. returned briefly to Mrs. Bowater's. There she received a letter from Fanny, begging her to try to use her influence with Mrs. Monnerie to secure a position for Fanny as a governess. During Miss M.'s stay with Mrs. Bowater she again met Mr. Anon, who declared his love for her. The midget told him that she was not able to return his love.

Before long Miss M. returned to London, where her pampered way of living did much to spoil her. During her stay Mrs. Bowater came with the news that she was going to South America to nurse her sick husband, a sailor. Shortly afterward Miss M.'s solicitors informed her that her small inheritance had dwindled because of the gifts and trifles she had bought and because of her loans to Fanny. When Miss M. confessed her troubles to Sir Walter Pollacke, he consented to become both her guardian and financial adviser. Meanwhile, Miss M. had not forgotten Fanny Bowater's request. Through the little person's persuasion, Mrs. Monnerie found a place for Fanny as morning governess and invited the girl to stay with her.

Mr. Anon wrote and proposed marriage, but Miss M. was horrified at the idea of repeating the performance of Tom Thumb and Mercy Lavinia Bump Warren. Then it became evident that Mrs. Monnerie was no longer amused by her little charge, for Fanny had become her favorite. To celebrate Miss M.'s birthday, Percy Maudlen planned a banquet in her honor, but the party was a dismal failure so far as Miss M. was concerned. The menu disgusted her, and when Percy proposed a toast Miss M. responded by drinking down her glass of chartreuse at a single gulp and staggering drunkenly down the table. In this condition she hurled at Fanny a reference to the unfortunate suicide of the curate.

Such actions deserved punishment. Mrs. Monnerie sent Miss M. in disgrace to Monks' House, her summer place in the country. One afternoon Miss M. saw the caravans of a circus passing the gate. Because she knew that she could no longer count on Mrs. Monnerie for support, Miss M. was desperate and she suddenly decided to hire herself to the circus. The owner engaged her to ride a pony in the ring, and she agreed to appear for four nights for fifteen guineas. She also told fortunes. She was a great success, the most popular attraction of the circus.

Her solitude during the day at Monks' House was interrupted by the arrival of Fanny Bowater. Fanny seemed to know of her escapades at the circus, and the two quarreled violently. Then Mrs. Monnerie arrived. She was in a high state of excitement over the news of the midget who was so popular at the circus. She had even made up a party to attend the performance on the last night. When Miss M. flatly refused to perform, Mrs. Monnerie sent her, like a child, to bed.

At the last minute Miss M. felt that she must appear at the circus to keep her contract. Setting out on foot, she encountered Mr. Anon, and they went on to the circus together. Although he tried to persuade her not to appear, she exhibited herself in the tent, unrecognized, in her disguise, by all of the members of Mrs. Monnerie's party except Fanny. Mr. Anon, determined that he would take her place in the riding act, put on her costume and rode into the ring. Thrown from the pony, he died in Miss M.'s arms.

Through a legacy from her grandfather, Miss M. became financially independent, and settled down at Lyndsey with Mrs. Bowater as her housekeeper. But one night Miss M. disappeared mysteriously, leaving a note saying that she had been called suddenly away. She was never seen again, and her memoirs were eventually presented to the public by her faithful friend, Sir Walter Pollacke.

MEMOIRS OF A PHYSICIAN

Type of work: Novel
Author: Alexandre Dumas, father (1802-1870)
Type of plot: Historical romance
Time of plot: Eighteenth century
Locale: Paris and environs
First published: 1846-1848

Principal characters:
BARON DE TAVERNEY
PHILIPPE, his son
ANDRÉE, his daughter
GILBERT, in love with Andrée
KING LOUIS XV OF FRANCE
M. DE CHOISEUL, the king's minister
MADAME JEANNE DU BARRY, the king's favorite
ARMAND DE RICHELIEU, a political opportunist
JOSEPH BALSAMO (COUNT DE FÉNIX), a sorcerer and revolutionary
LORENZA FELICIANI, his wife
ALTHOTAS, his instructor in magic
M. DE SARTINES, a lieutenant of police
JEAN JACQUES ROUSSEAU, the philosopher

Critique:

Memoirs of a Physician is an intricate plot of court intrigue in the closing days of the reign of Louis XV, with *dramatis personae* as diverse as the scheming Duc de Richelieu, the philosopher Rousseau, and the favorite-dominated king. Manipulating all these by means of his magical control of natural forces and the power invested in him as a representative of the secret brotherhood of Freemasonry is the mysterious figure of Joseph Balsamo. The climax is as lurid as any modern thriller. For its full historical value this volume should be read as one of a series of five, all concerned with the court life of France at the time of Louis XV and XVI. Called the Marie Antoinette romances, the novels are Memoirs of a Physician (including Joseph Balsamo), The Queen's Necklace, The Taking of the Bastille, The Countess de Charny, in that order, and, lastly, The Chevalier of the Maison-Rouge.

The Story:

At the court of Louis XV of France the Duc de Richelieu plotted with Madame du Barry, the king's favorite, to replace M. de Choiseul as the king's minister. They consulted a Count de Fénix, who turned out to be the reputed sorcerer Joseph Balsamo; ten years earlier the necromancer had predicted that Madame du Barry would one day be queen of France. Balsamo used his wife Lorenza as an unwilling medium for his sorcery. Through her he was able to give Richelieu and Madame du Barry compromising information contained in a letter sent by the Duchess of Grammont to her brother, de Choiseul, showing that the minister was encouraging the revolt of parliament against the king and attempting to bring about war with England. Fortified with this information, Richelieu forced the king to dismiss his minister.

The philosopher Rousseau, standing in the crowd gathered outside the palace after the king at a "bed of justice" had defied parliament, was urged to attend a secret meeting where he would be initiated into the mystic order of Freemasonry. Rousseau declared he could do more for the world by not joining the order. The chief of the council, who was Balsamo, read a communication from Swedenborg which warned them of a traitor in their midst.

In order to demonstrate to the surgeon Marat, a member of the secret fraternity, that body and soul can be separated and then reunited and that the soul has a greater knowledge than the body, Balsamo hypnotized one of Marat's patients. As the patient's crushed leg was amputated, Balsamo made the patient sing. He also hypnotized Marat's maid, drew from her an admission of the theft of her master's watch, and, still in the condition of sleep, made her repeat the contents of a letter she could not read while awake.

Andrée, daughter of the impoverished Baron de Taverney, had recently been saved from the violence of a mob by Gilbert, a son of the people, but she was ignorant of this circumstance because Balsamo had brought her home in his carriage. After the girl had been settled at the Trianon through the request of the dauphiness, her beauty charmed the king completely, and he commissioned Richelieu to present her with a necklace worth several million livres, but she declined the gift. Richelieu, escorting de Taverney through the gardens after they had supped with the king, was heard by Gilbert, hidden in a dense thicket, advising the baron to send his daughter to a convent. Philippe, Andrée's brother, who held a commission in the royal army, paid a farewell visit to his sister; she confided to him her fears and forebodings. After his departure, Andrée threw herself on a bench and wept. Gilbert approached and declared his love for her, but Andrée rebuffed him.

In his mansion, Balsamo was summoned to Lorenza's room, where she begged him to release her so that she could retire to a convent. When he refused, she plunged a dagger into her breast. After commanding Lorenza to sleep, Balsamo ascended to the chamber of the alchemist Althotas, who reminded him that in a week the aged man would be one hundred years old, by which time he must have the last three drops of blood of a child or a young female to complete the elixir which would preserve him for another half century. Balsamo, having promised his help, was returning to the sleeping Lorenza when he was interrupted by the arrival of Richelieu, who had come for a special sleeping draught for Andrée. Richelieu had already left instructions that a love potion be given the king which would cause him to fall in love with the first woman he saw on waking.

Gilbert overheard Nicole, Andrée's maid, tell her lover that Richelieu had arranged for them to escape together after first drugging Andrée and leaving her door unlocked; later he saw them ride off. Andrée, plunged into a hypnotic sleep by the drink, descended the stairs of her apartment in a trance and passed the astounded Gilbert. A flash of lightning disclosed the concealed figure of Balsamo, who ordered Andrée to tell what had happened at his house in Paris after Lorenza had tried to kill herself and he had put her to sleep. Andrée, describing Lorenza's flight, told how she had taken with her a box of papers and, on reaching the street, had inquired the address of the lieutenant of police, M. de Sartines. At this news Balsamo leaped to his horse and without releasing Andrée from her trance, dashed off for Paris.

Andrée, left alone, sank to the ground. Gilbert, a witness of this scene at a distance, rushed toward her, lifted her up, and carried her back to her chamber. As he placed her on the couch he heard a step. Hastily he blew out the candle. Realizing that the visitor was the king, Gilbert fled. King Louis, seeing Andrée lying pale and immobile and thinking her dead, also fled in panic.

Balsamo, riding toward Paris, knew that his only hope of preventing Lorenza from revealing his secrets to the police lay in his magic power over her. Abruptly he reined in his horse and with all the force at his command willed Lorenza to fall asleep wherever she was. From Sèvres, he sent a hasty note to Madame du Barry in Paris. Lorenza, meanwhile, had arrived at the office of the police, but before she could give him Balsamo's address she fell to the floor, overcome by a strange dizziness. A valet carried her into an adjoining room. M. de Sartines burst open the coffer, however, and a clerk deciphered the secret papers which implicated Balsamo in plans affecting the king and the government.

At that moment Balsamo, under the name of the Count de Fénix, was announced. Seeing that the coffer had been opened, he threatened to blow out M. de Sartines' brains. Madame du Barry, acting quickly on receipt of Balsamo's letter, arrived at that moment, and M. de Sartines surrendered the coffer to her. She in turn handed it to Balsamo with all the papers intact.

On his return to his chambers Balsamo found Lorenza there in convulsions. His determination to kill her ebbed as he gazed on her beauty, and an overpowering love for her swept his being and caused him to feel that if he surrendered his control over her he might still earn some heavenly recompense. For three days the very thought plunged him into a happiness he had never before experienced, while in her trance Lorenza dreamed aloud her own mysterious love. On the third day, after she had asked him to test her ability still to see through space in spite of intervening material obstacles, Balsamo willed her to report what Madame du Barry was doing. Lorenza reported that the king's favorite was on her way to see him.

Balsamo put Lorenza into a still deeper sleep. As he was leaving her he fancied he heard a creak. Looking back, he saw only her sleeping form. In her sleep Lorenza thought she saw part of the ceiling of her room descend, and from this moving trap a Caliban-shaped creature creep toward her. Powerless to escape, she felt him place her on the circular trap, which then ascended slowly toward the ceiling.

Madame du Barry, worried because she had been followed, told Balsamo that she had saved him from arrest when M. de Sartines had handed the king the deciphered names from the coffer. In appreciation, Balsamo presented her with a vial containing a draught which would ensure her twenty years of additional youth. After her departure Balsamo returned to Lorenza's couch, only to find her gone. He ascended to his instructor's room and there discovered the body of Lorenza. To his horror he realized that Althotas drained from her the blood needed for his elixir.

Cursing his master, from whose hands the vial with the precious liquid slipped and broke, Balsamo fell unconscious on the lifeless body of his wife. He stirred only when notified by his servant that "the five masters" were waiting to see him. They had come from the secret fraternity to pronounce sentence on him as a traitor. Having watched his movements, they had seen Lorenza leave his home with a coffer which contained secret names in cipher. Later he himself had arrived at the police office, and Lorenza had departed alone; but he had left with Madame du Barry, whom he had summoned there to receive the secret information for which he was paid. The paper which had revealed their secrets had been left with the police, they charged, but Balsamo had brought away the coffer in order to avoid implication. As a result of this betrayal, five of their prominent agents had been arrested. Balsamo did not defend himself. When he asked only for a few minutes to bring proof that would speak for him, they let him go. He returned, bearing the body of Lorenza which he let slip from his arms to fall at their feet. In consternation, his judges fled.

Althotas, enraged at his pupil and fearing death for himself, set fire to his precious manuscripts and perished in the flames. All night the fire roared in the rooms above, while Balsamo, stretched beside Lorenza's body, never moved. The vaulted walls were thick, however, and the fire finally burned itself out.

Andrée recovered from her prostration and retired to a convent. Baron de Taverney, repudiated by the king and Richelieu, slunk back to his impoverished estate. Philippe sailed for America, and Gilbert followed. Balsamo vegetated in his mansion, from which he was supposed to have reappeared during the violence of the French Revolution. As for the king, on May 9, 1774, his physician pronounced him suffering from smallpox. His daughter, Madame Louise of France, left her convent cell to attend him, and he was given extreme unction. Madame du Barry was sent to the chateau of the Duchess d'Aiguillon. The next day the king died, and Louis XVI came to a throne about to be engulfed in the flames of rebellion and anarchy.

MEMOIRS OF AN INFANTRY OFFICER

Type of work: Novel
Author: Siegfried Sassoon (1886-   )
Type of plot: Social chronicle
Time of plot: 1916-1917
Locale: France and England
First published: 1930

Principal characters:
GEORGE SHERSTON, an infantry officer
DAVID CROMLECH, his friend
AUNT EVELYN, his aunt

Critique:

This novel—the second of a series which also includes *Memoirs of a Fox-Hunting Man* and *Sherston's Progress*—is almost a caricature of what many people regard as typical English behavior. The war is a very casual, very personal thing, almost devoid of import and strategy. The officers who meet Sherston briefly are men who exhibit just the right amount of detachment and regard for good form. Underneath the well-bred tolerance for the real discomfort and danger of trench warfare there is a thread of revolt which culminates in Sherston's letter informing his colonel that the war is needlessly being prolonged. Even the authorities, however, are too well-bred to take the letter seriously, and Sherston falls back into nonchalance. The book is quiet but effective satire on upper-class English life.

The Story:

Spring arrived late in 1916 in the trenches near Mametz. Sherston had made up his mind to die, because under the circumstances there seemed to be little else to do. The battle of the Somme had exhausted him. Colonel Kinjack could see that Sherston was looking for trouble and so, to forestall any unpleasantness, he sent Sherston to the Fourth Army School at Flixécourt for a month's training.

The beds at the school were clean and comfortable, and the routine was not too onerous. Sherston settled back to forget the war. He attended a big game hunter's lectures on sniping and practiced with a bayonet. To him it was a little incongruous to listen to advice from civilians and army men who had never been close to real war. All the instructors concentrated on open warfare; they were sure that the trenches would soon be abandoned.

One hot Saturday afternoon he went back to his outfit, where the talk was all of an impending raid. There seemed to be some jealousy involved, for a Canadian raid a short time before had been a great success.

Sherston, sure he would accompany the raiders, wrote a farewell letter to his Aunt Evelyn, a letter in which he slyly assumed the attitude of the "happy warrior." Entering a dugout, he was a little surprised to see the raiders putting burnt cork on their faces. Their appearance reminded him ridiculously of a minstrel show. Requested to take the raiders up to headquarters, he jumped at the opportunity to present his plea to the commanding officer.

To his disappointment, Colonel Kinjack brusquely told him he had to stay behind to count the raiders when they returned. So he was condemned to stand in the trench and wait.

As soon as the raiders were well over the parapet, the explosions began. The men struggled back defeated when the second belt of German wire proved invulnerable. They had all tossed their bombs and retired. Sherston began to go out into No Man's Land to bring

MEMOIRS OF AN INFANTRY OFFICER by Siegfried Sassoon. By permission of the author and the publishers, Doubleday & Co., Inc. Copyright, 1930, by Coward-McCann Inc.

in the casualties. A gray-haired lance corporal was glad of his wound, for he had been waiting eighteen months for a chance to go home. O'Brien, the major, was killed, and Sherston had to drag him out of a shell crater. Luckily the Germans, perhaps out of pity, stopped firing.

The result of the raid was two killed and ten wounded. In the newspapers, the account was somewhat changed. Aunt Evelyn read that the party entered the German trenches without difficulty, displayed admirable morale, and withdrew after twenty-five minutes of hand-to-hand fighting.

The big push, the summer offensive, was in the air. Before Sherston really had time to think much about impending events, he was given a leave. At first it was strange to be back in England, where everyone seemed to know about the projected onslaught. Out of deference to one who would take part in it, however, they seldom mentioned it. Aunt Evelyn soon found out about the raid when Sherston grandly announced that he was due for a military cross. She was horrified, for she thought her nephew was still in the transport service.

On his way back to France he stopped in the Army and Navy Store and bought two pairs of wire cutters. Then, because he was late in returning from leave, he bought a salmon and two bottles of brandy to appease his colonel.

When the offensive began, Sherston's company advanced fifteen hundred yards in four hours. Then the guides became confused, and all forward progress stopped. According to the General Staff, the Germans were supposed to be out of the Mametz Woods, but they were still there. The company waited.

Sherston was going along a communications trench when his companion, Kendle, was killed by a sniper. Furious at the unexpected killing, Sherston took a mills bomb in each hand and went over the top. After a while he was looking down into a well-ordered trench filled with Germans. Fortunately they were just leaving, and he jumped into Wood Trench, until lately the German front line. Then he lost his perspective. Not knowing what to do with the trench, he returned to his own lines. His colonel reproved him severely for not "consolidating" the trench or even reporting the incident.

During the battle of Bazentin Ridge Sherston was kept in reserve in the transport lines. In this brief respite, he met his old friend, David Cromlech. For a while they shared experiences, but both were reluctant to talk about the battle of the Somme. David irritated the other officers greatly by his habit of making bold pronouncements about sacred things. For instance, he said that all sports except boxing, football, and rock climbing were snobbish and silly.

When Sherston was finally recalled to his battalion, it was with the expectation that he would go into action at once. As it turned out, however, he came down with enteritis before he arrived in the front lines. It was an escape, really, for he was removed to the base hospital and eventually was sent back to England.

At the military hospital in Oxford, Sherston recovered enough to go canoeing occasionally. By the end of August he was back with Aunt Evelyn on a month's sick leave with a possibility of extension. Several letters from fellow officers kept him informed about his battalion, mostly reports on men killed. He remained fairly cheerful, however, by riding in the local fox hunts. In February he went back to Rouen.

The Germans were retreating from the Hindenburg Line, and the British were on the offensive in the battle of Arras. To his surprise and gratification, Sherston was put in charge of a hundred bombers who were clearing the trenches. He carried out his task with great skill and bravery. When the mission was nearly accomplished, he was struck by a rifle bullet.

Back in England again, he rebelled

against going into action a third time. With the help of Tyrrell, a pacifist philosopher, he composed a defiant letter to his colonel, saying that he refused to take part in the war any longer because he was sure it was being unnecessarily continued by those in power. He was sure, above all, that the Germans would surrender if the Allies would publish their war aims. Expecting to be court-martialed for this breach of discipline, he was resolved to accept even execution.

To his chagrin, the superiors refused to take him seriously. He went before a board which investigated his sanity. Then David Cromlech was called in to talk to him at Clitherland Camp. Unable to persuade him to recant by any other means, David finally told Sherston that if he refused to retract his statements he would be confined in a lunatic asylum for the duration of the war. Sherston knew David was only telling a friendly lie, but he did not want to see his friend proved a liar. He decided to admit his mistake and see the war through to its finish.

THE MENAECHMI

Type of work: Drama
Author: Titus Maccius Plautus (c. 255-184 B.C.)
Type of plot: Farce
Time of plot: Third century B.C.
Locale: Epidamnum, a city of Macedonia
First presented: Late third or early second century B.C.

Principal characters:
MENAECHMUS OF EPIDAMNUM
MENAECHMUS SOSICLES, his twin brother
MESSENIO, Menaechmus Sosicles' servant
WIFE OF MENAECHMUS OF EPIDAMNUM
EROTIUM, a courtesan, Menaechmus of Epidamnum's mistress
PENICULUS, a parasite, hanger-on to Menaechmus of Epidamnum

Critique:

The *Menaechmi* is one of the best-known of Plautus' plays (Shakespeare leaned heavily on it for *The Comedy of Errors* (1592-1594). Although its plot is not remarkably complex, Plautus handles the action with considerable histrionic dexterity, carefully signaling in advance so that the audience may always be in a position to relish the misunderstandings and confusion of the characters. Binding itself to a very narrow unity of time and place, the action takes place before the house of Erotium in little more than the time actually represented. This limitation creates a number of problems in verisimilitude, but the play moves so rapidly that the audience has no opportunity to grow uneasy at the improbable coincidences or the obtuseness of the characters. The *Menaechmi* has no apparent social or moral theme, but it manifests good showmanship throughout.

The Story:

When the two Menaechmi were seven years old, one, later to become Menaechmus of Epidamnum, accompanied his merchant father from their home in Syracuse to Tarentum. There, fascinated by the confused activity, the boy wandered away, became lost, and was finally picked up by another merchant who took him to the merchant's own home in Epidamnum and adopted him. The boy's family was so grief-stricken at his loss that his name was given to the remaining son. This boy, Menaechmus Sosicles, grew up, and when he came of age and inherited his father's property, he went out to pursue an aimless quest of his brother.

Menaechmus of Epidamnum had by this time inherited his foster father's wealth, married a somewhat shrewish woman, and acquired a mistress. On the day Menaechmus Sosicles arrived in Epidamnum on his undirected search, Menaechmus of Epidamnum had quarreled with his suspicious wife and had parted from her, secretly bearing one of her robes as a gift to Erotium, his mistress. Delivering the robe, he instructed Erotium to prepare an elaborate meal for their evening's entertainment; then he left to attend to some business at the Forum.

Shortly afterward, Menaechmus Sosicles happened to arrive before Erotium's house and, much to his dismay, was addressed familiarly, first by one of her servants and then by Erotium herself. Confusion followed, but Menaechmus Sosicles finally decided that this was merely Erotium's way of trying to seduce him; and so he gave his servant Messenio his wallet for safekeeping and accompanied the courtesan into the house.

When he came back out later, having consumed the food which Menaechmus of Epidamnum had ordered for himself and his parasite, Erotium gave him the robe so that he could have it altered for

2326

her. As he walked away, intent on selling the robe for his own gain, he was accosted by Peniculus, Menaechmus of Epidamnum's parasite, indignant at having missed a banquet to which he had been invited only a short time before and convinced that he had been purposely affronted. Menaechmus Sosicles finally dismissed Peniculus with an insult, and the latter, believing himself grievously treated by his erstwhile benefactor, went to Menaechmus of Epidamnum's wife and revealed to her that her husband was not only keeping another woman but had given his mistress his wife's robe as well. When Peniculus had finished, Menaechmus of Epidamnum came by on his way from the Forum to Erotium's house, and, in concealment, the two overheard him soliloquizing in a way that substantiated Peniculus' whole story. Satisfied with what she heard, the wife stepped forward and accosted her husband. There followed a confused argument in which Menaechmus of Epidamnum alternated between dissembled ignorance regarding the theft of the robe and genuine dismay regarding his assumed presence at the banquet Erotium had given. At last, seeing that Peniculus had revealed all, he agreed to get the robe and return it. When he went to Erotium and, unaware that Menaechmus Sosicles had already taken the robe, tried to explain his dilemma, she assumed he was trying to defraud her, grew angry, and slammed her door in his face.

Meanwhile, Menaechmus Sosicles, still carrying the robe, met the angry wife, who assumed that he was Menaechmus of Epidamnum returning the robe as he had promised. While the whole situation was still in confusion, the wife's father arrived to take her part. Menaechmus Sosicles decided to feign madness to get rid of the two and was so successful in his attempt that they went off in search of a physician and men to restrain him.

But when these people were assembled, they met Menaechmus of Epidamnum instead of his brother. They would have carried him off if Messenio had not happened along and, mistaking Menaechmus of Epidamnum for his brother, beaten off the assailants. When the others had fled, Messenio asked for his freedom in return for saving his "master's" life; his request was granted by the amazed Menaechmus of Epidamnum, and Messenio went off to collect his master's belongings and return them.

On the way, however, he met Menaechmus Sosicles. Gradually the nature of the confusion came to light. The two brothers finally confronted each other and exchanged the information that was a necessary prelude to formal recognition. Menaechmus of Epidamnum decided to sell his property and return to Syracuse with his brother. Messenio was freed again, this time by his own master, and was made auctioneer for the sale of the property. Everything was to be converted into cash, including Menaechmus of Epidamnum's wife.

LE MENTEUR

Type of work: Drama
Author: Pierre Corneille (1606-1684)
Type of plot: Farce
Time of plot: Seventeenth century
Locale: Paris
First presented: 1643

Principal characters:

DORANTE, a student newly arrived in Paris
GERONTE, his father
CLITON, his valet and confidant
ALCIPPE, his friend, engaged secretly to Clarice
PHILISTE, a friend to both Alcippe and Dorante
CLARICE, a young précieuse, betrothed to Alcippe
LUCRECE, her friend and fellow conspirator
SABINE, the maid and confidante of Lucrece

Critique:

Although Corneille began his career at the famous Hôtel de Bourgogne with *Mélite* in 1629, his reputation as a writer of comedy rests solely on *Le Menteur* (*The Liar*), based on an episode from *Truth Suspected,* by Juan Ruiz de Alarcón (c. 1581-1639). The actor-producer-manager of the Royal Players, Pierre Le Messier, acted the title role with great success, though he was known chiefly as a tragedian. Written in Alexandrines—six iambic feet per line with rhyming couplets—the play has not been satisfactorily translated into English. Another reason for the play's diminished effectiveness in English lies in the clever play on words and the use of double meanings which defy exact translation.

The Story:

Dorante, a young gallant who had come to Paris in order to get his social education and not to take a wife as his father Geronte wished, hired Cliton, a valet who had military and amatory connections, as his mentor. The young man wished to be schooled in the ways of the world, though the only advice he ever took from his man was to spend freely.

Quite by planned accident Clarice, tired of waiting for her lethargic lover Alcippe to conclude their secret arrangements to marry, tripped onto the waiting arm of the newly arrived student. Although a rustic, Dorante immediately accommodated himself to the situation and exchanged euphemistic compliments with the young coquette, much to his valet's despair. The brazen liar captivated not only Clarice but her companions, especially Lucrece, who was silent throughout, by his false accounts of the wars he had fought in and the deeds he had accomplished in Germany during the last four years.

The arrival of Alcippe put the girls to flight, but not before Alcippe saw Clarice talking to his old friend Dorante—who quite ecstatically informed his companions that he had had amazing amatory adventures during his month's stay in Paris. Last night, for example, he had entertained a beautiful lady and five companions on five boats with four choirs of instruments playing all night and with dancing until dawn after a sumptuous repast of six courses, and so on. Cliton attempted to break into this mad monologue, but with no result, for Dorante's philosophy was to tell the big lie of wars and adventures in order to be believed. His stories were so plausible and his manner so persuasive that the two young ladies fell in love with him, his friend Alcippe burned with jealousy because he thought his fiancée had been on the

LE MENTEUR by Pierre Corneille, from CHIEF PLAYS OF CORNEILLE. Translated by Lacy Lockert. By permission of the publishers, Princeton University Press. Copyright, 1952, 1957, by Princeton University Press.

barge, and his friend Philiste was completely mystified when he tried to reconcile the tales with what he later found to be the unvarnished and unromantic truth. The one flaw in the liar's plans was that in his conversation with Cliton, who had gained information about the young women from a coachman, Dorante confused Clarice with Lucrece.

Into this confused web of mendacity and misplaced affections came the good-natured Geronte, who without his son's knowledge pressed the young man's suit for marriage with the daughter of an old friend. The girl was Clarice, ready and willing to be wooed after all the time she had spent waiting for Alcippe's advances. The old man and the young girl contrived a meeting that evening under her balcony and incognito, though she doubted that she could judge her suitor's character from such a distance and under such unintimate circumstances. A friend then suggested that she receive him at Lucrece's house and as Lucrece.

Alcippe, consumed with jealousy, angrily accused Clarice of infidelity. Although she denied his charges, she refused to seal their engagement with two kisses, her hand, and her faith. Alcippe, thinking himself the injured party, swore revenge.

Meanwhile, the tolerant father retracted his offer of his son's hand in marriage to Clarice because the young scoundrel had invented a touching story to escape the wedding planned for him. The story, a cape-and-sword melodrama, concerned his marriage to a poor girl whose father found them alone; in his anxiety to disguise their presence his gun went off, his sword was broken, his barricade smashed, and her reputation threat-could he do but marry sweet Orphise? Cliton's despair changed to admiration, now that he realized how useful his master's ability at lying could be. Though Cliton tried to acquaint him with his mistake about the shy, virtuous, and quiet Lucrece with whom Dorante had not spoken, the bewitched swain swore

he would keep his appointment under her balcony. Alcippe wrote a letter breaking off his friendship with Dorante and demanding satisfaction. In one short day, his second in the big city, the provincial student had quarreled, made love, and reported a marriage. To lie effectively, Cliton observed, one must have a good memory.

Confronted by his accuser, Dorante told Alcippe and Philiste that he had known Clarice for several years but was not interested in her; he had, he said, taken a beautiful married woman with him on the barge, a woman whom Alcippe could not possibly know. He cautioned Alcippe not to believe all he heard and not to be led by the green-eyed monster. When Philiste revealed to Alcippe that the young dandy had only yesterday arrived from the college at Poitiers—proof that while he might be valorous, his deeds were imaginary—Alcippe asked the innocent scoundrel's pardon.

Clarice, by the time she had exchanged places on the balcony with Lucrece, also knew about the lies Dorante had told. Lucrece thought his actions a sign of love. Confronted, Dorante denied all accusations save one; he declared that he had pretended marriage in order to wed his Lucrece—at this point there was consternation on the balcony—whom he would marry that next day as proof of his sincerity. By group action he was ordered hence, so shocked were the young ladies at his effrontery—or naïveté.

Dorante now promised Cliton not to lie any more, or at least to give a signal when he did. He immediately lied by saying that the rumor of his fight with Alcippe was true and that the unfortunate challenger had been left for dead. He lied again when he claimed that the secret of Alcippe's recovery lay in the magic of a Hebrew word. Hebrew, he claimed, was one of his ten languages. He lied also to Sabine, the servant, in order to get back in Lucrece's good graces, and he invented new names so that his father could send his daughter-in-law his good wishes; the duped father was pleased to learn a grandchild was even now six months along. His lies were met by counter-lies told by the clever Sabine, who lied for money and kept herself in constant employment by delivering letters and arranging assignations.

By now neither Dorante, Lucrece, nor Clarice knew whom they loved. Clarice declared herself in favor of Alcippe, whose father finally settled the marriage arrangements. Dorante then observed that she had only been flirtatious and curious, while the real Lucrece—he declared that he had fallen in love with a name and henceforth changed only the face to fit it—was much deeper. The father, declaring as he did so that he would never again help his scoundrel of a son, arranged quite docilely for his marriage. Lucrece, who swore she would love the liar when she could believe him, was suddenly converted to belief when she saw that his avowals were true in spirit. Cliton, of course, knew as much all along.

THE MERCHANT OF VENICE

Type of work: Drama
Author: William Shakespeare (1564-1616)
Type of plot: Tragi-comedy
Time of plot: Sixteenth century
Locale: Venice
First presented: c. 1596

Principal characters:
SHYLOCK, a Jewish money-lender
PORTIA, a wealthy young woman
ANTONIO, an impoverished merchant, Shylock's enemy, championed by Portia
BASSANIO, Portia's husband, Antonio's friend
NERISSA, Portia's waiting-woman
GRATIANO, Nerissa's husband, Bassanio's friend
JESSICA, Shylock's daughter
LORENZO, Jessica's husband

Critique:

Though the closing scenes of *The Merchant of Venice* keep it from becoming a tragedy, it is essentially a serious study of the use and misuse of wealth, of love and marriage. The encounter between the greedy, vengeful Jew, Shylock, and the wise and fine Portia, gives the play a theme of grave beauty.

The Story:

Bassanio, meeting his wealthy friend, Antonio, revealed that he had a plan for restoring his fortune, carelessly spent, and for paying the debts he had incurred. In the town of Belmont, not far from Venice, there lived a wealthy young woman named Portia, who was famous for her beauty. If he could secure some money, Bassanio declared, he was sure he could win her as his wife.

Antonio replied that he had no funds at hand with which to supply his friend, as they were all invested in the ships which he had at sea, but he would attempt to borrow some money in Venice.

Portia had many suitors for her hand. According to the strange conditions of her father's will, however, anyone who wished her for his wife had to choose among three caskets of silver, gold, and lead the one which contained a message that she was his. Four of her suitors, seeing that they could not win her except under the conditions of the will, departed. A fifth, a Moor decided to take

his chances. The unfortunate man chose the golden casket, which contained only a skull and a mocking message. For his failure he was compelled to swear never to reveal the casket he had chosen and never to woo another woman.

The Prince of Arragon was the next suitor to try his luck. In his turn he chose the silver casket, only to learn from the note it bore that he was a fool.

True to his promise to Bassanio, Antonio arranged to borrow three thousand ducats from Shylock, a wealthy Jew. Antonio was to have the use of the money for three months. If he should be unable to return the loan at the end of that time, Shylock was to have the right to cut a pound of flesh from any part of Antonio's body. In spite of Bassanio's objections, Antonio insisted on accepting the terms, for he was sure his ships would return a month before the payment would be due. He was confident that he would never fall into the power of the Jew, who hated Antonio because he often lent money to others without charging the interest Shylock demanded.

That night Bassanio planned a feast and a masque. In conspiracy with his friend, Lorenzo, he invited Shylock to be his guest. Lorenzo, taking advantage of her father's absence, ran off with the Jew's daughter, Jessica, who did not hesitate to take part of Shylock's fortune with her.

Shylock was cheated not only of his daughter and his ducats but also of his entertainment, for the wind suddenly changed and Bassanio set sail for Belmont.

As the days passed, the Jew began to hear news of mingled good and bad fortune. In Genoa, Jessica and Lorenzo were making lavish use of the money she had taken with her. The miser flinched at the reports of his daughter's extravagance, but for compensation he had the news that Antonio's ships, on which his fortune depended, had been wrecked at sea.

Portia, much taken with Bassanio when he came to woo her, would have had him wait before he tried to pick the right casket. Sure that he would fail as the others had, she hoped to have his company a little while longer. Bassanio, however, was impatient to try his luck. Not deceived by the ornateness of the gold and silver caskets, but philosophizing that true virtue is inward virtue, he chose the lead box. In it was a portrait of Portia. He had chosen correctly.

To seal their engagement, Portia gave Bassanio a ring. She declared he must never part with it, for if he did it would signify the end of their love.

Gratiano, a friend who had accompanied Bassanio to Belmont, spoke up. He was in love with Portia's waiting-woman, Nerissa. With Portia's delighted approval, Gratiano planned that both couples should be married at the same time.

Bassanio's joy at his good fortune was soon blighted. Antonio wrote that he was ruined, all his ships having failed to return. The time for payment of the loan being past due, Shylock was demanding his pound of flesh. In closing, Antonio declared that he cleared Bassanio of his debt to him. He wished only to see his friend once more before his death.

Portia declared that the double wedding should take place at once. Then her husband, with her dowry of six thousand ducats, should set out for Venice in an attempt to buy off the Jew.

After Bassanio and Gratiano had gone, Portia declared to Lorenzo and Jessica, who had come to Belmont, that she and Nerissa were going to a nunnery, where they would live in seclusion until their husbands returned. She committed the charge of her house and servants to Jessica and Lorenzo.

Instead of taking the course she had described, however, Portia set about executing other plans. She gave her servant, Balthasar, orders to take a note to her cousin, Doctor Bellario, a famous lawyer of Padua, in order to secure a message and some clothes from him. She explained to Nerissa that they would go to Venice disguised as men.

The Duke of Venice, before whom Antonio's case was tried, was reluctant to exact the penalty which was in Shylock's terms. When his appeals to the Jew's better feelings went unheeded, he could see no course before him except to give the money-lender his due. Bassanio also tried to make Shylock relent by offering him the six thousand ducats, but, like the Duke, he met only a firm refusal.

Portia, dressed as a lawyer, and Nerissa, disguised as her clerk, appeared in the court. Nerissa offered the duke a letter from Doctor Bellario. The doctor explained that he was very ill, but that Balthasar, his young representative, would present his opinion in the dispute.

When Portia appealed to the Jew's mercy, Shylock answered with a demand for the penalty. Portia then declared that the Jew, under the letter of the contract, could not be offered money in exchange for Antonio's release. The only alternative was for the merchant to forfeit his flesh.

Antonio prepared his bosom for the knife, for Shylock was determined to take his portion as close to his enemy's heart as he could cut. Before the operation could begin, however, Portia, examining the contract, declared that it contained no clause stating that Shylock could have any blood with the flesh.

The Jew, realizing that he was defeated, offered at once to accept the six thousand ducats, but Portia declared that he was not entitled to the money he had already refused. She stated also that Shylock, an alien, had threatened the life of a Venetian citizen. For that crime Antonio had the right to seize half of his property and the state the remainder.

Antonio refused that penalty, but it was agreed that one half of Shylock's fortune should go at once to Jessica and Lorenzo. Shylock was to keep the remainder, but it too was to be willed the couple. In addition, Shylock was to undergo conversion. The defeated man agreed to those terms.

Pressed to accept a reward, Portia took only a pair of Antonio's gloves and the ring which she herself had given Bassanio. Nerissa, likewise, managed to secure Gratiano's ring. Then the pair started back for Belmont, to be there when their husbands returned.

Portia and Nerissa arrived home shortly before Bassanio and Gratiano appeared in company with Antonio. Pretending to discover that their husbands' rings were missing, Portia and Nerissa at first accused Bassanio and Gratiano of unfaithfulness. At last, to the surprise of all, they revealed their secret, which was vouched for by a letter from Doctor Bellario. For Jessica and Lorenzo they had the good news of their future inheritance, and for Antonio a letter, secured by chance, announcing that some of his ships had arrived safely in port.

Type of work: Drama
Author: William Shakespeare (1564-1616)
Type of plot: Farce
Time of plot: Sixteenth century
Locale: England
First presented: c. 1597

Principal characters:

SIR JOHN FALSTAFF, a rogue
FENTON, a young gentleman
SLENDER, a foolish gentleman
FORD, and
PAGE, two gentlemen living at Windsor
DOCTOR CAIUS, a French physician
MISTRESS FORD, Ford's wife
MISTRESS PAGE, Page's wife
ANNE PAGE, daughter of the Pages
MISTRESS QUICKLY, servant of Doctor Caius

Critique:

Never was there a more lovable, merrier rogue than Sir John Falstaff. Indeed he has become the very essence of all stumbling, drunken scoundrels, but scoundrels against whom no one can long hold a grudge. It is to Falstaff that *The Merry Wives of Windsor* owes its great popularity. The plot is simple but highly amusing, a story of women plotting toward the ruination of one man and the complete subjection of another. The resulting situations are hilarious. The subplot of love conquering all is another favorite of the theater. But it is Falstaff, the lovable oaf, who brings the reader back to this play again and again.

The Story:

Sir John Falstaff was, without doubt, a rogue. True, he was fat, jolly, and in a way lovable, but he was still a rogue. His men robbed and plundered the citizens of Windsor, but he himself was seldom taken or convicted for his crimes. His fortunes being at low ebb, he hit upon a plan to remedy that situation. He had met Mistress Ford and Mistress Page, two good ladies who held the purse strings in their respective houses. Falstaff wrote identical letters to the two good ladies, letters protesting undying love for each of them.

The daughter of one of the ladies, Anne Page, was the center of a love triangle.

Her father wished her to marry Slender, a foolish gentleman who did not love her or anyone else, but who would marry any girl that was recommended to him by his cousin, the justice. But Mistress Page, on the other hand, would have her daughter married to Doctor Caius, a French physician then in Windsor. Anne herself loved Fenton, a fine young gentleman who was deeply in love with her. All three lovers paid the doctor's housekeeper, Mistress Quickly, to plead their cause with Anne, for Mistress Quickly had convinced each that she alone could persuade Anne to answer yes to a proposal. Mistress Quickly was, in fact, second only to Falstaff in her plotting and her trickery.

Unknown to poor Falstaff, Mistress Ford and Mistress Page compared the letters received from him, alike except for the lady's name. They decided to cure him of his knavery once and for all. Mistress Ford arranged to have him come to her house that night when her husband would be away. Mistress Page wrote that she would meet him as soon as she could cautiously arrange it. In the meantime two former followers of Falstaff had told the two husbands of that knave's designs on their wives. Page refused to believe his wife unfaithful, but Ford became jealous and planned to spy on his wife. Disguising himself as Mr. Brook, he called on Falstaff. His story was that he loved Mistress Ford but could not win her love, and he came to pay Falstaff to court her for him. His stratagem was successful; he learned from Falstaff that the knight already had a rendezvous with the lady that very night.

At the appointed time, having previously arranged to have several servants assist in the plot, the two ladies were ready for Falstaff. While Falstaff was trying to make love to Mistress Ford, Mistress Page rushed in and said that Ford was on his way home. Quickly the ladies put Falstaff in a clothesbasket and had him carried out by the servants, to be dumped into the Thames. Ford did arrive, of course, for, unknown to his wife, he knew Falstaff was to be there. But after looking high and low without finding the rogue, he apologized to his wife for his suspicions. Mistress Ford did not know which had been the most sport, having Falstaff dumped into the river or listening to her husband's discomfited apologies.

The ladies had so much fun over their first joke played on Falstaff that they decided to try another. Mistress Ford then sent him another message, this one saying that her husband would be gone all of the following morning, and she asked Falstaff to call on her at that time so that she could make amends for the previous affair of the basket. Again Ford, disguised as Brook, called on Falstaff, and again he learned of the proposed assignation. He learned also of the method of Falstaff's previous escape and vowed the old roisterer should not again slip through his fingers.

When Mistress Ford heard from Mistress Page that Ford was returning unexpectedly, the ladies dressed Falstaff in the clothes of a fat woman whom Ford hated. Ford, finding the supposed woman in his house, drubbed the disguised knight soundly and chased him from the house. Again Ford searched everywhere for Falstaff, and again he was forced to apologize to his wife in the presence of the friends he had brought with him to witness her disgrace. The two ladies thought his discomfiture the funniest part of their joke.

Once more the wives planned to plague poor Falstaff, but this time they took their husbands into their confidence. When Mistress Page and Mistress Ford told about the letters they had received from Falstaff and explained the details of the two adventures already carried out, Ford felt very contrite over his former suspicions of his wife. Eagerly the husbands joined their wives in a final scheme intended to bring Falstaff to public shame. The ladies would persuade Falstaff to meet them in the park at midnight. Falstaff was to be disguised as Herne the Hunter, a horned legendary huntsman said to roam the wintry woods each midnight. There he would be surrounded by Anne Page and others dressed as fairies and elves. After he had been frightened half to death, the husbands would accost him and publicly display his knavery.

But a quite different event had also been planned for that night. Page plotted to have Slender seize Anne in her disguise as the fairy queen and carry her away to marry her. At the same time Mistress Page arranged to have Doctor Caius find Anne and take her away to be married. But Anne had other plans. She and Fenton agreed to meet in the park and under cover of the dark and confusion flee her parents and her two unwelcome suitors.

All plans were put into effect. Falstaff, after telling the supposed Brook that on this night he would for a certainty win Mistress Ford for him, donned the horns of a stag and met the two ladies at the appointed place. Quickly the fairies and witches surrounded him, and the women ran away to join their husbands and watch the fun. Poor Falstaff tried to pretend that he was asleep or dead, but the merry revelers burned his fingers with tapers they carried, and pinched him unmercifully. When Falstaff threw off his disguise, Ford and Page and their wives laid hold of him and soundly scolded him for his silly gallantry and bombast. The wives ridiculed his fat and his ugliness and swore that none would ever have such a fool for a lover. But such was Falstaff's nature that no one could hate him for long. After he had admitted his guilt and his stupidity they all forgave him.

While all this merriment was going on, Anne and Fenton had stolen away to be married. They returned while the rest were busy with Falstaff. But Page and his wife were in such good humor over all that had occurred that they forgave the young lovers and bestowed on them their blessing. Then the whole company, Falstaff with them, retired to Page's house, there to laugh again over the happenings of that night.

MESSER MARCO POLO

Type of work: Novelette
Author: Donn Byrne (1889-1928)
Type of plot: Exotic romance
Time of plot: Thirteenth century
Locale: Venice and China
First published: 1921

Principal characters:
MARCO POLO, the Venetian
KUBLA KHAN, Emperor of China
GOLDEN BELLS, Kubla Khan's daughter
LI PO, court poet
SANANG, court magician

Critique:

A mixture of three elements gives this simple tale a unique flavor. A modern Irishman tells the adventures of a Christian Italian in pagan China. Irish mysticism mingles with the mystery of the East to produce a romantic and tragic love story based upon the visit of Marco Polo to the court of Kubla Khan. The author succeeds in bringing together, in one framework, folk tale, history, and imagination. His simple narrative style is of a kind very rarely found among modern authors; it suggests the fireside stories and poems of the past which passed from generation to generation by word of mouth.

The Story:

On the first night of spring young Marco Polo deserted his work in his father's counting-house and wandered restlessly through the streets of Venice. He entered a wine shop in the hope of talking with some of the foreign people gathered there. The people inside were gambling and drinking, except for one man who sat by himself at a table. Marco recognized him as a Chinese sea captain and sat down to talk to him. In a friendly argument over the merits of their native countries, the sea captain got the better of young Marco by describing the beauty of Golden Bells, the daughter of Kubla Khan.

From that night on, the image of Golden Bells haunted Marco Polo. When his father and uncle, Nicholas and Matthew Polo, returned from China, Marco told them that he wished to go with them on their next trip. Kubla Khan had told the Polos to bring a Christian missionary back with them from Venice, and they chose young Marco to play the part. He was delighted, for he had convinced himself that it was his mission to convert Golden Bells to Christianity.

The wise old Pope gave his blessing to Marco as he started out for China, but he warned the young man not to expect to convert many pagans. Marco, his uncle, and his father set out with their camel caravan for the court of Kubla Khan. Marco saw on the way many strange countries and cities. At last the travelers came to the Desert of the Singing Sands. Many deserted or died until there were only six of the caravan left. When a great sandstorm came upon them, Marco struggled until his strength gave out and he lay down to die.

Meanwhile Golden Bells sat in the garden of Kubla Khan and talked with Li Po, the court poet. Sanang, the court magician, joined them. He told Golden Bells that he could see in his crystal ball the troubles of Marco Polo. Golden Bells felt pity for the young man and begged Sanang to save him from death in the Desert of the Singing Sands. Through his magic power Sanang called upon the Tartar tribesmen to rescue Marco. Golden Bells was joyful when the old magician assured her the young man had been saved. Li Po smiled and said he would write a marriage song for her. She said that she was in love with no one, but she refused to sing any more the sad "Song of the Willow Branches."

The desert tribesmen brought Marco before Kubla Khan and Golden Bells. The emperor asked him to tell something about the Christian religion. Marco quoted the Beatitudes and related the life of Christ, but Kubla Khan and his court were not impressed by that story of gentleness and love. Golden Bells alone, of all the court, told Marco that she was his convert.

Marco began to instruct Golden Bells and told her all the Bible stories he knew. She was charmed by his voice. He tried to explain to her what sin was, but she could not believe that the beauty of a woman was a curse. Finally, when he had told her all he knew of Christianity, he spoke of returning to Venice. Golden Bells was heartbroken. At last Marco took her in his arms.

For three years they lived happily; then Golden Bells died. Marco remained on for fourteen years in the service of the emperor. One evening Kubla Khan came to Marco with Li Po and Sanang and told him that he should return to Venice, for some of the people in the land were jealous of Marco's power. It was for his own good that he should return.

Marco refused to go. He did not wish to leave the place where he had been happy. Only a sign from the dead Golden Bells would make him leave. Then Sanang cast a magic spell and Li Po sang a magic song. A ghostly moonlight appeared at the end of the palace garden, and there, slim in the moonlight, stood Golden Bells. With her pleading eyes and soundless lips she begged Marco to return to Venice; then she disappeared. Marco was overcome with grief, but he promised to go. As he took leave of his three old friends, he said that he was going home to be an exile in his own land. The sunshine and the rain of China—and the memory of Golden Bells—would be always in his heart.

THE METAMORPHOSES

Type of work: Collection of narrative poems
Author: Ovid (Publius Ovidius Naso, 43 B.C.-A.D. 18)
First transcribed: Before A.D. 8

Unlike most Greek and Roman authors, Ovid wrote almost entirely to entertain. The tone of the literature of the ancient world, whether written by Greeks or Romans, is ordinarily edifying, but that tradition Ovid discarded. For this reason, and because of the subject matter of Ovid's *Ars amatoria* (*Art of Love*), Europeans and Americans have usually been doubtful of Ovid's true literary stature. Anyone who has read Ovid seriously will usually agree, however, that to take his writings as they were intended—to entertain—opens the door to granting his writings a conspicuous place in Roman literature.

The *Metamorphoses* is generally conceded to be Ovid's finest work. In this collection of poems Ovid managed to draw together artistically most of the stories of Greek and Roman legend. More than two hundred of the myths of the ancient world have been rendered into an organic work, the unifying theme being that of transformation from one kind to another, as Jove changed himself into a swan, Narcissus was transformed into a flower, Tereus was turned into a bird, and Midas was given the ears of an ass. These stories were arranged by Ovid into fifteen books, containing in the original Latin almost twelve thousand lines of sweetly flowing verse written in the dactylic hexameters common in classical poetry. The poems were written when Ovid was a mature man of perhaps fifty, shortly before Augustus Caesar banished him to the little town of Tomi on the shores of the Black Sea, far from the city that Ovid loved. Although Ovid wrote that he destroyed his own copy of the *Metamorphoses*, apparently because he was dissatisfied with his performance, he also seemed to feel that the work would live after him. In his epilogue to the *Metamorphoses* he wrote:

Now I have done my work. It will endure,
I trust, beyond Jove's anger, fire, and sword,
Beyond Time's hunger. The day will come, I know,
So let it come, that day which has no power
Save over my body, to end my span of life
Whatever it may be. Still, part of me,
The better part, immortal, will be borne
Above the stars; my name will be remembered
Wherever Roman power rules conquered lands,
I shall be read, and through all centuries,
If prophecies of bards are ever truthful,
I shall be living, always.

As if it were necessary for a work of literary art to have some edifying or moral purpose, the poems have sometimes been regarded primarily as a useful handbook on Greek and Roman mythology. Certainly the work does contain a wealth of the ancient legends, and many later writers have become famous in part because they were able to build on the materials Ovid put at their disposal. However, the *Metamorphoses* deserves remembrance as a work of art in its own right.

Modern writers view stories about the gods of the pagan Pantheon in a different light from that in which such tales were regarded in the time of Ovid and Augustus Caesar. Where we can smile, Ovid's light, even facetious, tone must have been regarded by serious Romans as having more than a little touch of blasphemy. Perhaps his irreverent attitudes may even have been a partial cause for his exile, for rulers have always been sensitive people and Augustus was at the time attempting moral reforms. It must be kept in mind, too, that Ovid, after treating good-humoredly of the other gods, turned at the end of the *Meta-*

morphoses to describe the transformation of Julius Caesar to godhood. How seriously he meant to be taken, from the tone of the poem, is open to question.

Ovid began the collection with a description of how the universe came into being with the metamorphosis of Chaos, the unshaped stuff, into Cosmos, the ordered universe. Having described how the Lord of Creation, "Whatever god it was," established order in the universe, he proceeded to give a picture of the four ages. Like other ancients, Ovid had a different concept of the past from that of modern times. He began his account with the Golden Age, when justice and right existed everywhere, when law and punishment were absent because they were unnecessary. When Saturn was sent to the land of shadowy death, wrote Ovid, and Jove became chief of the gods, then came the Age of Silver, when men first built houses to guard themselves against the seasons and planted fields to provide themselves with a harvest. Next came the Age of Bronze, when warlike instincts and aggression came into being, to be succeeded in its turn by the Iron Age, when modesty, truth, and righteousness were displaced by trickery, violence, and swindling. So bad was this age that Jove struck down the living and nature brought forth a new race of men who were, as Ovid put it, "men of blood." Of this race, all except Deucalion and Pyrrha, a righteous man and woman, were wiped from the face of the earth by Jove, who with Neptune's aid caused a flood to cover the globe. Ovid's stories of the Creation and the Flood, told in a pagan environment, are strikingly similar to the stories of the same phenomena told, in keeping with Judaic tradition, in the Old Testament.

Much of Ovid's poetry in the *Metamorphoses* deals with love. It is not romanticized, sentimentalized love that Ovid presented, however, for he recognized the physical reality of men and women for one another, and his gods and goddesses exhibit human passions. In love, as Ovid described it, there is often found a strain of cruelty and brutality; the veneer of civilization is thin enough to let his readers sense the savagery of violence, revenge, and cruelty underlying human culture. In this connection one recalls Lycaon boiling and broiling the flesh of a human hostage before the altar of Jove, Tereus raping Philomela and then cutting out her tongue to keep the deed a secret, a satyr being flayed alive by Apollo, the son of Latona, for trying to surpass him at playing the flute, sixteen-year-old Athis having his face battered to mere splinters of bone by Perseus, and Pelias' daughters' letting their father's blood at the behest of Medea. In these stories gory details are described in the account of each brutal act; brains, blood, broken bones, and screams of agony and hate fill the lines. Love and hate, both powerful, basic human emotions, are close in Ovid's *Metamorphoses*.

Mere enumeration does not do Ovid's collection of stories in the *Metamorphoses* the justice it deserves. Practically every phase of the Graeco-Roman mythology is at least represented in the fifteen divisions of the work. The stories are artfully drawn together with consummate skill. Yet the noteworthy fact in assessing Ovid's mastery of his materials and craft is that he himself was a skeptic who did not believe in these stories as being true in the sense of really having happened. Without the sincerity of belief, he nevertheless wrote in such a way that he induces in the reader that mood which Coleridge, almost two thousand years later, described as the "willing suspension of disbelief."

Ovid placed in his pages believable personalities. His men and women, his gods and goddesses, hate and love as human beings have always done. The twentieth-century reader recognizes in himself the same surges and flows of emotion that he finds in Ovid's poetry. Our world is, in this way, little different from the Roman empire of Ovid and Augustus, despite technological advances.

Another element of Ovid's style that comes through in translation is the large amount of specific detail. At almost any point in the *Metamorphoses* there is a vivid picture of the people or the action, as when Myrrha, in "Cinyras and Myrrha," flings herself, face down, to cry into her pillow; when Pygmalion lavishes gifts of pet birds, sea shells, lilies, and lumps of precious amber on his beloved statue; or when Dorylas, in "The Battle of the Centaurs," is wounded by Peleus and dies trailing his entrails, treading and tangling them with his centaur's hoofs. We are reminded in such stories that Ovid's Rome had a culture that included not only greatness in art but also the grim and bloody scenes of death by violence within the confines of the arena at the Coliseum.

MICAH CLARKE

Type of work: Novel
Author: Arthur Conan Doyle (1859-1930)
Type of plot: Historical romance
Time of plot: Late seventeenth century
Locale: England
First published: 1888

Principal characters:
  MICAH CLARKE, an English youth
  JOSEPH CLARKE, his father
  DECIMUS SAXON, an old soldier
  REUBEN LOCKARBY, Micah's friend
  SIR GERVAS, a Cavalier
  THE DUKE OF MONMOUTH, pretender to the throne

Critique:

Micah Clarke is one of a group of historical romances by the writer who will always be best known for his creation of Sherlock Holmes. Micah Clarke is a stirring adventure story as well as a careful reconstruction of the events of 1685, when the Duke of Monmouth attempted to seize the English throne. The pictures of the determined Protestants who preferred death to a Catholic king are unforgettable.

The Story:

At Havant, near Portsmouth, young Micah Clarke grew up under the domination of his strong Puritan father, Joseph Clarke. He led a vigorous, active life, but he spent much time praying and hymn singing. From his father he heard many tales of Cromwell and the Puritans, for Joseph had fought in the wars of those troubled times. Save for a year at an Established Church school, Micah's education was taken in hand by his father himself. At the age of twenty, Micah was the strongest man in the village.

As was their custom, Micah and his good friend Reuben set out to fish in Langston Bay. They pulled up to their favorite fishing ground just as the sun was setting, threw out the large anchor stone, and set their lines. Not far away a king's ship stood in for the channel. The two youths watched her until their attention was drawn to a large brig not over a quarter mile distant. The ship seemed to be out of control, for she yawed as if there were no hand at the tiller. While they watched, they heard two musket shots aboard the brig. A few minutes later a cannon shot sounded and the ball passed close to their boat as the brig came about and headed down the channel. Reuben urged his friend to pull hard, for there was a man in the water. They could soon see him swimming easily along, and as they came alongside the swimmer expertly hoisted himself aboard. He was a tall, lean man, over fifty but wiry and strong. Their passenger looked them over coolly, drew out a wicked knife, and ordered them to head for the French coast. But when Micah lifted his oar and threatened to knock the man over the head, their passenger gave in meekly and handed over his knife with good grace. He told them that he had jumped overboard from the brig after he and his brother, the captain, had exchanged musket shots during a quarrel.

As they headed shoreward, the stranger heard Reuben use the name Clarke. Instantly the man became interested and asked Micah if he were the son of Joseph Clarke. When Micah replied that he was, the stranger pulled out his pouch and showed them that he carried a letter for Joseph Clarke, as well as for twenty others in the district. Reassured, Micah took the man home, where he learned that the stranger was Decimus Saxon, a mercenary soldier recruiting soldiers for the army of the Duke of Monmouth, the Protestant pretender who was coming to wrest his throne from Catholic King James. Joseph was too old to fight, but mindful of his duty he permitted Micah to go to the wars. With many prayers Micah set out in Saxon's company to meet Monmouth, who was soon to land somewhere in Devonshire. Even though he was a good member of the Church of England, Reuben went with them for friendship's sake.

Saxon soon threw off his sanctimonious manner, and to Micah's dismay showed himself a hardened man of the world. One night at an inn Saxon fought a king's officer over a card game and they were forced to flee, pursued by a body of horsemen and dogs. Only by stout courage and luck were they able to kill the dogs and go on their way.

That night they found shelter in the hut of a recluse, Sir Jacob Clancy. The hermit had lost all his estates through helping Charles II to gain his throne. Now renounced by the Stuart kings, he worked at his alchemy in solitude. When he heard that his guests were going to join the rebel Monmouth, he pressed on Micah some bars of gold to give to the Protestant pretender, and also a scroll on which was written:

"When thy star is in the trine
Between darkness and shine
Duke Monmouth, Duke Monmouth
Beware of the Rhine."

On another night the trio stayed at an inn kept by a buxom widow. The landlady cast sheep's eyes at Saxon, and that soldier seemed mightily interested. Reuben and Micah listened anxiously as he muttered to himself the advantages of keeping an inn. Saxon was shocked when a powdered and perfumed knight came into the tavern and kissed the widow heartily. In anger he left the table and the newly-arrived fop took his seat.

Micah soon learned that the newcomer was Sir Gervas, a London dandy who had gambled and drunk away all his estates. When Sir Gervas heard that Micah was going to join Monmouth, he nonchalantly agreed to go with them.

Afterward Saxon returned to the dining-room. No longer thinking of settling down as an innkeeper, he welcomed Sir Gervas as a good recruit to the cause.

The Protestants were rallying at Taunton, the strong center of the Dissenters. The mayor, Stephen Timewell, was a wealthy wool merchant and a staunch enemy of Rome, and so in Taunton the ragged but rugged horde of Dissenters found a secure headquarters. On their arrival, Saxon was made a colonel and Micah and Reuben became captains of infantry. Sir Gervas headed a hundred musketeers. In all the turmoil of drill and inspections, the most prominent figures were the gowned clergy, who intoned prayers and hymns for the godly rebels who were to fight the Lord's battles against Papist King James.

Micah thrilled to see the arrival of Monmouth at the head of his small but growing army. Because of his strength and manly bearing, Micah soon found his way into Monmouth's inner circle. At a council meeting Micah gave over the gold and the scroll entrusted to him by Sir Jacob Clancy. Monmouth blanched at the prophecy, but after nervously exclaiming he would be fighting in England, not in Germany, he ignored the warning.

The Protestants needed at least one great and powerful lord to support their cause. So far Monmouth had rallied the peasants, the ministers, and a few reckless cavaliers. He knew, however, that his forces were too weak to meet the royal army. After prolonged debate the Protestants decided that the Duke of Beaufort was the most likely convert. Lord of all Wales, he had always been an enemy of Catholicism, and he was under obligations to Monmouth. Micah was chosen to bear a message to the noble lord.

Micah set off alone to make the long trip from Taunton to Bristol. Near the channel he half dozed on his horse during the night. Suddenly he was knocked from the saddle, bound, and dragged to a cave, where he learned that smugglers had kidnaped him because they had mistaken him for a tax collector. When he was able to establish his identity and errand, the smugglers changed their attitude; they even took him and his horse in a lugger up the channel to Bristol.

Micah tried to talk to Beaufort alone, but he was forced to deliver his papers in full sight of the duke's court. Beaufort became very angry at the idea of deserting King James and had Micah imprisoned in a dungeon. Expecting to be hanged as a traitor, Micah resigned himself to his last night on earth. But during the night a rope dropped mysteriously from an opening in the ceiling. Climbing up, Micah saw that his deliverer was Beaufort himself. The duke explained that he had not dared say anything in council, but if Monmouth could get to Bristol Beaufort would join him.

Micah carried the news back to Monmouth, who announced his immediate decision to march toward Bristol. The ragged army encamped at Sedgemoor and decided to make a stand there. As Monmouth looked over the battlefield, he was startled to hear the natives refer to a big ditch nearby as the "rhine." Indeed the rhine was an omen, for the small band of Protestant zealots proved no match for the king's men. As the battle raged, Monmouth fled in a vain attempt to save his own skin.

Micah himself was captured and sentenced to be sold as a slave. Saxon saved his life. Using money which he had blackmailed from Beaufort, Saxon bought Micah's release. Thankfully Micah set out for the continent to become a man-at-arms in the foreign wars.

MICHAEL AND HIS LOST ANGEL

Type of work: Drama
Author: Henry Arthur Jones (1851-1929)
Type of plot: Social tragedy
Time of plot: Nineteenth century
Locale: England and Italy
First presented: 1896

Principal characters:
THE REVEREND MICHAEL FEVERSHAM, vicar at Cleveheddon
ANDREW GIBBARD, a parish clerk
ROSE GIBBARD, his daughter
AUDRIE LESDEN, Michael's mistress
SIR LYOLF FEVERSHAM, Michael's uncle
FATHER HILARY, a priest

Critique:

Although *Michael and His Lost Angel* was not one of Henry Arthur Jones' most popular plays at the time of its presentation, he himself considered it his most serious and best work. The play, which has become a familiar anthology piece, is the tragic story of a man's loss of faith in himself, for the death of Audrie Lesden is secondary to the disintegration of Michael Feversham's own soul. The character development is excellent, accurately portrayed, with deep insight into a minister's struggle with his own conscience.

The Story:

The Reverend Michael Feversham regretted that he must deal harshly with Rose, the daughter of his clerk, Andrew Gibbard. Because the girl had sinned, and Andrew had lied about Rose and her now dead child, Michael sternly insisted upon a public confession before the whole congregation of Cleveheddon Church. Only in that way, he believed, could Andrew and his daughter be absolved of their sin and deceit. Later Michael sent the girl away to an Anglican religious house where she could start life anew.

Andrew owed everything he had in life to Michael, but he could not forgive him for exposing Rose to the scorn of the smug, self-righteous parishioners. He recognized, however, the moral fervor which had prompted Michael's attitude and convictions.

Michael, having dedicated his life to his church and his people, felt that he was watched over by his dead mother, whose picture hung in his study. She was his guardian angel, he thought, knowing everything he said or did. He knew he must try always to be worthy of her guardianship.

When Audrie Lesden came to his parish, he was afraid he would be unworthy of his guardian angel's love and care. Audrie was a wealthy woman, reported a widow, who had been attracted to Michael because of a book he had written. Although she subscribed large sums for Michael's project of restoring the minster of Saint Decuman, an ancient Gothic church at Cleveheddon, she was a worldly woman, one torn in half by her emotions and desires. She wanted to be a good woman, to be worthy of Michael, but she wished also to enjoy the pleasures of the world. Sir Lyolf Feversham, Michael's kinsman, warned the young clergyman against her. Michael, thinking her possessed of great possibilities for good or evil, fought against her influence and pleaded with her to use him only as her spiritual adviser. At the same time he found himself almost helpless against her charm.

Andrew Gibbard watched Michael's struggle with an evil pleasure which he too fought against. He knew that the vicar had acted as he thought right in his daughter's case, but he was human enough to enjoy seeing a saintly man learn what temptations of the flesh were like.

The ancient shrine on Saint Decuman's Island in the Bristol Channel was a place to which Michael often went for study and meditation. One day Audrie took an excursion steamer to the island and remained behind after the boat had returned to the mainland. It was then impossible for her or Michael to return to Cleveheddon before the next day. She and Michael spent the night on the island. Although he did his best to resist her, he found himself weak. They sinned, just as Rose Gibbard had sinned. Afterward Michael tried to conceal the truth, more to protect Audrie than himself, but Andrew finally uncovered the clergyman's secret. He did not reproach Michael; in fact, he promised to keep silent. For the next several months, however, Michael could sense Andrew's scorn because the vicar did not make the same confession he had forced from Andrew and his daughter.

Audrie went to Michael with some disturbing news. She had heard from her husband, whom she had allowed everyone to believe dead. Their married life had been wretched, she said, and at last she had paid him to go to America and never bother her again. Now he was returning to England. Michael advised her to go back to her husband; that course, he said, was the road to true repentance for their sin. After Audrie had left Cleveheddon she continued to send him money for the restoration of the minster. Although the money was sent anonymously, Michael knew the gifts came from her. Andrew also guessed the source of the donations.

When the minster of Saint Decuman had been restored, Michael sent for Rose Gibbard. Having decided that he could no longer live with his own conscience if he did not confess publicly, he wanted the girl to witness his disgrace so that she would know that he could be just and unsparing with himself as well. Andrew tried to dissuade him from his plan, but

Michael was firm. Then Andrew really forgave Michael and blessed him.

At the church, shortly before the dedication service, Audrie came to Michael again. Her husband had died and she hoped that she and Michael might love each other honorably at last. But Michael felt that their sin had been too great ever to allow them happiness with each other. He sent her away after making her promise not to attend the service the next day.

Before the reconsecration of the minster the next morning, Michael bared his sin to his congregation. He told them that he could no longer be their vicar because he was not worthy, and he asked the people to pray for him after he left the parish.

A year later Michael was living in a monastery at Majano, Italy. He was almost ready to change his faith and join the Catholic Church in order to find peace of mind. Also at Majano were Sir Lyolf and Father Hilary, a priest whom Michael had known at Saint Decuman's shrine. Longing for Audrie had made the young clergyman almost physically ill. Even his mother's picture brought him no happiness; he felt that his guardian angel had justifiably deserted him because of his wickedness.

During his absence from the monastery Audrie arrived. She was sick and soon to die, and she wanted to see Michael once more. Sir Lyolf was greatly concerned over her condition. When Michael returned, Sir Lyolf reminded him of his promise that he would go to Audrie if she ever needed him. Michael was almost beside himself when he saw her and realized that she was dying. Audrie, still torn between love for him and love for the world, said that she would become his guardian angel, that they would never part again. His mother, she whispered, would forgive. As she died in his arms, Michael threw himself on her body and cried to Father Hilary that he was willing to suffer all but that he must meet Audrie again. He asked the priest to help him to believe.

MID-CHANNEL

Type of work: Drama
Author: Arthur Wing Pinero (1855-1934)
Time: c. 1900
Locale: London
First presented: 1909

Principal characters:
THEODORE BLUNDELL, a stockbroker
ZOE BLUNDELL, his wife
LEONARD FERRIS, Zoe's friend
ETHEL PIERPOINT, Zoe's protégée

Realistic drama tends to depend upon motivational interrelationships of characters within a specific environment or society for its impact. Henrik Ibsen, by his careful and selective writing and arrangement, made a place for realism in the modern theater. Believability of character was important, but more significant was the door that Nora slammed at the end of Ibsen's *A Doll's House* (1879). Its impact was heard around the world. Thereafter a new and important use was to be made of the theater, and the social thesis play became a recognized and valuable adjunct to the literature of the stage.

By the end of the nineteenth century many playwrights were following Ibsen's example. Henry Arthur Jones, Arthur Wing Pinero, Bernard Shaw, and others cast their works in the selectively realistic mold of the Norwegian. The success of these writers and the durability of their works depend on their language and characterization, not on their plots, many of which are remarkably similar. Upon reading the plays of Pinero and Jones, in particular, one is struck by their old-fashioned language and by their stereotyped characters. On the other hand, Shaw's brittle wit and absolute addiction to the language itself keeps his plays as fresh and true today as when they were written.

Pinero, writing concurrently with Shaw in an England that was still relatively ignorant of modern drama, achieved, in 1893, his first real success with *The Second Mrs. Tanqueray*, which remains his most durable play. He became known as a craftsman of the well-made play, chiefly concerned with social commentary. However, time has heightened a certain pretentiousness in his plays and in his concern with what were then accepted as ultrarealistic characters.

Pinero's plays depend heavily upon plot complications rather than the inevitability of circumstance for their action. What should seem headlong and unavoidable is rather a series of deviously contrived twists of storytelling designed to keep the spectator at all times interested. Pretentiously tragic, his plays now seem merely melodramatic. The transparent and pat endings remove the total impact of a higher, more energizing form of theater; resolutions are mechanical and forced.

The late nineteenth-century dramatists were unconsciously setting a trap for their successors, for the melodramatic form which they evolved almost automatically continues to harass playwrights to this day. Escapes from it have been few. Shaw managed because of his wit, deliberate artifice, and a rebellious spirit. Those who inadvertently copied Ibsen in search of tragedy were almost invariably doomed to conventions of theme and situation.

Mid-Channel appeared in 1909, after Pinero had written a series of successes that began with *The Second Mrs. Tanqueray* in 1893. As theater, it abounds in plot complications and moral preachments which make for interest but remove a unifying force from the play. The central character, Zoe Blundell, does contribute a certain cohesiveness, but because of the monotony of Pinero's prose, interest in her lags.

Zoe and Theodore Blundell are wealthy and fashionable, but their marriage is in mid-channel; there is little love in their relationship, and there are no children. To amuse herself, Zoe has taken on a series of men younger than she, whom she calls her tame robins. They squire her about in the social world and sip endless cups of tea while they amuse and entertain her. One of them, Leonard Ferris, makes the mistake of falling in love with her. She and Theodore finally agree to separate after another of their petty quarrels, and when Zoe goes to Italy to forget, Leonard follows her. Theodore takes a mistress during her absence.

When Zoe returns in bad health, a mutual friend tries to effect a reconciliation; but the old bickering begins again, making an adult relationship impossible.

In the meantime Zoe's young friend, Ethel Pierpoint, has confessed her love for Leonard. Leonard, on the rebound from Zoe, goes to Ethel and they plan marriage. Zoe admits having had an affair with Leonard while they were in Italy, and Theodore swears that he will divorce Zoe and force Leonard to marry her. When Zoe finds that Leonard is committed to Ethel, she ends it all by throwing herself from an upstairs window in her estranged husband's flat.

Zoe has some fascination as a tormented character. Wealthy and spoiled, childless and unhappy, she presents a rather touching picture of a woman approaching middle age who has never fulfilled her place as wife and mother. Yet she seems constantly at fault and unable to control herself as a social being. Interesting relationships exist between Zoe and her tame robins. They are her favorites until they become involved with other women; then, petulantly and jealously, they are dismissed. She exerts considerable control over them, while they, spineless and lacking in ambition, do her bidding.

Zoe and Theodore are characters caught in a circumstance of their own making. They are in mid-channel and must go one way or the other, or sink. They are both pictured as intelligent people, aware of their own shortcomings, yet they seem powerless to do anything about their failing marriage. Pride, ambition, thoughtlessness, and coldness all enter into their union, but on a petty, commonplace level. They are people of few redeeming qualities except for charm and money.

Zoe's suicide at the end of the play is an action difficult to explain in the light of all that has gone before. Pinero suggests that she has no choice, having been provided with all the possibilities for happiness but finding herself unable to use them. Actually, it is more Pinero the playwright than Zoe the character who has no choice but to come to this ending. Ibsen might have left it all unresolved, with the events of the future left to the imagination of the viewer, but with careful hints presented along the way to suggest other possibilities. But in the English theater of sensibility, a satisfactory conclusion to all entanglements was demanded. Theatergoers were not yet ready to face reality unless it condoned a fulfillment of moral obligations. The realistic form was a new and foreign thing, provocative and unpleasant; its redeeming feature was the lesson it taught.

As a stylist, Pinero lacked the technique of handling the inevitability of action in his plots. Circumstances invented rarely have as much force and impact as circumstances which inevitably flow from other events. Predictable actions are never as convincing as actions that arise from character itself. Zoe is, ultimately, an unsuccessful character because she reacts within a carefully structured framework, lacking the motivations that make for believability and importance as an individual caught up in an unavoidable turmoil.

MIDDLEMARCH

Type of work: Novel
Author: George Eliot (Mary Ann Evans, 1819-1880)
Type of plot: Psychological realism
Time of plot: Nineteenth century
Locale: England
First published: 1871-1872

Principal characters:
DOROTHEA BROOKE, an idealistic girl
EDWARD CASAUBON, her scholarly husband
WILL LADISLAW, Casaubon's cousin
TERTIUS LYDGATE, a doctor
ROSAMOND VINCY, whom he married
CELIA, Dorothea's sister
SIR JAMES CHETTAM, Celia's husband

Critique:

In this story of the provincial English life of the mid-nineteenth century, George Eliot has contrived a work of art that exemplifies a theme both noble and coherent. The lives of her characters, as she reveals them, indicate the truth of the writer's statement that ideals are often thwarted when applied to an imperfect social order. This novel is an ample picture of many aspects of English social life during the Victorian period.

The Story:

Dorothea Brooke and her younger sister, Celia, were young women of good birth, who lived with their bachelor uncle at Tipton Grange near the town of Middlemarch. So serious was Dorothea's cast of mind that she was reluctant to keep jewelry she had inherited from her dead mother, and she gave all of it to her sister. Upon reconsideration, however, she did keep a ring and bracelet.

At a dinner party where Edward Casaubon, a middle-aged scholar, and Sir James Chettam both vied for her attention, she was much more attracted to the serious-minded Casaubon. Casaubon must have had an inkling that his chances with Dorothea were good, for the next morning he sought her out. Celia, who did not like his complexion or his moles, escaped to other interests.

That afternoon Dorothea, contemplating the wisdom of the scholar, was walking and by chance encountered Sir James; he, in love with her, mistook her silence for agreement and supposed she might love him in return.

When Casaubon made his proposal of marriage by letter, Dorothea accepted him at once. Mr. Brooke, her uncle, thought Sir James a much better match; Dorothea's acceptance merely confirmed his bachelor views that women were difficult to understand. He decided not to interfere in her plans, but Celia felt that the event would be more like a funeral than a marriage, and frankly said so.

Casaubon took Dorothea, Celia, and Mr. Brooke to see his home so that Dorothea might order any necessary changes. Dorothea, intending in all things to defer to Casaubon's tastes, said she would make no changes in the house. During the visit Dorothea met Will Ladislaw, Casaubon's second cousin, who seemed to be hardly in sympathy with his elderly cousin's marriage plans.

While Dorothea and her new husband were traveling in Italy, Tertius Lydgate, an ambitious and poor young doctor, was meeting pretty Rosamond Vincy, to whom he was much attracted. Fred Vincy, Rosamond's brother, had indicated that he expected to come into a fine inheritance when his uncle, Mr. Featherstone, should die. Vincy, meanwhile, was pressed by a debt he was unable to pay.

Lydgate became involved in petty local politics. When the time came to choose a chaplain for the new hospital of which

Lydgate was the head, the young doctor realized that it was to his best interest to vote in accordance with the wishes of Nicholas Bulstrode, an influential banker and founder of the hospital. A clergyman named Tyke received the office.

In Rome, Ladislaw encountered Dorothea and her middle-aged husband. Dorothea had begun to realize too late how pompous and incompatible she found Casaubon. Seeing her unhappiness, Ladislaw first pitied and then fell in love with his cousin's wife. Unwilling to live any longer on Casaubon's charity, Ladislaw announced his intention of returning to England and finding some kind of gainful occupation.

When Fred Vincy's note came due, he tried to sell a horse at a profit but the animal turned out to be vicious. Caleb Garth, who had signed his note, now stood to lose a hundred and ten pounds because of Fred's inability to raise the money. Fred fell ill, and Lydgate was summoned to attend him. Lydgate used his professional calls to further his suit with Rosamond.

Dorothea and her husband returned from Rome in time to hear of Celia's engagement to Sir James Chettam. Will Ladislaw included a note to Dorothea in a letter he wrote to Casaubon. This attention precipitated a quarrel which was followed by Casaubon's serious illness. Lydgate, who attended him, urged him to give up his studies for the time being. To Dorothea, Lydgate confided that Casaubon had a weak heart and must be guarded from all excitement.

Meanwhile all the relatives of old Mr. Featherstone were waiting impatiently for his death, but he hoped to circumvent their desires by giving his fortune to Mary Garth, daughter of the man who had signed Fred Vincy's note. When she refused it, he fell into a rage and died soon afterward. When his will was read, it was learned he had left nothing to his relatives; most of his money was to go to a Joshua Riggs, who was to take the name of Featherstone, and a part of his fortune was to endow the Featherstone Almshouses for old men.

Plans were made for Rosamond's marriage with Lydgate. Fred Vincy was ordered to prepare himself finally for the ministry, since he was to have no inheritance from his uncle. Mr. Brooke, having gone into politics, enlisted the help of Ladislaw in publishing a liberal paper. Mr. Casaubon had come to dislike Ladislaw intensely after his cousin had rejected further financial assistance, and he had forbidden Ladislaw to enter his house.

Casaubon died suddenly. A codicil to his will gave Dorothea all of his property as long as she did not marry Ladislaw. This strange provision caused Dorothea's friends and relatives some concern because if publicly given out, it would appear that Dorothea and Ladislaw had been indiscreet.

Mr. Brooke, on the advice of his Tory friends, gave up his liberal newspaper and thus cut off his connection with Ladislaw. The latter realized that Dorothea's family was in some way trying to separate him from Dorothea but he refused to be disconcerted about the matter. He resolved to stay on in Middlemarch until he was ready to leave. When he heard of the codicil to Casaubon's will, he was more than ever determined to remain so that he could eventually disprove the suspicions of the village concerning him and Dorothea.

Meanwhile Lydgate and Rosamond had married, and the doctor had gone deeply in debt to furnish his house. When he found that his income did not meet his wife's spendthrift habits, he asked her to help him economize. He and his wife began to quarrel. His practice and popularity decreased.

A disreputable man named Raffles appeared in Middlemarch. Raffles knew that Ladislaw's grandfather had amassed a fortune as a receiver of stolen goods and that Nicholas Bulstrode, the highly respected banker, had once been the confidential clerk of Ladislaw's ancestor. More than that, Bulstrode's first wife had been his employer's widow. Upon money inherited from her, money which should have gone to Ladislaw's mother, Bulstrode had built his own fortune.

Already blackmailed by Raffles, Bulstrode reasoned that the scoundrel would tell Ladislaw the whole story. To forestall trouble, he sent for Ladislaw and offered him an annuity of five hundred pounds and liberal provision in his will. Ladislaw, feeling that his relatives had already tainted his honor, refused, unwilling to be associated in any way with the unsavory business. Deciding to leave Middlemarch, Ladislaw went to London without the assurance that Dorothea loved him.

Lydgate drifted deeper into debt. When he wished to sell what he could and take cheaper lodgings, Rosamond managed to make him hold on, to keep up the pretense of prosperity a little longer. At the same time Bulstrode gave up his interest in the new hospital and withdrew his financial support.

Faced at last with the seizure of his goods, Lydgate went to Bulstrode and asked for a loan. The banker advised him to seek aid from Dorothea and abruptly ended the conversation. But when Raffles, in the last stages of alcoholism, returned to Middlemarch and Lydgate was called in to attend him, Bulstrode, afraid the doctor would learn the banker's secret from Raffles' drunken ravings, changed his mind and gave Lydgate a check for a thousand pounds. The loan came in time to save Lydgate's goods and reputation. When Raffles died, Bulstrode felt at peace at last. But it soon became common gossip that Bulstrode had given money to Lydgate and that Lydgate had attended Raffles in his final illness. Bulstrode and Lydgate were publicly accused of malpractice in Raffles' death. Only Dorothea took up Lydgate's defense. The rest of the town was busy with gossip over the affair. Rosamond was anxious to leave Middlemarch to avoid public disgrace. Bulstrode also was anxious to leave town after his secret, which Raffles had told while drunk in a neighboring village, became known. But he became ill and his doctors would not permit him to leave his bed.

Dorothea, sympathetic with Lydgate, determined to give her support to the hospital and to try to convince Rosamond that the only way Lydgate could recover his honor was by remaining in Middlemarch. Unfortunately, she came upon Will Ladislaw, to whom poor Rosamond was pouring out her grief. Afraid Rosamond was involved with Ladislaw, Dorothea left abruptly. Angered at the false position Rosamond had put him in, Ladislaw explained that he had always loved Dorothea, but from a distance. When Dorothea forced herself to return to Lydgate's house on the following morning, Rosamond told her of Ladislaw's declaration. Dorothea realized she was willing to give up Casaubon's fortune for Ladislaw's affection.

In spite of the protests of her family and friends, they were married several weeks later and went to London to live. Lydgate and Rosamond lived together with better understanding and prospects of a happier future. Fred Vincy became engaged to Mary Garth, with whom he had long been in love. For a time Dorothea's family disregarded her, but they were finally reconciled after Dorothea's son was born and Ladislaw was elected to Parliament.

2352

A MIDSUMMER NIGHT'S DREAM

Type of work: Drama
Author: William Shakespeare (1564-1616)
Type of plot: Romantic comedy
Time of plot: Remote antiquity
Locale: Athens
First presented: 1595

Principal characters:
THESEUS, Duke of Athens
LYSANDER, and
DEMETRIUS, in love with Hermia
BOTTOM, a weaver
HIPPOLYTA, Queen of the Amazons
HERMIA, in love with Lysander
HELENA, in love with Demetrius
OBERON, king of the fairies
TITANIA, queen of the fairies
PUCK, fairy page to Oberon

Critique:

The capriciousness, the changeableness of lovers is obviously the theme of the perennially romantic and entertaining comedy, *A Midsummer Night's Dream.* Shakespeare presents a group of lovers so irresponsible in their actions that their freakish behavior can be explained only by the intervention of supernatural beings. All of the lovers in the play switch their affections from time to time, but they are not responsible for their infidelity; love makes them irrational. The play is a delightful comedy, one of the favorites by the master dramatist. It enjoys frequent revivals by noted producers and actors and will undoubtedly always retain its popularity.

The Story:

Theseus, the Duke of Athens, was to be married in four days to Hippolyta, Queen of the Amazons, and he ordered his Master of the Revels to prepare suitable entertainment for the nuptials. But other lovers of ancient Athens were not so happy as their ruler. Hermia, in love with Lysander, was loved also by Demetrius, who had her father's permission to marry her. When she refused his suit, Demetrius took his case to Theseus and demanded that the law be invoked. Theseus upheld the father, which meant that Hermia must either marry Demetrius, be placed in a nunnery, or be put to death. Hermia swore that she would enter a convent before she would consent to become Demetrius' bride.

But Lysander plotted with Hermia to steal her away from Athens, take her to the home of his aunt, and there marry her. They were to meet the following night in a woods outside the city. Hermia confided the plan to her good friend Helena. Demetrius had formerly been betrothed to Helena, and although he had switched his love to Hermia he was still desperately loved by the scorned Helena. Helena, willing to do anything to gain even a smile from Demetrius, told him of his rival's plan to elope with Hermia.

Unknown to any of the four young people, there were to be others in that same woods on the appointed night, Midsummer Eve. A guild of Athenian laborers was to meet there to practice a play the members hoped to present in honor of Theseus and Hippolyta's wedding. The fairies also held their midnight revels in the woods. Oberon, king of the fairies, desired for his page a little Indian prince, but Oberon's queen, Titania, had the boy. Loving him like a son, she refused to give him up to her husband. In order to force Titania to do his bidding, Oberon ordered his mischievous page, called Puck or Robin Goodfellow, to secure the juice of

2353

"Love in Idleness," a purple flower once hit by Cupid's dart. This juice, when placed in the eyes of anyone sleeping, caused that person to fall in love with the first creature seen on awakening. Oberon planned to drop some of the juice in Titania's eyes and then refuse to lift the charm until she gave him the boy.

While Puck was on his errand, Demetrius and Helena entered the woods. Making himself invisible, Oberon heard Helena plead her love for Demetrius and heard the young man scorn and berate her. They had come to the woods to find the fleeing lovers, Lysander and Hermia. Oberon, pitying Helena, determined to aid her. When Puck returned with the juice, Oberon ordered him to find the Athenian and place some of the juice in his eyes so that he would love the girl who doted on him.

Puck went to do as he was ordered, while Oberon squeezed the juice of the flower into the eyes of Titania as she slept. But Puck, coming upon Lysander and Hermia as they slept in the woods, mistook Lysander's Athenian dress for that of Demetrius and poured the charmed juice into Lysander's eyes. Lysander was awakened by Helena, who had been abandoned deep in the woods by Demetrius. The charm worked perfectly; Lysander fell in love with Helena. That poor girl, thinking that he was mocking her with his ardent protestations of love, begged him to stop his teasing and return to the sleeping Hermia. But Lysander, pursuing Helena, left Hermia alone in the forest. When she awakened she feared that Lysander had been killed, for she believed that he would never have deserted her otherwise.

Titania, in the meantime, awakened to a strange sight. The laborers, practicing for their play, had paused not far from the sleeping fairy queen. Bottom, the comical but stupid weaver who was to play the leading role, became the butt of another of Puck's jokes. The prankster clapped an ass's head over Bottom's own foolish pate and led the poor fool a merry chase until the weaver was at the spot where Titania lay sleeping. Thus when she awakened she looked at Bottom, still wearing the head of an ass. She fell instantly in love with him and ordered the fairies to tend his every want. This turn pleased Oberon mightily. When he learned of the mistake Puck had made in placing the juice in Lysander's eyes, however, he tried to right the wrong by placing love juice also in Demetrius' eyes, and he ordered Puck to have Helena close by when Demetrius awakened. His act made both girls unhappy and forlorn. When Demetrius, who she knew hated her, also began to make love to her, Helena thought that both men were taunting and ridiculing her. And poor Hermia, encountering Lysander, could not understand why he tried to drive her away, all the time protesting that he loved only Helena.

Again Oberon tried to set matters straight. He ordered Puck to lead the two men in circles until weariness forced them to lie down and go to sleep. Then a potion to remove the charm and make the whole affair seem like a dream was to be placed in Lysander's eyes. Afterward he would again love Hermia, and all the young people would be united in proper pairs. Titania, too, was to have the charm removed, for Oberon had taunted her about loving an ass until she had given up the prince to him. Puck obeyed the orders and placed the potion in Lysander's eyes.

The four lovers were awakened by Theseus, Hippolyta, and Hermia's father, who had gone into the woods to watch Theseus' hounds perform. Lysander again loved Hermia and Demetrius still loved Helena, for the love juice remained in his eyes. Hermia's father persisted in his demand that his daughter marry Demetrius, but since that young man no longer wanted her and all four were happy with their partners, he ceased to oppose Lysander's suit. Theseus gave them permission to marry on the day set for his own wedding to Hippolyta.

Titania also awakened and, like the

others, thought that she had been dreaming. Puck removed the ass's head from Bottom and that poor bewildered weaver made his way back to Athens, reaching there just in time to save the play from ruin, for he was to play Pyramus, the hero. The Master of the Revels tried to dissuade Theseus from choosing the laborer's play for the wedding night. Theseus, however, was intrigued by a play that was announced as both tedious and brief as well as merry and tragic. So Bottom and his troupe presented *Pyramus and Thisbe*, much to the merriment of all the guests.

After the play all the bridal couples retired to their suites, and Oberon and Titania sang a fairy song over them, promising that they and all their children would be blessed.

THE MIKADO

Type of work: Comic opera
Author: W. S. Gilbert (1836-1911)
Type of plot: Social satire
Time of plot: Middle Ages
Locale: Titipu, Japan
First presented: 1885

> *Principal characters:*
> Ko-Ko, Lord High Executioner of Titipu
> THE MIKADO OF JAPAN
> NANKI-POO, his son, disguised as a minstrel
> POOH-BAH, Lord High Everything Else
> YUM-YUM, PITTI-SING, and PEEP-BO, wards of Ko-Ko
> KATISHA, an elderly lady in love with Nanki-Poo
> PISH-TUSH, a noble lord

Critique:

The Mikado, or The Town of Titipu, is one of the many works of the famous light opera collaborators, Sir William Gilbert and Sir Arthur Seymour Sullivan (1842-1900). Although they began their creative careers independently, their greatest fame is the result of the work they did as co-workers, Gilbert as librettist and Sullivan as composer, after 1871. The Mikado is a comic opera in two acts. Like most of the Gilbert and Sullivan productions, it contains much light humor and pointed satire.

The Story:

Ko-Ko had become the Lord High Executioner in the town of Titipu in old Japan, and to his courtyard came many knights and lords to flatter and cajole the holder of so dread and august an office.

One day a stranger appeared at Ko-Ko's palace, a wandering minstrel who carried his guitar on his back and a sheaf of ballads in his hand. The Japanese lords were curious about his presence there, for he was obviously not of noble birth and therefore could expect no favors from powerful Ko-Ko. At last Pish-Tush questioned him about his business with Ko-Ko. Introducing himself as Nanki-Poo, the minstrel announced that he sought Yum-Yum, the beautiful ward of Ko-Ko, with whom he had fallen in love while playing the second trombone in the Titipu town band a year before. He had heard that Ko-Ko was to be executed

for flirting, a capital offense in the land of the Mikado, and since Ko-Ko was to die, he hoped that Yum-Yum would be free to marry him.

Pish-Tush corrected the rash young man, telling him that the Mikado had revoked the death sentence of Ko-Ko and raised him at the same time to the great and noble rank of the Lord High Executioner of Titipu. Nanki-Poo was crestfallen, for he realized that the ward of an official so important would never be allowed to marry a lowly minstrel.

Pooh-Bah, another nobleman, secretly resented the fact that he, a man of ancient lineage, had to hold minor office under a man like Ko-Ko, previously a mere tailor. But Pooh-Bah was interested in any opportunity for graft; he was even willing to betray the so-called state secret of Ko-Ko's intention to wed his beautiful ward. Pooh-Bah advised Nanki-Poo to leave Titipu and by all means to stay away from Yum-Yum.

Meanwhile, Ko-Ko had been preparing a list of the types of criminals he intended to execute—autograph hunters, people who insist upon spoiling tête-à-têtes, people who eat peppermint and breathe in one's face, the man who praises every country but his own, and apologetic statesmen.

Uncertain of the privileges of his new office, the Lord High Executioner consulted the Lord High Everything Else about the money to be spent on his impending marriage. Pooh-Bah advised him, first as Private Secretary, and gave one opinion; then as Chancellor of the Exchequer he expressed a contrary point of view. He had a different opinion for every one of his many offices and official titles. They were interrupted, however, by the appearance of Yum-Yum and her sisters Peep-Bo and Pitti-Sing. Ko-Ko attempted to kiss his bride-to-be, but she openly expressed her reluctance and distaste.

When the three sisters saw Nanki-Poo loitering nearby, they rushed to greet him, astonished to find him in Titipu. Ko-Ko, baffled and displeased by their schoolgirl mirth, demanded an introduction to the stranger.

When Yum-Yum and Nanki-Poo had a few moments alone with each other, the minstrel revealed his true identity as the son of the Mikado, and confessed the reasons for his flight from court. Katisha, a middle-aged woman in the court, had misunderstood acts of Nanki-Poo as overtures of romance. She mentioned them to the Mikado. He in turn misunderstood his son's conduct and requested that Nanki-Poo marry Katisha. Nanki-Poo, already in love with Yum-Yum, fled the court in the disguise of a minstrel and went to Titipu.

That same day Ko-Ko received from the Mikado a communication which instructed him to execute somebody within a month. Otherwise the office of Lord High Executioner would be abolished; Ko-Ko would be beheaded for neglecting his duties, and the city of Titipu would be ranked as only a village. Perplexed by this sudden and unhappy news, Ko-Ko saw no solution until he discovered Nanki-Poo carrying a rope with which to hang himself. Seeing a way of escape, Ko-Ko bargained with Nanki-Poo, promising him a luxuriant life for thirty days, if at the end of that time the minstrel would allow himself to be executed officially. Nanki-Poo agreed on the condition that he could marry Yum-Yum at once.

This acceptable solution was upset, however, by the arrival of Katisha, who recognized Nanki-Poo and tried to claim him for her husband. When she learned that he was to marry Yum-Yum, she attempted to reveal his true identity, but her voice was not heard above the singing and shouting instigated by Yum-Yum.

Hearing of the proposed marriage of Yum-Yum and Nanki-Poo, Pooh-Bah informed Ko-Ko that the wife of a beheaded man must be buried alive, a law which would mean Yum-Yum's death if Nanki-Poo were executed. Again lost as to a way out of his problem, Ko-Ko was spurred to action by the unexpected arrival of the Mikado himself. Desperate, he concealed Nanki-Poo and showed the Mikado a forged certificate of Nanki-Poo's execution.

But when the Mikado read the name of the victim, he announced that the heir-apparent had been executed. According to law, Ko-Ko's life must now be forfeited.

Luckily for Ko-Ko, Nanki-Poo and Yum-Yum appeared at that moment. Man and wife at last, they were ready to start on their honeymoon. Seeing his son happily married and not dead as he had supposed, the Mikado forgave everyone concerned in Ko-Ko's plot—the unfortunate Lord High Executioner, however, only after he had wed the jilted Katisha.

THE MILL ON THE FLOSS

Type of work: Novel
Author: George Eliot (Mary Ann Evans, 1819-1880)
Type of plot: Domestic realism
Time of plot: Nineteenth century
Locale: England
First published: 1860

Principal characters:
MR. TULLIVER, owner of the mill on the Floss
MRS. TULLIVER, his wife
TOM TULLIVER, their son
MAGGIE TULLIVER, their daughter
AUNT GLEGG, and
AUNT PULLET, sisters of Mrs. Tulliver
PHILIP WAKEM, Maggie's suitor
LUCY DEANE, cousin of Tom and Maggie
STEPHEN GUEST, Lucy's fiancé

Critique:

This book is more than a revelation of manners and conventions. It is the happy union of knowledge with sympathy, of understanding with determination to reveal some of the real differences between people. There is also bitterness in this book, a kind of grimness which is basic. People who get on in the book are those who are iron-willed, who go after what they want and subdue all emotions and desires that lie close to the heart. Those who try to live both by bread and by spirit end tragically, as do Tom and Maggie Tulliver, both unfitted for the roles life chose for them.

The Story:

Dorlcote Mill stood on the banks of the River Floss near the village of St. Ogg's. Owned by the ambitious Mr. Tulliver, it provided a good living for him and his family, but he dreamed of the day when his son Tom would climb to a higher station in life.

Mrs. Tulliver's sisters, who had married well, criticized Mr. Tulliver's unseemly ambition and openly predicted the day when his air castles would bring himself and his family to ruin. Aunt Glegg, richest of the sisters, held a note on his property, and when he quarreled with her over his plans for Tom's edu-

cation, Mr. Tulliver determined to borrow the money and repay her.

For Tom, who had inherited the placid arrogance of his mother's people, life was not difficult. He was resolved to be just in all his dealings and to deliver punishment to whomever it was due. His sister Maggie grew up with an imagination beyond her years of understanding. Her aunts predicted she would come to a bad end because she was tomboyish, dark-skinned, dreamy, and indifferent to their wills. Frightened by ill luck in her attempts to please her brother Tom, her cousin Lucy, and her mother and aunts, Maggie ran away, determined to live with the gipsies. But she was glad enough to return. Her father scolded her mother and Tom for abusing her. Her mother was sure Maggie would come to a bad end because of the way Mr. Tulliver humored her.

Tom's troubles began when his father sent him to study at Mr. Stelling's school. Having little interest in spelling, grammar, or Latin, Tom found himself wishing he were back at the mill, where he might dream of someday riding a horse like his father's and giving orders to people around him. Mr. Stelling was convinced that Tom was not only obstinate but also stupid. Returning home for the Christmas holidays, Tom learned that Philip Wakem, son of a lawyer who was his father's enemy, would also enter Mr. Stelling's school.

Philip Wakem was a cripple, and so Tom was not able to beat him up as he should have liked at first. Philip could draw, and he knew Latin and Greek. After they overcame their initial reserve, the two boys became useful to one another. Philip admired Tom's arrogance and self-possession and Tom needed Philip's knowledge to help him in his studies. But their fathers' quarrel kept a breach between them. Tom felt that Philip needed to be watched, that he was the son of a rascal.

When Maggie came to visit Tom, she met Philip, and the two became close friends. Then, after Maggie had been sent away to school with her cousin Lucy, Mr. Tulliver became involved in a lawsuit. Because Mr. Wakem defended the opposition, Mr. Tulliver said his children should have as little as possible to do with Philip.

Mr. Tulliver lost his suit and stood to lose all his property as well. In order to pay off Aunt Glegg, he had borrowed money on his household furnishings. Now he hoped Aunt Pullet would lend him the money to pay the debt against which his household goods stood forfeit. He could no longer afford to keep Maggie and Tom in school. Then Mr. Tulliver learned that Mr. Wakem had bought up his debts, and the discovery brought on a stroke. Tom made Maggie promise never to speak to Philip Wakem again. Mrs. Tulliver wept because her household things were to be put up at auction. In the ruin which followed, Tom and Maggie rejected the scornful offers of help from their aunts.

Bob Jakin, a country lout with whom Tom had fought as a boy, turned up to offer Tom partnership with him in a venture where Tom's education would help Bob's native business shrewdness. But both were without capital. For the time being Tom took a job in a ware-house and studied bookkeeping each night.

Mr. Wakem bought the mill but permitted Mr. Tulliver to act as its manager for wages. It was Wakem's plan eventually to turn the mill over to his son. Tulliver, not knowing what else to do, stayed on as an employee of his enemy, but he asked Tom to sign a statement in the Bible that he would wish the Wakems evil as long as he lived. Against Maggie's entreaties, Tom signed his name. Finally Aunt Glegg gave Tom some money which he invested with Bob Jakin. Slowly Tom began to accumulate funds to pay off his father's debts.

Meanwhile Maggie and Philip had been meeting secretly in the glades near the mill. One day he asked Maggie if she loved him. She put him off. Later, at a family gathering, she betrayed her feeling for Philip in a manner which aroused Tom's suspicions. He made her swear on the Bible not to have anything more to do with Philip, and then he sought out Philip and ordered him to stay away from his sister.

Shortly afterward Tom showed his father his profits. The next day Mr. Tulliver thrashed Mr. Wakem and then suffered another stroke, from which he never recovered.

Two years later Maggie, now a teacher, went to visit her cousin, Lucy Deane, who was also entertaining young Stephen Guest in her home. One difficulty Lucy foresaw was that Philip, who was friendly with both her and Stephen, might absent himself during Maggie's visit. Stephen had already decided that Lucy was to be his choice for a wife, but at first sight he and Maggie were attracted to one another. Lucy, blind to what was happening, was pleased that her cousin Maggie and Stephen were becoming good friends.

Maggie asked Tom's permission to see Philip Wakem at a party Lucy was giving. Tom replied that if Maggie should ever consider Philip as a lover, she must expect never to see her brother again.

Tom stood by his oath to his father. He felt his dignity as a Tulliver, and he believed Maggie was apt to follow the inclination of the moment without giving consideration to the outcome. He was right. Lacking the iron will which marked so many of her relatives, Maggie loved easily and without restraint.

Meanwhile Lucy's father had promised to try to buy back the mill for Tom. Learning of this plan, Philip hoped to persuade his father to sell the mill. For this service Philip felt sure Tom would forget his old hatred.

At a dance Stephen Guest tried to kiss Maggie. She evaded him and the next day avoided Philip Wakem as well. She felt she owed it to Lucy not to allow Stephen to fall in love with her, and she felt that she owed it to her brother not to marry Philip.

She was carried along by the tide. Her relatives would not let her go back into teaching, for Tom's good luck continued and he repossessed his father's mill. Both Stephen and Philip urged her to marry them without the knowledge of each other's aims. Certainly, Lucy did not suspect Stephen's growing indifference to her.

One day Stephen took Maggie boating and tried to convince her to run away with him and be married. She refused his offer. Then the tide carried them beyond the reach of shore and they were forced to spend the night in the boat.

Maggie dared the wrath and judgment of her relatives when she returned and attempted to explain to Lucy and the others what had happened. They refused to listen to her. Tom turned her away from the mill house, with the word that he would send her money but that he never wished to see her again. Mrs. Tulliver resolved to go with Maggie, and Bob Jakin took them in.

Maggie slowly began to realize what ostracism meant, for one by one people deserted her. Only Aunt Glegg and Lucy offered any sympathy. Stephen wrote to her in agony of spirit, as did Philip. Maggie wanted to be by herself. She wondered if there could be love for her without pain for others.

That autumn a terrible flood ravaged St. Ogg's. Knowing that Tom was at the mill, Maggie attempted to reach him in a boat. The two were reunited and Tom took over the rowing of the boat. But the full force of the flood overwhelmed them and they drowned, together at the end as they had been when they were children.

THE MILL ON THE PO

Type of work: Novel
Author: Riccardo Bacchelli (1891-   )
Type of plot: Historical romance
Time of plot: 1812-1872
Locale: The region of the Po River, near Ferrara
First published: 1938-1940

Principal characters:
LAZZARO SCACERNI, a miller on the Po
DOSOLINA, his wife
GIUSEPPE, his son
CECILIA, his daughter-in-law

Critique:

The epic sweep and poetic fervor of The Mill on the Po give Bacchelli's novel a significant place in Italian fiction of the twentieth century. Its story fills two volumes of a projected trilogy and embraces the stormy period of Italian unification. Political events, however, are not the prime consideration of the author, except as they affect the lives of people who are caught in the backwash of historical events. His chief interest is centered in the obscure heroes who struggle to obtain peace and security without becoming submerged by the mighty forces of history and nature.

The Story:

In 1817 a new water mill appeared on the Po River, near the city of Ferrara. Its owner was young Lazzaro Scacerni, who had become a miller in an odd fashion indeed. Nevertheless, he was no stranger to the river—his father had been a ferryman at Ariano before dying in the peasant uprising of 1807. Shortly afterward the boy Lazzaro had been sent, along with other orphans, to serve as cabin boy in the navy. When he became older, he went over to the army pontoniers, and in 1812 he found himself a part of Napoleon's ill-fated Russian campaign.

It was in Russia that the story of the mill really started. During the terrible retreat, a dying captain gave Lazzaro a mysterious receipt, which the illiterate young Scacerni could not read. He guarded it closely, however, as he straggled homeward from a debacle in which fourteen out of every fifteen Italian soldiers had perished. Finally regaining the neighborhood of Ferrara, Lazzaro led a hand-to-mouth existence while waiting for a chance to make use of his one asset. He learned to read well enough to decipher the name and address attached to the receipt, and subsequent search led to Ezekiel the Jew, in Ferrara's ghetto. The receipt was for jewels, plundered from Spanish churches by Lazzaro's benefactor. His windfall once assured, Lazzaro cannily pondered its best use. Millers, he decided, were least affected by times of adversity, and he arranged with a friendly old shipwright to build him a mill. In due time it was finished, christened St. Michael's, and put into operation.

As the years passed, the miller prospered. One, two, and finally three boys were hired for helpers as his trade grew. His success inspired more envy than affection among his neighbors, but not a few of their wives and daughters succumbed to his dashing gallantries. Nearly forty and wearying of bachelorhood, Lazzaro fell in love with Dosolina, poor but delicately beautiful and twenty years his junior. Lazzaro bought a house, married Dosolina, and settled down to enjoy his prosperity.

But fate was not always to smile. Floods came, the bane of the Po River millers, and smugglers, crossing between Italy and Austria, insolently adopted his mill for a rendezvous. On the birth night of his son Giuseppe, Lazzaro's troubles reached a climax. While Dosolina was writhing in difficult labor, the desperate Lazzaro fought to save his mill from the swollen menace of the Po. Slipping on the wet deck, he broke a leg but continued to direct his helpers, two of whom worked manfully. The third was malformed Beffa, who secretly hated his master and who had become a tool of the smugglers. Shedding all restraint, Beffa openly exulted over his master's plight and scornfully asserted that the miller had been cuckolded—whereupon Lazzaro reached out, seized Beffa with his muscular arms, and hurled him into the river.

Dosolina recovered, and the mill was saved; but Beffa's damp dismissal caused Lazzaro to receive disturbing threats from Raguseo, king of the smugglers. A gang feud, however, broke out among the outlaws soon afterward, disposing of both Raguseo and Beffa. Lazzaro breathed more easily thereafter. One danger was over, but another seemed constant, for intermittent floods continued to threaten St. Michael's Mill. One day a large mill washed ashore near Lazzaro's own, its only occupant a young girl orphaned by the flood. To Cecilia her mill meant home; she was very happy when the Scacernis befriended her and reëstablished her mill alongside theirs. From that time on Lazzaro regarded the girl almost as his own daughter.

He was much less pleased, however, with the character and disposition of his own son. Bandy-legged, crafty, and cowardly, Giuseppe cared nothing about his father's trade except its profit. He early showed great skill, as well as great avarice, in business dealings of any kind, and he was held in contempt, except by his mother. During the late 1840's he began successfully trafficking in grain with the hated Austrians, but the same years brought new distress to his family. Roving bands of partisans, now Italian and now Austrian mercenaries, infested the countryside and disturbed the peace and security of the Scacernis. Finally, both

mills were commandeered by the Austrians, and Lazzaro and Cecilia were required to transfer them to the opposite side of the river.

After a few months the mills were allowed to return, but the political atmosphere was still cloudy and confused among the rival claims and interests of the papacy, the Italian nationalistic movement, and Austria. Lazzaro, who was growing old and querulous, found much to complain about. Only at the mills, in the company of his helpers and Cecilia, did he feel comfortable; and even there he sometimes railed at the open smuggling which carried scarce grain across the river to Austria. He was outraged when he learned that Giuseppe took a leading role in such transactions.

Suddenly an unexpected family affair arose which gave concern to both the elder Scacernis, though for entirely different reasons. Giuseppe, apparently inattentive to women, had long slyly coveted Cecilia for his wife, in spite of her obvious indifference to him. Not daring to risk her mockery by a proposal, he went about winning his goal by characteristic trickery. Meanly playing on her fondness for his father, Giuseppe blandly announced that Lazzaro had broken a law by possessing concealed firearms. His son could exert influence to head off his arrest and punishment—but only for a price, Cecilia's consent to marry him. Cecilia, taken by surprise, was confused, angry, and ignorantly fearful. Her devotion to Lazzaro, however, was greater than her repugnance for his son, and in the end Giuseppe had his way.

Lazzaro, unaware of Cecilia's sacrifice, felt baffled and hurt by what he considered her poor judgment. In turn, Dosolina regarded her new daughter-in-law as little better than a river gipsy and quite unworthy of her son. Neither of the parents, however, had long to lament the marriage. In 1855 Dosolina was the victim of a wave of cholera which swept all Europe. The next morning Lazzaro was found dead beside her.

The structure of Italy changed: time

was bringing Austrian defeat, the end of papal rule, and the dawn of a united nation. These things, of course, meant little to Cecilia Scacerni. But the small warmth of her nature found, at last, a suitable outlet. Her first-born and favorite, Lazzarino, was vigorous and intelligent, a reminder of his grandfather in more than name. Even his grasping, mean-natured father openly adored him.

But Lazzarino was not destined to match his grandfather in years. Miserable at mockery of his father's cowardice, he ran off to join Garibaldi's volunteers. News of his death staggered Cecilia, but its effect on Giuseppe was catastrophic. Grief gnawed at his reason, and the destruction of his house and crops by flood completed his downfall. Howling obscenely, he was carted off to the asylum. Left alone, Cecilia looked about her with calm courage. There was work to do, and she would see that it was done.

THE MINISTRY OF FEAR

Type of work: Novel
Author: Graham Greene (1904-   )
Type of plot: Psychological melodrama
Time of plot: World War II
Locale: London and environs
First published: 1943

> *Principal characters:*
> ARTHUR ROWE, a middle-aged Englishman who has killed his wife
> ANNA HILFE, an Austrian refugee
> WILLI HILFE, Anna's brother and a fifth-column leader
> DR. FORESTER, English dupe of Willi Hilfe

Critique:

This novel records a train of incidents halfway between horror and insanity, while demonstrating how fifth-column agents worked in England during World War II. The ministry of fear was, of course, an organization of fascist agents operating in England and using as their tools people who had something in their pasts which they preferred to hide. In addition, there are descriptions of the blitz of 1940, when the German bombers obliterated a large section of London. The scenes describe not only the destruction and the confusion attendant upon it but also the reactions of Londoners who suffered through the raids day after day and night after night. As a whole, the novel captures the madhouse-like quality which hung for so many years over England and the rest of the world; the very disruption of values in human life is brought home to even an insensitive reader.

The Story:

Arthur Rowe, a middle-aged Englishman, happened one day onto a fête in blitz-torn London. In an effort to recapture some spirit of the brighter past, he entered the grounds. While there he had his fortune told, and the seer told him the weight of a cake which was to go to the person who guessed the weight correctly. Rowe won the cake and started to leave, but the clergyman who was in charge of the affair tried to get the cake back again. Rowe, angered, gave a pound note to the cause and left.

That same night, just before the German bombers flew up the Thames to terrorize the city, Rowe had his first visitor in months, a man who had just rented rooms in the same house. The visitor behaved very oddly. When given a piece of cake by Rowe, he crumbled it as if looking for something. Then, while Rowe was out of the room, the man slipped something into Rowe's tea. Rowe, returning, smelled the peculiar odor of the tea, but before he could say or do anything a bomb fell wrecking the house. He regained consciousness to find the house demolished.

The next day the worried Rowe, who had few friends to whom he could turn because he had killed his wife in a mercy killing, went to a detective agency, where he hired a man named Jones to watch after him and discover why someone wished to take his life. Rowe then went to the relief office which had been in charge of the fête at which he had won the cake. There he found a young woman, Anna Hilfe, and her brother Willi in charge of the office. The two said they were Austrian refugees. Willi Hilfe went with Rowe to the home of the fortune-teller in an effort to uncover the reason for the attempt on Rowe's life.

At the fortune-teller's home the two men were invited to stay for a seance. During the seance the man sitting next to Rowe was murdered with Rowe's knife.

Rowe, with Willi's aid, escaped from the house before the police arrived. He went to an air-raid shelter and remained there through the night. He wrote a letter to the police, but before he posted it he called Anna, who told him that "they" were still after him. "They" were supposed to be Nazi agents. Still Rowe could not understand why he had become a marked man. Anna agreed to aid Rowe and told him to send an address where he could be reached.

After talking to her, Rowe called the detective agency, only to find that Jones, the man he had hired, had disappeared and that the head of the agency had called the police in on the case. Rowe wandered aimlessly about the city until the afternoon, when he met a man who asked him to take a valise full of books to a Mr. Travers at a hotel. When Rowe arrived at the hotel, he was escorted to Travers' room. There he found Anna waiting for him. In fear of their lives, the two waited for the air raids to begin. They believed that Nazi agents would kill them during the noise and confusion of the raids. Then a bomb fell on the hotel. Rowe awoke in a private nursing home without any memory beyond his eighteenth year.

Anna visited him several times in the nursing home, and Rowe fell in love with her during the visits. She would not tell him of his past, and claimed that the head of the institution, Dr. Forester, wanted the recovery to be slow enough not to cause shock. One day a military officer being treated in the home confided that he had seen someone digging on the island in a pond on the grounds. The officer was immediately put into a strait jacket, while Rowe was confined to his room without newspapers or his clothes on the pretext that he had suffered a mild relapse.

Convinced that some evil was afoot, Rowe escaped from the room and visited the officer. His visit with the officer confirmed his suspicions. Within a few hours the doctor returned and, extremely angry at Rowe, threatened him, too, with a strait jacket. With the help of an attendant,

Rowe escaped and went to Scotland Yard. He turned himself in as the murderer of the victim at the seance, but to his surprise he was told that no one had been murdered there. The police turned him over to a counter-intelligence agent, who told Rowe that the murder had been a fraud to drive him into hiding and that the nursing home was actually a front for fifth-column activities.

The agent, Rowe, and a man from the hotel where Rowe had been injured went to the tailor shop run by the man who had supposedly been murdered. During the interview the tailor placed a phone call and after it was completed killed himself. The agent, angry at losing the man before learning any information, told Rowe that he had inadvertently been given a cake containing secret film which had been taken by Nazi agents from British documents.

Rowe and the agent then went to the home of the fortune-teller. There they failed to find the film, and they got no information. The last stop of the trip was at the nursing home. There they found the military officer dead, killed by Dr. Forester, who, Rowe now remembered, had been at the fortune-teller's home on the night of the supposed murder. The doctor was also dead, having been killed by the attendant who had helped Rowe to escape.

Without telling the counter-intelligence agent, Rowe called the number he had seen the tailor dial. When the call was answered, he found Anna at the other end. Going to her apartment, Rowe discovered that it was her brother Willi who was the head of the fifth-column ring. With Anna's help Rowe almost got the film. Anna, torn between love for her brother and for Rowe, allowed Willi to escape. Rowe, whose memory was almost complete, followed Willi and regained the film at the railroad station. He returned Willi's gun to him with but one bullet in it. Willi then went to the washroom and killed himself, but not before he had revealed the last piece of information which Rowe had failed to remember, the fact that Rowe had killed his first wife to put her out of pain. With the film in his possession, ready to give to the police, Rowe returned to Anna's apartment to tell her of her brother's death and to declare his love to her. Anna, even though he had driven her brother to his death, pledged her love for him as well.

MINNA VON BARNHELM

Type of work: Drama
Author: Gotthold Ephraim Lessing (1729-1781)
Type of plot: Romantic comedy
Time of plot: Eighteenth century
Locale: Germany
First presented: 1767

Principal characters:
MAJOR VON TELLHEIM, a discharged officer
JUST, his servant
PAUL WERNER, his sergeant
MINNA VON BARNHELM, in love with Tellheim
FRANZISKA, her maid

Critique:

Minna von Barnhelm is important for two reasons. First, it was a beginning of a drama native to Germany, with much appeal for its original audience: the historical background touched their patriotism; its treatment of German soldiers and German women aroused their sympathy; and its amusing blend of comedy and pathos touched their hearts. Secondly, it ranks high in Lessing's canon. Modern readers follow the action easily, for the unity of plot and setting keeps the play in small compass.

The Story:

Major von Tellheim had been wounded in the right arm, and after heroic deeds he had been discharged from the army. Crippled and poor, he had been put out of his room at the inn; in his absence his effects had been placed in a mean chamber with no view. The landlord had perhaps been justified. Two ladies had arrived asking for good accommodations, and Tellheim was behind in his rent.

Tellheim's servant, Just, sat in the inn parlor muttering about the injustice done to his master. The landlord came in and gave Just several drinks, but the worthy servant would not cease his complaints. Tellheim, entering in time to hear some of the dispute, ended the controversy by saying that the bill would be paid and that he would move out immediately. The landlord declared he was not afraid the bill would not be paid, for he had found a rich purse in Tellheim's writing desk.

When they were alone, Tellheim explained to Just that the money in the purse belonged to Werner, his sergeant; it was a trust. For immediate needs Tellheim asked his servant to pawn a ring for eighty louis. He tried to dismiss Just with a month's wages, but the servant preferred to work on for nothing. Then a widow came in to repay a loan Tellheim had made to her dead husband. Tellheim sent her away, vowing her husband owed him nothing. Werner tried to help the major by giving him all he could realize from the sale of his farm, but Tellheim would accept no help.

The ladies who had taken Tellheim's rooms were Minna von Barnhelm, a rich girl of twenty-one, and Franziska, her maid. Minna was agitated, for she had come in search of Tellheim. They had been betrothed, but she had had no word from him since the peace.

The landlord, who was inquisitive about his guests, came to their room to fill out an official form. When his questions became too personal, Minna, to turn the conversation, asked about the soldier whose room they had taken. The landlord contemptuously declared that he was only a discharged officer and showed her the ring Just had pawned with him. Minna recognized it at once as the ring she had given Tellheim. In the joy of her recognition, she put money to redeem it on the table and asked the landlord to bring in Tellheim at once.

When Tellheim first saw Minna, he spoke to her as a lover; but he promptly recovered himself and addressed her more formally. Hurt, Minna demanded a direct answer as to whether he still loved her. Tellheim admitted that he did. Crippled as he was, however, penniless, and discharged from service, he was no longer a suitable husband.

Tellheim wrote a note to Minna in which he explained fully why he could no longer expect to marry her. While Just was delivering the note, he fell into conversation with Franziska, who asked about the rest of Tellheim's servants. Just admitted that he alone was left. The valet had decamped with Tellheim's wardrobe; the huntsman had been imprisoned for treachery during the war, and the footman had run up debts in Tellheim's name.

The curious landlord attempted to get the story behind the reunion of Minna and Tellheim, but Franziska gave him little satisfaction. When he attempted to get a hundred louis for the pawned ring, she reminded him tartly that the loan was only eighty louis.

Werner returned to the inn with his pockets full of money. He emphatically denied that Tellheim was poor; all the sergeant's money really belonged to the major. When Franziska told him about the pawned ring, Werner tried to pass off the matter by saying that so many women give rings to soldiers. Undoubtedly Tellheim had twenty rings. Franziska left in anger, but she left Werner meditating on her charms.

Werner, meeting Tellheim, tried to give him the money he had collected by selling all his goods. He was put out by Tellheim's refusal because he felt old comrades in arms should help each other.

Franziska brought Tellheim's letter to Minna back to the major with word that Minna had not read it. Instead, she expected him to take her riding. Werner, seeing that the major was really fond of Minna, confessed to Franziska his falsehood about the twenty rings. She teased him coquettishly about his ready tongue. When she went back to Minna, her mistress told her she had a plan to recapture Tellheim.

Minna's scheme was to let Tellheim think that she, too, was poor after being disinherited; Franziska would tell him that her uncle, Count von Bruchsal, had cut her off because he objected to her marriage to Tellheim. In preparation for the plot, Minna took off the ring Tellheim had given her and put on the ring she had redeemed from the landlord.

Lieutenant Riccaut, seeking Tellheim, arrived at the inn. He announced that he was a great friend of Tellheim's and that he had good news for the major. A high government official had told him that Tellheim would soon have a letter from the king restoring his commission and righting his financial troubles. Minna, delighted with the news, questioned Riccaut about himself. He was a gambler who had had bad luck for a long time. Minna gave him money to start up a bank again. Riccaut promised to repay the money and let her have a third of the profits. As their talk continued, Minna was repelled to realize that Riccaut was a sharper rather than a gentleman gambler.

Tellheim had a long interview with Minna. He rehearsed again his misfortunes and added that he was under suspicion by the war ministry. Instructed to levy a war tax on the people in Minna's neighborhood, he had nobly advanced the money out of his own fortune. After the peace he had tried to collect from the government, but he was discharged under suspicion of double-dealing. Obviously he could not marry Minna and be dependent on her.

Minna pretended anger at his reasoning and gave him back the ring she had recovered from the landlord. After she left, Franziska told Tellheim that Minna was also poor. In great relief he straightway went in search of her to get her back.

Thinking Minna destitute, Tellheim asked Werner for all the money he could get. Soon Tellheim would go to the wars in Asia as a mercenary soldier, and Werner and Minna would go with him to the Orient. The delighted Werner brought in all the gold he could lay his hands on.

The plan never materialized, however. An orderly brought a letter from the king in which Tellheim learned his bill against the government would be honored and that he was recommissioned in the army. Tellheim's jubilation ended when he learned that Minna had not given him back her engagement ring after all, but rather the ring he had pawned. He interpreted her redemption of the pledge as proof that Minna had sought him out to break the engagement. The lovers were reconciled, however, by the arrival of Count von Bruchsal. The count declared his love for them both and sanctioned their marriage.

Werner thought he had as good luck as his master, for he became engaged to Franziska.

A MIRROR FOR WITCHES

Type of work: Novel
Author: Esther Forbes (1894?-   )
Type of plot: Psychological realism
Time of plot: Seventeenth century
Locale: Massachusetts
First published: 1928

> Principal characters:
> JARED BILBY, an English sea captain
> HANNAH, his wife
> DOLL, his adopted daughter
> MR. ZACHARIAS ZELLEY, a minister
> TITUS THUMB, in love with Doll
> LABOUR AND SORROW THUMB, twins, his sisters
> GOODY GREENE, an old herb woman
> THE BLOODY SHAD, her pirate son and Doll's demon prince
> MR. KLEAVER, the surgeon

Critique:

Esther Forbes is probably the outstanding woman writer of historical novels in America today. She is primarily interested in New England, where she lives and where her ancestors have lived since Massachusetts was settled. She was peculiarly equipped to write *A Mirror for Witches,* since witches are common to the folklore and history of her region and it is said that one of her ancestors died in jail after being charged with witchcraft. While the nineteenth-century Hawthorne used this kind of material symbolically, and others have used it romantically or sentimentally, Esther Forbes has written originally and brilliantly in making *A Mirror for Witches* a psychologically realistic novel. Under the same title, a successful modern ballet has been based on this tale of demonism and witchcraft in early Puritan times.

The Story:

Mr. Jared Bilby, captain of an English brig, landed his ship in Britanny on a day when the French burned over two hundred witches and warlocks. Attracted by the holocaust, he saw a tiny girl trying to pass the guards in order to reach her burning mother. Bilby sheltered the child and took her home. He thought she would forget her past, for she lay in a swoon for days. But she remembered only the evil of the years before she met Bilby.

Bilby called the little one his dolly and soon the child was known as Bilby's Doll. They adored each other, but Bilby's wife Hannah hated the child as soon as she saw her. Hannah, who had been barren for years, had recently become pregnant. One searing look from Doll withered Hannah to the marrow, and she believed thereafter that Doll had blasted her unborn child.

Bilby took his family to America. On the ship they met Mr. Zelley, a minister who became friendly and settled close to them at Cowan Corners, near Salem.

Goody Greene, a kindly woman looked on with disfavor by the townspeople because she associated with Indians in her search for herbs, was called to account by the churchmen because she had let fall in church a poppet she had made for Doll. No one would visit her, but suspicion fell away from her and centered on Doll when Hannah became strangely ill. Hannah told everyone that Doll was a witch who had cast a spell on Bilby so that it pleased him to pamper and fondle her. Mr. Zelley also befriended the girl.

To join their properties, Bilby proposed a marriage between Doll and Titus, the son of Deacon Thumb. Titus, a virtuous young man, was attracted to Doll and willing to wed. One day the Thumbs' black bull Ahab was missing. Titus got up early the next morning to catch the animal at a watering hole. The bull, ridden by an Indian, came crashing down to the water. Titus called out and shot at the Indian. In the twinkling of an eye Doll stood before him, her hands over her heart. Titus knew the bullet had gone through her, but there was no blood on her gown. He wanted to make love to Doll, but he felt only like a protecting big brother until after he had left her, when again he greatly desired her. From then on he began to pine away.

Bilby wished to speed the marriage. When Titus came courting, Doll frantically locked up the house, but at last she let him in. When he asked her to marry him, she bit his hand. He flung her away so hard that she hit her head and lay helpless. Titus wept.

Without telling Doll, Bilby had the marriage banns proclaimed the next Sunday. After Mr. Zelley had announced them, Doll screamed at her foster father. Cursed as he was, he took to his bed and died four days later. Doll kept herself hidden during his illness, but on the fourth day she went looking for Goody Greene. Tracing the herb woman's footsteps into the woods, Doll became lost. Lying down to sleep, she was startled to hear her father calling her. Then she knew that he was dead and she offered herself to the Evil One if he would only release Bilby's soul. Before and after sleeping she saw a host of evil signs and knew that she was a witch with powers for evil. On her return home Mr. Zelley assured her that her father had died from natural causes.

No one came to see Hannah and Doll during the winter except Mr. Zelley, who spoke to each separately because the women kept apart. When spring came, Doll noticed that by thought she could make the bull Ahab rush at Titus, and by twisting her fingers compel the deacon to break into fits of coughing. She kept looking for an agent of the Devil to instruct her in arts of evil.

Doll was lonely. The only house in which she was welcome was Goody Greene's. When she went there, Doll could feel a presence in the room which the woman would not identify. She could even see a bulge against the bed curtains. In the cellar, where she went for herbs, Doll was frightened by a little imp that looked like an Ethiopian.

In May there was a fire at the Thumbs'. Fascinated but terrified because fires reminded her of her parents' death, Doll went to watch the blaze. Ahab, penned in the burning barn, came thundering out as the roof fell in. Doll ran up a short ladder to the top of a haystack. There she found her demon prince, dressed like a sailor and carrying the imp she had seen in the cellar. The fiend called his imp the Bloody Shad.

Doll spent the summer nights happily with her demon lover, who taught her to say her prayers backwards. He told her that her parents were safe in hell and that she would have a short life, then life everlasting. Before he left her for good he told her that he would come back to be with her when she lay dying.

Shortly afterward three pirates were caught and executed at Boston harbor. One, called the Bloody Shad, carried a monkey that resembled a tiny imp.

Without her demon, Doll was lonely again. She spent much time in the Thumbs' pasture talking to Ahab, who was friendly with her but savage with anyone else. At last Titus' mother persuaded him to pen the beast. One day Doll met Titus' small twin sisters and gave them pumpkin seed poppets. Without telling their mother about them, the children ate the seeds and became deathly sick. Mrs. Thumb was sure Doll had withered the children's vitals when she learned that Doll had given them the poppets. The children screamed that Doll was visiting them and pinching them, but no one could see her. Strange things blamed on Doll happened to people in nearby towns. Convinced that Doll was a witch, Deacon Thumb and Mr. Kleaver, the surgeon, had her jailed.

At her trial the judges were at first convinced that Hannah's hatred for Doll had produced all the complaints against the girl. The twins, brought into the court, went into convulsions at the sight of her. When she touched them, the devil went out of them into her and they quieted. Then Doll, in reciting the Lord's prayer, said the last half backwards. When Doll spoke of her lover, Goody Greene claimed that he had been her pirate son, but the old woman was thrown out of court. The judges seemed so sympathetic that Doll told them why she thought she was a witch. She insisted, however, that she had never harmed the twins.

Held for a jury trial, Doll was put in irons. Mr. Zelley, going to comfort her, was confused by a third presence he could feel in the cell. Doll told him that her demon had come back to be with her. When she was found dead one dismal morning, her face was peaceful.

THE MISANTHROPE

Type of work: Drama
Author: Molière (Jean Baptiste Poquelin, 1622-1673)
Type of plot: Comedy of manners
Time of plot: Seventeenth century
Locale: Paris
First presented: 1666

Principal characters:
ALCESTE, in love with Célimène
PHILINTE, friend of Alceste
ORONTE, in love with Célimène
CÉLIMÈNE, a young widow
ÉLIANTE, cousin of Célimène

Critique:

Molière, born Jean Baptiste Poquelin, is the outstanding French writer of comedies, above all, comedies of manners; and he is sometimes compared in the breadth and humanity of his genius with Shakespeare. *The Misanthrope* is a comedy with a rather sad conclusion; but the merit of the play rests on its depiction of manners. We can see in *The Misanthrope* Molière's objective analysis of his own time, for he exposes to the public eye the frivolity and inconsistency of his contemporaries.

The Story:

Alceste had been called a misanthrope by many of his friends, and he took a rather obstinate delight in the name. This characteristic led him to quarrel heatedly with his good friend Philinte, who accepted uncritically the frivolous manners of the day. When Philinte warmly embraced a chance acquaintance, as was customary, Alceste maintained that such behavior was hypocritical, especially since Philinte hardly knew the man.

Philinte reminded Alceste that his lawsuit was nearly ready for trial, and that he would do well to moderate his attitude toward people in general. His opponents in the suit were doing everything possible to curry favor, but Alceste insulted everyone he met and made no effort to win over the judges.

Philinte also taunted Alceste on his love for Célimène, who, as a leader in society, was hypocritical most of the time.

Alceste had to admit that his love could not be explained rationally.

Oronte interrupted the quarrel by coming to visit Alceste, who was puzzled by a visit from suave and elegant Oronte. Oronte asked permission to read a sonnet he had lately composed, as he was anxious to have Alceste's judgment of its literary merit.

After some affected hesitation, Oronte read his mediocre poem. Alceste, too honest to give false praise, condemned the verses and even satirized the poor quality of the writing. Oronte instantly took offense at this criticism, and a new quarrel broke out. Although the argument was indecisive, there were hints of a possible duel.

Alceste then went to call on Célimène. As soon as he saw her, he began perversely to upbraid her for her frivolous conduct and her hypocritical attitude toward other people. Although Célimène could slander and ridicule with a keen wit and a barbed tongue while a person was absent, she was all flattery and attention when talking with him. This attitude displeased Alceste.

The servant announced several callers, including Éliante. To Alceste's dismay, they all sat down for an interminable conversation. The men took great delight in naming over all their mutual acquaintances, and as each name was mentioned, Célimène made unkind remarks. The only gentle person in the room was Éliante, whose good sense and kind heart were in striking contrast with Célimène's caustic wit. Eliante was overshadowed, however, by the more brilliant Célimène. The men all declared they had nothing to do all day, and each swore to outstay the other, to remain longer with Célimène. Alceste determined to be the last to leave.

A guard appeared, however, to summon Alceste before the tribunal. Astonished, Alceste learned that his quarrel with Oronte had been noised about, and the authorities intended to prevent a possible duel. Loudly protesting that except for an order direct from the king nothing could make him praise the poetry of Oronte, Alceste was led away.

Arsinoé, an austere woman who made a pretense of great virtue, came to call on Célimène. She took the opportunity to warn Célimène that her conduct was creating a scandal, because her many suitors and her sharp tongue were hurting her reputation. Célimène spoke bitingly of Arsinoé's strait-laced character.

Arsinoé decided to talk privately with Alceste, with whom she was half in love. She comforted him as best she could for being so unfortunate as to love Célimène, and complimented him on his plain dealings and forthright character. Carried away by the intimacy of her talk, Arsinoé offered to do much for Alceste by speaking in his favor at court. But the two concluded that the love of Alceste for Célimène, though unsuitable from almost every point of view, was a fast tie.

Éliante and Philinte were in the meantime discussing Alceste and his habit of antagonizing his friends through his frankness. Philinte told her of Alceste's hearing before the tribunal. He had insisted that Oronte's verses were bad, but he had nothing more to say. Éliante and Philinte began to discover a mutual liking. If Eliante ever lost her fondness for Alceste, Philinte intended to offer himself as a lover.

Alceste received an unflattering letter, purporting to come from Célimène, which described him in malicious terms. After much coy hesitation, Célimène admitted that she had sent the letter and expressed surprise at Alceste's indignation. Other suitors appeared, each holding a letter and each much upset. On comparing notes, they found that they had all been ridiculed and insulted.

Meanwhile, Alceste had made up his mind to ask Éliante to marry him, but reconsidered when he realized that his proposal would seem to spring from a desire to avenge himself on Célimène. To the misanthrope there seemed to be no solution except to go into exile and live a hermit's life.

When Célimène's suitors clamored for an explanation, she told them that she had written the letters because she was tired of the niceties of polite conversation. For once she decided to say what she really thought. This confession was shocking to the suitors who thought frankness and rudeness were unpardonable crimes. Hypocrisy, flattery, cajolery, extravagances—these were the marks of a gentle lady. Protesting and disdainful, they left together, never to return.

Only Alceste remained. Even the coquettish and malicious heart of Célimène was touched. When Alceste repeated his vows of fidelity and asked her once more to marry him, she almost consented. But when Alceste revealed that he wanted them to go into exile and lead quiet, simple lives, she refused. Célimène could never leave the false, frivolous society she loved.

Now completely the misanthrope, Alceste stalked away with the firm resolve to quit society forever, to become a hermit, far removed from the artificial sham of preciosity. Philinte and Éliante, more moderate in their views, however, decided that they would marry.

MISCELLANIES

Type of work: Poetry
Author: Abraham Cowley (1618-1667)
First published: 1656

Abraham Cowley and his works are difficult to classify. Cowley himself was essentially a pre-Restoration poet, but his verse does not fit well into the classifications normally made of poetry in the period between 1600 and 1660. At various times his work has been compared to that of John Donne and John Milton. The comparison of Cowley's poetry to Donne's has been made because of the conceits to be found in both, to Milton's because of Cowley's use of Biblical subject matter in his *Davideis,* an unfinished epic poem.

Most representative of Cowley's work is the 1656 edition titled *Miscellanies,* a volume published shortly after the poet's return to England from France. Cowley, dispossessed of his fellowship at Cambridge University had joined friends among the followers of Charles I at Oxford during the early years of the Civil War. When many of the Royalists fled to France, Cowley was among them. In exile he assisted the English queen in her correspondence with the king in England. The *Miscellanies* volume, according to Cowley's preface, was an attempt on his part to preserve in print all his poetical works that he considered worth keeping for posterity. His avowed motivation was that he intended to write no more verse, and he wished to publish his own edition, lest after his death an edition containing spurious or inferior writings be foisted upon the public, as had already happened in the cases of Shakespeare, Fletcher, and Jonson.

The *Miscellanies* consists of four parts. The first is a collection of poems on a variety of themes, some written when Cowley was quite young; the second includes the poems Cowley had published earlier as *The Mistress,* a series dealing with love in various aspects; the third part he labeled *Pindarique Odes,* transla-

tions from Pindar and free imitations in English of that poet's work; the fourth and last portion of the volume contains the four books of the *Davideis.*

In the first section there are odes on wit, on the king's return from Scotland, on Prometheus, on the pleasures of wine over the pangs of love, on friendship, and also imitations, in English, of both Horace and Martial. A light but pleasant poem is "The Chronicle," an example of *vers de société* dealing with the experiences of a young man in love with a long series of young women. Of note also is a poem celebrating the publication of the first two books of Sir William Davenant's *Gondibert* (1651). The best, certainly the sincerest poems of the *Miscellanies* group, are those written on the deaths of persons the poet had known and respected in life. The most outstanding of these is "On the Death of Mr. William Hervey." Although the poem may seem to the twentieth-century reader extravagant in its tone, diction, and imagery, it compares favorably with the best elegiac poetry of the time. Other elegiac poems in the collection are those on Sir Henry Wotton; Mr. Jordan, a master at Westminster School; Van Dyck, the painter, and Richard Crashaw, the poet. Of little interest, other than historic, are some English paraphrases of Anacreon.

Most critics have been less inclined to favor *The Mistress, or Several Copies of Love Verses,* first published in 1647 and included in the *Miscellanies.* Like much of the love poetry of the earlier part of the seventeenth century, *The Mistress* is bound too closely by conventions in many respects. It supposedly deals with a courtship and the lady's reception of the suit over a period of three years. That Cowley actually loved a woman of higher social rank and courted her with this poetry is doubtful, for the suffering lover, the stand-offish lady of higher degree, and extravagant protestations of love are typical of the love poetry of the time— usually mere convention. Cowley's unusual figures of speech, written apparently under the influence of John Donne, have until recent years been the target of critics. With the revived interest and renewed sympathy for the metaphysical poets and their techniques, however, Cowley's exercise of his exceptionally learned and fertile fancy has been viewed less stringently. In this section the poem entitled "The Spring" represents Cowley at his best, while "Written in Juice of Lemmon" shows him at his poorer level of performance.

For about a century the ode, particularly the Pindaric ode as it was established by Cowley, was a favorite verse form among English poets and poetasters until the eighteenth century, when Dr. Samuel Johnson, literary arbiter of the era, pronounced against it. Undoubtedly the freedom of meter exercised by Cowley in his *Pindarique Odes* and introduced by him was a decisive factor in the popularity of the form, for as they were written by Cowley the odes appear deceptively easy. Current literary opinion is against Cowley's odes, declaring them too flat and imitative.

The last portion of the *Miscellanies* is taken up with the unfinished *Davideis*, four of the twelve books originally planned on the model of the *Aeneid*. Cowley's strong religious convictions led him to choose the figure of David, traditional ancestor of Jesus, as the hero for an epic poem. In these four books he packed much of his learning, often in wide and only loosely connected digressions. Critics have argued the fitness of the subject; Cowley himself seems to have changed his mind about its suitability, since he left the work unfinished.

As he announced in the preface to the *Miscellanies*, Cowley wrote almost no poetry after publication of that edition. In the twentieth century his poetry attracts little attention beyond that given by students of literature. The poems seem to have little to say to modern readers that has not been said better by other poets.

THE MISER

Type of work: Drama
Author: Molière (Jean Baptiste Poquelin, 1622-1673)
Type of plot: Romantic comedy
Time of plot: Seventeenth century
Locale: Paris, France
First presented: 1668

Principal characters:
HARPAGON, a miser
CLÉANTE, his son
ÉLISE, his daughter
VALÈRE, Élise's lover
MARIANE, loved by Cléante and Harpagon
ANSELME, father of Valère and Mariane

Critique:

The genius of Molière has not been dimmed by time, for his plays are as popular today as they were to past generations. Almost every year sees a major theatrical company producing one of his dramas. *The Miser (L'Avare)* ranks with his best. Filled with satire, humor, and love interest, it meets all requirements for romance and comedy. Harpagon is often compared with Shylock as his equal in avarice and miserliness. All of the characters are clear-cut and well presented. The plot is exciting and fast-moving. It is little wonder that this and the other plays of Molière never lose their popularity.

The Story:

Valère, the steward of Harpagon's house, was in love with his employer's daughter Élise. Valère was sure that he was of a good family, but until he could find his relatives he had little hope that Harpagon would give his consent to a marriage between his daughter and his steward. Harpagon was a miser of such great avarice and stinginess that he loved nothing but money. He lived in constant fear that someone would rob him of the large sum he had buried in his garden. Valère knew that his only hope lay in insinuating himself into Harpagon's affection by flattering the old man beyond belief.

Harpagon's son Cléante was also in love. The object of his love was Mariane, a poor girl who lived with her widowed mother. But Cléante's love was as hopeless as that of his sister Élise and Valère. Since Mariane had no money, Harpagon would not consent to a marriage, and Cléante kept his love for the girl from his father. What he did not know was that his father had seen Mariane and wanted her for himself. He had been a widower for many years and the young girl's beauty made him desire her. He must first, however, secure a dowry for her; his miserliness was stronger than his love.

Élise learned from her father that against her wishes she was to be married to Anselme, a wealthy man of fifty. The fact that Anselme would take his daughter without a dowry was too good a proposition for Harpagon to pass by. Élise appealed to Valère for help. The clever lad pretended to agree with her father while he whispered to her to take heart and trust him to prevent the marriage. If all else failed, he and Élise would flee from the house and be married without her father's consent.

Cléante was so determined to marry Mariane that he arranged through an agent to borrow from a money-lender. Never was a higher rate of interest demanded. Cléante was to pay twenty-five percent interest and take part of the loan in goods which he must sell. With no choice but to agree, he went to meet the money-lender. He was horrified to find his own father. Harpagon was equally angry that his son should be such a spendthrift

2377

that he must borrow money at such high rates. The two parted without completing the loan, Cléante to try to arrange a loan elsewhere and Harpagon to try to secure a dowry for Mariane.

Harpagon arranged a party in honor of Mariane, whom he had not as yet met. He cautioned the servants to be very sparing with the food and drink, as it was an injustice to one's guests to stuff them full. Although Mariane found Harpagon repulsive, she was bound by her poor mother's wish to take a rich husband. When Mariane learned that Harpagon was the father of her beloved Cléante, she detested him more than ever. Cléante got a small measure of revenge on his father by taking a huge diamond ring from his father's finger and presenting it to Mariane after telling her that Harpagon wanted her to have it. The miser was helpless; he could not get it back unless he admitted his stinginess to the girl he wished to marry.

After Harpagon tricked Cléante into admitting his love for Mariane, the old man vowed more than ever to have her for himself. Cléante cursed his father and swore that the old miser should never have the girl, and Harpagon disinherited his son. Then a servant rushed in with the news that Harpagon had been robbed of his buried money. All else was forgotten by the miser as he cried out for help. He suspected everyone of stealing the money, even himself. He would have the whole household hanged, and if the money were not found he would hang himself.

A jealous servant told Harpagon that Valère had taken the money. Harpagon ordered the magistrate to arrest the steward, even though there was no true evidence against him. Anselme arrived in time to hear Valère shouting to Harpagon that he would marry Élise in spite of the miser's objections. Anselme said that he would bow out of the courtship, for he had no desire to take the girl against her wishes. Harpagon was furious. Where else could he find a wealthy son-in-law, particularly one who would demand no dowry? He pressed the magistrate to arrest Valère, but that young man stopped the official with the announcement that he was the son of Don Thomas d'Alburci, a nobleman of Naples who had had to flee his native city.

Valère said that he and a manservant had survived a shipwreck and made their way to Paris. He produced the family seals to prove his identity. Then Mariane rushed to him and told him that she was his sister, that she and her mother had also been saved from the wreck and had thought the rest of the family dead. But there was more joy to come for the reunited brother and sister. Anselme was their father, the former Don Thomas d'Alburci, who had also been saved. Thinking his loved ones dead, he had settled in Paris under the name of Anselme.

These revelations made no difference to Harpagon. He still insisted that Valère return his money. While he was ranting, Cléante entered the room and said that he had found the money and would return it to his father as soon as his father gave him permission to marry Mariane. That was no hard choice for Harpagon to make. He would gladly exchange Mariane, even his own children, for his money. Anselme also gave his consent to the marriage. Harpagon insisted that Anselme pay for both weddings. This the kind father was willing to do, and the happy couples and Anselme went off to tell Mariane's mother the glad news. Harpagon had an errand of his own. He went to examine his cashbox, the true love of his mean and stingy nature.

LES MISÉRABLES

Type of work: Novel
Author: Victor Hugo (1802-1885)
Type of plot: Social chronicle
Time of plot: About 1815 to 1835
Locale: France
First published: 1862

Principal characters:
JEAN VALJEAN, also known as Father Madeleine
FANTINE, a woman befriended by Valjean
COSETTE, her daughter
M. JAVERT, inspector of police
MARIUS PONTMERCY, in love with Cosette
M. THÉNARDIER, known also as Jondrette, a rogue
EPONINE THÉNARDIER, his daughter

Critique:

Les Misérables is a romantic novel, packed with exciting incidents. It is also a sociological study of poverty and slum life. Victor Hugo spent fourteen years on the book, a fact which probably accounts for the numerous digressions and additions to the story. The core of this extremely long novel is the life story of a criminal, Jean Valjean, who serves as an example of the misery and contradictions of society with which the author was especially concerned at the time of writing. Les Misérables is both a powerful social document and an extremely interesting and dramatic narrative. Hugo's masterpiece, it is one of the great novels of the world.

The Story:

In 1815, in France, a man named Jean Valjean was released after nineteen years in prison. He had been sentenced to a term of five years because he stole a loaf of bread to feed his starving sister and her family, but the sentence was later increased because of his attempts to escape. During his imprisonment he astonished others by his exhibitions of unusual physical strength.

Freed at last, he started out on foot for a distant part of the country. Innkeepers refused him food and lodging because his yellow passport revealed that he was an ex-convict. Finally he came to the house of the Bishop of Digne, a saintly man who treated him graciously, fed him, and gave him a bed. During the night Jean stole the bishop's silverware and fled. He was immediately captured by the police, who returned him and the stolen goods to the bishop. Without any censure, the priest not only gave him what he had stolen, but also added his silver candlesticks to the gift. The astonished gendarmes let the prisoner go. Alone with the bishop, Jean was confounded by the churchman's attitude, for the bishop asked only that he use the silver as a means of living an honest life.

In Paris, in 1817, lived a beautiful girl named Fantine. She gave birth to an illegitimate child, Cosette, whom she left with M. and Mme. Thénardier to bring up with their own children. As time went on, the Thénardiers demanded more and more money for Cosette's support, yet treated the child cruelly and deprived her even of necessities. Fantine, meanwhile, had gone to the town of M— and obtained a job in a glass factory operated by Father Madeleine, a kind and generous man whose history was known to no one, but whose good deeds and generosity to the poor were public information. He had arrived in M— a poor laborer, and by a lucky invention he was able to start a business of his own. Soon he built a factory and employed many workers. After five years in the city he was named mayor and was beloved by all the citizens. He was reported to have

2379

prodigious strength. Only one man, Javert, a police inspector, seemed to watch him with an air of suspicion. Javert was born in prison. His whole life was influenced by that fact and his fanatical attitude toward duty made him a man to be feared. He was determined to discover the facts of Father Madeleine's previous life. One day he found a clue while watching Father Madeleine lift a heavy cart to save an old man who had fallen under it. Javert realized that he had known only one man of such prodigious strength, a former convict named Valjean.

Fantine had told no one of Cosette, but knowledge of her illegitimate child spread and caused Fantine to be discharged from the factory without the knowledge of Father Madeleine. Finally Fantine became a prostitute in an effort to pay the increasing demands of the Thénardiers for Cosette's support. One night Javert arrested her while she was walking the streets. When Father Madeleine heard the details of her plight, and learned that she had tuberculosis, he sent Fantine to a hospital and promised to bring Cosette to her. Just before the mayor left to get Cosette, Javert confessed that he had mistakenly reported to the Paris police that he suspected Father Madeleine of being the ex-convict, Jean Valjean. He said that the real Jean Valjean had been arrested at Arras under an assumed name. The arrested man was to be tried two days later.

That night Father Madeleine struggled with his own conscience, for he was the real Jean Valjean. Unwilling to let an innocent man suffer, he went to Arras for the trial and identified himself as Jean Valjean. After telling the authorities where he could be found, he went to Fantine. Javert came there to arrest him. Fantine was so terrified that she died. After a day in prison Jean Valjean escaped.

Valjean, some time later, was again imprisoned by Javert. Once more he made his escape. Shortly afterward he was able to take Cosette, a girl of eight,

away from the Thénardiers. He grew to love the child greatly, and they lived together happily in the Gorbeau tenement on the outskirts of Paris. When Jarvert once more tracked them down, Valjean escaped with the child into a convent garden, where they were rescued by Fauchelevant, whose life Valjean had saved when the old peasant fell beneath the cart. Fauchelevant was now the convent gardener. Valjean became his helper, and Cosette was put into the convent school.

Years passed. Valjean left the convent and took Cosette, her schooling finished, to live in a modest house on a side street in Paris. The old man and the young girl were little noticed by their neighbors. Meanwhile the blackguard Thénardier had brought his family to live in the Gorbeau tenement. He now called himself Jondrette. In the next room lived Marius Pontmercy, a young lawyer estranged from his aristocrat grandfather because of his liberal views. Marius was the son of an officer whose life Thénardier had saved at the battle of Waterloo. The father, now dead, had asked his son some day to repay Thénardier for his deed. Marius never suspected that Jondrette was really his father's benefactor. When the Jondrettes were being evicted from their quarters, however, he paid their rent from his meager resources.

During one of his evening walks Marius met Cosette and Valjean. He fell in love with the girl as he continued to see her in the company of her white-haired companion. At last he followed her to her home. Valjean, noticing Marius, took Cosette to live in another house.

One morning Marius received a begging letter delivered by Eponine Jondrette. His neighbors were again asking for help, and he began to wonder about them. Peeping through a hole in the wall, he heard Jondrette speak of a benefactor who would soon arrive. When the man came, Marius recognized him as Cosette's companion. From Eponine he later learned Cosette's address, but before he saw Cosette again he overheard the Jondrettes plotting against the man whom he believed to be Cosette's father. Alarmed, he told the details of the plot to Inspector Javert.

Marius was at the wall watching when Valjean returned to give Jondrette money. While they talked, numerous heavily-armed men appeared in the room. Jondrette then revealed himself as Thénardier. Marius, horrified, did not know, whom to protect, the man his father had requested him to befriend or the father of Cosette. Threatened by Thénardier, Valjean agreed to send to his daughter for more money, but he gave a false address. When this ruse was discovered, the robbers threatened to kill Valjean. Marius threw a note of warning through the hole in the wall as Javert appeared and arrested all but Valjean, who made his escape through a window.

Marius finally located Cosette. One night she told him that she and her father were leaving for England. He tried to get his grandfather's permission to marry Cosette. It was refused. In despair, he returned to Cosette and found the house where she had lived empty. Eponine met him there and told him that his revolutionary friends had begun a revolt and were waiting for him at the barricades. Because Cosette had disappeared, he gladly followed Eponine to the barricades, where Javert had been seized as a spy and bound. During the fighting Eponine gave her life to save Marius. As she died, she gave him a note which Cosette had given her to deliver. In it Cosette told him where she could be found.

In answer to her note, Marius wrote that his grandfather would not permit his marriage, that he had no money, and that he would be killed at the barricade. Valjean discovered the notes and set out for the barricades. Finding Javert tied up by the revolutionists, he freed the inspector. The barricades fell. In the confusion Valjean came upon the wounded Marius and carried him into the Paris sewers.

After hours of wandering he reached a locked outlet. There Thénardier, unrecognized in the dark, met him and agreed to open the grating in exchange for money. Outside Valjean met Javert, who took him into custody. Valjean asked only that he be allowed to take Marius to his grandfather's house. Javert agreed to wait at the door, but suddenly he turned and ran toward the river. Tormented by his conscientious regard for duty and his reluctance to return to prison the man who had saved his life, he drowned himself in the Seine.

When Marius recovered, he and Cosette were married. Valjean gave Cosette a generous dowry, and for the first time Cosette learned that Valjean was not her real father. Valjean told Marius only that he was an escaped convict, believed dead, and he begged to be allowed to see Cosette occasionally. But gradually Marius banished him from the house. Then Marius learned from Thénardier that it was Valjean who had rescued Marius at the barricade. Marius and Cosette hurried to Valjean's lodgings, to find him on his deathbed. He died knowing that his children loved him and that all his entangling past was now clear. He bequeathed the bishop's silver candlesticks to Cosette, with his last breath saying that he had spent his life in trying to be worthy of the faith of the Bishop of Digne. He was buried in a grave with no name on the stone.

MISS JULIE

Type of work: Drama
Author: August Strindberg (1849-1912)
Type of plot: Naturalism
Time of plot: Nineteenth century
Locale: A country estate in Sweden
First presented: 1888

Principal characters:
MISS JULIE, a headstrong gentlewoman of twenty-five
JEAN, Miss Julie's lover and her father's valet
CHRISTINE, a cook, fiancée of Jean

Critique:

Strindberg termed this long, one-act play a naturalistic tragedy in his author's preface to the drama, which represented an effort on his part to popularize the naturalism of French literature in the literature of Sweden. In his preface Strindberg declared that the impetus for the play's content came from his reading of the novels of the Goncourt brothers rather than the fiction of Zola, who is generally considered the fountainhead of naturalism in European literature. Readers will quickly note the emphasis which Strindberg placed on the environment of the three characters in this play, especially on the importance environment played in the shaping of Julie's personality. Such elements of determinism are, of course, the hallmarks of naturalism.

The Story:

Miss Julie's broken engagement to the county attorney was quite a scandal to the servants in the house. Miss Julie, daughter of a count, had made the man actually jump over her horsewhip several times, giving him a cut with the whip each time. He had finally put an end to such conduct and the engagement by snatching the whip, breaking it, and striding away from the manor.

On Midsummer Eve, a great holiday held throughout the Swedish country-side a few weeks later, Miss Julie entered into the festivities and danced with the servants. She dared to do so because her father had gone to the city and was not expected to return. Although the servants disliked her entrance into their fun, they were powerless to make their dislike known; she was their mistress. Her father's valet, Jean, left the festivities after dancing once with Miss Julie. He retreated to the kitchen, where his fiancée, Christine the cook, gave him a little supper.

But Miss Julie gave Jean no peace. She came into the kitchen and dragged him out to dance with her again, even though she knew that he had promised to dance with Christine. After dancing another time with Miss Julie, Jean escaped once more to the kitchen. He was afraid that Christine was angry. She assured him, however, that she did not blame him for what had happened. Just then Miss Julie returned to the kitchen and demanded that Jean dance with her again after he had changed from his livery into a tailcoat. While he was changing, Christine fell asleep in a chair. When he returned Miss Julie asked him to get her something to drink. Jean got a bottle of beer for her and another for himself.

After finishing the beer, Miss Julie teased Christine by trying to wake her up. Christine, moving as if asleep, went to her own room. After she had gone, Miss Julie began to ogle Jean, who warned his mistress that it was dangerous to flirt with a man as young as he. But

MISS JULIE by August Strindberg, from PLAYS BY AUGUST STRINDBERG, SECOND SERIES. Translated by Edwin Björkman. By permission of the publishers, Charles Scribner's Sons. Copyright, 1913, by Charles Scribner's Sons. Renewed, 1941, by Edwin Björkman.

Miss Julie paid no attention to him. Jean, falling in with her mood, told about his early life as a cotter's child and how, even as a small child, he had been in love with his young mistress. They talked so long that the other servants came to look for the valet. Rather than expose themselves to the comments and the scandal of having drunk together in the kitchen, Jean and Miss Julie went into Jean's room. They were there a long time, for the servants stayed in the kitchen and danced and sang. During that time Miss Julie gave herself to Jean.

After the servants had gone, neither Jean nor Miss Julie knew just what to do. They agreed only that it was best for them to leave the country. Jean suggested that they go to Como, Italy, to open a hotel. Miss Julie asked Jean to take her in his arms again. He refused, saying that he could not make love to her a second time in her father's house, where she was the mistress and he the servant. When she reminded him of the extravagant language he had used a little while before, he told her the time had come to be practical.

To cheer her, Jean offered Miss Julie a drink of wine from a bottle he had taken from the count's cellar. She saw whose it was and accused Jean of stealing. An argument followed, with bitter words on both sides. When they had both calmed a little, Miss Julie tried to tell Jean how she had come to be what she was. She said that she had been brought up to do a man's work by her mother, because the mother had hated to be a slave to men. She told also how her mother had revenged herself on Miss Julie's father by taking a brick manufacturer as her lover and how her mother's lover had stolen great sums of money from the count. From her mother, said Miss Julie, she had learned to hate men and to wish to make them her slaves. He understood then why she had treated her fiancé as she had with the whip. Miss Julie ended her recital with the recommendation that she and Jean go abroad at once. To her sugges-

tion that when they ceased enjoying one another they should commit suicide, Jean, far more practical, advised her to go away by herself. Miss Julie, helpless in the urgency of the situation, did as Jean suggested and prepared to leave.

While Miss Julie was upstairs dressing, Christine came into the kitchen. It was morning. Seeing the glasses on the table, she knew that Miss Julie and Jean had been drinking together. She guessed the rest, and Jean admitted what had happened. Christine, angry at Miss Julie, told Jean that fine people did not behave so with the servants. Christine urged him to go away with her as soon as possible. Loving him, she did not intend to lose him to her mistress.

Christine persuaded Jean to get ready to go to church with her, since it was Sunday morning. When they were both dressed, Miss Julie and Jean met in the kitchen. The mistress carried a bird cage. When Jean said she could not take her pet finch with her, she ordered him to kill it. Seeing her bird die, Miss Julie's love turned to hate. Despising him for killing in cold blood the pet she had loved so much, she raged at Jean and told him that her father would soon return. Then he would learn what had happened. Miss Julie declared she would welcome her father's discovery; she wished now only to die.

When Christine appeared ready for church, she told Miss Julie bluntly that she would not allow her mistress to run off with the man who had promised to become her husband. Miss Julie then tried to persuade Christine to go with them to Como. While the two women talked, Jean left the room. He returned a few moments later with his razor. Christine, refusing to join in the flight, left for church after saying that she had spoken to the men at the stables about not letting anyone have horses until the count's return.

After Christine's departure Miss Julie asked Jean what he would do if he were in her position. He indicated the razor in

2383

his hand. At that moment the valet's bell rang. The count had returned. Jean, answering the bell, received instructions to have boots and coffee ready in half an hour. His master's voice reduced Jean once again to the mental attitudes of a servant. Miss Julie, almost in a state of trance, was filled with ecstasy at the thought of freeing herself by committing suicide. She took the razor Jean gave her and left the kitchen with it in her hand.

MISS LONELYHEARTS

Type of work: Novel
Author: Nathanael West (Nathan Weinstein, 1903?-1940)
Type of plot: Social satire
Time of plot: Late 1920's
Locale: New York City
First published: 1933

Principal characters:
MISS LONELYHEARTS, an advice-to-the-lovelorn columnist on the New
York *Post-Dispatch*
BETTY, his girl friend
WILLIE SHRIKE, the paper's feature editor, his boss
MARY SHRIKE, the boss's wife
PETER DOYLE, a cripple
FAY DOYLE, his wife

Critique:

If it took seventeen years after his early death for the works of Nathanael West to achieve either critical or popular success, one may say with some assurance that the present acclaim is on fairly solid ground. Of the four novels in his *Complete Works* (1957), *Miss Lonelyhearts* is regarded most highly. Bitter in its satire, brief, episodic and unique in its treatment, ironic and hopeless in its outlook, *Miss Lonelyhearts* is not so much a tale of newspapering as it is West's grotesque picture of the miserable, monstrous, often disgusting life man has made for himself in his despair.

The Story:

Miss Lonelyhearts found it hard to write his lovelorn column in the New York *Post-Dispatch*: the letters were not funny, there was no humor as desperate people begged for help. Sick-of-it-all, for example, with seven children in twelve years, was pregnant again and ill, but being a Catholic she could not consider an abortion and her husband would not let her alone; Desperate, a sixteen-year-old girl, a good dancer with a good shape and pretty clothes, would like boy friends, but cried all day at the big hole in the middle of her face (should she commit suicide?); Harold S., fifteen, wrote that his sister Gracie, thirteen, deaf, dumb,

and not very smart, had something dirty done to her by a man, but Harold could not tell their mother Gracie was going to have a baby because her mother would beat her up. Shrike, the feature editor and Miss Lonelyhearts' tormentor, was no help at all: instead of the same old stuff, he said, Miss Lonelyhearts ought to give his readers something new and hopeful.

At Delehanty's speak-easy, where Miss Lonelyhearts went to escape his problems, his boss still belabored him about brooding and told him to forget the Crucifixion and remember the Renaissance. Meanwhile, he was trying to seduce Miss Farkis, a long-legged woman with a childish face. He also taunted the columnist by talking of a Western sect which prayed for a condemned slayer with an adding machine, numbers being their idea of the universal language.

Miss Lonelyhearts' bedroom walls were bare except for an ivory Christ nailed with large spikes, and the religious figure combined in a dream with a snake whose scales were tiny mirrors in which the dead world took on a semblance of life. First he was a magician who could not move his audience by tricks or prayer; then he was on a drunken college spree with two friends. Their attempt to sacrifice a lamb before barbecuing it, with Miss Lonelyhearts chanting the name of

Christ, miscarried when the blade broke on the altar and the lamb slipped out of their bloodied hands. When the others refused to go back to put the lamb out of its misery, Miss Lonelyhearts returned and crushed its head with a stone.

One day, as he tried to put things in order, everything went against him: pencils broke, buttons rolled under the bed, shades refused to stay down, and instead of order on the skyline he found chaos. Miss Lonelyhearts remembered Betty, who could bring order into his world, and he went to her apartment. But he realized that her world was not the world and could never include the readers of his column; his confusion was significant and her order was not. Irritated and fidgety, he could neither talk to her nor caress her, although two months before she had agreed to marry him. When she asked if he were sick, he could only shout at her; when she said she loved him, he could only reply that he loved her and her smiling through tears. Sobbing that she felt swell before he came and now felt lousy, she asked him to go away.

At Delehanty's he listened to talk of raping a woman writer, and as he got drunker he heard friends mock Shrike's kidding him; but whiskey made him feel good and dreams of childhood made the world dance. Stepping back from the bar, he collided with a man holding a beer. The man punched him in the mouth. With a lump on his head, a loose tooth and a cut lip, Miss Lonelyhearts walked in the fresh air with Ned Gates. In a comfort station they met an old man with a terrible cough and no overcoat, who carried a cane and wore gloves because he detested red hands. They forced him to go to an Italian wine cellar. There they told him they were Havelock Ellis and Krafft-Ebing and insultingly mocked him with taunts of his homosexuality. When Miss Lonelyhearts twisted his arm —imagining it was the arm of Desperate, Broken-hearted, or Sick-of-it-all—the old man screamed, and someone hit the columnist with a chair.

Instead of going to the office after Shrike phoned him, Miss Lonelyhearts went to the speak-easy; he knew Shrike found him too perfect a butt for his jokes to fire him. Needing a woman, he phoned Mary, Shrike's wife, whom he had never seduced, although she hated her husband and used Miss Lonelyhearts to arouse Shrike. At a night club, in a cab, and at her apartment door, Miss Lonelyhearts tried to talk Mary into sleeping with him; but Shrike opened the door, ending that scheme.

The next day Miss Lonelyhearts received a letter from Fay Doyle, unhappily married to a cripple, asking for an appointment. Although he first threw the letter away, he retrieved it, phoned her to meet him in the park, and took her to his apartment. In the intervals of making love, she told of her married life and her child Lucy, whose father was not Doyle.

Physically sick and exhausted in his room for three days, he was comforted by Betty, who tried to get him to quit his Lonelyhearts job. He said he had taken the job as a joke, but after several months the joke had escaped him. Pleas for help made him examine his values and he became the victim of the joke. While Betty suggested he go to the country with her, Shrike broke into the room, taunted him to escape to the South Seas, hedonism, art, suicide, or drugs, and ended by dictating an imaginary letter from the columnist to Christ.

After he had been ill for a week, Betty finally persuaded Miss Lonelyhearts to go with her to her aunt's Connecticut farm. They camped in the kitchen, sat near a pond to watch frogs, deer, and a fawn, and slept on a mattress on the floor. They walked in the woods, swam in the nude, and made love in the grass. After several days they returned to the city. Miss Lonelyhearts knew that Betty had failed to cure him; he could not forget the letters. He vowed to attempt to be humble. In the office he found a lengthy letter from Broad Shoulders, telling of her troubles with a crazy husband.

About a week later, while Shrike was pulling the same familiar jokes in Delehanty's, the bartender introduced Miss Lonelyhearts to Peter Doyle, a cripple whose wife wanted the columnist to have dinner at their house. After labored conversation, Doyle gave him a letter about his problems: he must pull his leg up and down stairs for $22.50 a week; his wife talked money, money, money; a doctor prescribed a six months' rest. When their hands touched under the table, they were at first embarrassed, but then held hands in silence.

As they left the speak-easy, very drunk, to go to Doyle's, the cripple cursed his wife and his foot. Miss Lonelyhearts was happy in his humility. When Mrs. Doyle tried to seduce the columnist, he failed to respond. Meanwhile, her husband called himself a pimp and at his wife's request went out to get gin. Failing to find a message to show Mrs. Doyle her husband loved her, and disgusted by her obscene attempts to get him to sleep with her, Miss Lonelyhearts struck her again and again before he ran out of the house.

Following a three days' illness, Miss Lonelyhearts was awakened by five people, including Shrike and his wife, all drunk, who wanted to take him to a party at the editor's home. Betty was one of the party. Shrike wanted to play a game in which he distributed letters from Miss Lonelyhearts' office file and made taunting comments. When the columnist could stand it no longer, he followed Betty out, dropping unread the letter given him, which Shrike read to the crowd. It was from Doyle, accusing Miss Lonelyhearts of trying to rape the cripple's wife.

Miss Lonelyhearts told Betty he had quit the Lonelyhearts job and was going to look for work in an advertising agency. She told him she was going to have a baby. Although he persuaded her to marry him and have the baby instead of an abortion, by the time he left her he did not feel guilty; he did not feel, in fact, for his feeling, conscience, sense of reality, and self-knowledge were like a rock.

The next morning he was in a fever. The Christ on his wall was shining, but everything else in the room seemed dead. When the bell rang and he saw Doyle coming up the stairs, he imagined the cripple had come to have Miss Lonelyhearts perform a miracle and make him whole. Misunderstanding the outspread arms, Doyle put his hand in a newspaper-wrapped package as Betty came in the door. In the struggle the gun Doyle carried went off and Miss Lonelyhearts fell, dragging the cripple with him.

MISS RAVENEL'S CONVERSION

Type of work: Novel
Author: John William De Forest (1826-1906)
Type of plot: Historical romance
Time of plot: The Civil War period
Locale: New England and Louisiana
First published: 1866

Principal characters:
CAPTAIN COLBURNE, a Federal officer
COLONEL CARTER, his superior
LILLIE RAVENEL, a Southern belle
DR. RAVENEL, her father
MRS. LARUE, a relative of the Ravenels

Critique:

It is unfortunate that *Miss Ravenel's Conversion from Secession to Loyalty* has been neither well-known nor widely read, for in its war scenes and in its fidelity to human nature it is, as William Dean Howells said, "of an advanced realism before realism was known by that name." Without labored detail, it presents civil war; without grisly enterprise, it depicts civil war. With an artist's fine sensitivity it unfolds a tender love story. De Forest's style and tastes are quite modern; possibly these facts account for the failure of his novel to achieve popularity when first published and for its later obscurity. But it is a versatile book, well-developed in plot, character, and background. Much to the writer's credit is his skillful handling of character and situation so that Lillie Ravenel's final acceptance of Colburne is without loss of dignity or womanliness.

The Story:

Edward Colburne, of New Boston, met Miss Lillie Ravenel shortly after the outbreak of the Civil War and not long after she had come to New England with her father, Dr. Ravenel, who had been forced to leave Louisiana on account of his refusal to support the Confederacy. Lillie was a loyal daughter of the South, Colburne an equally adamant supporter of the North.

Among Lillie's acquaintances was Lieutenant Colonel Carter, on leave because of an injury. Colonel Carter was a general favorite with the ladies, and Colburne could find only one defect in his attractive personality; he drank too much. Carter, foreseeing that the war would be a long one, hoped to enlist more troops. Colburne, a loyal Yankee, agreed to recruit a company of his own.

Lillie's flirtation with Carter alarmed her father. He liked Colburne, instead, but his daughter did not encourage that young man's attentions.

After saying farewell to Lillie, Colonel Carter and Captain Colburne set out under orders which eventually led them to New Orleans. Some time later Dr. Ravenel and Lillie returned to their former home. Lillie found the city changed; women spoke bitterly about the Yankee soldiers. When Dr. Ravenel, having no other practice in the city, accepted a position as head of a hospital held by Union forces, he added further insult to the pride of the local citizens. Because Colonel Carter had tried to help the doctor find employment, his efforts gained him a welcome in the Ravenel house, although the doctor did not approve of the officer's attraction for Lillie.

Dr. Ravenel's kinswoman, Mrs. Larue, was attracted to Carter. When the doctor reproved her, she turned her attentions to Colburne. Because the captain innocently rebuffed her attempted flirtation, Mrs. Larue took her revenge by telling

Lillie that he had dined with the Meurices, a Creole family that had aided the Northern invaders.

Colonel Carter, preparing to drive a Southern regiment from the area, declared his love to Lillie before he left. Dr. Ravenel, adamant, would not consent to Carter's proposal, for he thought the officer's character questionable. Lillie wept and her father suffered. After the engagement Carter, for his heroism, was appointed Lieutenant Governor of Louisiana and stationed in New Orleans. A constant visitor in the Ravenel house, he gradually overcame the doctor's distrust, and at last he and Lillie became engaged. Carter was again ordered to active duty. Returning to New Orleans on leave, he hurriedly married Lillie before rejoining his troops.

Dr. Ravenel left his post at the hospital in order to take charge of a plantation in nearby Taylorsville, where he hoped to rehabilitate freed slaves. To Lillie's horror, he asked her to teach his charges how to read. Letters came quite frequently from Carter, and Lillie waited for his return.

Colburne, wounded in the arm, was hospitalized for a short time. When Dr. Ravenel found Colburne in the hospital, which reeked of sickness and decay, he took his young friend to the plantation. There Colburne had to endure Lillie's constant prattle about her husband. Colburne's visit was interrupted by a Confederate raid. Taking command, the captain secured the Ravenels and the Negroes in a nearby fort. In command was Major Gazaway, a cowardly and uncertain officer who urged surrender when the Southerners attacked. Colburne literally took command while Gazaway huddled in a protected spot with Lillie. After the Confederate troops had been repulsed, Dr. Ravenel attended the wounded. Lillie had been impressed by Colburne's courage.

Reporting to Carter, Colburne found him celebrating a victory with whiskey and women. The young man felt sorry for Lillie. A few days later Carter established his wife in a local cottage, and Dr.

Ravenel returned to head the hospital in New Orleans. Colburne spent much time with the Carters. Carter, however, was gradually sinking under his debts. A summons to Washington took Colonel Carter away from his wife after he had borrowed two hundred dollars from Colburne. Another passenger on the ship with Carter was Mrs. Larue. Although he berated himself for his infidelity, Carter carried on an affair with Lillie's aunt.

Carter did try, unsuccessfully, to obtain a promotion for Colburne. In Washington he himself bowed to custom and beguiled senators and officials until he was promised promotion to the rank of a brigadier general. He called on Mrs. Larue in New York. They traveled together to New Orleans on the return trip. Carter borrowed one hundred dollars from the widow.

After his return Carter sank more deeply into debt. He and Mrs. Larue met frequently in a private room behind his office. When Lillie's baby was born, however, he promised himself to have nothing more to do with Mrs. Larue.

To alleviate his indebtedness, Carter began to speculate with government funds. Shortly afterward he received his appointment as brigadier general and was recalled to active duty. At that time Dr. Ravenel found and read a letter written to him by Mrs. Larue. Heartsick, the doctor tried to hide the news from Lillie. Unfortunately, she came upon the same letter and, accustomed to reading her father's mail, read it.

When Lillie became seriously ill, her father took her and the baby on a sea voyage, his intention being to take Lillie north after her recovery. The letter he wrote to his son-in-law, informing him of that decision, was delivered on the eve of a battle in which Carter was mortally wounded. Colburne grieved for the fallen officer and for the bereaved wife.

Gradually Lillie readjusted herself and devoted her time to her child. When Colburne, worn out and sick, returned to New Boston near the end of the war, Dr.

Ravenel undertook to cure him. During his convalescence, Colburne renewed his friendship with Lillie, who more and more began to display her old charm. Still in love with her, he was too hesitant to speak up boldly. When he finally asked her to marry him, Lillie realized that she truly loved him, better than she had loved any other.

MR. BRITLING SEES IT THROUGH

Type of work: Novel
Author: H. G. Wells (1866-1946)
Type of plot: Social criticism
Time of plot: World War I
Locale: England
First published: 1916

Principal characters:
MR. DIRECK, an American
MR. BRITLING, an English writer
HUGH, Mr. Britling's oldest son
TEDDY, Mr. Britling's secretary
LETTY, Teddy's wife
CISSIE, Letty's sister and Mr. Direck's sweetheart
HEINRICH, the Britling children's tutor

Critique:

In this book the author tries to show the effect of World War I upon the mind of one man. Mr. Britling passes from optimism to despair and back to optimism as he ponders questions of war, religion, morality, and social reform. For anyone who enjoys novels of theme this is a rewarding and inspiring book.

The Story:

Mr. Direck, secretary of a Boston cultural society, was in England for the purpose of persuading Mr. Britling, a famous writer, to deliver a series of lectures in the United States. Direck found England all that he had expected, as he traveled from London to Matching's Easy in Essex to meet Mr. Britling. However, Mr. Britling did not support the illusion. He neither dressed like an Englishman nor acted like an intellectual, and Direck was disappointed. But Mr. Britling's family and friends aroused his interest. Mr. and Mrs. Britling had three boys. The oldest, Hugh, was the son of Mr. Britling's first wife. In addition to the immediate family, an old aunt and a young German tutor, Heinrich, lived in the house. Mr. Britling's secretary Teddy, his wife Letty, and her sister Cissie, lived in a cottage nearby. Direck fell in love with Cissie, a vivacious and intelligent girl.

Largely because of Cissie, Direck entered with zest into the entertainments of the Britling household, and at times he almost forgot the real reason for his visit. Several times, however, he and his host had serious discussions. Once they spoke about possible war with Germany. Mr. Britling said the idea was nonsense; it had been expected for a long time and had never happened. Unknown to Direck and Mr. Britling, however, an attempt was at that moment being made to kill Archduke Francis Ferdinand of Austria. The fatal march of events had begun.

One morning Mr. Britling took Direck on a ride around the countryside. Mr. Britling, a poor driver, was involved in an accident with a motorcycle. He was not hurt, but Direck broke his wrist. He saw in the accident an opportunity to prolong his stay at Matching's Easy. Meanwhile, war brewed behind the scenes. France was unsettled. The British were troubled with civil war in Ireland. Heinrich anxiously questioned Mr. Britling about the war. Mr. Britling was still confident that Germany could not be so foolish as to fight the rest of the world.

When the time finally came for Direck to leave Matching's Easy, he decided that he could not go without confessing his love to Cissie. Because she had not yet made up her mind about her love for him, Direck left for a tour of Europe. He felt hopeful because Cissie had not definitely rejected him.

Mr. Britling, too, was involved in a love affair. He and his wife had ceased to love each other years before, but they cooperated admirably to run their pleasant household. Life ran smoothly at home. Away from home there was Mrs. Harrowdean, a widow. The love affair between her and Mr. Britling did not run smoothly. At the time they had ceased to see each other and were quarreling by mail.

The threat of war crept forward. Heinrich was called home for mobilization. He left sadly. He did not believe in war. The Britlings urged him to stay, but he said that he must serve his country.

Germany invaded France, and Russia invaded Germany. Although forced to readjust his thinking. Mr. Britling firmly believed that Germany could never win. With a troubled mind he drove into the country, half-determined to call on Mrs. Harrowdean, but on the way he began to think of what the war would mean to the world. Instead of going to see Mrs. Harrowdean, he returned home to his writing desk. The war had arrived to fill the mind of Mr. Britling to the exclusion of everything else.

When the Germans attacked Belgium, England declared war. Direck, who had been in Germany when war was declared, returned immediately to England, where he found Cissie thinking only of England and the war. Direck, being an American, remained only an interested spectator.

Gradually it dawned on Mr. Britling that Germany could not easily be beaten. The Britling household slowly became involved in the war. First Teddy volunteered, then Hugh. Mr. Britling at last got a job as a constable guarding bridges and public works. Mrs. Britling worked for the Red Cross. A Belgian refugee and his family came to live with them for a time. Later two squads of soldiers were billeted in their barn.

Mr. Britling did a lot of thinking in his attempt to adjust his mind to Germany's attitude in the war. To most Englishmen, the war was a game to be played and won against an honorable enemy; to many Germans, the war was a campaign of hate. Mr. Britling thought often of Heinrich. There had to be other Germans as good as Heinrich, for not all of them could be evil. Then he realized that the British were growing as cruel and hardened as the enemy. This war, after all, was no different from the ones that had gone before, and men on both sides were victims of their own foolishness and stupidity.

Hugh lied about his age and managed to be sent to the front in Flanders. Teddy was there too, and one day Letty received a telegram which said that he was missing. Mr. Britling was so disturbed that writing was now impossible. Direck, still a civilian, left for the continent to learn news of Teddy. Then a telegram announced that Hugh had been killed. The war was leaving its mark upon Mr. Britling of Matching's Easy.

Although Direck had found almost certain evidence that Teddy had been killed, Letty still believed him to be alive. Cissie tried to make her sister face the truth. Convinced, Letty went alone out into the fields with her grief. There she met Mr. Britling. He had become reconciled to Hugh's death because he had convinced himself that the boy had not died in vain. A better world was in the making; after the war things would be different.

Letty returned home, strangely quieted by what Mr. Britling had told her; she, too, had become reconciled to the idea of death. Suddenly she saw a familiar figure in front of the cottage. It was Teddy. He was alive, with one hand gone. Now it was Cissie who must begin to worry. Direck had volunteered in the Canadian Army.

Some weeks later Mr. Britling learned that Heinrich had died. He tried to compose a letter to Heinrich's parents, but the effort was useless. He wrote all night without being able to express what he felt. Hugh and Heinrich had both died for a reason. With the promise of a better world to come, now was not the time for despair. Mr. Britling rose from his desk and watched the morning begin. His mind was calm. It seemed as if the whole world was bathed in sunrise.

MR. FACEY ROMFORD'S HOUNDS

Type of work: Novel
Author: Robert Smith Surtees (1803-1864)
Type of plot: Picaresque satire
Time of plot: Nineteenth century
Locale: England
First published: 1865

Principal characters:

FACEY ROMFORD, a self-made M. F. H.

LUCY SPONGE, nee GLITTERS, an actress and sportswoman

MR. WATKINS, owner of Dalberry Lees

MRS. WATKINS, his wife

CASSANDRA CLEOPATRA, their daughter

MR. HAZEY, master of the Hard and Sharp Hunt

MRS. HAZEY, his wife

ANNA MARIA, their daughter

BILL, their son

MISS BETSY SHANNON, an actress

LOVETIN LONNERGAN, her suitor

GOODHEARTED GREEN, a sharp horse-trader

Critique:

Published a year after the writer's death, *Mr. Facey Romford's Hounds* is the most involved of Surtees' novels and in part a sequel to *Mr. Sponge's Sporting Tour.* A number of characters from the earlier novel appear in this posthumous work, notably Facey Romford, who played only a minor role in Sponge's adventures, and Mrs. Sponge, the former Lucy Glitters, that dashing actress and sportswoman. Like its predecessors, the novel belongs to the great comic tradition in English fiction. Unlike the others, it is less episodic in form, showing that Surtees at the end of his career was working toward the novel of plot. The story is boisterous, aggressive, and satirical. Surtees, who wrote about life as he saw it, was an unappreciated novelist of manners as well as a chronicler of sport, and his downright honesty and hearty humor won for him the dislike of the fox-hunting fraternity, a prejudice which in criticism at least exists to this day. Yet Surtees reflected an age and a whole society in his books, and we go back to him for our best picture of one important segment of that society, country sporting life. At a time when most of the nineteenth-century writers have been re-claimed and evaluated, the comparative neglect of Surtees' novels is difficult to understand.

The Story:

Facey Romford had the reputation of being the most impudent man in the country. Because his first name was Francis and he kept a hound or two, strangers sometimes mistook him for the rich and sporting Francis Romford, Esq., owner of Abbeyfield Park. Facey, always willing to profit by the other Mr. Romford's name and reputation, never contradicted that false impression. In fact, he kept for use on some of his own correspondence a broad seal of the right Mr. Romford's crest, a turbot sitting on its tail on a cap of dignity, taken from an envelope in which Squire Romford had redirected a dunning shoemaker's bill intended for Facey but delivered in error at Abbeyfield Park.

Facey lived on expectations. Early in life he had elected himself heir to his cattle-jobbing uncle, Mr. Francis Gilroy, whose farm he was supposed to look after during the old man's business trips. Living in lodgings in the village, Facey spent his days hunting and fishing on other men's properties, his evenings playing on his flute or estimating the amount he would someday inherit. On occasion, under the influence of a third glass of gin, the figure rose as high as thirty thousand pounds.

Uncle Gilroy died suddenly, leaving all his worldly goods to the wife and numerous progeny he had been maintaining secretly in a London suburb. When his sharp-tongued widow arrived with her brood to take possession of the farm, Facey realized there was no hope for him in that quarter. But he was never one to let the grass grow under his feet. Before word of the Widow Gilroy's coming could spread through the district he carried word of his uncle's death to Mr. Jogglebury Crowdey, a neighbor, secured a check for fifty pounds from that unwary gentleman, cashed it, and set out immediately for London.

There his first act was to look up Soapey Sponge, an old acquaintance who had once tricked him out of seven pounds ten in a card game. In palmier days Soapey had married Lucy Glitters, the actress, and set up a cigar and betting establishment. When an unfeeling government passed laws against betting houses, however, the business ceased to prosper. Although lovely Mrs. Sponge never sold her husband's cheap cigars under sixpence or gave change for a shilling, they had a hard time making ends meet. Facey found the shop but no Mr. Sponge, for Soapey, seeing the caller first, went out the back way. Whether Facey called early or late, Soapey was never at home, and since he called frequently he spent much of his time in Mrs. Sponge's company.

One day, while looking into a saddlery window, Facey had his great idea. He would become a master of hounds. A short time later *Bell's Life in London* carried an advertisement stating that a gentleman was prepared to treat a country where he could enjoy shooting and fishing as well. In the correspondence which followed, Facey's letters sealed with the turbot crest proved sufficiently impressive to members of the Heavyside Hunt. Their wives, learning from Burke that Francis Romford, Esq., was a bachelor, decided that he was a possible match for unmarried daughters, and without further delay Facey became master of the Heavyside hounds. To celebrate, he bought Mrs. Sponge a tiara of brilliants, but when he went to deliver his gift he was greeted by the news that Soapey had bolted for Australia with all the loose cash on hand. On Facey's advice Lucy sold the furnishings of the store to a secondhand dealer, packed her clothes, and went to stay with her mother while she waited for something to turn up.

At Minshull Vernon, meanwhile, Facey found the Heavyside hounds a splay-footed, crooked-legged pack. On his first day out he was forced to ride a borrowed mount, but even so his daring horsemanship put to shame the fat, timid huntsman, Jonathan Lotherington. The members were so enthusiastic about their new M. F. H. that few cared when the disgruntled huntsman resigned. Facey immediately appropriated Lotherington's horses, the property of the hunt, for his own use. Planning to improve his pack, he wrote, under the turbot crest, to the huntsmen of the best packs in the kingdom and engaged their draughts. In this way he secured a fine lot of hounds without the necessity of paying for them, for some of the huntsmen were pleased to oblige Francis Romford, Esq., without cost and those who presented bills received such abusive letters denouncing their hounds as overrunning, sheep-worrying beasts that they were ashamed to press their demands further.

Facey next consulted Mr. Goodhearted Green, a shady horse-trader, and bought from him three mounts of good appearance but vicious habits, Honest Robin, Brilliant, and Leotard. At Tattersall's he hired two disreputable grooms and whippers-in, Daniel Swig and Tom Chowey. Although his horses and grooms were such as only he could manage, Facey might have had a long career with the Heavyside Hunt if he had not been tempted to make a handsome profit by selling Leotard to Mrs. Rowley Rounding. After Leotard had dumped his new mistress into a mud puddle, the horse was sent back to Facey. Insisting that the sale had been without condition and to Colonel Chatterbox, the lady's intermediary, he refused to return the money. Because some of the hunt sided with Mrs. Rounding, Facey planned to prove Leotard a suitable lady's mount by having Lucy Sponge, a magnificent horsewoman, ride him in the next meet.

Having been drunk the night before, Swig and Chowey were in no condition to ride on the day of the hunt, and Facey asked Lucy to act as whipper-in. His scheme had unforeseen results. Lucy, dressed in a fashionable London habit, rode with such ease and skill that the members unanimously judged Leotard a perfect horse for a lady. But if she won the approval of the gentlemen, Lucy also aroused the envy and dislike of their wives. Claiming that her performance and presence were an outrage to the proprieties, they insisted that the M. F. H. must go. Facey was not to be bought off lightly, however, and as a result he found himself with fifty excellent hounds in his kennels and money in his pockets. Deciding that the way to fortune was to keep hounds, hunt a country, and get his sport at the expense of others, he advertised his services once more.

As luck would have it, the Larkspur Hunt in Doubleimupshire needed a M. F. H. for the remainder of the season. Again the turbot seal did its work, and before long Facey was engaged for a subscription of two thousand pounds a year. The seal also brought offers from people anxious to let their houses to the new master. At last Facey decided on Beldon Hall, the property of Lord Viscount Lovetin, who, living abroad, vaguely remembered a Francis Romford at Eton. Supposing Facey to be the same Romford, and without consulting his agent, Mr. Lonnergan, his lordship announced his willingness to rent his house at a nominal fee to so desirable a tenant.

Lucy had enjoyed her taste of country life at Minshull Vernon. Having no intention of returning to London, she persuaded Facey that it would be to his advantage for him to have a lady exhibit his horses. Finally it was decided that she would pass as his half-sister, Mrs. Somerville, the widow of an Indian officer, and that her mother, to be known as Mrs. Sidney Benson, would be installed at Beldon Hall to keep her daughter company. To prepare for their venture into society, Facey ordered new outfits for himself and his grooms, while Lucy required the newest creations of London dressmakers and milliners. The turbot seal and Lord Viscount Lovetin's address did the rest. There was no question of payment on the part of tradesmen, little intention to pay on the part of the new tenants of Beldon Hall.

Wishing to convert some coach houses into kennels, Facey sent Proudlock, the keeper, to ask Mr. Lonnergan's permission to make the change. The agent was away but his son, Lovetin Lonnergan, sent back word that Mr. Romford might do as he liked. Acting on that reply, Facey broke open the nobleman's wine cellar. He also wrote to Goodhearted Green and bought six more horses of uncertain habits to add to the three already in his starting stud. Lucy, meanwhile, had opened the rooms of the mansion and bullied Mrs. Mustard, the housekeeper, and her three slatternly daughters, locally called the Dirties, into somewhat presentable appearance and behavior.

The whole country was eager to meet the new M. F. H. and his sister. Among the early callers were Mr. and Mrs. Watkins and their daughter Cassandra Cleopatra, of Dalberry Lees. In his seedy younger days Watkins had emigrated to Australia. There he had struck it rich in the diggings, even richer when he married the daughter of an ex-convict who had made a fortune in land speculation. Anxious to display their wealth and to find Cassandra's equal in marriage, they had returned to England to establish themselves as a landed family. Mrs. Watkins was not one to hold back when opportunity arose to exhibit her daughter's simpering charms to an eligible bachelor.

Facey's first day out with the Larkspur Hunt was a great success. The hounds raised a fox in a wood near Pippin Priory and after the long, spirited chase Facey showed his mettle when he put his horse to a flooded river, leaving the others to ride around by the bridge. The hunt was delighted with the day's run and their new master. Reports of Facey's prowess finally reached Mr. Hazey of Tarring Neville, a shrewd horse-trader and master of the Hard and Sharp Hunt. So great was his curiosity that he and his son Bill rode over to Beldon Hall to pay their respects.

Enterprising Mrs. Watkins invited Facey and Lucy to dine with them and stay overnight for a meet at Dalberry Lees the next morning. The dinner and the hunt breakfast were on a grand scale, but the lady's plans came to nothing because the fox she had ordered for a draw in her gardens failed to arrive on time. Facey, who had nothing but contempt for bag foxes, rode away disgusted. Returning home that evening, he found the fox, sent to him with Mrs. Watkins' compliments, caged in his front hall. He gave orders that the animal was to be turned loose early in the morning, when he and Lucy would ride after it with only a few hounds.

The next day's chase carried them as far as Tarring Neville, where they breakfasted after the fox had gone to earth. Mr. and Mrs. Hazey made much of their unexpected guests, and their daughter Anna Maria, forewarned by her anxious mother, was especially attentive to the Larkspur M. F. H. A few days later came an invitation asking Facey and Lucy to dine at Tarring Neville and hunt with the Hard and Sharp pack the next day. They went, but Facey formed no high opinion of the Hard and Sharp hounds or their master.

Mrs. Watkins, not to be outdone by Hazey hospitality, decided to organize a stag hunt. Mr. Stotfold and his stag were engaged for the occasion and the chase was started from Dalberry Lees. The affair was a fiasco. The stag created havoc on the premises of a young ladies' finishing school and mired itself at last in the mud of a tilery. Facey decided to stick to fox hunting.

Christmas promised to be a gay season at Beldon Hall. Lucy had invited down from London a good friend of her theatrical days, buxom, jolly Betsy Shannon. Introduced to the gentry as Miss Hamilton Howard, she soon had the swains of the neighborhood vying for her smiles. Betsy's success led Lucy to her great resolution—she would give a party. Once more the turbot seal worked its magic. Caterers came from London with great hampers of food and drink, for a simple at home had become in the planning an elaborate ball. Facey, who had voted for a few people with rabbit-pie and cheese or sandwiches and sherry, was dismayed when he estimated the cost of Lucy's expensive entertainment, but after several glasses of champagne he unbent so far as to entertain the guests with several tunes on his flute. Disaster threatened when the coachmen and grooms, tired of waiting in the cold outside, invaded the house and carried away the food laid for a second supper, but not even that rumpus dashed the spirits of the guests. Everyone agreed that the ball had been the affair of the season.

The next day Goodhearted Green showed up unexpectedly with a prospective new horse for Facey. At the infirmary ball, a short time later, he was presented to the country as Sir Roger Ferguson. And on that memorable night young Lovetin Lonnergan made his offer to Miss Hamilton Howard and was accepted.

Once more Leotard was to involve Facey in difficulties. Mr. Hazey, having admired the horse and Lucy's performance in the saddle, wished to purchase the mount for a third-hand sale to the

Countess of Caperington. Lucy finally agreed to part with the animal for one hundred and fifty pounds. The countess paid two hundred guineas for a headstrong horse that first carried his mistress afield and then threw her over his tail. During the wrangling for refund of the Caperington guineas the countess decided to see for herself the famous Mrs. Somerville who rode Leotard with such ease. Attending a meeting of the Larkspur Hunt, she recognized Lucy as a former friend of the days when she herself had been the cigar-smoking, actress-wife of dissipated Sir Harry Scattercash. The countess greeted her old friend haughtily, calling her Mrs. Sponge and a pernicious woman.

The awkward situation might have been explained away if Lord Lovetin had not chosen that particular time to return to England, where to his surprise he found the wrong Mr. Romford comfortably installed in Beldon Hall. Disputing the possession of the premises with his lordship, Facey demanded a large bonus if he was to leave the house immediately. During the proceedings he continued to hunt his hounds as usual, but Lucy went to stay with Betsy, who in the meantime had married young Lonnergan. The opinion of the Larkspur Hunt was divided, some of the members declaring that their Mr. Romford might be the wrong man for Lord Lovetin but that he was the right Mr. Romford for them. Among his defenders were the Watkinses. Having recently lost much of their wealth through unfortunate speculations in Australia, they saw in Facey their final hope for Cassandra Cleopatra. At last Facey, deciding that he could hunt from Dalberry Lees as easily as he could from Beldon Hall, led the eager Miss Watkins to the altar.

When both parties realized that they had been tricked, and harsh words had been spoken, it was decided that Facey and his bride should go to Australia and there try to save the wreck of Mr. Watkins' fortune. Facey, who had prudently collected his subscription money, was willing. In Melbourne he accidentally ran into his old acquaintance Soapey Sponge, who had done uncommonly well for himself in the mines. When news of Soapey's prosperity reached England, Lucy dropped the name of Somerville in favor of Sponge and sailed to share her husband's prosperity. Last reports stated that all parties were happily reunited in Australia and that Soapey and Facey had established a private bank. Everyone expected them to set up next a pack of hounds.

MR. MIDSHIPMAN EASY

Type of work: Novel
Author: Frederick Marryat (1792-1848)
Type of plot: Adventure romance
Time of plot: Napoleonic wars
Locale: Mediterranean Sea and European coastal waters
First published: 1836

Principal characters:
JACK EASY, a midshipman
GASCOIGNE, another midshipman
MESTY, an Ashantee Negro
AGNES REBIERA, Easy's Sicilian sweetheart

Critique:

Marryat wrote from experience, having himself been a captain in the British navy, and his book gives a fully detailed account of life aboard a war vessel, including vivid accounts of several battles at sea. Unlike many other stories about the British or American navy in the early nineteenth century, he did not charge the naval system of discipline with being too harsh. Rather, he tried to show that it developed the best that was in a man. Marryat thought poorly of the theories of equality which had been popularized in France during the French Revolution.

The Story:

Jack Easy was the son of a wealthy landowner in the county of Hampshire, England. Jack's father and mother had almost spoiled the boy for any good in the world, the former by his over-simplified philosophy of equality, and the latter by her doting. Fortunately for the young lad, the family physician, Doctor Middleton, rescued him from his home and put him in a school where he began to learn that the survival of the fittest was the way of the world. When he left school, it was decided he should go to sea as midshipman with Captain Wilson, a poor relation who was indebted to Mr. Easy for a loan of one thousand pounds and who was in command of the warship *Harpy*.

Jack soon made friends aboard the *Harpy* through the use of his fists in beating down bullies among the ship's company and through the obvious goodwill which the captain showed him. It was hard at first for the young man to become accustomed to life aboard the warship. The duties of a midshipman kept him busy, but the small living quarters and the discipline proved irksome to the son of a philosopher who preached a doctrine of equality.

Jack's first naval adventure occurred when the ship was not far from Tarragona. In command of a boat during the capture of a Spanish vessel by a boarding party, he was left behind when the *Harpy* sailed away. Captain Wilson thought that Easy's boat had been sunk with all hands. The following night Easy's boat captured another Spanish vessel by boarding. Easy ordered the crew and passengers, including an elderly Sicilian and his wife and two beautiful daughters, overboard into a small boat. A few days later, after Easy had vainly tried to find the *Harpy*, the crew landed on an island and refused to return to the captured ship. But an Ashantee Negro, Mesty, was loyal to Easy because the midshipman had befriended him and had treated him as an equal. Through the efforts of Mesty, the men were brought back on board in a docile condition and Easy again set sail to look for the *Harpy*. After a week had passed, Easy and his crew found the British warship engaged with a Spanish vessel. The timely aid of gunfire from Easy's prize helped the *Harpy* take its opponent. Everyone, including Captain Wilson, was amused at the flag which Easy had flown in the engagement. Having no British flag aboard the prize, he had hoisted a lady's green petticoat.

The first stop for the *Harpy* in the Mediterranean was at Malta. There Easy fought a duel. Thinking he had killed his man, he and a fellow midshipman, Gascoigne, ran away in a native boat they had hired. A storm drove their small craft to the Sicilian shore, where the two young sailors hid in a cart and there fell asleep. When they awakened they found themselves in the yard of a great house. Hearing loud cries, they rushed into the house in time to prevent the owner from being murdered by two relatives. The man and his family proved to be the passengers whom Easy had put into a small boat when he had taken his prize a month earlier. Before Don Rebiera sent them to Palermo, Easy had fallen deeply in love with the Sicilian nobleman's daughter, Agnes.

At Palermo the two midshipmen went aboard a British frigate which took them back to Malta to rejoin the *Harpy*. Since Easy's opponent in the duel had not died, Captain Wilson forgave their escapade.

A few weeks later the *Harpy* was sailing off the coast of Africa. In another battle to board a vessel, Easy distinguished himself a second time. The prize was taken back to Malta, where Captain Wilson learned that he had been promoted to the command of a larger ship, the *Aurora*. When he left the *Harpy*, Captain Wilson took Easy, Gascoigne, and Mesty with him.

Separated from the fleet during a storm, the *Aurora* was struck by lightning and set afire. Many of her officers and men were killed or injured. Both Easy and Gascoigne were heroic in their efforts to help stop the blaze and get the ship seaworthy enough to reach Malta for repairs. Back at Malta, Easy and Gascoigne had still further adventures. Chosen to accompany a Sicilian nobleman who was visiting the ship, they recognized him as one of the men who had tried to assassinate Don Rebiera. The impostor was arrested by the authorities and returned to Sicily.

Several weeks later the *Aurora* sighted a galley, filled with criminals, sinking off the Sicilian coast. A party was sent to release the prisoners and set them ashore. During the operation Easy recognized the man who had attempted to assassinate Don Rebiera and who had been sent to the galleys just a few weeks before. He notified Captain Wilson, who immediately informed the authorities on the island and then permitted Easy, Gascoigne, and Mesty to go ashore to warn their friends. Easy and his companions arrived at Don Rebiera's home in time to warn the household of its danger. A battle of a day and a night ensued. At the end of that time Sicilian troops arrived and rescued the besieged house and its defenders from the band of escaped galleyslaves under the leadership of Don Rebiera's enemy.

The next day Easy asked Agnes' father if he might marry her. The father, indebted to Easy and knowing that his daughter loved the young midshipman, could not give his permission immediately because of the Church. His family confessor threatened excommunication if the marriage took place.

Not to be daunted, Easy and Gascoigne, with the help of Mesty, pretended to have broken their legs in a carriage accident. Captain Wilson was forced to leave them behind to convalesce when the *Aurora* left port. As soon as the ship had sailed, Mesty was sent with a bribe to the confessor. The priest, in his turn, tried to get Mesty's aid in poisoning Easy in order to prevent the marriage. Mesty promised to help the priest but administered the poison to the confessor instead. Don Rebiera then withdrew his objection to the marriage if he could have the written permission of the midshipman's father, since Easy was still under age. Easy eagerly reported to the *Aurora* to resign from the navy and return to England to get his father's permission to marry.

Back in England, Easy learned that his mother had died and his father had become insane. While the son was straightening out the affairs of the family, the father also died, leaving Easy a large fortune. Since the seas were not a safe place to travel as a passenger in a merchant vessel, Easy bought a small ship. Armed with cannon and letters of marque, he sailed for Sicily. There he married Agnes.

He and his bride returned to England after Easy had helped to secure Gascoigne's resignation from the navy. Neither Easy nor Gascoigne went to sea again, but settled down as country gentlemen on Easy's large estate in Hampshire.

MISTER ROBERTS

Type of work: Novel
Author: Thomas Heggen (1919-1949)
Type of plot: Humorous satire
Time of plot: Last months of World War II
Locale: Southwest Pacific
First published: 1946

Principal characters:

DOUGLAS ROBERTS, First Lieutenant, U. S. S. Reluctant
CAPTAIN MORTON, skipper of the Reluctant
ENSIGN KEITH, USNR
BOOKSER, a seaman
FRANK THOMPSON, radio man

Critique:

Mister Roberts, first published serially in The Atlantic Monthly, became a national best seller soon after its appearance in book form. The subject matter offers relief from the general run of war literature; the style ranges from almost poetic prose to screaming farce. An air of lusty masculinity pervades the narrative. Heggen has perfectly reproduced the uninhibited idiom of men at war. The success of the novel led Heggen, with Joshua Logan, to dramatize it into an equally successful play. Heggen's artistic motive in writing the novel must surely have been his wish to show the public that the backwashes of the war also have their tragedy and comedy, and even their romance, despite their apparent lack of color.

The Story:

Douglas Roberts, First Lieutenant on the Reluctant, a U. S. Navy supply ship in the Pacific, was the guiding spirit of the crew's undeclared war against the skipper, Captain Morton, an officious, childish, and unreasonable officer. The Reluctant was non-combatant, plying among islands left in the backwash of the war. None of its complement had seen action, and none wanted action except Roberts, who had applied without success for transfer to a ship of the line.

In the continuously smoldering warfare between the captain and the other officers and the men of the ship, Roberts scored a direct hit on the captain's fundament with a wad of lead-foil shot from a rubber band while the captain was watching movies on board. Ensign Pulver, who spent most of his time devising ways of making the skipper's life unbearable, manufactured a giant firecracker to be thrown into the captain's cabin at night. The premature and violent explosion of the firecracker put the entire Reluctant on a momentary battle footing. Ensign Pulver was burned badly.

Ensign Keith came to the Reluctant by way of middle-class Boston, Bowdoin College, and accelerated wartime naval officer training. He was piped aboard in the blazing sunshine of Tedium Bay, hot in his blue serge uniform but self-assured because Navy Regulations prescribed blues when reporting for duty. Despite the discomfort of a perspiration-soaked shirt and a wilted collar, Ensign Keith immediately showed the crew that they would have to follow naval regulations if he had his way aboard ship. One night, however, while he was on watch, he came upon a drinking and gambling party presided over by Chief Dowdy. Keith was hoodwinked by the men into trying some of their drink. Not much later, under the influence of Chief Dowdy's "pineapple juice," Keith had become roaring drunk, all regulations and service barriers forgotten. His initiation completed, Ensign Keith never again referred to rules and regulations.

At a forward area island base, where the *Reluctant* had docked to unload cargo, the crew quickly learned that the military hospital was staffed by real live nurses. Every available binocular, telescope, and range-finder on board was soon trained on the nurses' quarters. Interest rose to fever-pitch when it was discovered that a bathroom window shade in quarters was never lowered. Officers and men soon came to know the nurses by their physical characteristics, if not by formal introduction. One day a nurse came aboard and overheard two seamen making a wager concerning her physical characteristics. That same day the bathroom shade was lowered, never to be raised again.

For days in advance the ship's complement planned their shore leave in Elysium, a civilized port of call. Seaman Bookser, the spiritual type, was the butt of many jokes concerning his liberty plans. At Elysium half of the men were given shore leave. From sundown until the following dawn they were brought back by jeep and truck. They had fought with army personnel, insulted local citizens, stolen government property, wrecked bars and saloons, and damaged the house of the French consul. Further shore leave was canceled. Bookser, the spiritual seaman, was driven up to the dock in a large car on the day of departure. Beside him was a beautiful young woman whom he kissed long and passionately before leaving her. Astonished at Bookser and proud of him at the same time, the crew made him the hero of the stop at Elysium.

Roberts listened to V-E Day reports on the ship's radio. The apathy of his fellow officers toward events happening in Europe led him to pitch the captain's pet potted palm overboard late that night. At the same time Roberts stirred up the noise-hating captain by slamming a lead stanchion against a stateroom bulkhead. Roberts was not caught, nor did he give himself up during the captain's mad search for the culprit. The crew manufactured a medal and presented it to Roberts for valor above and beyond the call of duty—a seaman had seen Roberts in action on V-E night.

Frank Thompson, a radio man and the ship's monopoly expert, was informed by wire that his baby, whom he had never seen, had died in California. Thompson, anxious to go to the funeral and to be with his wife, applied for permission to fly to the States. The captain refused. Roberts advised him to go to a nearby island to see the chaplain and the flag secretary. Thompson went, but he was told that no emergency leave could be permitted without his captain's approval. He then walked alone in a deserted section of the island for several hours before he returned to the *Reluctant* and took his usual place at the head of the monopoly table.

Not long after V-E Day, Roberts received orders to report back to the States for reassignment. The night before he left the *Reluctant* he spent with his special friends among officers and men, drinking punch made of crew-concocted raisin brew and grain alcohol from dispensary supplies. The effect of Roberts' leaving the ship was immediate. No longer was there a born leader aboard. All functions and activities in ship's routine went wrong; no longer was there any one man upon whom the officers could depend to maintain their balance in the tedium of a dull tropic supply run. No longer did the enlisted men have an officer upon whom they could depend as a link between them and the ship's authorities.

Roberts was assigned to duty aboard a destroyer which was part of a task force bombarding the Japanese home islands. Not long before V-J Day, Ensign Pulver received a letter from a friend aboard the same ship. The letter stated that a Japanese kamikaze plane had broken through anti-aircraft defenses and had crashed into the bridge of the destroyer. Among those killed in the explosion was Roberts, who was in the officers' mess drinking coffee with another officer. Mr. Roberts had seen action at last.

MR. SPONGE'S SPORTING TOUR

Type of work: Novel
Author: Robert Smith Surtees (1803-1864)
Type of plot: Picaresque satire
Time of plot: Nineteenth century
Locale: England
First published: 1853

> *Principal characters:*
> MR. SOAPEY SPONGE, a cockney sportsman
> LUCY GLITTERS, an actress
> JAWLEYFORD, a sportsman
> PUFFINGTON, another sportsman
> JOGGLEBURY, a carver of canes

Critique:

Mr. Sponge's Sporting Tour is one of a number of novels dealing with the lower classes who are striving to emulate the aristocracy. This novel differs somewhat from the others in two ways: it has a reasonably coherent plot, and it is much more picaresque in tone. Sponge is quite plainly a sharper, out to live well on the bounty of his fellows. He is the one character we follow rather closely in a number of related situations. The hero is different from Surtees' renowned and clumsy Jorrocks in that Sponge is a skillful, dedicated hunter of foxes.

The Story:

Soapey Sponge led a remarkably consistent life while he was in London. Each day he appeared at the same pub or betting stall at exactly the same time. No man had a better knowledge of London's streets and transportation. In fact, he spent all his spare time studying his street guide. He affected loud clothes, and he was intimate with grooms and horse dealers.

Just outside London was a small farm run by Buckram, a sharp horse trader. Sponge, in need of mounts for the hunting season, decided to visit him. Buckram had two horses to show, Hercules and Multum in Parvo; both could be bought cheaply, for they were incurably vicious. Sponge, an expert horseman, concluded a deal whereby he could take the horses on an installment basis. Since he would need

a groom if he were to cut a figure among fox hunters, he engaged Leather, Buckram's slippery factotum. Leather had neither morals nor standing, but Sponge believed he could make him behave acceptably.

The hunt at Laverick Wells had become popular among certain of the sporting fraternity, and Sponge decided to try his luck there first. He sent Leather and the horses on ahead to prepare for his coming. Leather was too efficient, however; he puffed his master up too much. He extolled Sponge's rich wardrobe and extensive stables to such an extent that the whole town was sick of Sponge before he even arrived.

Waffles, the master of the hunt, determined to show up the newcomer by substituting a drag hunt for the real fox hunt. All the town knew of the substitution and secretly hoped Sponge would come to grief. On the day of the hunt Sponge mounted Hercules in private. By the time he joined the crowd the horse was considerably subdued. The drag hunt was thrilling. The pack ran through all the bogs and flinty pastures, through all the stout fences. The casualties were numerous, but Sponge kept on bravely. Riding ahead of Waffles, he was first at the supposed kill.

The daring horsemanship of Sponge changed the atmosphere a great deal; now he was admired and his horse was praised.

Waffles made indirect overtures to buy Hercules; by pretending indifference Sponge closed the deal at three hundred guineas. As a favor, Waffles allowed a friend to ride Hercules soon afterward. That animal, vicious as always, took the bit in his teeth and crashed through the window of a drapery shop.

After four weeks Waffles was heartily sick of his bargain and told people of his unlucky deal. When Buckram turned up and offered twenty pounds for Hercules, Waffles was glad to let the horse go. But Sponge pretended that Lord Bullfrog, Hercules' former owner, was incensed at the report that he had sold Sponge a vicious horse. Sponge supposedly agreed to return Hercules and get his money back. Waffles had to admit the horse was gone, he knew not where. To avoid a lawsuit for slander, he paid over two hundred and fifty pounds to Sponge to quiet Lord Bullfrog.

At Laverick Wells, Sponge had met Jawleyford, a boaster who had invited him to Jawleyford Court to hunt with Lord Scamperdale's hounds. Jawleyford had invited Sponge in so general a way that he never expected him to accept. But Sponge, thick-skinned, wrote a note announcing his acceptance and then appeared before Jawleyford could think up a good excuse for putting off the visit. The host and hostess consoled themselves with the idea that Sponge was rich and might make a match with one of their daughters.

Sponge was a most disagreeable guest. His appetite was prodigious. He smoked cigars in the house, read his beloved guide to London's streets, and paid no attention at all to the daughters. The family was relieved every time he rode out to hunt with Scamperdale's pack.

Sponge's mount was quite unmanageable on the first hunt. In spite of Sponge's best efforts he ran among the hounds and hurt some of them. Scamperdale was furious. He had no love for Jawleyford and his guest seemed a dangerous man to have around. Back at Jawleyford Court, rumor eventually began to circulate that Sponge was no rich hunter but a penniless adventurer. As hints to leave became stronger, Sponge was relieved to have an invitation from Puffington, a neighbor who kept his own pack of hounds.

At Puffington's house, a rich bachelor establishment, Sponge was well situated for a time. He was puzzled for a while by the cordiality of his reception, but Spraggon, Lord Scamperdale's man, soon made the situation clear. Somehow Puffington had the notion that Sponge was a sports writer intent on gathering material for hunting stories. Spraggon induced Puffington to give Sponge thirty pounds to secure a flattering writeup. After pocketing the commission Sponge gladly paid him for his help, Spraggon sat down to dictate a story on the Puffington hounds.

As it turned out, Spraggon had no definite ideas on writing a hunting story. Sponge used a blotchy pen. In addition, neither of them knew much about spelling. They sent their completed effort to the local weekly paper, where it was edited by a spinster who had only contempt for hunting. When Puffington saw the garbled story, he was furious. Learning that Sponge had written it, he retired to his room with a supposed illness and instructed the butler to give strong indications that Sponge was to leave.

In the nick of time Jogglebury came over to invite Sponge for a visit. Jogglebury was no hunter; he was too fat and asthmatic even to stoop over. But he had a young son due to be christened, and Mrs. Jogglebury badly wanted a rich godfather. So Sponge was invited.

Jogglebury was a niggardly host. When he agreed to take Sponge to a neighboring hunt, he stopped so often to hack out likely looking saplings that they missed the pack completely. Jogglebury lived only for his hobby of carving canes in the likeness of famous men. Sponge could scarcely stay long with the Joggleburys; he detested children, and his hosts soon gave him to understand that he was wearing his welcome thin.

At last Sponge found a refuge with Sir Harry Scattercash, a rake married to a former actress who smoked cigars. Sir Harry and his party were much more interested in liquor than in hounds, but Sponge stayed on long enough to fall in love with Lucy Glitters, an actress whom he admired greatly for her daring riding in the field. After their marriage, Lucy and Sponge stayed on with Sir Harry until the bailiffs arrived to attach the property. Then they set out for London, where Sponge opened up a betting establishment and seemingly prospered. It was soon commonly supposed that he was a rich man.

MR. WESTON'S GOOD WINE

Type of work: Novel
Author: T. F. Powys (1875-1953)
Type of plot: Quasi-mysticism
Time of plot: November 20, 1923
Locale: Folly Down, a village in western England
First published: 1927

Principal characters:
MR. WESTON, a wine merchant and author
MICHAEL, his trusted assistant
THE REVEREND MR. GROBE, rector at Folly Down, a disbeliever in God
TAMAR GROBE, the rector's daughter
MR. GRUNTER, a sexton
MR. BUNCE, the innkeeper in Folly Down
JENNY BUNCE, his daughter, in love with Mr. Bird
MR. BIRD, a teacher of the gospel to animals, in love with Jenny Bunce

Critique:

T. F. Powys has said of himself that he thinks too much of God, and this novel, like most of his literary endeavors, reflects his preoccupation with things religious. Like his other novels, also, this one presents a small English village as a microcosm of the earth's macrocosm. An invalid for a large part of his life, Powys has had to limit his literature to his experience in a small portion of the world. It would seem, however, that his works bear out Thomas Hardy's doctrine that the humanity of a small district can reflect the universality of mankind. Certainly the portrayal of the Deity and His attitudes toward the earth and man, as found in *Mr. Weston's Good Wine*, reflect an unorthodox set of religious doctrines, a position which Powys presents but does not try to justify.

The Story:

On the evening of November 20, 1923, an old Ford car stopped on a hill overlooking Folly Down, a village in western England. Within the car Mr. Weston, a wine merchant, conferred with Michael, his assistant, about possible customers in the village. They had a large book which listed the names of the inhabitants, and Michael had detailed knowledge about them which only a supernatural being could possess. As they talked, their com-

ing was forecast to the village of Folly Down by an electrical sign displayed atop the car.

Down in the village many people noticed the sign on the hill; they could scarcely avoid seeing it, for it lit up the sky. As the men gathered in the inn for their evening beer, they began to speak of the peculiar sign, but the conversation drifted to the cause of all the pregnancies among the village maidens. Most of the men blamed M Grunter, the sexton, but Mr. Bunce blamed God. While they argued the question, the men noticed the clock had stopped. Mr. Grunter announced that eternity had come. He seemed to be correct, for all over the village time stood still at seven o'clock.

Mr. Weston arrived in the parlor of the inn and announced his wares. Although no one was interested in buying, they all felt an affection for the man and believed that they had known him somewhere before. When asked if he knew whether God or Mr. Grunter was responsible for the misfortunes of the village maidens, Mr. Weston referred them to Mr. Grobe, the rector, and then went himself to visit the clergyman.

Mr. Grobe was a melancholy man, for the accidental death of his vivacious and pretty wife had proved to him, clergyman though he was, that there was no

God Life weighed heavily upon him that evening; his bottle of London gin was empty. From Mr. Weston he ordered a bottle to try. He did not see the merchant leave a bottle, but after Mr. Weston's departure Mr. Grobe found, in place of his large Bible, a vast flagon of delicious wine, a flagon that remained full as long as he drank. Much later, although the clocks still pointed to seven o'clock, Mr. Weston appeared with a small bottle which he said gave eternal peace. After being assured he would meet his long-dead wife, Mr. Grobe drank from the small bottle and died peacefully.

While he was gone from the rectory, Mr. Weston had seen a number of the village people and transacted business with them. He had seen Tamar Grobe, who had looked all her life for an angel to marry, in whose arms she would be so happy that she would die. Mr. Weston sent her to see his assistant Michael, who waited under an old oak tree, the village trysting place where so many of the maidens had lost their virtue. There, in Michael's company, Tamar found happiness. They went to the church, where Mr. Weston married them and entered their names in the register.

After the couple had gone, Mr. Grunter found the wine merchant in the church. He thought at first that Mr. Weston was the devil, but he soon discovered that Mr. Weston had every right to be there. He agreed to aid Mr. Weston in some further transactions that evening.

Mr. Weston met Jenny Bunce, a simple-hearted girl who wanted only to marry a good man, like Mr. Bird, and care for him as long as she lived. But her father thought Mr. Bird a fool and had said that they could marry only when Mr. Bird's well ran with wine. Mr. Weston told Jenny to curl up in his car and wait while he went to see Mr. Bird. Mr. Weston found Mr. Bird an honest, virtuous man who preached the gospel to animals as well as men, when they would listen. Like Mr. Grunter and Mr. Grobe, Mr. Bird recognized Mr. Weston. Un-

like the other two, Mr. Bird was willing to listen to a chapter from the book Mr. Weston had written long before he became a wine merchant. Mr. Weston recited to him the One Hundred Fourth Psalm.

Then Mr. Weston asked for a drink from Mr. Bird's well, which, much to the owner's surprise, ran wine. Jenny Bunce's father happened along and in his surprise agreed to the wedding. Mr. Weston took Jenny Bunce and Mr. Bird to church and married them.

Two men whom Mr. Weston visited while the clocks stood still were the rascally sons of Squire Mumby. Because they were responsible for the large number of illegitimate children in Folly Down, Mr. Weston took them to the churchyard to see the corpse of a girl who had committed suicide after she had been with them. Failing to recognize Mr. Weston or understand his motives, they left him in a huff. Before they had gone far they were chased by a wild beast that had hoofs and a roar like a lion's, a beast which Mr. Weston controlled on a very light chain.

The Mumby boys were so frightened that they ran to the cottage of the evil woman who pandered to their desires and, finding two of their victims there, promised to marry the girls. The strange beast walked about the cottage for several minutes. The evil old woman died crying out that the devil was taking her down to hell.

After the Mumby boys had left the churchyard, Mr. Weston helped Mr. Grunter bury the corpse of the dead girl. The interment depressed Mr. Grunter until Mr. Weston told him to look at the sky. There, among a band of angels, Mr. Grunter saw the dead girl's soul singing happily. On his way home Mr. Grunter passed the oak tree which had seen the dead girl's downfall. Thinking sorrowfully of her life's end, Mr. Grunter called down a curse in her name. The effect was instantaneous; lightning struck and shattered the tree. The lightning also killed

Tamar Grobe, who was lying beneath its branches with Michael. Unscathed, Michael gave a signal, whereupon two angels appeared and carried the dead girl to heaven.

A short time later Michael and Mr. Weston met and decided that their business in Folly Down was complete. Climbing into the battered old car that had brought them, they drove out of the village by the same road they had come. As they left Folly Down, all the clocks again began telling time. Much to everyone's surprise, it was only ten o'clock.

At the top of the hill, where they had sat discussing the inhabitants of the village some time before, Mr. Weston stopped the car and turned off the motor and lights. Mr. Weston remarked that the beast in the rear of the car might like to return to his element in fire, and so Michael set a match to the gas tank. When the flames died away, everything had disappeared. Mr. Weston and Michael were gone from human sight.

MRS. DALLOWAY

Type of work: Novel
Author: Virginia Woolf (1882-1941)
Type of plot: Psychological realism
Time of plot: 1920's
Locale: London
First published: 1925

Principal characters:
  CLARISSA DALLOWAY
  RICHARD DALLOWAY, her husband
  PETER WALSH, a former suitor
  ELIZABETH, Mrs. Dalloway's daughter
  MISS KILMAN, Elizabeth's friend
  SALLY SETON, an old friend of Clarissa and Peter

Critique:

Mrs. Dalloway is a cleverly written book. The author has used the stream-of-consciousness method, encompassing within a single day the activities of Clarissa Dalloway's life and the lives of other people as well. There is little action but much intense probing of memory.

The Story:

Mrs. Clarissa Dalloway went to make last-minute preparations for an evening party. During her day in the city she enjoyed the summer air, the many sights and people, the general bustle of London. She met Hugh Whitbread, now a court official, a handsome and sophisticated man. She had known Hugh since her youth, and she knew his wife, Evelyn, as well, but she did not particularly care for Evelyn. Other people came down to London to see paintings, to hear music, or to shop. The Whitbreads came down to consult doctors, for Evelyn was always ailing.

Mrs. Dalloway went about her shopping. While she was in a flower shop, a luxurious limousine pulled up outside. Everyone speculated on the occupant behind the drawn curtains of the car. Everywhere the limousine went, it was followed by curious eyes. Mrs. Dalloway, who had thought that the queen was inside, felt that she was right when the car drove into the Buckingham Palace grounds.

The sights and sounds of London reminded Mrs. Dalloway of many things. She thought back to her youth, to the days before her marriage, to her husband, to her daughter Elizabeth. Her daughter was indeed a problem and all because of that horrid Miss Kilman who was her friend. Miss Kilman was something of a religious fanatic, who scoffed at the luxurious living of the Dalloways and felt sorry for Mrs. Dalloway. Mrs. Dalloway hated her. Miss Kilman was not at all like the friend of her own girlhood. Sally Seton had been different. Mrs. Dalloway had really loved Sally.

Mrs. Dalloway wondered what love really was. She had loved Sally, but she had loved Richard Dalloway and Peter Walsh, too. She had married Richard, and then Peter had left for India. Later she learned that he had married someone he met on shipboard. She had heard little about his wife since his marriage. But the day was wonderful and life itself was wonderful. The war was over and she was giving a party.

While Mrs. Dalloway was shopping, Septimus Smith and his wife were sitting in the park. Septimus had married Lucrezia while he was serving in Italy, and she had given up her family and her country for him. Now he frightened her because he acted so queerly and talked of committing suicide. The doctor said that there was nothing wrong with him, nothing wrong physically. Septimus, one of the first to volunteer for war duty, had gone to war to save his country, the England of Shakespeare. When he got back, he was a war hero and he was given a good job at the office. They had nice lodgings and Lucrezia was happy. Septimus began reading Shakespeare again. He was unhappy; he brooded. He and Lucrezia had no children. To Septimus the world was in such horrible condition that it was unjust to bring children into it.

When Septimus began to have visitations from Evans, a comrade who had been killed in the war, Lucrezia became even more frightened and she called in Dr. Holmes. Septimus felt almost completely abandoned by that time. Lucrezia could not understand why her husband did not like Dr. Holmes, for he was so kind, so much interested in Septimus. Finally she took her husband to Sir William Bradshaw, a wealthy and noted psychiatrist. Septimus had had a brilliant career ahead of him. His employer spoke highly of his work. No one knew why he wanted to kill himself. Septimus said that he had committed a crime, but his wife said that he was guilty of absolutely nothing. Sir William suggested a place in the country, where Septimus would be by himself, without his wife. It was not, Sir William said, a question of preference. Since he had threatened suicide, it was a question of law.

In the meantime Mrs. Dalloway returned home. Lady Bruton had invited Richard Dalloway to lunch. Mrs. Dalloway had never liked Millicent Bruton; she was far too clever. Then Peter Walsh came to call, and Mrs. Dalloway was surprised and happy to see him again. She introduced him to her Elizabeth. He asked Mrs. Dalloway if she were happy; she wondered why. When he left, she called out to him not to forget her party. Peter thought, Clarissa Dalloway and her parties! That was all life meant to her. He had been

divorced from his wife and had come to England. For him, life was far more complicated. He had fallen in love with another woman, one who had two children, and he had come to London to arrange for her divorce and to get some sort of a job. He hoped Hugh Whitbread would find him one, something in the government.

That night Clarissa Dalloway's party was a great success. At first she was afraid that it would fail. But at last the prime minister arrived and her evening was complete. Peter was there, and Peter met Lady Rossetter. Lady Rossetter turned out to be Sally Seton. She had not been invited, but had just dropped in. She had five sons, she told Peter. They chatted. Then Elizabeth came in and Peter noticed how beautiful she was.

Later, Sir William Bradshaw and his wife entered. They were late, they explained, because one of Sir William's patients had committed suicide. For Septimus Smith, feeling altogether abandoned, had jumped out of a window before they could take him into the country. Clarissa was upset. Here was death, she thought. Although the suicide was completely unknown to her, she somehow felt it was her own disaster, her own disgrace. The poor young man had thrown away his life when it became useless. Clarissa had never thrown away anything more valuable than a shilling into the Serpentine. Yes, once she had stood beside a fountain while Peter Walsh, angry and humiliated, had asked her whether she intended to marry Richard. And Richard had never been prime minister. Instead, the prime minister came to her parties. Now she was growing old. Clarissa Dalloway knew herself at last for the beautiful, charming, inconsequential person she was.

Sally and Peter talked on. They thought idly of Clarissa and Richard, and wondered whether they were happy together. Sally agreed that Richard had improved. She left Peter and went to talk with Richard. Peter was feeling strange. A sort of terror and ecstasy took hold of him, and he could not be certain what it was that excited him so suddenly. It was Clarissa, he thought. Even after all these years, it must be Clarissa.

MRS. DANE'S DEFENCE

Type of work: Drama
Author: Henry Arthur Jones (1851-1929)
Type of plot: Social criticism
Time of plot: Early twentieth century
Locale: Near London
First presented: 1900

Principal characters:
MRS. DANE, a woman of questionable reputation
SIR DANIEL CARTERET, a distinguished jurist
LIONEL CARTERET, his adopted son, in love with Mrs. Dane
MRS. BULSOM-PORTER, a gossip
MR. JAMES RISBY, her nephew
LADY EASTNEY, Mrs. Dane's friend
JANET COLQUHOUN, her niece

Critique:

Mrs. Dane's Defence belongs to the period of dramatic literature which saw the introduction of naturalism into the English theater. The attempt to portray people as they really are was coupled with another new tendency in drama—humanitarianism. Although Mrs. Dane's sin was not condoned, her weakness was forgiven by those who were really her friends. Henry Arthur Jones was one of the early so-called Modern dramatists, the school founded by Ibsen just before the turn of the century.

The Story:

Young Lionel Carteret was madly in love with Mrs. Dane, a woman three years older than he. The difference in their ages was not too important to those who loved the young man, but the nature of Mrs. Dane's reputation made them try to dissuade Lionel from his attachment. Mrs. Bulsom-Porter, a local gossip, had been told by her nephew, James Risby, that Mrs. Dane was actually one Felicia Hindemarsh.

Miss Hindemarsh had, five years previously, been involved in a horrible scandal in Vienna, when she had had an affair with a married man for whom she worked as governess. The wife, learning of the affair, had committed suicide; the man himself was still in an insane asylum. Risby, however, had since told Mrs. Bulsom-Porter that he had been mistaken. Although he at first thought that Mrs. Dane was Felicia Hindemarsh, he was now completely convinced that he had been wrong. In fact, he declared that Mrs. Dane did not even much resemble the sinful Miss Hindemarsh. But his retraction meant little to Mrs. Bulsom-Porter, who knew absolutely nothing of Mrs. Dane except that she was attractive and charming. Those qualities were enough to make Mrs. Bulsom-Porter hate her, and she continued to spread the story about Mrs. Dane's past, without admitting that there might be some doubt about her story.

Lionel had the year before been deeply in love with Janet Colquhoun, but had been persuaded by Sir Daniel Carteret, his foster father, to wait before he asked her to marry him. Sir Daniel tried to make Lionel see that his latest infatuation might also pass away, but Lionel would not listen to that well-meaning advice. He accused Sir Daniel of never having known love. What the young man did not know was that many years before Sir Daniel had been in love with a married woman. They had decided to defy the conventions and go away together, but on the night of their departure her son had become dangerously ill. She had stayed with her child, and she and Sir Daniel had then renounced their affections. The woman had been Lionel's mother. After her death, and the subsequent death of her husband, Sir Daniel had adopted Lionel, giving him his name and his love. The young man was so dear to Sir Daniel that he could not stand to see the boy ruin his life by marrying Mrs. Dane, at least while she had a cloud on her reputation.

Sir Daniel and Lady Eastney, Mrs. Dane's friend, set about to try to solve the mystery once and for all. Although Risby had retracted his story, Mrs. Bulsom-Porter would not stop spreading the scandal until she was proved wrong beyond a doubt. Mrs. Dane herself would do nothing to stop the gossip, but at last Sir Daniel persuaded her to tell him enough about her background to allow an investigation. While he was trying to piece together the facts, Mrs. Bulsom-Porter employed a detective to go to Vienna and find evidence to prove Mrs. Dane was Miss Hindemarsh.

When the detective returned from Vienna, Mrs. Dane met him first and begged him to declare her innocence. She offered him any sum not to reveal what he had learned. Consequently, when he was asked by Mrs. Bulsom-Porter and Sir Daniel to reveal his findings, he said that those in Vienna who had known Felicia Hindemarsh swore that there was absolutely no resemblance between her and the photograph of Mrs. Dane which he had shown them. His account satisfied everyone but Mrs. Bulsom-Porter. Sir Daniel, Lady Eastney, and even her own husband insisted that she sign a retraction and a public apology, but she refused. She still hoped to catch Mrs. Dane in a lie.

Because it might be necessary for Mrs. Dane to sue Mrs. Bulsom-Porter for slander, Sir Daniel continued his own investigation. He talked again with Mrs.

Dane in an attempt to find out everything about her history. She told him that she had lived in Canada for several years, a fact which made it difficult to trace her past. Then she betrayed herself by mentioning her uncle's name, for when Sir Daniel looked up that name and her relative's place of residence, he found a reference to a Reverend Mr. Hindemarsh.

At first Mrs. Dane claimed that Felicia Hindemarsh was her cousin, and that she had tried to conceal the fact because of the disgrace, but at last she was forced to confess that she was in reality Felicia. Risby and the detective had known the truth but had shielded her because they thought she had suffered enough for her sin.

Because Mrs. Bulsom-Porter was a troublemaker who needed to be cured of her vicious ways, and because no one else wished to make Mrs. Dane suffer more, Sir Daniel and Lady Eastney forced Mrs. Bulsom-Porter to make a public apology for the scandal she had caused. No one would ever know that she had been right all the time. Lionel wanted to marry Mrs. Dane anyway, but Sir Daniel persuaded her to forsake him, even though she loved him sincerely. Mrs. Dane had had a child as a result of her unfortunate earlier affair, and Sir Daniel knew that even though Lionel loved her he would forever remember that she had lied once and might lie again. Also, the man in the case was still living, though insane, and the wise Sir Daniel knew that these facts were no foundation for a successful marriage. Since Lionel would never forsake her, Mrs. Dane must use her love for him wisely and disappear from his life forever. She agreed, never doubting the wisdom of Sir Daniel's decision, and left the region without telling Lionel goodbye.

Because Sir Daniel had been so kind and wise in dealing with Mrs. Dane and Lionel, Lady Eastney accepted the proposal that Sir Daniel had made to her sometime before. She knew that she would always feel secure with him. Although Lionel thought that he could never be happy or fall in love again, he promised to try to carry out his foster father's wishes.

Janet, who had tried hard to pretend that their last year's love was over, kissed Lionel understandingly, promising him better times to come.

THE MISTRESS OF THE INN

Type of work: Drama
Author: Carlo Goldoni (1707-1793)
Type of plot: Romantic comedy
Time of plot: Mid-eighteenth century
Locale: Florence, Italy
First presented: 1752

Principal characters:
MIRANDOLINA, mistress of the inn
THE CAVALIER DI RIPAFRATTA, a woman-hater
THE MARQUIS DI FORLIPOPOLI, in love with Mirandolina
THE COUNT D'ALBAFIORITA, also in love with Mirandolina
FABRICIUS, a serving-man, also in love with Mirandolina

Critique:

This play, *La Locandiera* in the original, is one of the sprightliest comedies to flow from any dramatist's pen. From beginning to end the situations and dialogue are sparkling and vivacious. Nowhere in the play do the misogyny of the Cavalier di Ripafratta and the wiles of Mirandolina become vicious or biting. Because an atmosphere of gaiety pervades the entire work, no reader can take the pretensions of the noblemen with anything but delight. Goldoni's characters are only creatures of the stage, but during the reading there is enough of what Coleridge called "a willing suspension of disbelief" to make the comedy entirely plausible. While the play is unpretentious, it does reveal the ability of Goldoni to construct a well-knit plot that holds together in every respect.

The Story:

A Florentine innkeeper died and left his young and pretty daughter, Mirandolina, mistress of his inn. The girl continued to run the hostelry with much success, for she was as shrewd as she was pretty. On his deathbed her father had made her promise to marry Fabricius, a faithful young serving-man in the inn. She had promised the father to obey his wishes, but after her father's death she made excuses for not marrying. She told Fabricius that she was not yet ready to settle down to married life, although she loved him very much. Actually, Mirandolina liked to have men fall in love with her, and she did her best to make fools of them in every way possible. She took all and gave nothing.

A short time after her father's death two noblemen staying at her inn fell in love with her. One was the Marquis di Forlipopoli, a destitute man who, despite his lack of money, was excessively proud of his empty title. The other love-smitten lodger was the Count D'Albafiorita, a wealthy man who boasted of his money. The two men were constantly at odds with each other, each feeling that his suit should be viewed more favorably by Mirandolina. In private she laughed at both of them.

The Count gave Mirandolina expensive diamond brooches and earrings, and he also spent a great deal of money as a patron of the inn. The Marquis, having no money to spend, tried to impress Mirandolina with his influence in high places and offered her his protection. Occasionally he gave Mirandolina small gifts, which he openly stated were much better than the Count's expensive presents because little gifts were always in the best taste.

Pleased at the attentions of the Count, the Marquis, and her faithful Fabricius, Mirandolina was somewhat taken aback

THE MISTRESS OF THE INN by Carlo Goldoni. Translated by Helen Lohmann. By permission of the publishers, Longmans, Green & Co., Inc. Copyright, 1926, 1927, by Helen Lohmann.

when a guest of another kind stopped at her inn. Her new guest, the Cavalier di Ripafratta, professed to be a woman-hater. Even when he received a letter telling of a beautiful girl with a great dowry who wished to marry him, he became disgusted and angry and threw away the letter. Although his attitude toward Mirandolina was almost boorish, she seemed much taken with a man who was immune to her charms. More than a little piqued by his attitude she vowed to make him fall in love with her.

Seizing an opportunity presented by the Cavalier's demand for better linens, Mirandolina went to his room and by engaging him in conversation struck up a friendship of sorts. She told him that she admired him for being truly a man and able to put aside all thoughts of love. The Cavalier, struck by her pose, said that he was pleased to know such a forthright woman, and that he desired her friendship.

Mirandolina followed up her initial victory by cooking extra dishes for the Cavalier with her own hands and serving them to him in his room with her own hands, much to the displeasure of the Marquis and the Count because the former was of much greater rank and the latter was far more wealthy. Mirandolina's strategy began to have immediate success. Within twenty-four hours the Cavalier found himself in love with the woman who served him so well and was so agreeable to his ways of thinking.

The Cavalier, however, was much disturbed by his new-found love and vowed that he would leave for Leghorn immediately. He believed that out of Mirandolina's sight he would soon forget her. He had already given orders to his servant to pack for his departure when Mirandolina learned of his plans. She herself went to present his bill and had little trouble in beguiling him to stay a little longer. At the end of the interview, during which the Cavalier professed his love, Mirandolina fainted. The Marquis and the Count ran into the room to see

what had happened. The Cavalier, furious at them for discovering Mirandolina in his room, threw the bottle of restorative at them. The Marquis vowed to have satisfaction, but when the Cavalier accepted his challenge the Marquis showed his cowardice by refusing to fight a duel.

The Cavalier, now almost beside himself with love, sent a solid gold flask to Mirandolina, who refused to accept it and threw it into a basket of clothes to be ironed. Fabricius, seeing the flask, became jealous. He was also displeased by the offhanded treatment he had been receiving from the girl who had promised to marry him. Mirandolina finally appeased him by saying that women always treat worst those whom they love best.

Later in the day, while Mirandolina was busy ironing the linen, the Cavalier came to her and asked why she had rejected his suit. He refused to believe that she had been playing a game with him, just as she had been doing with the Count and the Marquis. In addition, he became angry because Fabricius continually interrupted the interview by bringing in hot flatirons for Mirandolina to use on the linen. After a lengthy argument, during which the Cavalier became furious and refused to let Fabricius bring in the irons, Mirandolina left the room.

After Mirandolina left, the Marquis entered and began to taunt the Cavalier for having fallen victim to the innkeeper's charms. The Cavalier stormed out of the room. Looking about, the Marquis, very much embarrassed for money, saw the gold flask. Intending to sell it, he picked it up and put it in his pocket. At that moment the Count entered and the two began to congratulate themselves on Mirandolina's success in making a fool of their latest rival. They could not help remembering, however, that she had done things for him that she had not done for them: cooked special foods, provided new bed linen, and visited with him in his room. Finally, having come to the conclusion that they were as foolish as the

Cavalier, they resolved to pay their bills and leave the inn.

While Mirandolina was bidding them goodbye, the Cavalier pushed his way into the room and tried to force a duel upon the Count. But when he seized the Marquis' sword and attempted to pull it from the scabbard, he found only the handle. Mirandolina tried to calm him and send all three away. She bluntly told the Cavalier that she had simply used her wiles to make him love her because he boasted of being a woman-hater. Then, declaring her promise to her father that she would marry Fabricius, she took the serving-man by the hand and announced her betrothal to him. The Cavalier left angrily, but the Count and the Marquis received the news more gracefully. The Count gave the newly betrothed couple a hundred pounds, and the Marquis, poor as he was, gave them six pounds. Both men left the inn wiser in the ways of women than they were when they arrived.

MITHRIDATE

Type of work: Drama
Author: Jean Baptiste Racine (1639-1699)
Type of plot: Historical tragedy
Time of plot: First century B.C.
Locale: Nymphée, on the Bosphorus
First presented: 1673

Principal characters:

MITHRIDATE, King of Pontus
MONIME, betrothed to Mithridate and already declared queen
PHARNACE, and
XIPHARES, sons of Mithridate by different wives
ARBATE, Mithridate's confidant and governor of Nymphée
PHOEDIME, Monime's confidante
ARCAS, a servant

Critique:

Presenting a theme borrowed from history, *Mithridate* is a tragedy which conforms absolutely to Racine's literary ideal: a simple action with few events. In this work Racine was much more faithful to actual fact than he had been in his earlier plays. He simply added a love story to the historical pageant to turn it into a drama: an old man in love with a young woman and jealous of his two sons. The two main characters are interesting in their complexity. Mithridate offers a contrast between the indomitable will power of the warrior and the blindness and confusion of the unhappy lover. Monime seems to combine harmoniously all the gentleness and strength of Racine's heroines. The style is versatile. Rhetorical and sometimes epic in Mithridate's speech, it also takes on an exquisite softness to express the subtlest shades of sentiments. *Mithridate* is the only one of Racine's tragedies with a happy ending.

The Story:

Mithridate, the Pontine king who had been fighting against the Romans for forty years, had just been defeated and was believed dead. Xiphares, the son who was, like his father, an enemy of Rome, deplored sincerely the loss of Mithridate. The other son, Pharnace, favorable to the Romans, was all the more pleased because he was in love with Monime, the old king's betrothed; now he hoped to win her for himself.

Xiphares had told Arbate that he had no claims to the states Pharnace was to inherit and that his brother's feelings toward the Romans were of little interest to him. His concern for Monime was another matter. The truth was that Xiphares himself had long been in love with Monime, even before his father saw her. Although he had remained silent as long as she was betrothed to his father, he was now determined that Pharnace would be compelled to kill him in order to have her.

When Monime begged Xiphares to protect her against Pharnace, whom she did not love, Xiphares finally declared his love to her. At first he was afraid that she might receive his avowal with anger. Monime, however, was secretly in love with Xiphares. They might have opened their hearts to each other at that time if Pharnace had not appeared.

Pharnace urged Monime to support his cause in Pontus. She thanked him but explained that she could not favor a friend of the Romans who had killed her father. When Pharnace hinted that another interest was prompting her, Xiphares confirmed his suspicions by defending Monime's freedom. The brothers then realized that they were rivals.

At that moment Phoedime, Monime's confidante, arrived to tell them that the report of Mithridate's death was false and that the king was returning. Monime and Xiphares, each having sensed at last the other's feelings, were stunned. Monime deliberately bade them farewell and left. Now Pharnace knew that Monime and Xiphares loved each other, and Xiphares knew that Pharnace loved Monime and was expecting the arrival of the Romans. Both, afraid of their father's anger, would be forced to keep each other's secret when they met him.

After everyone had gone to meet Mithridate at the harbor, Phoedime was surprised to find Monime still in the palace. Monime explained her realization that Xiphares had suffered as much as she did all the time they had been separated after their first meeting in Greece. Aware that she had betrayed her love without even speaking, she felt that she could never see Xiphares again because she also feared Mithridate's anger. She left hurriedly because she heard the noise of Mithridate's arrival and she did not want to face him.

The king was surprised to find his sons in Nymphée instead of in their own states. Suspiciously, he asked whether they were in love with Monime and inquired of Arbate why he had allowed them to enter the city. The governor told him that Pharnace had declared his love to Monime. Arbate said nothing, however, about Xiphares' feelings. Mithridate, relieved that his favorite son had remained faithful, was afraid that Monime might have responded to Pharnace's love. At that moment Monime appeared and he asked to be left alone with her. Mithridate told her that he wished to have their wedding performed as soon as possible. Seeing her sad resignation and suspecting that she was in love with Pharnace, he summoned Xiphares and asked his trusted son to try to turn her affections away from his brother.

Xiphares also feared that Monime might love Pharnace. Aware of his fear, Monime was unable to hide her true feelings. At the same time she declared her intention to follow her duty to Mithridate.

A short time later Mithridate called for his two sons and explained to them his plan to attack the Romans in Italy. Pharnace would leave on a mission to the Parthians, his purpose being to marry the daughter of their king, with whom Mithridate wished to make an alliance necessary to his plans. When Pharnace refused, his resistance aroused his father's anger. Pharnace, thinking that his brother had betrayed him, tried to get revenge by disclosing the love of Xiphares for Monime.

At first Mithridate refused to listen to Pharnace. Then, tortured by jealousy, he resorted to a stratagem in order to learn the truth. He announced to Monime his desire to have her marry Xiphares. When she showed surprise, asking if he were trying to test her love, he pretended to believe that she wanted to marry Pharnace instead. He declared that he would go with Xiphares to find death in battle, while she would stay with Pharnace. Monime, misled by the king's apparent sincerity, admitted that she loved Xiphares and was loved by him. After her departure Mithridate prepared to take a terrible revenge on his son.

When Xiphares came to bid Monime farewell, she accused herself of having caused his ruin by her weakness. Hearing the king approaching, he left hurriedly. Monime then reproached Mithridate for his infamous stratagem. Ordered to marry him at once, she gently but firmly refused.

At that point Mithridate was in a quandary over killing Xiphares, the son who was not only his rival in love but also his best ally against the Romans. While he was debating with himself, Arbate appeared with the announcement that Pharnace, aided by the Romans, had risen in revolt. Believing that Xiphares had also betrayed him, the king ordered Arcas, his faithful servant, to kill Monime.

Meanwhile, convinced that Xiphares

was dead, Monime had attempted to strangle herself, but Phoedime had prevented her. Still wishing to die, she welcomed the poison Arcas brought her. Before she could drink it, however, Arbate came on the run and took the potion away from her. He brought word that Xiphares had routed the Romans and that Mithridate was dying. The king, believing himself defeated, had chosen to die by his own sword.

Forgetting all jealousy, Mithridate blessed Monime and Xiphares, the faithful son who would succeed to the throne and avenge his father's death.

MOBY DICK

Type of work: Novel
Author: Herman Melville (1819-1891)
Type of plot: Symbolic allegory
Time of plot: Early nineteenth century
Locale: The high seas
First published: 1851

Principal characters:
ISHMAEL, the narrator
QUEEQUEG, a savage harpooner
AHAB, captain of the *Pequod*
STARBUCK, the first mate
STUBB, the second mate
FEDALLAH, Captain Ahab's Parsee servant

Critique:

Moby Dick, or, *The White Whale* is undoubtedly one. of the finest novels in American literature. On one level it has an appeal for children, and on another a deep and penetrating significance for all men. Melville intended to indicate in this work the disaster which must result when man constitutes himself a god and sets out to eliminate a force established by God throughout the universe. The whale symbolizes evil, but Ahab, in believing that alone he could hope to destroy it, was also evil. Here is a universal problem, handled with skill and understanding.

The Story:

Ishmael was a schoolmaster who often felt that he must leave his quiet existence and go to sea. Much of his life had been spent as a sailor, and his voyages were a means for ridding himself of the restlessness which frequently seized him. One day he decided that he would sign on a whaling ship, and packing his carpetbag he left Manhattan and set out, bound for Cape Horn and the Pacific.

On his arrival in New Bedford he went to the Spouter Inn near the waterfront to spend the night. There he found he could have a bed only if he consented to share it with a harpooner. His strange bedfellow frightened him when he entered the room, for Ishmael was certain that he was a savage cannibal. After a few moments, however, it became evi-dent that the native, whose name was Queequeg, was a friendly person, for he presented Ishmael with an embalmed head and offered to share his fortune of thirty dollars. The two men quickly became friends, and decided to sign on the same ship.

After some difficulty, they were both signed on as harpooners aboard the *Pequod,* a whaler out of Nantucket. Although several people seemed dubious about the success of a voyage on a vessel such as the *Pequod* was reported to be, under so strange a man as Captain Ahab, neither Ishmael nor Queequeg had any intention of giving up their plans. They were, however, curious to see Captain Ahab.

For several days after the vessel had sailed there was no sign of the captain, as he remained hidden in his cabin. The running of the ship was left to Starbuck and Stubb, two of the mates, and although Ishmael became friendly with them, he learned very little more about Ahab. One day, as the ship was sailing southward, the captain strode out on deck. Ishmael was struck by his stern, relentless expression. In particular, he noticed that the captain had lost a leg and that instead of a wooden leg he now wore one cut from the bone of the jaw of a whale. A livid white scar ran down one side of his face and was lost beneath his collar, so that it seemed as though he were scarred from head to foot.

2423

For several days the ship continued south looking for the whaling schools. The sailors began to take turns on masthead watches to give the sign when a whale was sighted. Ahab appeared on deck and summoned all his men around him. He pulled out an ounce gold piece, nailed it to the mast, and declared that the first man to sight the great white whale, known to the sailors as Moby Dick, would have the gold. Everyone expressed enthusiasm for the quest except Starbuck and Stubb, Starbuck especially deploring the madness with which Ahab had directed all his energies to this one end. He told the captain that he was like a man possessed, for the white whale was a menace to those who would attempt to kill him. Ahab had lost his leg in his last encounter with Moby Dick; he might lose his life in the next meeting. But the captain would not listen to the mate's warning. Liquor was brought out, and at the captain's orders the crew drank to the destruction of Moby Dick.

Ahab, from what he knew of the last reported whereabouts of the whale, plotted a course for the ship which would bring it into the area where Moby Dick was most likely to be. Near the Cape of Good Hope the ship came across a school of sperm whales, and the men busied themselves harpooning, stripping, melting, and storing as many as they were able to catch.

When they encountered another whaling vessel at sea, Captain Ahab asked for news about the white whale. The captain of the ship warned him not to attempt to chase Moby Dick, but it was clear by now that nothing could deflect Ahab from the course he had chosen.

Another vessel stopped them, and the captain of the ship boarded the *Pequod* to buy some oil for his vessel. Captain Ahab again demanded news of the whale, but the captain knew nothing of the monster. As the captain was returning to his ship, he and his men spotted a school of six whales and started after them in their rowboats. While Starbuck and Stubb rallied their men into the *Pequod's* boats, their rivals were already far ahead of them. But the two mates urged their crew until they outstripped their rivals in the race and Queequeg harpooned the largest whale.

Killing the whale was only the beginning of a long and arduous job. After the carcass was dragged to the side of the boat and lashed to it by ropes, the men descended the side and slashed off the blubber. Much of the body was usually demolished by sharks, who streamed around it snapping at the flesh of the whale and at each other. The head of the whale was removed and suspended several feet in the air, above the deck of the ship. After the blubber was cleaned, it was melted in tremendous try-pots, and then stored in vats below deck.

The men were kept busy, but their excitement increased as their ship neared the Indian Ocean and the probable sporting grounds of the white whale. Before long they crossed the path of an English whaling vessel, and Captain Ahab again demanded news of Moby Dick. In answer, the captain of the English ship held out his arm, which from the elbow down consisted of sperm whalebone. Ahab demanded that his boat be lowered at once, and he quickly boarded the deck of the other ship. The captain told him of his encounter, and warned Captain Ahab that it was foolhardy to try to pursue Moby Dick. When he told Ahab where he had seen the white whale last, the captain of the *Pequod* waited for no civilities, but returned to his own ship to order the course changed to carry him to Moby Dick's new feeding ground.

Starbuck tried to reason with the mad captain, to persuade him to give up this insane pursuit, but Ahab seized a rifle and in his fury ordered the mate out of his cabin.

Meanwhile, Queequeg had fallen ill with a fever. When it seemed almost certain he would die, he requested that the carpenter make him a coffin in the shape of a canoe, according to the custom of his tribe. The coffin was then placed in the cabin with the sick man, but as yet there was no real need for it. Queequeg recovered from his illness and rejoined his shipmates. He used his coffin as a sea chest and carved many strange designs upon it.

The sailors had been puzzled by the appearance early in the voyage of the Parsee, Fedallah. His relationship to the captain could not be determined, but that he was highly regarded was evident. Fedallah had prophesied that the captain would die only after he had seen two strange hearses for carrying the dead upon the sea, one not constructed by mortal hands, and the other made of wood grown in America. But he said that the captain himself would have neither hearse nor coffin for his burial.

A terrible storm arose one night. Lightning struck the masts so that all three flamed against the blackness of the night, and the men were frightened by this omen. It seemed to them the hand of God was motioning them to turn from the course to which they had set themselves and return to their homes. Only Captain Ahab was undaunted by the sight. He planted himself at the foot of the mast and challenged the god of evil which the fire symbolized for him. He vowed once again his determination to find and kill the white whale.

A few days later a cry rang through the ship. Moby Dick had been spotted. The voice was Captain Ahab's, for none of the sailors, alert as they had been, had been able to sight him before their captain. Then boats were lowered and the chase began, with Captain Ahab's boat in the lead. As he was about to dash his harpoon into the side of the mountain of white, the whale suddenly turned on the boat, dived under it, and split it into pieces. The men were thrown into the sea, and for some time the churning of the whale prevented rescue. At length Ahab ordered the rescuers to ride into the whale and frighten him away, so he and his men might be picked up. The rest of that day was spent chasing the whale, but to no avail.

The second day the men started out again. They caught up with the whale and buried three harpoons in his white flanks. But he so turned and churned that the lines became twisted, and the boats were pulled every way, with no control over their direction. Two of them were splintered, and the men hauled out of the sea, but Ahab's boat had not as yet been touched. Suddenly it was lifted from the water and thrown high into the air. The captain and the men were quickly picked up, but Fedallah was nowhere to be found.

When the third day of the chase began, Moby Dick seemed tired, and the Pequod's boats soon overtook him. Bound to the whale's back by the coils of rope from the harpoon poles they saw the body of Fedallah. The first part of his prophecy had been fulfilled. Moby Dick, enraged by his pain, turned on the boats and splintered them. On the Pequod Starbuck watched and turned the ship toward the whale in the hope of saving the captain and some of the crew. The infuriated monster swam directly into the Pequod, shattering the ship's timbers. Ahab, seeing the ship founder, cried out that the Pequod—made of wood grown in America—was the second hearse of Fedallah's prophecy. The third prophecy, Ahab's death by hemp, was fulfilled when rope from Ahab's harpoon coiled around his neck and snatched him from his boat. All except Ishmael perished. He was rescued by a passing ship after clinging for hours to Queequeg's canoe-coffin, which had bobbed to the surface as the Pequod sank.

THE MOCK ASTROLOGER

Type of work: Drama
Author: Pedro Calderón de la Barca (1600-1681)
Type of plot: Farce
Time of plot: Seventeenth century
Locale: Madrid
First presented: c. 1624

Principal characters:
MARÍA, a girl of Madrid
JUAN DE MEDRANO, an impoverished young nobleman
DON CARLOS, his friend
DON DIEGO, a wealthy nobleman in love with María
MORÓN, his servant
BEATRIZ, María's servant
LEONARDO, María's father
DOÑA VIOLANTE, a woman in love with Juan

Critique:

If Lope de Vega wrote plays at an early age, Calderón was no less precocious. When his *El mejor amigo, el muerto (Death, the Best Friend)* was published in 1657, it was announced as the work of a nine-year-old boy. And in his letter of 1680 to his friend the Duke of Veragua, he stated that *El carro del cielo (Cart of Heaven)* was completed when he was thirteen. Very likely he was practicing the art of playwriting before he was graduated from the University of Salamanca in 1619—certainly immediately afterward. At any rate, Hartzenbusch dates *The Mock Astrologer* before 1622 because of its mingling of Tirso de Molina and Lope de Vega, and all critics put it before 1625, when Calderón went into military service. Because of the many pirated copies by publishers and actors, it quickly appeared in several authorized versions before being included, with additional scenes, in Part II of his *Collected Plays* in 1637, a volume reissued posthumously by Calderón's friend, Juan de Vera Tassis, in 1682. In this satire on grafters and impostors there is no deep philosophy and little beyond a fast moving farce. The first scene of Act II provides a good sample of the belabored language of Gongorism as Diego pleads his love in baroque style and María replies in language no less flowery and figurative. Only the servant brings the speakers down to earth. There is no moral lesson,

unless Morón's insistence that one cannot trust a woman with a secret is so regarded.

The Story:

Looking from the balcony of her Madrid home, María watched Juan de Medrano ride by, courting her from a distance as he had been doing for two years, and she was moved to confess to her servant Beatriz that she much preferred him to the more aggressive Don Diego. But Juan was at last tired of seeing María only at a distance. That afternoon he came to call, with the excuse that next day he was leaving for the wars in Flanders. María postponed their farewells until that night, when Beatriz would bring Juan to her mistress' room.

Don Diego, also deciding on direct action, next arrived with a highly rhetorical demand for her affections. Claiming inability to understand his proposal, María turned him down in the same kind of jargon. Angered, Don Diego directed his servant Morón to try to learn from Beatriz how his mistress might be approached. Though the gift of a gold chain did not open her mouth, the gracioso knew she would in time tell him everything.

Juan had another secret. He wanted his friend Don Carlos to spread the story of his departure for the army, while really providing him with lodgings. The first

2426

step was to send his farewells to Doña Violante, an errand gladly performed by Don Carlos because with Juan away he thought he could win the lady for himself.

The next morning, as she was sneaking Juan out of María's house, materialistic Beatriz reflected on how silly aristocratic ladies were. They would not be seen talking to a man on the street for fear of gossip; instead, they entertained him secretly in their rooms. But this time the secret was not kept. Morón wormed out of Beatriz all the details of Juan's visit and ran with them to his master. Don Diego elaborated on the story while passing it on to his friend Antonio, and it grew greater as the latter tried to get the true facts from Don Carlos. Exasperated and resentful, Don Diego decided to confront María and levy on her affections.

When Don Diego mentioned Juan's nocturnal visit to María, the girl was sure that her servant had gossiped indiscreetly. To protect Beatriz, whom he loved, Morón explained that Don Diego was an astrologer who could summon up demons and who knew the past and the future. Don Diego did not deny this claim. In fact, when María's father Leonardo came up to them, he was predicting an impoverished husband for her. The father, having had experiences with magicians, did not believe in them, and he would have unmasked Don Diego if Morón had not cleverly saved his master from disclosure.

Don Diego's friends, passing on the story, convinced Doña Violante of Don Diego's powers, and she begged him to materialize the absent Juan. To his protest that his power could not cross water, she replied that, according to a letter just delivered by Don Carlos, he was in Zaragoza. At Don Diego's prompting, Doña Violante wrote Juan a letter inviting him to visit her. The note, mysteriously delivered by Don Carlos, brought Juan to her house. There he frightened her and he himself became thoroughly confused, since he knew nothing about the pretended astrologer.

Juan was more eager than ever to see María. Since Leonardo did not know him, he presented himself as a friend of Leonardo's brother, just arrived from Zaragoza. María gave him a ribbon with a costly pin and told him to sell it in order to provide himself with spending money. Then, scheming to bring him back to her, she told her father that the pin had been stolen. Leonardo hurried to consult Don Diego. Since Beatriz had already babbled the new developments to Morón, Don Diego appeared to have miraculous powers, and Leonardo went in search of Juan. Discovered and fearing for María's reputation, Juan confessed to the theft. Angered, Leonardo refused Juan's request to marry María.

His supposed magic prowess brought Don Diego nothing but trouble. Even his servant was claiming a share in his strange powers and was trying to send another servant on an aerial journey to his home town. Then Don Diego angered Doña Violante by refusing her a spell that would kill Juan and María. Meanwhile, he was no further advanced in his own courtship. The conflicting prophesies he had given, hoping that some might come true, caused everyone to turn against him. Then Beatriz explained how he had secured his information. Finally, the mock astrologer renounced all claims to magic powers, but not before he had accomplished one good deed. His action in the jewel robbery reunited María and Juan after the whole truth had been revealed.

MODERN CHIVALRY

Type of work: Novel
Author: Hugh Henry Brackenridge (1748-1816)
Type of plot: Picaresque satire
Time of plot: First years of the United States
Locale: Pennsylvania
First published: 1792-1815

Principal characters:
CAPTAIN JOHN FARRAGO, a gentleman of Pennsylvania
TEAGUE O'REGAN, the captain's Irish servant, a rascal
DUNCAN FERGUSON, another servant of the captain

Critique:

The application of the term novel to *Modern Chivalry* is almost incorrect; it is, rather, a bulky, episodic narrative that is almost completely devoid of plot. The real importance of the novel lies in the fact that it heralded the appearance of something new in early American fiction: satire. It is a brilliant and ironic inquiry into the faults and weaknesses of political activities during the first years of the United States, written by a man who had taken part in the incidents of those years, including the Whiskey Rebellion. Like all great satires, it was written, not with the aim of simply finding fault, but with the aim of improving what the author saw as weaknesses in the persons and institutions of mankind. Currish as the satire is, and unkind as it sometimes appears to be to the Irish as they are seen in the person of Teague O'Regan, the book is also humorous in a quizzical and often reflective way. Among other things, *Modern Chivalry* brought the spirit of Cervantes, Rabelais, and Montaigne to the American frontier.

The Story:

Captain John Farrago, a Pennsylvanian in his fifties, decided to get on his horse and, accompanied by his servant Teague O'Regan, to travel about the country. He wanted to see how things were getting on and to observe human nature.

His first adventure was at a horse-race. After the race the crowd became embroiled in arguments. When the captain tried to calm them, in the name of reason, he had his head broken for his pains. Starting out again the next morning, Captain Farrago came to a village where the election of a legislator was taking place. The candidate, a weaver, was not, in the captain's opinion, worthy of the office, and so he spoke out against the backwoods politician. Much to his dismay, the villagers wanted to send Teague, Captain Farrago's servant, as their elected representative. The captain finally convinced his Irish servant, who had far more brawn than brains, that he was better off as a servant of one man than as the servant of many.

A short time later the captain found the carcass of a very large owl. Upon taking it to a town, he met a philosopher who offered to have him made a member of the philosophical society on the basis of his discovery. When Captain Farrago refused, the philosopher asked if the servant Teague might be made a member. Once again the captain had to convince simple Teague that he was better off as a private servant than he would be chasing over the country after dangerous animals.

That same night Teague got into a scrape at an inn, where he tried to get into bed with a girl who raised a great hue and cry. Teague, a cunning chap, shifted the blame to a young clergyman by claiming that the clergyman had attempted to molest the girl and that he, Teague, had been her rescuer. The tale got out, and Captain Farrago finally had to bribe Teague with half a crown to tell the truth to the presbytery in order to clear the innocent preacher's good name. Teague, by means of blarney and flattery, convinced the presbytery that he wished to be a candidate for the ministry; only the captain's intercession with an explanation that Teague would have to give up his vices and enter into a war with the devil himself prevented the gullible clergymen from taking Teague, ignorant as he was, into the ministry.

Sometime later Captain Farrago met a Miss Fog. In his efforts to court the young lady, who had a considerable fortune, Captain Farrago only managed to insult her. Miss Fog's other suitor, Jacko, then challenged the captain to a duel. Captain Farrago, after warning the man who delivered the challenge that such conduct was against the law, kicked him out of his quarters. Calling in Teague, the captain offered to let him fight the duel if he wished; Teague, a coward, refused to do so, whereupon Captain Farrago sent a letter telling Jacko that he would not duel because one of them might be hurt or killed for no reason at all. That was the end of the matter.

Not long afterward a man approached Captain Farrago and asked to hire Teague from the captain. The man, a maker of treaties with the Indians, wanted to use Teague as a bogus chief of the Kickapoo tribe. He pointed out that the government wanted treaties and that he was going to provide treaties; he received a good salary for his work, in addition to making money from the gifts that were given to his bogus chieftains. Captain Farrago, an honest man, refused to be a party to the scheme. Fearing that Teague might take to the idea of easy money, Captain Farrago told him to stay away from the maker of treaties, lest the latter take Teague's scalp. Simple-minded Teague, fearful for his life, stayed his distance, and the man gave up his fraudulent plan.

Having kept his servant from becoming everything thus far, the captain soon faced a new problem. Teague imagined himself in love with a beautiful young woman considerably above his station, and nothing Captain Farrago could say swayed him from his illusion. In a final effort to bring Teague to his senses, Captain Farrago told the girl's brother what was happening. The brother, by a judicious and heavy application of a horsewhip, cured Teague of his matrimonial aspirations for the time being.

Later in their wanderings the captain and Teague stopped overnight at the home of a widow who took a fancy to Teague. Teague, anxious to improve his lot, flattered the woman, and the two quickly decided to get married, much to Captain Farrago's disgust. Only the captain's friendly warning to Teague that the widow might prove to be a witch or sorceress, so quickly had she won his affection, turned the servant away from the probability of marriage. As it was, he was anxious to be gone, lest some spell be cast upon him.

Shortly afterward Teague disappeared while he and Captain Farrago were in a city. All the captain's efforts, including a visit to a house of prostitution, were in vain so far as locating Teague was concerned. At last the Irishman was discovered by the captain in a theater, where Teague was being used in place of a comedian who imitated the Irish. Teague was anxious to keep his place, until the theater manager gave him a cudgeling for paying attentions to the manager's mistress.

Captain Farrago determined to make something better of his servant while they were in the city. Dressing him smartly and impressing on him some semblance of manners improved Teague so much that the Irishman was given the post of exciseman in the customs service. Having lost Teague, Captain Farrago found himself a new servant, a Scot named Duncan Ferguson, who had recently arrived in America.

Teague, acting as an excise officer, was badly treated by the populace, who tarred and feathered him when he tried to collect duties in outlying towns. He returned hastily to Captain Farrago. Then the captain, upon the advice of a French friend, sent Teague to France. Arriving in France, Teague was taken up as a great common citizen, since there was no taint of the nobility about him. But Teague soon tired of France and returned to Captain Farrago's employ in America. Accompanied by his servant, the captain once again began his travels to observe human nature.

One day the captain arrived at a town where there was considerable discussion over the local newspaper. The citizens, dissatisfied with the editor, decided to let Teague write the editorials. When he proved unsatisfactory and was quickly dismissed, the town was glad to have the original editor return. Shortly afterward, with the captain's help, Teague wrote his memoirs. So successful was the volume that Teague was suggested for the professorship of rhetoric at the local college. Only the outrage of the faculty kept the plan from going through.

Teague's adventures finally proved too much for the Pennsylvania village, and so the captain, accompanied by Teague and a retinue of hangers-on, moved westward. Because of his learning and good sense, Captain Farrago soon became governor of a new territory, which he attempted to set to rights according to Greek and Roman tradition. Thus ended his travels, for he now found himself in such a position of responsibility that he had to cease his aimless wanderings in favor of a settled life.

A MODERN COMEDY

Type of work: Novel
Author: John Galsworthy (1867-1933)
Type of plot: Social chronicle
Time of plot: 1922-1926
Locale: England and America
First published: 1924, 1926, 1928

Principal characters:
SOAMES FORSYTE, the man of property
FLEUR MONT, his daughter
MICHAEL MONT, his son-in-law
JON FORSYTE, Fleur's former lover
MARJORIE FERRAR, an acquaintance of Fleur

Critique:

A *Modern Comedy* is part of the Forsyte Chronicles (1886-1926), in which Galsworthy pictures the life of a large, upper middle-class family against a carefully detailed background of English life. Solid and very readable, this novel is important as a social document aside from its value as literature. The volume is composed of three long sections—*The White Monkey, The Silver Spoon,* and *Swan Song*—originally published as separate novels, and two interludes. Galsworthy's social history is valuable as a record of the various currents of British life in the 1920's.

The Story:

Soames Forsyte was a member of the board of the Providential Premium Reassurance Society. Against his better judgment, the society had invested much of its holdings in foreign securities. Because the European exchange was so unstable, Soames insisted that the report to the stockholders be detailed. Not long afterward, Butterfield, a clerk in the P.P.R.S. office, overheard a conversation between Elderson, the manager, and a German. The German insisted that Elderson, who had received commissions on the society's investments in Germany, should see to it that the board made good any losses if the mark fell in value. Accused of bribery, Elderson denied the charge and dismissed Butterfield. When pressed, however, Elderson escaped to the

continent. The stockholders were outraged that the board had permitted Elderson to get away. Although Soames explained that any early revelation of the manager's dishonesty would have been futile, he received very little support from his listeners. He resigned from the board.

Michael Mont, Soames' son-in-law, was a publisher. When Butterfield lost his job with the P.P.R.S., Soames asked Michael to give the clerk employment. Butterfield prospered as a salesman of special editions.

Michael's wife, Fleur, had been spoiled by her father. She was restless, passionate, and not in love with her husband. Wilfred Desert, an artist, was deeply in love with her, but she knew that he could provide only adventure, not love. Wilfred finally left the country for Arabia. For a time the relationship of Michael and Fleur appeared happier, and Fleur gave birth to a son, whom they named Christopher.

Before she married Michael, Fleur had been in love with her cousin, Jon Forsyte, but because of a family feud she could not marry him. Jon had gone to America, where he fell in love with a Southern girl, Anne Wilmot, and married her.

A year or so after Christopher's birth, Michael entered Parliament. To help her husband and to provide herself with diversion, Fleur entertained many prominent people. One night Soames overheard one of Fleur's guests, Marjorie Ferrar, speak of her as a snob. He asked Marjorie to leave the house. Fleur was impatient with her father for interfering, but she criticized Marjorie for creating an unpleasant scene. Marjorie demanded an apology. After an offer of settlement from Soames, Marjorie still insisted on the apology and took her suit into court, Soames and his lawyer managed to prove that Marjorie was a woman of irresponsible morals. Fleur won the case, but the victory brought her so many snubs from former friends that she was more unhappy than ever.

Francis Wilmot, whose sister Anne had married Jon, arrived from America to see what England was like. He stayed for a time with Fleur and Michael but, having fallen in love with Marjorie Ferrar, he moved out after the unpleasantness between Marjorie and Fleur. Marjorie refused to marry him, however, and go to what she felt would be a dull life in America. Francis contracted pneumonia in a lonely hotel and would have died but for the kindliness of Fleur. He recovered and went back to America.

Fleur, discontented with her life in London, persuaded Soames to take her on a trip around the world. Michael could not leave until the current session of Parliament had adjourned. He was fostering Foggartism—a plan for a return to the land and for populating the dominions with the children of the British poor—and he felt that he must remain in London. It was arranged that he would meet Fleur and Soames in Vancouver five months later. Meanwhile, little Christopher would be in the care of his grandmother, Soames' wife.

While in Washington, Fleur, Michael, and Soames stayed at the hotel where Jon Forsyte and his mother, Irene, were also staying. It was Soames' first sight of his divorced wife in many years. He kept discreetly in the background, however, and saw to it that Fleur did not encounter Jon.

Back in London, with the Marjorie Ferrar affair almost forgotten, Fleur was eager for activity. When the general strike of 1926 began, she opened a canteen for volunteer workers. One day she saw Jon there. He had come over from France to work during the strike. Jon's conscience would not let him fall in love again with Fleur, but she managed to be near him as often as she could. After a single night together, Jon wrote that he could not see her again.

Foggartism having met with high disfavor and unpopularity, Michael became interested in slum improvement. Fleur, still smarting from Jon's rebuff, established a country rest home for working girls. Michael's work had taught him that the poor would never have consented to part with their children, even though keeping them would always mean privation and suffering. He realized that he was well out of Foggartism.

Soames, unhappy in an environment of post-war confusion and family unrest, spent more and more time among his collection of great paintings. One night, awakened by the odor of smoke, he discovered that his picture gallery was on fire. With the aid of his chauffeur, he managed to save many of his pictures by tossing them out the window. At last, when they could stay in the room no longer, they went outside, where Soames directed the firemen as well as he could. Then he saw that one of his heavily framed pictures was about to fall from the window above. He also saw that Fleur was deliberately standing where the frame would fall on her. He ran to push her out of the way, and received the blow himself. He died from exhaustion and from the injury. Fleur was further desolated because she knew that her own desire for death had killed her father. The death of Soames brought her to her senses, however. Michael was assured that her affair with Jon was over forever.

A MODERN INSTANCE

Type of work: Novel
Author: William Dean Howells (1837-1920)
Type of plot: Domestic realism
Time of plot: Nineteenth century
Locale: New England
First published: 1882

Principal characters:

MARCIA GAYLORD, a small-town girl
SQUIRE GAYLORD, her father
BARTLEY HUBBARD, her husband
ATHERTON, a Boston lawyer
BEN HALLECK, a moral man
KINNEY, a vagabond

Critique:

William Dean Howells had a long and distinguished career, and he was the author of nearly seventy books and countless shorter pieces. In his time his reputation as a man of letters was high. Although modern criticism places less value upon his work, *A Modern Instance* is representative of his restrained realism and still widely read for its sympathetic analysis of human character.

The Story:

In the little town of Equity, in northern New England, Bartley Hubbard was an up-and-coming young man. An orphan whose life had so far been one of great promise, he had a free and easy way about him and a ready tongue that made him a general favorite. Squire Gaylord was well pleased with his work as editor of the village paper, the *Free Press*, but not so well pleased when Bartley became engaged to Marcia Gaylord, the squire's only daughter.

One afternoon Bartley and Marcia went for a sleigh ride. In a swamp they met another cutter which overturned in deep snow while trying to pass them on the narrow trail. The women in the overturned vehicle were Mrs. Morrison and her daughter Hannah, who worked in the office of the *Free Press*. Bartley jumped out to help them. Mrs. Morrison got into the cutter by herself. Because Bartley lifted Hannah Morrison to her place, Marcia was angry enough to precipitate their first quarrel.

Hannah was the daughter of the town drunkard. Young Bartley encouraged her greatly, thinking to improve the quality of her work, but she interpreted his interest as love. Her father called on Bartley one morning, drunk as usual, and asked Bartley's intentions toward his daughter. The young editor was so vexed and infuriated that he ejected Hannah's father bodily. His foreman, Henry Bird, in his turn accused Bartley of stealing Hannah's affections. When he hit Bartley in the face, the latter retaliated with an open-handed slap. Henry fell, suffering a concussion when his head hit the floor.

The scandal was immense. Squire Gaylord took a legal view of the possibility that Bird might die. Marcia took the fight as proof of an affair between Bartley and Hannah and broke their engagement. Bartley resigned his job, even though Bird soon recovered. Bartley went to stay with Kinney, a crackerbox philosopher who cooked in a nearby logging camp.

At the camp Willett, the owner, came to visit with a fashionable party. Mrs. Macallister, one of the guests, flirted with Bartley, and he tried to curry favor by poking fun at the quaint Kinney. That same night Bartley and Kinney parted in anger, and the young man walked back to town.

After selling his horse and cutter, Bartley went to the station to catch the Boston train. Marcia caught up with him at the depot. Asking his forgiveness, she begged him to take her back. They were married that same day and left for Boston together.

In the city Bartley went to work. He turned his visit to the logging camp into a feature article which he sold for twenty-five dollars. That was the start of his fairly comfortable, although uncertain, income as a free-lance writer. Marcia and he could afford only one room, but they were happy together. Marcia's father, Squire Gaylord, came to see her once, to make certain she was married. He refused to meet her husband again.

About the time Marcia learned that she was pregnant, Bartley was offered a job as managing editor of *Events*, whose publisher was a shrewd, unprincipled man named Witherby. With a regular salary at last, Bartley moved his wife into a private house.

In college Bartley had known Ben Halleck, a member of one of Boston's older families. Marcia knew no one at all, and she often wondered why Bartley did not resume his acquaintance with the Hallecks. Now that Bartley had a better job, he did call on the Hallecks, and they at once befriended the Hubbards. Through them the young couple also got acquainted with Mr. Atherton, a conservative lawyer. Halleck cared no more for Bartley than he ever had, but he was sorry for trusting Marcia, saddled with a shallow husband. After the birth of her child Flavia, Marcia saw less and less of Bartley, who spent many of his evenings away from home.

Witherby offered to sell some stock in the newspaper. For this deal Bartley borrowed fifteen hundred dollars from Halleck. Before long he had assumed a prosperous air, and his drinking added greatly to his girth. After a quarrel with Marcia, one night, he stayed out late and became quite drunk. Halleck saw him on the street and rescued him from a policeman. When Halleck took the drunken man back to Marcia, his pity for the poor wife increased.

Kinney, visiting the Hubbards, entertained Bartley and another newspaperman with stories of his picturesque life. After he left, Bartley wrote up the tales and sold them to another paper without Kinney's permission. Witherby was upset at seeing Bartley's work in a rival newspaper, and when he learned that his managing editor had written the article in violation of ethical considerations he dismissed Bartley.

Bartley returned to free lancing. Halleck was absent from the city; hence Bartley could not repay the fifteen hundred dollars. He intended to do so, but he gambled with the money and before long lost several hundred dollars. Atherton and Halleck were confirmed in their suspicions of Bartley's moral weakness.

Marcia, returning from the Halleck house one evening, saw a drunken woman on the street. To her surprise she recognized Hannah Morrison. When she tried to talk with Hannah, the latter insisted that Bartley was to blame for her present status in life. Suspecting and believing the worst of Bartley, Marcia rushed home and accused him of having seduced Hannah. During the ensuing quarrel they separated, and Bartley took a train for Cleveland.

On the train Bartley's wallet was stolen; in consequence he was unable to send money back to Halleck. In Boston, Marcia regretted her hasty conclusions and stayed on at their house awaiting her husband's return. When creditors began to hound her, she enlisted Atherton's sympathetic aid. He and Halleck continued to look after the deserted wife. In time she thought of Bartley as dead, and Halleck wondered when he would be free to speak to her of his love.

By chance a western newspaper came into Halleck's hands, a paper in which Bartley had given notice of suit for divorce. Marcia, her small daughter, Squire Gaylord, and Halleck took a train to Indiana to contest the suit. They arrived in time to have the divorce set aside, but during the trial Marcia's father had a stroke from which he never recovered. After the trial Bartley drifted farther west and became the editor of a weekly paper in Whited Sepulchre, Arizona. He was shot there by a citizen of the town. When Bartley's death was reported, Halleck wondered whether morally he was free to ask Marcia to marry him.

A MODERN MIDAS

Type of work: Novel
Author: Maurus Jókai (1825-1904)
Type of plot: Philosophical romance
Time of plot: Nineteenth century
Locale: Hungary
First published: 1872

Principal characters:

MICHAEL TIMAR, a modern Midas
ALI TSCHORBADSCHI (EUTHRYN TRIKALISS), a Turkish political
    refugee
TIMÉA, his daughter
THÉRÈSE, a trader on No Man's Land
NAOMI, her daughter
ATHANAS BRASOWITSCH, a prosperous Hungarian trader
ATHALIE, his daughter
LIEUTENANT IMRE KATSCHUKA, betrothed to Athalie

Critique:

The name of Maurus Jókai is insep-
arably connected with the course of Hungarian history in the nineteenth century.
He began his career as a writer largely
through patriotic motives, and at one
time he was exiled because his books
were so highly regarded in the revolutionary circles of Hungarian Youth. Later he
served as a member of the Hungarian
Parliament and in the House of Mag-
nates. Although Hungarian has never
been a popular literary language, Jókai's
works were widely read and translated
into many languages during his lifetime.
Influenced chiefly by the romantic writers of England and France, he excelled
in the field of the imaginative romance,
one which depended for its effect upon a
wealth of incident and character, an involved plot mingling the ideal and the
fantastic, and an idyllic, pastoral atmosphere. *A Modern Midas*, the work of a
master of storytelling and romantic atmosphere, is typical of Jókai at his best.

The Story:

In the season of autumn gales a man
calling himself Euthryn Trikaliss and his
young daughter Timéa took passage up
the Danube on the *Saint Barbara*, a cargo
boat owned by Athanas Brasowitsch,
the wealthy merchant of Komorn, in
Hungary. Although Trikaliss posed as a
Greek trader, proprietor of the cargo of

grain carried by the vessel, the crew felt
that there was some mystery about him
and his lovely daughter, a suspicion confirmed when a Turkish gunboat was
sighted in pursuit. By quick wit and
daring, Michael Timar, supercargo of the
Saint Barbara, outwitted the pursuing
brigantine, brought the craft safely
through the perilous rocks of the Iron
Gate, and anchored it near an unnamed
island on the left bank of the river.

Seeing signs of habitation on the island, Michael went ashore in hopes of
buying fresh provisions for the *Saint
Barbara*. In the midst of several acres of
cultivated ground lived a woman who
gave her name only as Thérèse and her
daughter Naomi. Thérèse agreed to supply fruits, flour, kids, and cheese, but refused to take any money in return. She
and her daughter, she explained, lived by
barter, trading with farmers and smugglers of the district. When Michael returned to the boat for grain to offer in exchange for Thérèse's goods, he brought
Timéa and her father ashore with him.

During their overnight stay on the island another visitor, apparently an unwelcome one, appeared. He was Theodore Kristyan, who announced himself
as Naomi's betrothed. That night Michael
heard Kristyan demanding money of
Thérèse and threatening to report the
existence of the island to the Turkish

2436

government if she refused. Since she had no money to give him, he took a bracelet which had been Timéa's present to Naomi.

The next morning, after Kristyan's departure, Thérèse told Michael her story. Twelve years before her husband had endorsed the older Kristyan's note to Athanas Brasowitsch. Defaulting, the older Kristyan had run away, and Thérèse's husband had been ruined when he was forced to satisfy Brasowitsch's claims on his property. The unfortunate man committed suicide. Penniless, the widow had found a refuge for herself and her child on the island which she called No Man's Land. There they lived happily, persecuted only by the infrequent visits of Theodore Kristyan, to whom Naomi had been betrothed before his father's disgrace and her own father's death.

Euthryn Trikaliss seemed despondent when the *Saint Barbara* resumed the voyage up the river. That night the passenger called Michael to his cabin. After telling that he had taken a fatal dose of poison, he confided that he was not a Greek trader but Ali Tschorbadschi, a Turkish government official fleeing in disgrace from the sultan's wrath. Having recognized Kristyan as a spy of the sultan, he knew that the informer would hurry ahead to carry the news of Ali's coming, and he preferred death to capture. He asked Michael to take Timéa to Brasowitsch, a distant kinsman. Then, muttering some strange words about a red crescent, he died.

Ali was buried in the river. His fears proved correct. At Panscova Turkish officials came aboard the boat and demanded the person of Ali Tschorbadschi, but after Michael had reported the circumstances of his passenger's death and burial the *Saint Barbara* was allowed to proceed. Another disaster was to follow. Not far from Komorn the boat struck a snag and sank. Only at the risk of his own life was Michael able to save a small casket containing the thousand ducats which Ali had entrusted to him as pro-vision for Timéa's future.

Brasowitsch was furious when he heard that his ship had foundered with its valuable cargo of grain, and he had only a surly welcome for Timéa, who was still dazed by grief over her father's death. He and his vulgar wife having agreed that the orphan was to become a servant in their household, he paid no attention to Michael's suggestion that the grain be salvaged for Timéa's sake. He did, however, give Michael power of attorney to dispose of the cargo.

Among Michael's friends was Lieutenant Imre Katschuka, betrothed to Athalie, Brasowitsch's daughter. The officer informed Michael that army maneuvers were to be staged near Komorn, and he suggested that the sunken grain could be used to make bread for the troops. Acting on information supplied by Katschuka, Michael underbid Brasowitsch on the bread contract for the army and later, having purchased the cargo cheaply at a public auction, he proceeded to salvage the grain from the *Saint Barbara*. During the operations he found one sack marked with a red crescent instead of a black wheel. Opening the bag in private, he found in it a fortune in gold and jewels. This, then, was Timéa's real fortune, which he had bought at auction for ten thousand gulden.

Michael's first impulse was to take the fortune to Brasowitsch, as Timéa's guardian. His second was to keep the treasure and eventually provide for Timéa without allowing Brasowitsch to profit by using it in his own speculations. Having decided on the second course, he began a series of operations which soon made him the great man of the region. After disproving Brasowitsch's charges of bribery over the bread contract he offered the government a generous rental for the vacant Levetinczy estate. As Baron Michael Timar von Levetinczy he planted and bought and sold so shrewdly and successfully that he became known throughout all Hungary as a modern Midas.

Meanwhile he continued to visit the Brasowitsch household, where Timéa was ridiculed and humiliated by Brasowitsch's spiteful wife and arrogant daughter. Their cruelest jest was to let the poor child believe that she was the bride intended for Katschuka, with whom she had innocently fallen in love. The approaching wedding gave Michael an opportunity to plot Brasowitsch's ruin. Because Katschuka refused to marry Athalie without a dowry of one hundred thousand gulden, Brasowitsch, acting on hints supplied by Michael, mortgaged all his possessions to buy land where it was rumored the government intended to build a new fort. The merchant's intention was to resell the ground to the government at a high price. But on the day of the wedding the officials informed him that the fort was to be built on other lands owned by Michael. Brasowitsch had a stroke and died. Katschuka refused to go through with the wedding.

When the house and furnishings of dead Brasowitsch were sold at auction, Michael bought the property and presented it to Timéa with his offer for her hand. He was overjoyed when she accepted, for he believed that he was returning to her at last all that was hers by right. One stipulation Timéa made was that Athalie and her mother were to occupy the house as before. Michael reluctantly agreed to the request.

But the marriage proved unhappy. Timéa, although grateful to her husband, was still in love with Katschuka, and he with her. Ungrateful Athalie, hating all three, informed Michael of the true state of affairs and so added to his wretchedness. Wanting Timéa's love more than anything else, he tried in every way, but unsuccessfully, to win her unasked affection. Timéa was a faithful and dutiful wife, but no more.

During a visit to the Levetinczy estate Michael had a sudden impulse to return to No Man's Land, which he had secretly secured for Thérèse and Naomi. During his visit Kristyan appeared and ordered Thérèse to sign a contract which would have stripped the island of its valuable timber. To silence his threats, Michael informed him that he had secured from the Turkish and Hungarian governments a deed giving the rental of the island to the present colonists for ninety-nine years. When Michael left the island Kristyan tried to shoot him. Forgiving the act, Michael offered Kristyan an opportunity to make an honest living by acting as his South American agent in a new project, the shipment of Hungarian flour to Brazil.

The next spring Michael returned to No Man's Land. When Naomi frankly offered him her love, he accepted it without telling her that he was wealthy and already married. He returned to his home in the fall, to learn that Timéa had managed his enterprises during his absence and added greatly to his wealth. On his return to the island the next year he found that Naomi had borne his child, a boy named Dodi. Their grief was great when the baby died. Michael himself almost succumbed to fever. He was sad when the time came for him to leave the island in the fall, but he rejoiced to find another Dodi in the cradle when he returned the next year.

At last Michael decided that he could bear his double life no longer. For a time he thought of committing suicide and willing all his possessions to Timéa, but he found it impossible to contemplate giving up forever his idyllic life with Naomi. While he was trying to find a way out of his dilemma he went to inspect one of his fishing enterprises. There Kristyan arrived to accuse him of theft. Kristyan, having abused Michael's trust, had been sent to the galleys in Brazil and from his father, a fellow prisoner, he had heard the full story of Tschorbadschi's activities. Suspecting the source of Michael's wealth, he had returned to denounce his benefactor. He offered to hold his tongue, however, if Michael would give up No Man's Land and Naomi. While the two men talked, Kristyan, scoffing at all promises of great wealth for himself, took off his own ragged clothing and put on a suit belonging to Michael. Then he started off across a frozen lake to make his accusations. Michael followed with the intention of drowning himself. As he approached a crack in the ice he saw Kristyan's floating body. The knave had accidentally fallen in and had drowned.

The body found at the time of the spring thaws was identified as Michael's because of the suit the dead man wore and a purse in one of the pockets. Everyone mourned the death of the great Baron Levetinczy, who was honored by an impressive state funeral. After a proper period of mourning Timéa married Katschuka. Jealous Athalie went to prison after an attempt to kill Timéa on her wedding day. And on No Man's Land, surrounded by three generations of their descendants, Michael and Naomi lived to a contented and peaceful old age. All trade of the colony was carried on by barter. Wise old Michael would never allow money, the breeder of selfishness, misery, and crime, to be used or kept on the island where he ruled as a beloved patriarch.

MOLL FLANDERS

Type of work: Novel
Author: Daniel Defoe (1660-1731)
Type of plot: Picaresque romance
Time of plot: Seventeenth century
Locale: England and the American colonies
First published: 1722

Principal characters:
MOLL FLANDERS, a female rogue
ROBIN, her first husband
A SEA CAPTAIN, Moll's half-brother and husband
JEMMY E., a rogue

Critique:

The complete original title of this remarkable volume was as follows: *The Fortunes and Misfortunes of the famous Moll Flanders, who was born in Newgate, and during a life of continued variety, for threescore years, besides her childhood, was twelve years a Whore, five times a Wife (thereof once to her own brother), twelve years a Thief, eight years a transported Felon in Virginia, at last grew rich, lived honest, and died a penitent. Written from her own Memorandums.* As this title suggests, the heroine of the story is perhaps the world's best-known female picaroon. Like the story of *Robinson Crusoe,* this book is so convincingly written, with such a wealth of intimate detail, the reader feels it must be true.

The Story:

When her mother was transported to the colonies as a felon, eighteen-month-old Moll Flanders was left without family or friends to care for her. For a time she was befriended by a band of gipsies, who deserted her in Colchester. There the child was a charge of the parish. Becoming a favorite of the wife and daughters of the mayor, Moll received gentle treatment and no little attention and flattery.

At the age of fourteen Moll Flanders was again left without a home. When her indulgent instructress died, she was taken in service by a kindly woman of means,

receiving instruction along with the daughters of the family. In all but wealth Moll was superior to these daughters. During her residence there she lost her virtue to the oldest son of the family and secretly became his mistress. Later when Robin, the youngest son, made her a proposal of marriage, she accepted him. At the end of five years Robin died. Soon afterward Moll married a spendthrift draper, who quickly went through her savings and was imprisoned. In the meantime Moll took lodgings at the Mint. Passing as a widow, she called herself Mrs. Flanders.

Her next venture in matrimony was with a sea captain with whom she sailed to the Virginia colony. There she discovered to her extreme embarrassment that she was married to her own half-brother. After eight years of residence in Virginia she returned to England to take up her residence at Bath. In due time she became acquainted with a gentleman whose wife was demented. Moll helpfully nursed him through a serious illness. Later she became his mistress. When she found herself with child she made arrangements for her lying-in, sent the child to nurse, and rejoined her companion. During the six years in which they lived together, she gave birth to three children and saved enough money to support herself after the gentleman had regretted his indiscretions and left her.

Next the ambitious girl met a banker

with whom she carried on a mild flirtation. However, she left him to marry an Irishman named Jemmy E., supposedly a very wealthy gentleman of Lancashire. Moll had allowed him to believe she had means. She soon learned that her new husband was penniless. He had played on her the same trick she had used on him. Both rogues, they were a congenial couple, but eventually they decided to separate; he to follow his unlawful profession of highway robbery, she to return to the city. After Jemmy had left her, Moll found that she was again to become a mother. Lying-in at the house of a midwife, Moll was delivered of a healthy boy who was boarded out.

In the meantime Moll Flanders had been receiving letters from her admirer, the bank clerk. They met at an inn and were married there. On the day after the ceremony she saw her Lancashire husband, the highwayman, in the courtyard of the inn, and she was able to save him from arrest. For five years, until his death, Moll lived with the banker in great happiness. After his death she sold her property and took lodgings. Forty-eight years old and with two children as dependents, she was prompted by the devil to steal a bundle from an apothecary shop. Next she stole a necklace from a pretty little girl on her way home from dancing school. Thus Moll Flanders embarked on a twelve-year period as a thief. Sometimes she disguised herself in men's clothing. A chance encounter with a gentleman at Bartholomew Fair resulted in an affair which the two carried on for some time. Moll became, after a period of apprenticeship, the richest thief in all England. Her favorite disguise was that of a beggar woman.

Finally she was seized while trying to steal two pieces of silk brocade and was imprisoned in Newgate prison. There she saw again her former husband, the highwayman, committed at Newgate for a robbery on Hounslow Heath. Before going up for trial and sentence, Moll repented of her sins; nevertheless she was sentenced to death by the court. But through the kind offices of a minister, Moll Ilanders, now truly repentant, was given a reprieve. The next day she watched her fellow prisoners being carried away in carts for the fate which had been spared her. She was finally sentenced to transportation to America.

The highwayman, with whom she had become reconciled, was awarded a like sentence. The pair embarked for Virginia in the same ship, having made all arrangements for a comfortable journey, and stocked themselves with the tools and materials necessary for running a plantation in the new world. Forty-two days after leaving an Irish port they arrived in Virginia. Once ashore, Moll found that her mother had died. Her brother, whom she had once married, and her son were still living near the spot where she had disembarked.

Not yet wishing to meet her relatives, and not desiring to be known as a transported criminal in America, she arranged for transportation to the Carolina colony. After crossing Chesapeake Bay, she and the highwayman found the ship already overloaded. They decided to stay in Maryland and set up a plantation there. With two servants and fifty acres of land under cultivation, they soon prospered. Then Moll arranged an interview with her son in Virginia across the bay.

In due course she learned that her mother had willed her a plantation on the York River, a plantation complete with stock and servants. To her son she presented one of the stolen watches which she had brought from London. After five weeks she returned to Maryland, where she and her husband became wealthy and prosperous planters of good repute throughout all the colonies. This prosperity was augmented by the arrival of a second cargo of goods from England, for which Moll had arranged before she sailed. In the meantime the man who had been both brother and husband to Moll died and she was able to see her son without any embarrassment.

At the age of seventy years, Moll returned to England. Her husband soon joined her there, and they resolved to spend the rest of their lives in repentance for their numerous sins.

THE MONK

Type of work: Novel
Author: Matthew Gregory Lewis (1775-1818)
Type of plot: Gothic romance
Time of plot: The Spanish Inquisition
Locale: Madrid, Spain
First published: 1795

Principal characters:
FATHER AMBROSIO, the monk
MATILDA (ROSARIO), his evil mistress
LORENZO DE MEDINA, a young nobleman
AGNES, his sister
ANTONIA, a virtuous maiden
ELVIRA, her mother
THE MARQUIS RAYMOND DE LAS CISTERNAS, a wealthy relative of Elvira
MOTHER ST. AGATHA, prioress of St. Clare Convent
VIRGINIA DE VILLA FRANCA, a beautiful heiress

Critique:

Although not widely read today, *Ambrosio, Or, The Monk* won instant fame for its twenty-year-old author when it was first published, and it was one of the most popular books of its day. An excellent example of Gothic horror, the book is by modern standards fantastic, crude, and stilted. Lewis, attacked by many for his immorality, was praised by others for his honesty and his vividness of description. The story is pure romance, filled with mystery and terror. The book is important because its plot was the forerunner of later novels of mystery and romance.

The Story:

Whenever Father Ambrosio talked in the church, all Madrid went to hear him. He was the most learned, the most virtuous, the most admired monk in the city. Such was his own purity that he would tolerate no sin in others, and he berated the worshipers viciously. In the audience one day was a young girl named Antonia. The girl and her mother had come to Madrid to seek the financial aid of their relative, the Marquis Raymond de las Cisternas. At the church Antonia met Lorenzo de Medina, a wealthy young nobleman who, charmed by her sweetness, promised to petition Raymond in her behalf. Before he left the church, Lorenzo saw Raymond and learned that he was the man who had supposedly spurned Loren-

zo's sister Agnes and caused the heartbroken girl to enter the convent of St. Clare. Lorenzo challenged his former friend, but Raymond begged him to hear the story and then make his judgment.

The marquis did not know the fate at that moment befalling Agnes. Father Ambrosio had intercepted a note written to Agnes by Raymond, acknowledging that the child she would soon bear was his and laying plans for her escape from the convent. Ambrosio summoned Mother St. Agatha, the prioress, and Agnes was carried away to torture and probable death. The young girl begged Ambrosio for mercy, but he was cold to her pleas. Then she cursed him, calling on him to remember her when he himself yielded to temptation.

Ambrosio was to remember Agnes' words when he yielded to the passions of Matilda, an evil woman who had disguised herself as a novice at the monastery and who was known to the monks as Rosario. Ambrosio struggled with his conscience, but his lust overcame him and he surrendered himself completely to Matilda. He could not let the monks learn that a woman was in the monastery, however, for then he would be exiled and reviled by all who now honored him.

After hearing Raymond's story, Lorenzo forgave his friend for his supposed betrayal of Agnes. Agnes, persuaded by unscrupulous relatives that Raymond had

2443

deserted her, had in her sorrow entered the convent of St. Clare. Raymond found her there and by bribing the gatekeeper managed to see her each night. When she found that she was to have his child, she sent a note to him, and it was his note, in reply, planning the escape and their subsequent marriage, that Ambrosio had intercepted. Neither of them aware of the fate that had befallen her, Lorenzo joined with Raymond in the plan to rescue Agnes.

Before the proposed rescue, Lorenzo paid court to Antonia, but her mother Elvira, fearing that his family would not permit his union with a girl without noble family or fortune, begged him not to call again until he should secure his family's permission to marry Antonia. He was unable to consult his family until after his sister's rescue. When Agnes did not appear at the appointed time, Lorenzo went to the convent and demanded to see her. For several days Mother St. Agatha told him that Agnes was too ill to receive him. When he insisted, the prioress told him the girl had died while delivering a stillborn child. Wild with anger, Lorenzo and Raymond swore vengeance on the prioress. Raymond would not believe his beloved really dead.

In the meantime Ambrosio, satiated by his lust, learned to his horror that Matilda worked magic and consorted with the devil. Although his desire for Matilda was gone, his passion for women was still great and he turned his attention toward Antonia, who had come to beg him to go to her sick mother. The innocent girl did not suspect his intentions, but her mother did. Elvira came upon them once when the monk was attempting to ravish Antonia, but the girl was so innocent that she did not understand the monk's actions. Matilda came to his aid and cast a spell so that he could ravish Antonia as she slept. The plan would have succeeded if Elvira had not come into the room. When Elvira tried to call out for help, Ambrosio strangled her to death.

Raymond became ill after learning of Agnes' fate. Lorenzo, learning from another nun that Mother St. Agatha had murdered Agnes, laid plans to have the prioress seized. Ambrosio, meanwhile, had not given up his plan to possess Antonia. With the aid of a magic potion mixed by Matilda, he took the girl to a dungeon in the monastery and there ravished her. Immediately afterward he was penitent and begged her forgiveness, but she would not hear his pleas and tried to escape from him. Fearing her escape, he plunged a dagger into her heart. She lived only long enough to die in the arms of Lorenzo, who had suddenly appeared upon the scene.

Lorenzo had obtained from the cardinal an order to arrest Mother St. Clare and to have her tried for the murder of Agnes. News of the arrest turned the fury of the mob against the prioress and she and several of the other nuns were killed by the crowd. While the mob stormed the convent, Lorenzo was led by screams for help into the cellar of the convent. There in the darkness he found a pitiful figure clutching a baby. The woman's ravings were almost insensible, and she was all but dead of starvation. Lorenzo sent her to the home of Virginia de Villa Franca, a beautiful heiress. Searching the rest of the crypt, he came upon dying Antonia.

Ambrosio and Matilda were arrested by the Inquisition. Lorenzo and Raymond learned that the pitiful woman they had saved from death was Agnes, who had been imprisoned and starved by the prioress. The love of Raymond and the kind ministering of Virginia restored her to health, and she and Raymond were married. Lorenzo for a long time lay ill of grief for his lost Antonia, but at last the kindness of Virginia healed his spirit, and those two were married also.

The Inquisitors tortured Matilda and Ambrosio to make them confess their crimes and their sorcery. Matilda confessed and was condemned to death by fire. Ambrosio, refusing to confess, was to be tortured again the following day. That night Matilda came to his cell a free woman. The devil had released her and she begged the monk to give his soul to

Lucifer and thus escape death. The monk wrestled with his conscience until his fear of the torture overcame his fears of hell, and he sold his soul to the devil.

His freedom was short-lived. Lucifer took him through the sky to a high precipice. There he taunted him with the knowledge that he would have been released by the Inquisition had he been true to his faith. The monk heard also that through the accident of a mixed-up family relationship Antonia was his own sister and Elvira his mother. Ambrosio himself was to die. The devil had promised him only release from prison in exchange for his soul—not freedom. Lucifer held the monk high in the heavens, then dashed him to death on the rocks below.

MONKEY

Type of work: Novel
Author: Wu Ch'eng-en (c. 1505-c. 1580)
Type of plot: Fantasy
Time of plot: Seventh century
Locale: China, India, and various mythical regions
First published: Sixteenth century

Principal characters:

MONKEY, a monster with miraculous powers
BUDDHA, the founder of Buddhism and Lord of the Western Paradise
KWAN-YIN, a Bodhisattva (commonly known as the Goddess of Mercy)
HSÜAN TSANG (TRIPTITAKA), a Chinese Buddhist priest
T'AI TSUNG, the great Chinese emperor of the T'ang Dynasty
PIGSY, and
SANDY, monsters, Triptitaka's disciples

Critique:

Known in Chinese as the *Hsi Yu Chi* (*Record of a Journey to the West*), *Monkey* was inspired by the pilgrimage of the Chinese priest Hsüan Tsang to India in the seventh century. Except for the priest and a few other historical personages, the novel is fantastic, with the whole mythical universe as its background. It is interpreted as a satire, with the rebellious monkey against the bureaucratic heavenly government, and as an allegory, a Buddhist *Pilgrim's Progress*. For centuries, however, the Chinese, adults and children alike, have loved this absurd story of monsters simply because of its imagination, humor, and profound nonsense. Arthur Waley has translated thirty out of the original one hundred chapters, omitting many of the calamities the pilgrim and his disciples encountered. The story before the start of the pilgrimage is preserved almost in its entirety and this alone makes interesting reading. Wu Ch'eng-en was a sixteenth-century magistrate as well as a novelist.

The Story:

In the beginning there was a rock. The rock gave birth to a stone egg and the egg developed into the shape of a monkey. The monkey became alive and played with other monkeys. He was made their king.

One day, troubled by the thought of death, he bade farewell to the monkey tribe and set out on a journey to seek immortality. He became a pupil of the Patriarch Subodhi, from whom he learned seventy-two transformations and the cloud trapeze. When he showed off his newly learned magic of transformation by changing into a pine tree, this public display of magic enraged his master, who disowned him. Monkey went back to his cave. But now he did not have to travel over mountains and rivers. One leap carried him head over heels a hundred and eight thousand leagues.

He killed the demon who had molested his "little ones" during his absence. He got the magic iron staff from the Sea Treasury of the Dragon King. The weapon could reduce, at his will, to the size of an embroidery needle. In spite of all these powers, however, his allotted life span of 342 years had come to an end. In a dream he was taken to the Land of Darkness. Furiously, he crossed out his name in the Registers of Death, together with whatever names of other monkeys he could find.

His disturbance at the Palace of the Dragon King and the Court of Death having been reported to the Jade Emperor, Monkey was summoned to Heaven so that he could be constantly watched.

MONKEY by Wu Ch'eng-en. Translated by Arthur Waley. By permission of the publishers, The John Day Co., Inc. Copyright, 1943, by The John Day Co., Inc.

At first he was happy to have an appointment from the emperor, but upon learning how humble his position as groom in the heavenly stables really was, he returned to his monkeys.

As a rebel, he called himself "Great Sage, Equal of Heaven," and he defeated the heavenly hosts sent off to arrest him. The Jade Emperor consented to appoint him to the rank he wished. Then he disturbed the Peach Banquet, to which he was not invited. By the joint effort of the gods he was caught and imprisoned in the crucible of Lao Tzu, where for forty-nine days he was burned with alchemical fire before he escaped. It seemed nothing could stop him until Buddha came to help the heavenly powers. Monkey was placed under a five-peaked mountain, originally the five fingers of Buddha's hand, where he was to serve his penance.

Now Buddha wished that some believer from sinful China would come to the Western Continent to fetch the True Scriptures. Kwan-yin volunteered to help the man accomplish his journey.

The man was Hsüan Tsang. His father, a young scholar, had been murdered while on his way to take up his duties as governor of Chiang-chou. The murderer, a ferryman, assumed the dead man's name and took his wife and office. The wife would have committed suicide but for her unborn child. Immediately after the boy was born, she tied him to a plank with a letter written in blood tucked to his breast, and pushed the plank into the river. The child was picked up by the abbot of a temple, who learned the tragic story of the boy's birth from the blood-letter.

Hsüan Tsang was brought up as a monk. He did not know of his parentage until he was eighteen years old; then he met his mother and made plans to avenge his father. The false governor was executed, on the spot where he had committed his evil deed. Suddenly a body came floating up through the water. It was Hsüan Tsang's father, whom everyone had thought dead, but who had been saved by the Dragon King of the River. Thus the family was reunited. Hsüan Tsang chose to remain a monk.

The Emperor T'ai Tsung of T'ang made a visit to the World of Darkness. He had promised to celebrate a great mass for the salvation of the hungry ghosts, and Hsüan Tsang was chosen to preside over the ceremonies. Kwan-yin, appearing in the disguise of a ragged priest, interrupted the service by pointing out that there were Three Baskets (or Triptitaka) of Mahayana scriptures for a pilgrim to bring from India. Then she revealed herself in her glory and vanished. Hsüan Tsang volunteered to undertake the quest in spite of the length and perils of the journey. His request granted, he was given a new name, Triptitaka.

He had passed several dangers before he arrived at the mountain where Monkey had been imprisoned for five hundred years, waiting for the man who, according to Kwan-yin, would release him and whom he was to follow and protect and obey as his master. When Triptitaka said a prayer, the seal of the prison was lifted into the air and Monkey was freed.

Three other monsters had received similar instructions from Kwan-yin to wait for the priest of T'ang at three different places. Because they did not know the man when they saw him, they had to be defeated in battle before they joined the pilgrimage. A young dragon devoured Triptitaka's horse, but, learning his mistake, he allowed himself to be changed into a horse to serve the priest. Pigsy, a banished marshal of the heavenly hosts, now reincarnated in the shape of a pig, had to be driven away from his human wife and father-in-law. The last to join was Sandy, a man-eating monster with red hair and a blue face, also a banished heavenly marshal.

Monkey and Pigsy sometimes created trouble. Pigsy was cowardly, lazy, self-indulgent, clumsily shrewd, and jealous of the much more powerful Monkey. But he seemed to be Triptitaka's favorite. The brilliant Monkey could not be a paragon of obedience and on several occasions he quarreled with his master. But the priest needed only to say a certain spell, and the fillet on the monkey's head began to hurt him by becoming tighter. He had been tricked into wearing the cap with the fillet and now he could not take it off. This was the only control Triptitaka, with Kwan-yin's help, held over unruly Monkey.

The travelers passed the kingdom of Cock-crow, where a Lion Demon had murdered the king and, disguised as the monarch, usurped the throne. The ghost of the dead king asked help from Triptitaka. After the king had been fished up from a well and miraculously revived, the usurper was forced to flee. He turned out to be the gelded lion in the service of the Bodhisattva Manjusri.

The travelers came also to Cart-slow Kingdom, where Taoists were the privileged class and Buddhists were persecuted. Monkey challenged three Taoist magicians, who had won full confidence of the king, to a contest of miracles. The first magician could not recover his head, chopped off in the contest, and he fell dead, leaving the corpse of a headless tiger. The second magician was found to be only a white deer, now dead, since he was not able to close his ripped-open belly. The third was fried to death in boiling oil, leaving in the caldron the bones of a ram. Monkey survived every one of the ordeals.

Monkey and Pigsy changed into a boy and a girl as bait for the Great King of Miracles, who demanded annual human sacrifice. Although the monster proved no match for Triptitaka's disciples, he captured the priest and brought him down to the River That Leads to Heaven. There the monster, caught at last, in Kwan-yin's basket, turned out to be a golden fish. A big turtle carried Triptitaka across the river. The turtle had been perfecting himself for more than one thousand years, but he was worried because he could not yet achieve human form. Triptitaka promised to ask Buddha about the turtle's wish.

The travelers, finally arrived in the Blessed Region of Buddha, began to carry the scriptures to China. But Triptitaka had forgotten to ask about the turtle's prospects. The turtle, annoyed, took a dive, leaving the pilgrims, who had been riding on his back to recross the river, and the scriptures in the water. The pilgrims were all saved, but a part of the scriptures was lost. This was the "eighty-first calamity."

Carried back to paradise after completing their mission, Triptitaka and Monkey were both made Buddhas and Pigsy was promoted to be Cleanser of the Altar. Sandy, Golden Bodied Arhat, and the white horse, who had also aided Triptitaka, were set among the eight senior Heavenly Dragons. And Buddhism prospered in China.

MONSIEUR BEAUCAIRE

Type of work: Novelette
Author: Booth Tarkington (1869-1946)
Type of plot: Period romance
Time of plot: Early eighteenth century
Locale: Bath, England
First published: 1900

Principal characters:
>LOUIS-PHILLIPE DE VALOIS, Duke of Orleans, alias Victor, M. Beaucaire,
>   and M. de Chateaurien; nephew of King Louis XV of France
>DUKE DE WINTERSET, an English scoundrel
>LADY MARY CARLISLE, a shallow aristocrat
>MOLYNEAUX, a sympathetic Englishman
>BEAU NASH, social arbiter of Bath

Critique:

Booth Tarkington achieved international fame with the appearance of this slight and romantic story of disguise and intrigue. The truism embodied in *Monsieur Beaucaire*—that a man's name is unimportant, that it is the man himself who is important—is proved delightfully enough, not by a nobody but by a real prince, and at the expense of a snobbish English aristocracy. Beaucaire duels twice in Tarkington's Bath; in the historical Bath dueling was outlawed by social arbiter Beau Nash. The story was dramatized in 1901.

The Story:

Victor, alias Monsieur Beaucaire, the barber of the French ambassador to England, gambled with the socially elite of Bath for any amount. It was the early eighteenth century, when Bath society was under the leadership of Beau Nash. One night M. Beaucaire caught the English Duke de Winterset cheating at his table. But instead of hush money, Beaucaire exacted Winterset's promise to take him, a barber in disguise, to Lady Malbourne's ball, and there to introduce him to the young and beautiful Lady Mary Carlisle.

Winterset was disgusted beyond words, for he was sure the barber would be recognized and he himself shamed before his acquaintances. Beaucaire then shed the disguise he wore and appeared before Winterset as an entirely different person. He declared that he would be Monsieur le Duc de Chateaurien.

It was dawn when the ball ended. The gallant M. de Chateaurien, assisting Lady Mary to her sedan chair, begged her for a rose. She refused but managed to drop a flower to the ground for him to retrieve. Within a short time M. de Chateaurien became, along with Winterset, the cynosure of Bath society. But Winterset planned revenge for the way in which this upstart barber had blackmailed him. Unable to expose Beaucaire without ruining his own reputation, Winterset had a captain in his debt provoke M. de Chateaurien by insulting French womanhood. In the ensuing duel, Chateaurien was victorious; he sent Winterset a basket of roses. Another of Winterset's minions then daringly suggested that M. de Chateaurien was an impostor. The Frenchman, avowedly fighting to defend the honor of his sponsor, Winterset, was victorious a second time.

All the while M. de Chateaurien gained favor with Lady Mary. After a grand fête he was granted the privilege of riding beside her coach. As they talked, Lady Mary more than tacitly confessed her love for the supposed duke. Armed and masked horsemen suddenly attacked M. de Chateaurien and shouted that they intended to kill the barber. He defended himself skillfully, but was finally overcome by superior numbers. As he was being prepared for a lashing, his servants rode up in force and dispersed the attackers. Winterset, who was the leader of the attackers, returned to the coach and disclosed to Lady Mary that M. de Chateaurien was an impostor who had blackmailed Winterset into sponsoring his introduction to Bath society. To the horror of Lady Mary, M. de Chateaurien confessed that he was really a barber. Also he promised to see Winterset at the assembly in a week's time.

The assembly progressed under the watchful eye of Beau Nash. The Chateaurien affair was on every tongue, and Winterset, now the hero of Bath, was again Lady Mary's favorite. Beau Nash assured Winterset that the house and grounds were being guarded, that it would be impossible for the ridiculous barber to enter.

As the Marquis de Mirepoix, the French ambassador, and the Comte de Beaujolais entered the house, Lady Mary retired to a side room where she discovered Molyneaux, a Bath dandy, and M. de Chateaurien playing cards. She vilified Molyneaux for associating with a common barber, and she refused to heed M. de Chateaurien's plea to her to consider him not as a name, but as a man.

Winterset, upon being told of the barber's presence at the assembly, prepared to eject the impostor forcibly. The decorations and orders on the Frenchman's chest aroused indignation among the English gentry. Molyneaux returned from the ballroom with the Comte de Beaujolais, who addressed M. de Chateaurien as Phillipe. It soon became evident that M. de Chateaurien and de Beaujolais were brothers, and that de Beaujolais had come to England to escort Phillipe back to France now that certain family problems had been resolved.

M. de Chateaurien, or Prince Louis-Phillipe de Valois, Duke of Orleans, shamed the Englishmen present for their blindness. He said that the humblest French peasant would have recognized his high nobility if he had seen the sword fight of a week previous. He exposed Winterset as a base coward and a cheat. When Lady Mary asked the prince's forgiveness, he said that he would return to France and marry the lady that his uncle, King Louis XV, had chosen for him; he was sure that she would accept him whether he were Victor, the barber; M. Beaucaire, the gambler; M. Chateaurien, the gentleman, or Prince Louis-Phillipe, nephew of the king.

MONSIEUR D'OLIVE

Type of work: Drama
Author: George Chapman (c. 1559-1634)
Type of plot: Romantic comedy
Time of plot: Seventeenth century
Locale: An imaginary dukedom near France
First presented: 1604

Principal characters:
VANDOME, a gentleman
MONSIEUR D'OLIVE, a fop
ST. ANNE, a count
MARCELLINA, a countess
EURIONE, her sister

Critique:

The most entertaining part of this drama is the subplot, which is concerned with the action, or inaction, of d'Olive, a fluent, self-assured fop. D'Olive's ill-fated mission to France is a satire on certain English embassies of the seventeenth century that were distinguished by magnificent preparations and long delays. Also ridiculed is King James's wholesale creation of knights. Although these events are of little interest today, Chapman's treatment of them retains its power to amuse, mainly because of the delightful character of d'Olive.

The Story:

On returning home after three years of travel, Vandome was greeted with two pieces of bad news. First, he heard that his friend Marcellina, the wife of Count Vaumont, had gone into voluntary exile: shutting herself in her curtained chamber, she had resolved never again to be seen in the light. This unusual behavior had been her response to the unjust accusations of her husband. Before Vandome left on his travels, Marcellina had carried on with him a circumspect and perfectly acceptable platonic affair. When he left, she had spoken of him with such passion that Vaumont had been filled with jealousy and had asserted that the relationship went beyond the purely spiritual. Vaumont later realized that he had made an error, but it was too late to dissuade Marcellina from her action.

Vandome's second piece of bad news concerned the equally eccentric behavior of the Count St. Anne. St. Anne's wife, who was Vandome's sister, had died. His devotion to her was so great that he refused to have the corpse buried. Instead, he had her body embalmed and placed in a chair in his chamber. With sad music playing in the background, he was weeping out his life at her feet. When Vandome learned of these problems, he determined to find solutions.

Forcing his way past the servants, he entered Marcellina's chamber. He called her course of action stupid and implored her to abandon it, but she was unmoved and refused to answer him. Sharing her isolation was her sister Eurione, who had been a close friend of St. Anne's wife. Eurione claimed that she had gone into seclusion in honor of the dead woman. In reality, however, she had become a recluse because of her love for St. Anne, a love that developed from her observation of the amazing fidelity of the bereaved husband for his dead wife. Eurione now revealed to Vandome her feeling toward St. Anne, and asked his help.

Meanwhile, measures to help St. Anne were being contemplated in another quarter. Duke Philip had decided to ask the King of France to intervene. He planned to petition the king, who was the uncle of St. Anne's wife, to demand the burial of the corpse. Since it was necessary to send an emissary to the king, Monsieur d'Olive was recommended for the post. Two courtiers, Roderigue and Mugeron, had suggested d'Olive, partly for selfish reasons and partly for amusement. D'Olive—an idler, wit, and man about town—had agreed to consult with the duke, mostly for amusement. In his interview with Duke Philip, d'Olive declined to accept advice about the mission. Instead, he gave a learned talk on the advantages and disadvantages of using tobacco. Duke Philip, pleased with his wit, appointed him the ducal envoy.

Vandome, who had a marked physical resemblance to his dead sister, used this fact to establish a bond with St. Anne on his first visit to the widower. While St. Anne readily accepted the friendship of Vandome, he was deaf to suggestions that he seek a new love or that he bury his wife's body. On his second visit, Vandome declared love for Eurione and appealed to St. Anne for his help. The count, out of affection for his brother-in-law, agreed to visit Eurione and try to advance the suitor's cause.

D'Olive proceeded slowly with his preparations for his journey. Having dismissed St. Anne's affliction as stupidity, he turned his attention to the more important business of forming a retinue. He had no difficulty in collecting followers; in fact, they soon became a nuisance to him. Many people felt that a trip to France as members of an embassy would revolutionize their lives, that they would return with exquisite manners and new-found wisdom. After Mugeron had collected bribes from the applicants, d'Olive assigned them, according to his whim, to the rank of gentleman or yeoman.

When St. Anne visited Eurione, she adroitly succeeded in acting and speaking as the dead woman had done in life. Suddenly St. Anne discovered that all his deep emotions had been transferred to Eurione. After leaving her, he spoke aloud to himself of his passion, and was overheard by Vandome. Vandome, after first calling St. Anne a traitor, revealed that he had only feigned love for Eurione, that she was, in reality, in love with St. Anne.

All the attention that d'Olive had received as a result of his ambassadorship began to go to his head. While he was congratulating himself on his great fame Roderigue came and told him that the trip had been canceled because St. Anne had buried his dead wife. Mugeron rebuked d'Olive for having taken such a long time with his preparations. D'Olive, after first refusing to believe the news, decided to sever completely his connection with the court. His followers, he said, could take care of themselves.

Roderigue and Mugeron, who profited from having d'Olive in the court, were now faced with the problem of getting him back. They decided that his most vulnerable side was his interest in women. Accordingly, they forged a love letter to him from Hieronime, a lady of the court whom he liked. The letter told him to come in disguise to her chamber between two and three o'clock.

Vandome, having successfully solved St. Anne's problem, now turned his attention to Marcellina. Standing outside her window, he shouted that he brought bad news and that she must come out. When she had reluctantly come from her room, he told her that her husband had become a libertine. With help from Eurione, he fabricated a lurid story of Vaumont's activities. He claimed that Hieronime was the current object of his lasciviousness, and that she, disliking his attentions, was planning to expose him to public shame. When it was suggested that Vaumont might suffer castration or death for his behavior, Marcellina decided that she would break her vows in order to save him.

When Vandome's group arrived outside Hieronime's chamber, d'Olive was there, preparing to enter. Hidden nearby were Mugeron, Roderigue, and Duke Philip. Now that Marcellina's vows were fully broken, Vandome revealed his trickery, but to insure that she did not hurry back to her room he told Duke Philip that she had come out of seclusion to see

2452

the duke's wife, who was ill. When Mugeron and Roderigue revealed themselves to d'Olive, he was furious with them. The duke brought peace by stepping forth and assuring d'Olive that his services would be desired in the future.

MONSIEUR LECOQ

Type of work: Novel
Author: Émile Gaboriau (1835-1873)
Type of plot: Mystery romance
Time of plot: Nineteenth century
Locale: Paris
First published: 1869

>> *Principal characters:*
>> M. Lecoq, a young detective
>> Father Absinthe, an old detective
>> M. d'Escorval, an examining judge
>> M. Segmuller, another judge
>> May, a suspect
>> Tabaret, a consulting detective

Critique:

Monsieur Lecoq is of special interest to detective story fans. In this novel we find an exciting incident in the early career of the greatest of French detectives in fiction. The exposition of the methods and persistence of Lecoq is painstakingly detailed, and we see in embryo the future pride of the French Sureté. The novel is better in some respects than much of Gaboriau's work because there is not such an abundance of the melodramatic and the theatrical. But the inconclusive ending and the problem left in the air may prove a disappointment to readers familiar with the well-plotted detective story of modern times.

The Story:

A party of police agents left the Barrière d'Italie to make their nightly rounds in a tough, sparsely settled district inhabited by thugs and cheap crooks. In that precinct the police were careful always to go in groups. Their leader was old Gevrol, an unimaginative, fearless inspector.

About a hundred yards from Mother Chupin's wineshop they heard some loud cries, and the whole party rushed forward over the rough ground. The house was closed up tight; only bands of light through the shutters gave evidence of life within. One eager young officer climbed up on a box to peer through the shutters, and his evident horror at what he saw caused the officers to hasten their attempt to break into the house.

At Gevrol's order two men battered down the door. Inside on the mud floor were three bodies, two men dead and one wounded. Swaying on his feet was a stocky man with a revolver in his hand. On the stair hysterical Mother Chupin hid her face in her apron. One agent seized the murderer and disarmed him, while another man knelt beside the wounded victim, who was clothed in a soldier's uniform. Murmuring that he had received his just deserts, the man died.

Gevrol, diagnosing the affair as a drunken brawl, was pleased that the murderer had been so quickly caught. But the young officer who had peered through the shutters expressed doubts about the case. Gevrol patronizingly asked him if he suspected some mystery. When the young man said he did, Gevrol told him he could stay with the bodies until morning and investigate to his heart's content.

After the doctors had gone and a wagon had taken away the accused murderer and Mother Chupin, the young man stayed behind with a stolid, seasoned companion, grizzled Father Absinthe. The young detective was Lecoq, who, after drifting from one job to another for several years, had decided to join the police force. With Father Absinthe to help him, he eagerly looked around the house.

His first find was an earring, half buried

in the mud on the floor. It was a diamond earring, jewelry too expensive to be found in Mother Chupin's establishment. Encouraged, Lecoq went outside. There was enough snow on the ground for him to reconstruct some of the happenings prior to the murders. Two women, one young and one older, had come to the house. They had been running when they left. A man had met them outside the garden and had led them to a cab. There the traces were lost. Lecoq remembered also what the suspect had said when he was captured, "Lost! It is the Prussians who are coming!" Only a man who knew Napoleonic history would have used that allusion. He evidently had been expecting someone to return and help him.

Lecoq presented his lucid report to the examining judge in the morning. M. d'Escorval was greatly impressed with Lecoq's report. In spite of Gevrol's insistence that the case was merely a wineshop brawl, M. d'Escorval agreed with Lecoq and prepared to look fully into the affair. Disgruntled and jealous, Gevrol ever afterward was Lecoq's enemy.

As soon as the preliminaries were over, Lecoq hurried to the police station to attend the examination of the prisoner. To his disappointment, M. d'Escorval brusquely ordered him to wait in the corridor. Lecoq overheard enough of the examination to realize that the judge seemed unwell or upset. He asked only a very few routine questions, and the prisoner's answers were almost nonsensical. In a very short time the judge hurried out and drove rapidly away.

Lecoq was curious. Looking into the prisoner's cell, he surprised the man in the act of strangling himself. Lecoq removed the band from the prisoner's throat just in time. Continuing his investigation, he learned that the night before, after the murders, a drunken man had created a disturbance outside the jail. He was locked up for the night, in the same cell with the murderer. In the morning the police let him go. From the description, Lecoq believed him the accomplice,

the man who had waited outside the wineshop and helped the two women to their cab.

The next morning Lecoq had a fresh disappointment. M. d'Escorval fell and broke his leg while descending from his carriage. There was more delay while a new judge was assigned to the examination. The new examiner, M. Segmuller, listened attentively to Lecoq's analysis and agreed that there was a mystery behind the case. At last the prisoner was brought in for formal examination.

The murderer, giving his name as May, irritatingly insisted he had no given name. He said he was a circus performer, and he gave convincing imitations of a barker in French, English, and German. His story was that he had been attacked by the three men, and had shot them in self-defense. May was returned to his cell and Lecoq continued his patient investigation.

The quest for the murderer's identity was a long hunt. Lecoq and Father Absinthe, working for weeks on fruitless clues, were never successful in tracing the diamond earring. They found the cab that had picked up two women at the scene of the crime, but the women had left the cab at an apartment house, gone into the courtyard, and disappeared through a back door.

So it went with all clues. A visitor came to see the prisoner and showed a pass issued to a relative of Mother Chupin. Father Absinthe tried to trail the visitor but lost him. Lecoq learned of the visit later. He was sure the man was the drunk who had been locked up with the murderer that first night, the man whose general build Lecoq had reconstructed from the footprints in the snow. Then, by spending six days hidden in the garret above May's cell, Lecoq learned that the prisoner received cipher notes from the outside rolled in bits of bread. Lecoq even suspected Gevrol of helping May, but he could prove nothing.

In despair Lecoq pulled the old trick of letting the prisoner escape; then he followed him closely. May joined his accomplice outside a high wall. Lecoq watched while the accomplice boosted May over the wall into the garden of the Duke of Sairmeuse. The accomplice was captured, but no trace of May could be found, although Lecoq searched the duke's house thoroughly. He learned nothing from May's accomplice, an ex-convict.

As a last resort Lecoq consulted old Tabaret, the oracle of the force. The sage listened eagerly. Then he explained logically Lecoq's errors. M. d'Escorval had conveniently broken his leg because he knew who the prisoner was and did not dare prosecute him. Lecoq could not find May in the Duke of Sairmeuse's house because May was the duke.

Lecoq had to agree; an obscure detective could do nothing against a duke who undoubtedly was engaged in some mysterious intrigue. If he persisted in trying to arrest so great a noble, Lecoq himself would be convicted as a madman. Lecoq gave up the case, but he was determined that sooner or later he would get to the bottom of the whole affair.

MONT-ORIOL

Type of work: Novel
Author: Guy de Maupassant (1850-1893)
Type of plot: Social satire
Time of plot: Mid-nineteenth century
Locale: Auvergne, France
First published: 1887

Principal characters:

> CHRISTIANE ANDERMATT, a young married woman
> PAUL BRETIGNY, Christiane's lover
> WILLIAM ANDERMATT, Christiane's husband
> GONTRAN DE RAVENEL, Christiane's brother
> FATHER ORIOL, a wealthy peasant landowner
> CHARLOTTE, and
> LOUISE, Oriol's daughters

Critique:

There are two stories told in *Mont-Oriol*. One deals with the love intrigues of Christiane Andermatt, her brother, and her lover. The other describes the financial scheming of William Andermatt, Father Oriol, and the physicians at the health resort. The fact that the love affair carried on by Christiane and Paul Bretigny is often melodramatic and unconvincing is more than compensated for, however, by the skill and humor with which some of the minor characters, such as the crafty Oriol and Christiane's witty brother Gontran, are drawn.

The Story:

The Marquis of Ravenel, who was an enthusiastic patron of the baths at Enval, persuaded his young daughter Christiane and her husband, William Andermatt, to join him. On the advice of one of the doctors at the spring, Christiane agreed to take a series of baths, internal and external, in the hope that they would cure her childlessness.

When the young couple arrived, they were joined by Christiane's spendthrift brother Gontran and his friend, Paul Bretigny, who had come to the country to recover from a disappointing love affair. During their stay, learning that Father Oriol, a wealthy peasant landowner of the district, was going to blast out a huge rock which hindered cultiva-

tion of his fields, the party went to watch the event.

To everyone's surprise, a spring came gushing from the ground after the explosion. Andermatt decided that if the water were of medicinal value he would make Oriol an offer for it, for he hoped to build an establishment that would give the existing baths heavy competition. That same evening Andermatt, accompanied by Gontran, went to the Oriol house and placed his proposal before the peasant.

Oriol, whose bargaining ability was also one to be reckoned with, decided that he would have to be careful not to ask too much for the spring and the fields around it; on the other hand, he would not let the possibility of obtaining great wealth slip from his grasp. To inflame Andermatt's desire, he engaged a beggar named Clovis to help him. Clovis, who engaged in poaching by night and feigned rheumatism by day to escape the attentions of the police, was to bathe in the spring for an hour each day— for a fee. At the end of a month he was to be examined. If he were cured of his rheumatism, his condition would prove the medicinal value of the spring.

The unsuspecting Andermatt was enthusiastic about the projected plan, and he himself agreed to pay Clovis for undergoing treatment. Meanwhile he and Oriol agreed to sign a promise of sale.

In order that the Oriol family might be won over to his project, Andermatt decided to hold a charity fête and a lottery, in which the Oriol girls and Christiane would participate.

Andermatt returned to Paris, leaving Christiane at the baths. She and her family, accompanied by Paul Bretigny and the Oriol girls, made numerous excursions about the countryside. Paul began to confide in her, to tell her of his adventures, his love affairs. As their conversations became more intimate, she realized that he was paying court to her. To inflame his desire, she held him at arm's length until finally, as they were starting back from a jaunt at nightfall, he caught at her shawl while she walked in front of him and kissed it madly. She had all she could do to master her agitation before she joined the others in the carriage.

A few days later, when the party went to view the ruins of a nearby castle by moonlight, Paul threw himself at Christiane's feet and she submitted to him.

The following morning Andermatt returned. Losing no time, the financier set about reaching an agreement with Oriol. According to the terms decided upon after much discussion, the company which Andermatt had formed was assigned the lands along the newly-created stream and the crest and slope of the hill down which it ran. In return, Oriol was to receive one fourth of the profits to be made.

Andermatt rushed back to Paris after completing his arrangements. That night Paul went to Christiane's room. During Andermatt's absence they had nearly a month for uninterrupted lovemaking. It was a blow to both of them when they learned that Andermatt was arriving within a few days and that he was planning to take Christiane back to Paris with him when he left.

The financier brought several members of the newly-formed company with

him. The terms of the purchase were read and signed before the village notary, and Andermatt was elected president of the company, over the dissenting votes of Oriol and his son. It was agreed that the baths should be known as Mont-Oriol.

That night Paul sorrowfully said goodbye to his love. He felt that, although they might meet later in Paris, part of the enchantment of their affair would be gone forever. Christiane, on the other hand, was full of plans for future meetings and ways of evading the notice of her servants.

The first of July in the following year was set as the dedication date for the new baths at Mont-Oriol. Christiane, big with child, walked with her father and brother and Paul to watch the dedication of the three new springs. They were to be known as the Christiane, Charlotte, and Louise springs, the latter two named after the Oriol girls. But Clovis, who had seemed so successfully cured the previous summer, was again doubled up by his assumed rheumatism. He threatened to become a serious menace to business, for he declared to the guests who would listen that the waters had ultimately done him more harm than good. At last Andermatt was forced to reckon with him, and Clovis finally agreed to undergo treatment every year. It was decided that his return annually for the same treatment would only prove to the public the medicinal value of the baths.

Andermatt had planned an operetta and a display of fireworks for that evening. Gontran, observing that his sister was suffering from the heat of the room in which the entertainment was beginning, sneaked out and set off the rocket which was the signal for the fireworks display to start. Everyone dashed out, to Andermatt's disgust, but he took advantage of the unexpected interlude to have a serious conversation with Gontran. Having been informed that Oriol intended to give the lands around Mont-Oriol as his daughters' dowries, Andermatt proposed that Gontran, who was deeply in debt, should recoup his finances by marrying either Charlotte or Louise. Gontran, after meditating for a few moments, announced that he would open the ball to be held later that evening by dancing with Charlotte Oriol, the younger and prettier of the two sisters.

Christiane, too, made use of the interruption. She proposed to Paul that they walk along the road on which they had said goodbye the previous year. At that time he had fallen to his knees and kissed her shadow. Her hopes that he would repeat the act were dashed, for although the child she was carrying was his, her shadow betrayed too clearly her changed form.

Gontran paid court to Charlotte Oriol at the ball and the news of his interest in her soon became common gossip at the springs. The innocent girl responded so freely that Christiane and Paul, who were fond of her, began to fear that she would eventually find herself compromised. They were satisfied, however, when Gontran confided to them his intention to ask for her hand. When he asked Andermatt to sound out Oriol, the crafty peasant, realizing that his younger daughter would be easier to dispose of than the older, said that he planned to endow her with the lands on the other side of the mountain. Because those lands were of no use to Andermatt at the moment, Gontran realized that he would have to change his tactics.

He persuaded Louise that he had courted Charlotte only to arouse the older sister's interest. He managed to meet her frequently at the home of one of the doctors and on walks, and when the time seemed ripe he sent Andermatt once more to talk to Oriol. As the reward for his efforts he received a signed statement which assured him a dowry and the promise of the girl's hand.

Paul, unaware of Gontran's and Andermatt's designs, had been incensed by the sudden desertion of Charlotte. Gradually his feeling grew to love. One day her father found them together. Partly because he was in love, and partly because he did not want to compromise Charlotte, his immediate reaction was to propose. When he agreed to sign a statement as to his satisfactory income, the peasant gave his consent to the marriage.

The next morning Christiane learned that Paul was to marry Charlotte. Her informant was the doctor who came to examine her, for she felt ill. As soon as she heard that her lover was to marry, she went into labor from the shock. Fifteen hours later a little girl was born. She would have nothing to do with the baby at first, but when Andermatt brought the child to her she found the infant irresistible, and wanted it kept near her.

Because there was no one else to nurse her, the doctor's wife was chosen to keep Christiane company during her recovery. The talkative woman knew the Oriols well, and Christiane was able to learn from her most of the details of Paul's courtship. Upset by the realization that he had given Charlotte the same attentions she had once received, she fell into a delirium for a day. The next day her condition began to improve.

When the baby was a few days old, Christiane asked that Paul be sent to see her. He went, planning to beg her pardon, but he found there was no need to do so. Christiane, engrossed in the child, had only a few conventional words for him. Although he had hoped to see the infant that was partly his, he noted that the curtains of the cradle were significantly fastened in the front with some of Christiane's pins.

A MONTH IN THE COUNTRY

Type of work: Drama
Author: Ivan Turgenev (1818-1883)
Type of plot: Realistic comedy
Time of plot: The 1840's
Locale: Russia
First presented: 1850

> *Principal characters:*
> ARKADY ISLAYEV, a wealthy landowner
> NATALYA (NATASHA), his wife
> KOLYA, their son
> VERA, Natalya's ward
> LIZAVETA, a companion
> RAKITIN, a family friend
> BELYAYEV, a young tutor
> SHPIGELSKY, a doctor

Critique:

This play is comedy barbed with psychological realism and social satire. Turgenev has presented a timeless interlude with a little Russian coloring, for the kind of atmosphere found in Chekhov's work is only lightly sketched in. The characters run a range from a near-cuckolded husband to a buffoon doctor. The main action concerns the struggle between Natalya, an older woman, and her young ward, Vera. The courtship of a neighbor and the affairs of Lizaveta and the doctor are side actions. The play reads well, but it is a little long for modern staging.

The Story:

In her drawing-room, Natalya, a twenty-nine-year-old wife and mother, was talking confidentially to her good friend Rakitin. She admitted that her husband Islayev had one fault: he went into things too enthusiastically. He was with his workmen constantly, and he himself demonstrated how they should do their work. Her complaint ended, she bade Rakitin go on reading *The Count of Monte Cristo* to her. She really had no interest in the book, but it was being discussed by her friends.

It was read aloud in the big room, where a card game was in progress. Schaaf, the German tutor, had been winning until Lizaveta, companion to Islayev's mother, made a mistake; the German grumbled at her ineptness. The doctor, Shpigelsky, breezed in and, as was his wont, told a long, pointless story. He had really come to discuss privately with Natalya a friend of his who wished to marry Vera. Natalya, claiming that at seventeen Vera was too young, put off a definite answer.

Kolya, Natalya's little son, came running up, full of news about Belyayev's doings. Now the energetic young tutor, who had been there nearly a month, was making a kite. Vera, also coming from play, told how Belyayev could climb trees as nimbly as a squirrel. Islayev tried to induce Natalya and Rakitin to look over his new blowing machine, but only Rakitin was interested.

As the room gradually cleared, Natalya had a chance to talk with Belyayev at some length. She complimented him on his good singing voice and asked about his family. She was touched to learn that his mother was dead and that he had a sister also named Natalya. In spite of her friendly attitude, Belyayev was nervous and persisted in being formal and

A MONTH IN THE COUNTRY by Ivan Turgenev, from THE PLAYS OF IVAN S. TURGENEV. Translated by M. S. Mandell. By permission of the publishers, The Macmillan Co. Copyright, 1924, by The Macmillan Co. Renewed, 1952, by Dora Mandell.

polite with her.

In the garden Katya, the maid, was listening to the butler's proposal. She had some trouble in fending him off, and the arrival of Schaaf made matters a little more complicated. Schaaf archly sang a love song and tried to kiss her. She escaped by running into a raspberry patch.

Vera and Belyayev called her out after Schaaf left. They were working on the kite and, as they worked, they companionably shared Katya's raspberries. Belyayev told Vera much of his past life, of his studies in Moscow, of his poverty. Vera described her loneliness without friends her own age. Interrupted by the arrival of Natalya and Rakitin, they slipped out of the garden.

Natalya professed to Rakitin her uneasiness about Vera; the girl was very young and probably should not be so much alone with Belyayev. Rakitin began to suspect what was happening. Natalya had always been so frank and tender with him. Now she seemed preoccupied and talked distractedly. She even accused him of having a languid mind, and she no longer cared for his descriptions of nature.

Rakitin sought out Belyayev to get better acquainted with him. He was troubled when he discovered that the young tutor hid such an engaging manner underneath his gawky exterior. Although Belyayev thought of Natalya only as an older woman and his employer, Rakitin sensed a possible rival.

Shpigelsky brought Bolshintsov, a neighbor of forty, to the house and coached him carefully on what he was to say. Bolshintsov was shy with women, but, having decided to make an offer to Vera, he had enlisted the busybody doctor as an intermediary. If the match came off, Shpigelsky was to get three horses as his reward.

When Natalya could not disguise her increasing coldness toward Rakitin, he accused her of being attracted to Belyayev. Although she proclaimed that she still loved Rakitin, she could not deny the young tutor's charms. Rakitin delicately hinted that she owed her love to her husband and suggested that both he and Belyayev should leave the house.

With Vera, Natalya assumed a sisterly air and told her of Bolshintsov's proposal. She did not press the point too much after Vera laughed at the idea of marrying such a funny old man. Instead, with mature skill, she probed into her ward's feelings and got her to confess her love for Belyayev. Her suspicions confirmed, she was torn between her inclinations as a woman and her duty as wife and guardian.

Natalya, sending for Belyayev, warned him that Vera was quite immature and that it was easy for her to misinterpret friendship. When the young man finally understood that Vera was in love with him, he was amazed; he had no notions of love at all. He resigned his job and offered to leave the house immediately. Natalya, unable to bear his willingness to leave the house, asked him to defer his decision for a while.

Meanwhile, Shpigelsky was impressing Lizaveta by diagnosing the ills and attitudes of members of the family. He reminded her that she would not want to remain a companion all her life; hence he would make her an offer of marriage. Lizaveta, adopting a coquetish manner, began a coy reply, but the doctor kept on talking. He insisted on telling her all his faults and the extent of his fortune, and then proved to her he was a fine fellow because he had confessed his faults. Lizaveta promised to give him an answer the next day. To her surprise, Shpigelsky sang a peculiar song about a gray goat.

Vera made an effort to save the situation by telling Belyayev that she knew how Natalya had warned him of the girl's love. Bitter over Natalya's efforts to get her married off to Bolshintsov, she hoped that Belyayev would confess his love for her. The young man was unresponsive. Then Vera assured him that Natalya herself was in love with him.

When Natalya found them, Vera was openly reproachful. She accused her guardian of treating her as a child when she was a grown woman. Henceforth they would be equals and probably rivals. She left in an emotional state. When they were alone, Natalya confirmed that she was in love with Belyayev. Overwhelmed by her declaration, he could think only of going away.

Islayev began to suspect that all was not well in his household, for he knew that Rakitin had been much in his wife's company. Being a forthright man, he asked Rakitin outright if he were in love with Natalya. Rakitin admitted that he was, and he added that he was going away immediately. Islayev scarcely wanted him to leave, but his departure did seem a good solution. Rakitin made no mention of Natalya's infatuation for Belyayev.

Vera told Shpigelsky that she would accept Bolshintsov's offer because she could no longer remain under the same roof with Natalya. Belyayev, not trusting himself to meet Natalya, sent a farewell note by Vera. To Islayev, it seemed peculiar that so many people were leaving at once. Lizaveta also commented to Islayev's mother that she too would be going away one of these days.

THE MOON AND SIXPENCE

Type of work: Novel
Author: W. Somerset Maugham (1874-   )
Type of plot: Fictional biography
Time of plot: Nineteenth century
Locale: England, France, Tahiti
First published: 1919

Principal characters:
CHARLES STRICKLAND, an artist
DIRK STROEVE, his friend
BLANCHE STROEVE, Dirk's wife
ATA, Strickland's Tahitian wife
AMY STRICKLAND, Strickland's English wife

Critique:

A fictionalized biography of the French artist, Paul Gauguin, this novel attempts to portray the character of a pure artist, a man of renunciation. The material world meant nothing to Strickland; man meant nothing to him, either. He lived ruthlessly for his art. There is shrewd comment on the world's attitude toward a man who passes by the material and the sensual to fulfill some spiritual need. If by chance his intent is to help mankind, then he is proclaimed a saint; but if he is like Charles Strickland, and ignores mankind, he is vested with the spirit of the devil. Maugham passes no judgment on this painter. He merely presents him as he was.

The Story:

Charles Strickland, a dull stockbroker, lived in England with his wife and two children. Mrs. Strickland was a model mother, but her husband seemed bored with her and with his children. To everyone else, it was Strickland himself who seemed commonplace. The family had spent the summer at the seashore, and Strickland had returned ahead of his wife. When she wrote him that she was coming home, he had answered from Paris, simply stating that he was not going to live with her any more. With singleness of intention, Mrs. Strickland dispatched a friend to Paris to bring back her husband.

Strickland was living in a shabby hotel; his room was filthy, but he appeared to be living alone. Much to the discomfort of the friend, he candidly admitted his beastly treatment of his wife, but there was no emotion in his statements concerning her and her future welfare. When asked about the woman with whom he had allegedly run away, he laughed, explaining to Mrs. Strickland's emissary that he had really run off to paint. He knew he could if he seriously tried. The situation was incredible to Mrs. Strickland's friend. Strickland said he did not care what people thought of him.

Stubbornly, Strickland began to take art lessons. Although his teacher laughed at his work, he merely shrugged his shoulders and continued to paint in his own way. Back in England, the friend tried to explain to Mrs. Strickland the utter hopelessness of trying to reconcile her husband. She could not realize her defeat at first. If Strickland had gone off with a woman, she could have understood him. She was not able to cope with an idea.

Dirk Stroeve, a very poor painter with a delicate feeling for art, had married an Englishwoman and settled in Paris. Impossible as it seemed, Dirk, who had become acquainted with Strickland, thought the red-haired Englishman a great painter. But Strickland did not want any man's opinion. Indifferent to physical discomfort, he had not tried to sell his paintings in order to eat. When he needed money, he found odd jobs in and around Paris.

It was apparent that the Stroeves were very much in love. A buffoon and a fool, Dirk was constantly berating himself, but Blanche seemed to hold him in high esteem. When Strickland became very ill, Dirk rushed home to Blanche and pleaded with her to nurse the sick artist back to health. She bitterly professed her hatred of the man who had laughed at her husband's paintings, and she tearfully begged Stroeve not to bring that monster near her. Nevertheless, Dirk was able to persuade her to allow Strickland to come to their home.

Although she and Strickland rarely spoke to each other, Blanche proved a capable nurse. There seemed to be something electrifying in the air when they were together in the same room. Strickland recovered. Because he admired Strickland's work, Dirk was anxious that he stay and work in Dirk's studio. Strickland took possession of the studio. When Dirk finally gathered enough courage to ask him to leave, Blanche said that she would leave also. Dirk fell before her, groveling at her feet, and pleaded with her to stay, but his adoring demonstrations only bored her. When he saw that she would indeed return with Strickland to the filthy hovel which was the Englishman's studio, Dirk's generous soul could not bear to think that his beloved Blanche should live in such poverty. He said that she need not leave; he would go. Thanking her for having given him so much happiness, he left her with half of what he owned.

Dirk hung around Paris waiting for the time to come when Blanche would need him again after Strickland had tired of her. Once he followed her when she went shopping. He walked along with her, telling her of his devotion; she would not speak to him. Suddenly she slapped him in the face and walked away. One day the police informed Dirk that Blanche had swallowed oxalic acid. After she died, Dirk felt compelled to return to his studio. There he found a nude portrait of his wife, evidently the work of Strickland. In a mad passion of jealousy he started to hack at the picture with a knife, but he was arrested by the obvious fact that it was a wonderful piece of art. No matter what he felt, Dirk could not mutilate the painting. He packed his belongings and went back to Holland to live with his mother.

Strickland had taken Blanche Stroeve because he thought she had a beautiful body to paint. When he had finished the picture, he was through with her. Thinking that the picture was not satisfactory, he had left it in the studio. The death of Blanche and the misery of Dirk did not move him. He was an artist.

After Blanche's death Strickland went to Marseilles, and finally, after many wanderings, to Tahiti. There he painted his vivid awkward-looking pictures and left them with people all over the island in payment for lodging and food. No one thought the pictures worth anything, but years later some who had saved the pictures were pleasantly surprised to sell them for enormous sums of money to English and French collectors who came to the island looking for the painter's work.

At one of the hotels in Tahiti, Strickland had been befriended by a fat old woman, Tiare, who looked after his health and his cleanliness. She even found him a wife, a seventeen-year-old native girl named Ata. For three years Ata and her husband lived together in a bungalow just off the main road. These were perhaps the happiest years in Strickland's life. He painted, read, and loafed. Ata had a baby.

One day Ata sent to the village for a doctor. When the doctor came to the artist's bungalow, he was struck with horror, for to his experienced eye Strickland bore the thickened features of a leper. More than two years passed. No one went near Strickland's plantation, for the natives knew well the meaning of Strickland's disease. Only Ata stayed faithfully with him, and everyone shunned her just as they shunned Strickland. Two more years passed. One of Ata's children died. Strickland was now so crippled by the disease that he would not even permit the doctor to see him. He was painting on the walls of his bungalow when at last he went blind. He sat in the house hour after hour, trying to remember his paintings on the walls—his masterpieces. Caring nothing for the fame his art might bring, Strickland made Ata promise to destroy this work upon his death, a wish she faithfully carried out.

Years later a friend of Strickland, just returned from Tahiti, went to call on Mrs. Strickland in London. She seemed little interested in her husband's last years or his death. On the wall were several colored reproductions of Strickland's pictures. They were decorative, she thought, and went so well with her Bakst cushions.

THE MOONSTONE

Type of work: Novel
Author: Wilkie Collins (1824-1889)
Type of plot: Mystery romance
Time of plot: 1799-1849
Locale: India and England
First published: 1868

Principal characters:
JOHN HERNCASTLE, an adventurer
LADY VERINDER, his sister
RACHEL VERINDER, his niece
FRANKLIN BLAKE, Lady Verinder's nephew
GODFREY ABLEWHITE, a charity worker
DR. CANDY, a physician
SERGEANT CUFF, an inspector from Scotland Yard
ROSANNA SPEARMAN, a maid

Critique:

The Moonstone is often called the first and best of detective stories. The true story of the theft of the Moonstone is told by several different hands who were judged best able to describe the various phases of the solution of the plot. These papers have been brought together and studied by one of the suspects, and in due time the mystery is solved. There is not as much true detection in this novel as there is in the later detective story, but the fine characterization and the humor of the book compensate for any loss.

The Story:

In the storming of Seringapatam in India, in the year 1799, John Herncastle, a violent and cruel man, stole the sacred Hindu diamond called the Moonstone. The jewel had been taken years before from the forehead of the Moon-God in its Brahmin shrine, and Herncastle's theft was only one of a series. Since the stone had first been stolen three faithful Hindus had followed its trail, sworn to recover the gem and return it to the statue of the Moon-God. Herncastle took the gem to England and kept it in a bank vault. He saved himself from murder by letting the Hindus know that if he were killed the stone would be cut up into smaller gems, thus losing its sacred identity. Herncastle left the jewel to his niece, Rachel Verinder, at his death.

The stone was to be presented to Rachel on her birthday following her uncle's death, and young Franklin Blake, Lady Verinder's nephew, was asked by Herncastle's lawyer to take the gift to his cousin. Franklin took the stone to his cousin's estate and barely missed death at the hands of the Hindus before reaching his destination. On the advice of Gabriel Betteredge, the Verinders' old family servant, Franklin put the gem in the vault of a bank nearby until the birthday arrived, as the Hindus had been seen in the neighborhood about three weeks before. Franklin and Rachel fell in love, and even the appearance of Godfrey Ablewhite, a handsome and accomplished charity worker, failed to weaken Rachel's affection. Godfrey had been asked to attend the birthday celebration, together with a number of guests, including Dr. Candy, the town physician, and Mr. Bruff, the family lawyer.

While the guests at the birthday dinner were admiring the beauty of the jewel, they heard the beating of a drum on the terrace. Three Hindus had appeared, disguised as jugglers. One of the guests was Mr. Murthwaite, a famous traveler in the Orient, and at a sharply spoken word from him the Indians retreated. Watchdogs were released to protect the house that night. There was no disturbance to alarm the household, however, and everyone thought all had gone well until Rachel announced the jewel had disappeared from an unlocked cabinet in her dressing-room.

Over Rachel's protests, Franklin Blake insisted the police be called in. The Hindus were arrested and put in jail, but to the astonishment of everyone they were able to prove an alibi for the entire night.

Little about the crime was discovered until Sergeant Cuff of Scotland Yard arrived. He decided that some fresh paint from the door in Rachel's dressing-room must have come off on someone's clothes. Rachel, for some unknown reason, refused to allow a search for the stained clothing. Sergeant Cuff suspected that Rachel had staged the theft herself, and her actions seemed to substantiate his theory. He also thought that Rosanna Spearman, a maid with a criminal record, was a party to the plot, for he learned that Rosanna had made a new nightdress shortly after the theft. Sergeant Cuff guessed it was to take the place of another dress which was stained. Because the Verinders opposed his efforts, he dropped the case. The only other clue he had was that Rosanna might have hidden something in the rocks by the seashore. He suspected it was the stained dress. Rosanna committed suicide soon afterward by throwing herself into a pool of quicksand. Betteredge discovered she had left a letter for Franklin, who had departed from the country by the time it was found.

Rachel went to London with her mother, and in time became engaged to Godfrey Ablewhite. When Mr. Bruff told her Godfrey had secretly learned the terms of her mother's will before asking for her hand, Rachel broke the engagement. Franklin returned to England later in the year and went to visit Betteredge, who told him about Rosanna's letter. Franklin got the letter and learned from it that she had thought him guilty of the crime. The letter also gave him directions for recovering a box which, as Sergeant Cuff had thought, she had buried by the sea. The box proved to have the stained nightgown in it, but it was not Rosanna's nightgown. On the contrary, it was Franklin's!

Unable to account for this strange fact, Franklin returned to London, where he had a long talk with Mr. Bruff about the case. Mr. Bruff informed Franklin that the Moonstone must be in a certain bank in London, deposited there by a notorious pawnbroker named Luker. A mysterious attack upon the money-lender seemed to confirm this belief. Franklin told Mr. Bruff of the strange discovery of the nightgown. Mr. Bruff planned a surprise meeting between Franklin and Rachel, at which Franklin learned that Rachel had actually seen him come into the room and steal the stone. Because she loved him she had refused to let the investigation go on. Franklin tried to convince her he had no memory of the deed.

On Mr. Bruff's advice, Franklin returned to the country place and tried to discover what had happened to him that night. From Dr. Candy's assistant, Ezra Jennings, he learned that the doctor had secretly given him a dose of laudanum on the night of the theft, so that Franklin, suffering from insomnia, would get a good night's sleep. Jennings suggested administering a like dose to Franklin again, in the same setting, to see what he would do. Mr. Bruff and Rachel came down from London to watch the experiment.

With the help of Betteredge the scene was set and Franklin given the laudanum. Under its influence he repeated his actions on the night of the theft. Rachel watched him come to her room and take out a substitute stone. She was now convinced that his original act had been an attempt to protect her from the Hindus by removing the stone to another room. Before Franklin could recollect what he did with the stone after he left Rachel's room, however, the drug took full effect and he fell sound asleep.

The experiment explained how the stone disappeared from Rachel's room, but not how it got into a London bank through the hands of Luker. Mr. Bruff suggested that the gem might shortly be redeemed from Luker: Sergeant Cuff was called back into the case, and a watch set on the bank. One day Luker came into the bank and claimed the stone. On his way out he could have passed it to any of three people. All three men were followed. Two proved to be innocent citizens. Bruff's office boy trailed the third, a bearded man who looked like a sailor, to an inn where the suspect took lodgings for the night.

When Franklin and Sergeant Cuff arrived at the inn, they found the sailor dead and the box from the bank empty. Sergeant Cuff examined the dead man closely and then tore away a false wig and beard to expose the features of God-frey Ablewhite. From Luker they learned that Godfrey had seen Franklin go into Rachel's room the night of the robbery, and that Franklin had given Godfrey the stone with instructions to put it in the bank. Since Franklin had remembered nothing of this request the next day, Godfrey kept the jewel. The mystery solved, Rachel and Franklin were happily reunited.

Several years later Mr. Murthwaite, the explorer, told them of a great festival in honor of the Moon-God which he had witnessed in India. When the idol was unveiled, he saw gleaming in the forehead of the stone image the long-lost treasure of the god—the sacred Moon-stone.

LE MORTE D'ARTHUR

Type of work: Chronicle
Author: Sir Thomas Malory (1400?-1471)
Type of plot: Chivalric romance
Time of plot: Golden Age of chivalry
Locale: Britain
First published: 1485

Principal characters:
ARTHUR, King of Britain
QUEEN GUINEVERE, his wife
SIR MORDRED, his natural son
SIR LAUNCELOT,
SIR TRISTRAM, and
SIR GALAHAD, knights of the Round Table

Critique:

Le Morte d'Arthur is a monumental work which made the Arthurian cycle available for the first time in English. Malory took a body of legends which had gone from the folklore of Celtic Britain into French literature by way of Brittany, gave these tales a typically English point of view, and added, amended, and deleted for his own purposes, to produce a work which has had tremendous influence on literature ever since. Because of the episodic nature of its contents, the romance concerns itself at great length with figures associated with King Arthur, to the extent that Arthur, as a man, never quite materializes. But Arthur, as the symbol of knighthood at its full flower, pervades the book.

The Story:

King Uther Pendragon saw and loved Igraine, the beautiful and chaste Duchess of Cornwall. His desires being checked by Igraine's husband, King Uther made war on Cornwall and in that war the duke was killed. By means of magic, King Uther got Igraine with child; the couple were subsequently married. The child, named Arthur, was raised by a noble knight, Sir Ector. After the death of King Uther, Arthur proved his right to the throne by removing a sword from an anvil which was imbedded in a rock. From the Lady of the Lake he received his famous sword, Excalibur. When the independent kings of Britain rebelled and

made war on the young king, they were defeated. Arthur ruled over all Britain.

King Arthur married Guinevere, the daughter of King Leodegrance, who presented to Arthur as a wedding gift the Round Table and a hundred knights. Merlin the magician was enticed by one of the Ladies of the Lake into eternal imprisonment under a rock.

Five foreign kings invaded Arthur's realm and were defeated after a long war. To show his gratitude to God for his victory, King Arthur founded the Abbey of the Beautiful Adventure at the scene of his victory.

Sir Accolon, the paramour of Morgan Le Fay, enchantress sister of King Arthur, fought Arthur with Excalibur, which Morgan had procured from Arthur by black magic. Arthur was nearly overcome, but in the fight their swords were accidentally exchanged and the king defeated Accolon.

King Lucius of Rome sent ambassadors to Britain to demand tribute of King Arthur. When Arthur refused to pay, he was promised aid in war by all of the knights of his realm. In the war that followed, the British defeated Lucius and conquered Germany and Italy. Arthur was crowned Emperor of Rome.

Back in England, Sir Launcelot, a knight of the Round Table and Queen Guinevere's favorite, set out on adventures to further the honor and glory of himself and of his queen. After many

LE MORTE d'ARTHUR by Sir Thomas Malory. Published by Appleton-Century-Crofts, Inc.

long and arduous adventures, all of them triumphant, Sir Launcelot returned to Camelot, the seat of King Arthur, and was acclaimed the first knight of all Christendom.

Elizabeth, queen of King Meliodas of Liones, died in giving birth to a son, who was named Tristram because of the sad circumstances surrounding his birth. Young Tristram was sent with his preceptor, Gouvernail, to France, where he was trained in all the accomplishments of knighthood. When the king of Ireland demanded tribute from King Mark of Cornwall, Sir Tristram, defending the sovereignty of King Mark, his uncle, slew the Irish champion, Sir Marhaus, but was wounded in the contest. He was nursed by Isolde, princess of Ireland. Tristram and Isolde fell in love and promised to remain true to each other. Later, King Mark commissioned Sir Tristram to return to Ireland to bring back Isolde, whom the king had contracted to marry. During the return voyage from Ireland to Cornwall, Tristram and Isolde drank a love potion and swore undying love. Isolde married King Mark, and Sir Tristram later married Isolde La Blanche Mains, daughter of King Howels of Brittany. But Tristram, unable to remain separated from Isolde of Ireland, joined her secretly. At last, fearing discovery and out of his mind for love of Isolde, Tristram fled into the forest. In a pitiful condition he was carried back to the castle, where a faithful hound revealed his identity to King Mark. King Mark then banished Tristram from Cornwall for ten years. The knight went to Camelot, where he won great renown at tourneys and in knightly adventures. King Mark, hearing of Tristram's honors, went in disguise to Camelot to kill Tristram. Sir Launcelot recognized King Mark and took him to King Arthur, who ordered the Cornish sovereign to allow Sir Tristram to return to Cornwall. In Cornwall, King Mark attempted unsuccessfully to get rid of Tristram. But Tristram managed to avoid all the traps set for him, and he and Isolde escaped to England

and took up residence in Castle Joyous Guard.

An old hermit prophesied to King Arthur that a seat which was vacant at the Round Table would be occupied by a knight not yet born—one who would win the Holy Grail.

After Sir Launcelot was tricked into lying with Elaine, the daughter of King Pelles, the maid gave birth to a boy named Galahad. Some years later there appeared in a river a stone with a sword imbedded in it. A message on the sword stated that the best knight in the world would remove it. All the knights of the Round Table attempted to withdraw the sword, without success. Finally an old man brought a young knight to the Round Table and seated him in the vacant place at which the young knight's name, Sir Galahad, appeared magically after he had been seated. Sir Galahad withdrew the magic sword from the stone and set out, with other of Arthur's knights, in quest of the Holy Grail. During his quest, he was joined part of the time by his father, Sir Launcelot. Sir Launcelot tried to enter the Grail chamber and was stricken for twenty-four days as penance for his years of sin. A vision of Christ came to Sir Galahad, who, with his comrades, received communion from the Grail. They came to a near-Eastern city where they healed a cripple. Because of this miracle they were thrown into prison by the pagan king. When the king died, Sir Galahad was chosen king; he saw the miracle of the Grail and died in holiness.

There was great rejoicing in Camelot after the questing knights returned. Sir Launcelot forgot the promises he had made during the quest and began to consort again with Guinevere.

One spring, while traveling with her attendants, Guinevere was captured by a traitorous knight, Sir Meliagrance. Sir Launcelot rescued the queen and killed the evil knight. Enemies of Launcelot reported to King Arthur Launcelot's love for Guinevere. A party championing the king's cause engaged Launcelot in combat. All members of the party except Mordred, Arthur's natural son, were slain. Guinevere was sentenced to be burned, but Sir Launcelot and his party saved the queen from the stake and retired to Castle Joyous Guard. When King Arthur besieged the castle, the Pope commanded a truce between Sir Launcelot and the king. Sir Launcelot and his followers went to France, where they became rulers of that realm. King Arthur invaded France with the intent of overthrowing Sir Launcelot, and in Arthur's absence Mordred seized the throne of Britain and tried to force Guinevere to become his queen. Guinevere escaped to London, where she took refuge in the Tower. King Arthur, hearing of the disaffection of Sir Mordred, returned to England and in a great battle drove the usurper and his false knights back to Canterbury.

At a parley between King Arthur and Sir Mordred, an adder caused a knight to draw his sword. This action brought on a pitched battle in which Mordred was killed and King Arthur was mortally wounded. On his deathbed King Arthur asked Sir Bedivere to cast Excalibur back into the lake from which the sword had come. Sir Bedivere hid the sword twice, but was reproached by the king each time. Finally, Sir Bedivere threw the sword into the lake, where it was caught by a hand and withdrawn under the water.

King Arthur died and was carried on a barge down the river to the Vale of Avalon. When Sir Launcelot returned from France to avenge his king and queen, he learned that Guinevere had become a nun. Sir Launcelot retired to a hermitage and took holy orders. Sir Constantine of Cornwall was chosen king to succeed King Arthur.

THE MOTHER

Type of work: Novel
Author: Grazia Deledda (1872-1936)
Type of plot: Psychological realism
Time of plot: Early twentieth century
Locale: Sardinia
First published: 1920

Principal characters:
PAUL, a priest
MARIA MADDALENA, his mother
AGNES, his sweetheart

Critique:

The Mother is a searching study of a human problem, the age-old conflict arising out of the struggle between authority and inclination. The scene, as in most of this writer's work, is the island of Sardinia, with its poor peasants, its inbred superstitions, and its church-directed religion. The structure of the novel is compact in that the dramatic action covers only two days. The tragic ending is inevitable. The character of Maria Maddalena dominates the book, but Paul and Agnes become sympathetic creations. Grazia Deledda was awarded the Nobel prize for literature in 1926.

The Story:

Maria Maddalena had been an orphan, brought up in drudgery by aunts. Part of her work was to bring flour from the mill. If there were no other customers, the old man who waited on her would follow her out and kiss her by force behind the bushes. His whiskers pricked her. When her aunts learned what was happening, they forbade the girl to go near the mill again. To their surprise, the old man came to the house one day and asked for Maria in marriage.

Maria continued to live in her aunts' house; her husband stayed at the mill. Each day, when she visited him, he would steal flour and give it to her. Widowed shortly after she became pregnant, she supported her son by working as a servant. She refused to sully herself with the demanding servants and masters of the places in which she worked, for she wished to make her son a priest and she felt purity was required of her as well.

When her son Paul went to the seminary, she worked there to be near him. The bishop often commanded Paul to seek out his sacrificing mother and kiss her hand. During vacation periods they sometimes went back to their native village. One summer Paul visited the town prostitute several times. He was fascinated by her white skin; he thought it was so pale because her house was in constant shade. After that summer Paul threw off desires of the flesh and felt himself sanctified.

His studies completed, Paul was assigned to the remote village of Aar, a mountainous town where strong winds blew all the time. The mother was proud that her dreams were coming true as the population gathered in the square to meet the new priest. She settled down placidly in the presbytery to keep house for her son.

Aar had had no priest for some time. The former priest had been a drunkard and a gambler; some people said a sorcerer. They had half-liked him, however, and had never complained to the bishop because they were afraid of his magic. Prudently Maria had bars in the form of a cross put on the front door to ward off the evil eye, for it was common knowledge that the old priest had sworn to drive away any successor. But then, Maria was an ignorant woman.

One night Maria was desperately afraid. For some time Paul had had a mirror in his room; he cleaned his nails and washed with scented soap. He even let his hair grow long and tried to comb it over his tonsure. She knew what was happening. Agnes was the only member of the family left in the big house; Paul had begun to visit her on his parish rounds. From the sounds in his bedroom, Paul was again getting ready to go out that night.

Paul left hurriedly. Ashamed but desperate, his mother followed after him. She saw him go to the side gate of the big house and disappear inside. Finding the gate locked, she circled the grounds; all the entrances were shut. She returned home to wait for Paul.

Dozing as she waited, she thought the wicked old priest was sitting beside her, leering at her from his whiskered face. He drew off his socks and ordered her to mend them. Calmly enough, she asked him how she could mend socks for a dead man. The priest declared he was not dead; furthermore, he would drive them out of the village. When she called him wicked, he argued with her that God had put us on earth to enjoy ourselves.

With a start she awoke looking about her for the socks. She thought she heard ghostly footfalls leaving the presbytery. Earlier she had considered denouncing Paul to the bishop. Not sure of his guilt, however, she resolved to face the problem at once.

When Paul came in, he curtly told his mother that he had been calling on a sick person. Maria was determined, however, to leave the village, never to see him again unless he broke with Agnes. She wondered if her own son could be so selfish that he could not see he was endangering Agnes' soul as well as his own. In his chamber Paul fell into a troubled sleep after calling on God for help.

In the morning his mother waked him early. Before he left his room he wrote a letter renouncing Agnes. With a pale face he gave it to his mother and told her to deliver it to the girl in person.

After hearing confessions, he said mass. His sermon was cutting. The congregation was growing smaller each day; only on Sunday were the pews filled. Afterward he learned that Agnes had received his letter.

During the morning word came that King Nicodemus was dying. Nicodemus was a wild hunter who lived far up the mountain, where he had removed himself so he could do no harm to man. His relatives had brought him into the village when he was far gone in sickness. Paul, with his server Antiochus, went to the hut to give the hunter extreme unction. To their surprise, Nicodemus had disappeared. With his last strength he had left the hated village, to die in his own mountain cabin.

Later a woman brought to Paul a little daughter who was having a tantrum. The mother thought the girl possessed of a demon, for it took force to get her into the presbytery. Humoring the superstitious mother, Paul read the parable of the Gadarene swine. As he read, the girl became quiet and receptive. Maria and the others were sure Paul had exorcised an evil spirit.

The people of the village, believing him a miracle worker who could cast out demons, held a celebration for Paul. He was thankful when some of the merrymakers went home with him. He needed help that night to keep him from going to Agnes.

Antiochus lingered after the rest of the company to remind Paul of a promise to visit the boy's mother. Antiochus wanted to be a priest, and Paul had promised to speak about the plan. Wearily he set out. While he was impressing on his server's mother the sacrifices demanded of the priesthood, one of Agnes' servants came with the news that Agnes had fallen and was bleeding at the nose. Accepting his fate, Paul went to see her again.

Agnes was pale and older looking but not ill. She reproached him for the letter and inquired about his promise to marry her and take her away. Paul declared only a brother's love for her. Angry, Agnes said that he came at night and seduced young girls. She would so denounce him in church if he did not leave the village before morning.

Paul told his mother of the threat. Both were apprehensive of going to church; they were thankful to see Agnes' pew empty. But toward the end of the service she appeared, looking straight at Paul. As the services were ending he heard a cry. His mother had dropped dead. Paul went to her side. He saw Agnes staring at him.

MOTHER

Type of work: Novel
Author: Maxim Gorky (Aleksei Maksimovich Peshkov, 1868-1936)
Type of plot: Naturalism
Time of plot: First decade of the twentieth century
Locale: Russia
First published: 1907

Principal characters:
 PELAGUEYA VLASOVA, a revolutionary heroine
 PAVEL VLASOV, her son
 ANDREY,
 RYBIN,
 NIKOLAY IVANOVICH,
 SOFYA,
 SASHENKA, and
 NATASHA, the Vlasovs' revolutionary friends

Critique:

Although Maxim Gorky wrote primarily about the proletariat and in a naturalistic vein, he was not fundamentally concerned with politics, and his works exhibit a marked lyric talent that gives his writing a haunting poetic quality. Gorky's basic concern was with strong, vital, memorable characters rather than with dogma or morality. He envisioned a future in which these vigorous people would free themselves from their economic degradation and live as free, independent spirits. He was a visionary rather than a dogmatist. This fact is particularly evident in his novel *Mother*, in which Pelagueya Vlasova, through the love of her son, becomes converted to the revolutionary cause and gradually comes to love all the people as her children. Gorky was strongly attracted to these self-made people, to men and women with the courage to carry out their plans, and he makes the reader admire them as well. The lyric sweep of Gorky's vision in this novel is compelling.

The Story:

The factory workers in the small Russian community of Nizhni-Novgorod were an impoverished, soulless, brutal lot. Their work in the factory dehumanized them and robbed them of their energy; as a result they lived like beasts.

When Michael Vlasov, a worker, died, his wife Pelagueya felt that her son Pavel would lead the same anguished, brutal life. But gradually she noticed with joy and apprehension that Pavel was turning out differently, that he was given to reading. One day Pavel informed his mother that he was reading subversive literature and that a group of his Socialist friends were coming one evening to visit him. Pelagueya was naturally frightened, but when his friends arrived she noticed that they were much warmer, much more gentle than the people she had lived with all her life. Though they engaged in heated arguments, no one seemed to get angry at the others. Pavel's friends seemed full of hope and vitality, and Pelagueya quickly warmed up to them. She liked Pavel's friend, Andrey, in particular, for he was big-hearted and full of laughter. She liked Natasha too, a frail, gentle girl who read aloud during the meetings. Other members of the group were Sashenka, a commanding girl who loved Pavel, and Vyesovshchikov, the village misanthropist. They were an idealistic crowd, hopeful about the future of the workingman, and prepared to put their ideas into action. Gradually Pavel's home became the center of their activities, and Pelagueya agreed to take Andrey in as a roomer out of her motherly love for him.

Eventually Pavel's house became the

center of village suspicion as well. Pavel and his comrades had printed and distributed among the workmen leaflets which made plain their miserable conditions. Rumors were spread that the police were coming to search the house. Soon afterward the police dropped in unexpectedly and arrested Andrey and Vyesovshchikov. Several others had been arrested as well.

While the workers were generally hostile to Pavel because of his strangeness, he also inspired a certain confidence in them by virtue of his stern intelligence. Pelagueya was flattered that the sharp peasant, Rybin, an old bear of a man, should go to her son for advice. One day the workers were notified that their pay was going to be cut. The workers were behind Pavel when he made a speech to them and to the manager in protest against the cut; however, because of the speech, Pavel was arrested and sent to jail.

Pelagueya, distressed by her son's arrest, learned that about sixty others had been arrested along with him and that Andrey sent her his regards from prison. Deciding at last to become involved in her son's activities, she took a job as a caterer to the factory laborers and under cover of her work she distributed revolutionary literature. Meanwhile, she continued to see Pavel's Socialist friends.

Soon afterward Andrey was released from prison, and he returned to Pelagueya, who welcomed him with open arms. Rybin, claiming that the peasants were no better off than the workers, went to the country to stir up the peasantry against their oppressive masters.

With Andrey living in her house, Pelagueya felt happier, and under his friendly goading she learned to read and write. She visited Pavel in prison and slyly told him of her activities in distributing leaflets. Pelagueya's world expanded greatly now that she was involved in the Socialist cause; she had something to hope for beyond her selfish interests.

In the spring Pavel was released from prison. The Vlasov household continued

to be the hub of the local Socialist activities, and Pavel announced his intention of marching with the banner in the coming May Day parade, even though to do so would mean another jail sentence.

Not long afterward one of Pavel's friends rushed in to report that a spy had been murdered in the street. At first Pelagueya feared that Vyesovshchikov had committed the crime; later Andrey revealed that he had accidentally killed the spy and felt guilty about his deed. After two weeks of inquiring into the matter the police gave up the investigation.

May Day arrived and Pavel and Andrey were up early. The crowds had gathered in the streets and the two men walked through them with Pelagueya close behind. After they had made an abortive attempt to rouse the workers with speeches and songs, soldiers appeared, forced back the crowd, and arrested Pavel, Andrey, and their companions.

Pelagueya felt depressed after their arrest. In answer to her loneliness Nikolay Ivanovich came to her and invited her to live with him in the city. She accepted his invitation and moved to his apartment. Nikolay and his sister Sofya were well-bred Socialists. They treated Pelagueya with affection and respect, and she came to love them as though they were members of her own family.

Pelagueya and Sofya dressed as pilgrims and in that disguise distributed propaganda throughout the city and surrounding countryside. While delivering books to Rybin, Pelagueya saw the hardships of peasant life and the cruelty of the masters. She proved useful in aiding Vyesovshchikov to hide out from the police after he had escaped from prison. She nursed a dying comrade and during a riot at his funeral she helped a wounded boy at some danger to herself. She also visited Pavel in prison.

Learning that many of her comrades had been arrested, she decided to go alone to deliver her pamphlets in the country village. On arriving there she saw that Rybin had been arrested and cruelly beaten. That night she stayed with sympathetic peasants and gave them copies of her leaflets.

Returning to the city, she aided a fugitive peasant and told Nikolay about her trip. Shortly thereafter she helped a comrade to escape from prison. Her efforts for the workers made her realize how family allegiances could interfere with loyalty to the cause; she understood now why Pavel would never get married.

After about six months in jail Pavel and his comrades were finally brought to trial. The judges were cold, impersonal, and aloof. Several of Pavel's friends declined to testify in his defense. As the trial proceeded Pavel made a rousing speech in which he denounced the decadence of the masters and praised the youth and vision of the Socialists. After Andrey had further taunted the judges, Pavel and his companions were finally sentenced to exile in Siberia.

In the meantime the police were hunting down the Socialists. Nikolay was arrested shortly after the trial. Pavel's speech had been printed and Pelagueya had promised to deliver copies to a remote town. On the train she recognized a police spy and knew she had been trapped. When the police tried to arrest her, she shouted to the other occupants of the train about her mission and their servitude. She opened her bag and handed out the leaflets even while the police were beating her.

MOURNING BECOMES ELECTRA

Type of work: Drama
Author: Eugene O'Neill (1888-1953)
Type of plot: Romantic tragedy
Time of plot: Shortly after the Civil War
Locale: New England
First presented: 1931

Principal characters:
  EZRA MANNON, a Civil War general
  CHRISTINE, his wife
  ORIN, his son
  LAVINIA, his daughter
  CAPTAIN ADAM BRANT, Christine's lover
  HAZEL NILES, and
  PETER NILES, cousins of the Mannons
  SETH, the Mannon caretaker

Critique:

The plot of *Mourning Becomes Electra* is based on the Greek tragedy of Electra and her brother Orestes. In keeping with the nature of the story, O'Neill chose for his time and setting the Civil War era, a period not too far off to be forgotten by the American public and yet remote enough to be viewed in legendary aspect. The Orestes of the Greek plays had killed his mother because she had murdered his father. According to Greek ethics, it was a son's duty to avenge his father, and Orestes had acted justly according to the gods, who in the end saved him from punishment. Because such a conclusion would not be acceptable to a modern audience, O'Neill created Orin's madness to complete his tragedy. The separate parts of this trilogy are entitled *Homecoming, The Hunted, The Haunted.*

The Story:

The Civil War was over, and in their New England home Christine and Lavinia Mannon awaited the homecoming of old Ezra Mannon and his son Orin. Lavinia, who adored her father, detested Christine because of Ezra's love for his wife. Christine, on the other hand, jealously guarded Orin's love because she hated her husband and her daughter. In this house of hidden hatred, Seth, the

gardener watched the old mansion and saw that Lavinia also despised Captain Brant, who was a steady caller at the Mannon home.

The Mannons, descended from old New England stock, had their family skeleton. Dave Mannon, Ezra's brother, had run off with an Indian woman named Marie Brantôme. Seth, seeing the antagonism between Lavinia and her mother, disclosed to Lavinia that Captain Brant was the son of Marie and Dave Mannon.

Embittered by her mother's illicit romance with Brant and jealous of Christine's hold on Ezra, Lavinia forced Christine to send her lover away. But Christine was too powerful a woman to succumb to her daughter's dominance. She urged the grudge-bearing Brant to send her some poison. It was common knowledge that Ezra had heart trouble, and Christine was planning to rid herself of the husband whom she hated so that she would be free to marry Brant. Lavinia cruelly reminded her mother that her favorite offspring was Orin, who was born while Ezra had been away during the Mexican War.

The family jealousies were obvious by the time Ezra came home. Ezra, a kind, just man, realized that Christine shrank from him while she attempted to pretend concern for his health. That night in their bedroom Ezra and Christine quarreled over their failing marriage. Ezra had a heart attack, and when he gasped for his medicine Christine gave him the poison instead. As he lay dying in Lavinia's arms, the helpless man feebly but incoherently accused Christine of guilt in his murder. Lavinia had no proof, but she did suspect her mother's part in Ezra's death.

Peter and Hazel Niles, cousins of the Mannons, came to the mansion after Ezra's death. Peter was a rejected suitor of Lavinia, and Hazel was in love with Orin. Lavinia spied upon her mother constantly. When Orin came home, the two women vied for his trust, Lavinia trying to create suspicion against her mother and Christine attempting to regain her son's close affection. Uncomfortable under her daughter's looks of silent, sneering accusation, Christine finally realized that Lavinia had found the box of poison. While Hazel, Peter, and Christine tried to make a warm welcome for Orin, Lavinia hovered over the group like a specter of gloom and fatality. Able to get Orin alone before Lavinia could speak to him, Christine told her son about Lavinia's suspicions concerning Captain Brant and Ezra's death, and she tried to convince Orin that Lavinia's distraction over Ezra's death had warped her mind.

Orin, whose affection for his mother had made him dislike Ezra, believed Christine, but the returned soldier swore that if he ever discovered that the story about Captain Brant were true, he would kill Brant. Desperately Christine told Lavinia that Orin's trust had been won, that Lavinia need not try to take advantage of his credulity; but Lavinia stared at her mother in silent defiance. Under her daughter's cold stare Christine's triumphant manner collapsed into a pathetic plea that Lavinia should not endanger Brant's life, for Orin had threatened to kill him.

Lavinia slyly hinted the truth to Orin, and his old childhood trust in his sister led him to believe her story in part, unwillingly however, for he was still influenced by love for his mother. Lavinia hinted that Christine might run to Brant at the first opportunity. Orin agreed to wait for proof, and if sufficient proof were offered, then to kill Brant. Lavinia instructed Orin to maintain his pretense that he believed her to be mad.

Shortly after Ezra's funeral, Christine did go to Brant. Orin and Lavinia had pretended to be paying a call on a nearby estate, but they followed their mother to Brant's ship, where they overheard the lovers planning to run off together. Although Orin was consumed with jealous hatred of Brant, Lavinia restrained him from impulsive action. When Christine had gone, Orin went into the cabin and shot Brant. Then the brother and sister rifled the ship's cabin and Brant's pockets to make the death appear to have been a robbery and murder.

Orin and Lavinia returned to the Mannon mansion and told Christine what they had done. At the sight of his mother's grief Orin fell to his knees, pleading with her to forgive him and to give him her love. Fearing he had lost his mother's affection, the bewildered boy rushed from the room, but Lavinia faced her mother victoriously. Christine went into the house and shot herself. Orin, in a frenzy of grief, accused himself of his mother's murder.

Lavinia took her brother on a long sea trip to help him overcome his feeling of guilt. When they returned, Orin was completely under Lavinia's control, reciting in toneless speech the fact that Christine had been an adulteress and a murderess, and that Orin had saved his mother from public hanging. He was changed in appearance and spirit; it was plain that strange thoughts of grief and guilt preyed on his mind. During the trip Lavinia had grown to look and behave like Christine.

Lavinia was now able to accept Peter's love, but when Orin saw his sister in Peter's embrace, he became angered for a brief moment before he congratulated Peter and Lavinia. When Orin became engaged to Hazel, Lavinia was afraid to leave Orin alone with the girl for fear he would say too much about the past.

Orin began to write a family history, urged by a remorseful desire to leave a record of the family crimes. Becoming jealous of Lavinia's engagement to Peter, he threatened to expose her if she married him. Orin kept hinting to Lavinia that, like Christine, she was planning to poison him as Christine had poisoned the man who held her in bondage. Finally, driven to distraction by Orin's morbid possessive attitude toward her and by his incessant reminding of their guilt, Lavinia suggested to the crazed mind that he kill himself. As Peter held Lavinia in his arms, Orin went to the library to clean his pistol. His death was assumed to have been an accident.

Hazel suspected some vile and sinister fact hidden in Orin's accidental death. She went to Lavinia and pleaded with her not to ruin Peter by marrying him, but Lavinia denied that there was any reason to put off the marriage. While she spoke, however, Lavinia realized that the dead Mannons would always rule her life. The others had been cowards, and had died. She would live. She sent Peter away. Then she ordered Seth the gardener to board up the windows of the mansion. Alone, the last surviving Mannon, Lavinia entered the old house to spend the rest of her life with the dead.

MUCH ADO ABOUT NOTHING

Type of work: Drama
Author: William Shakespeare (1564-1616)
Type of plot: Romantic comedy
Time of plot: Thirteenth century
Locale: Italy
First presented: 1598

Principal characters:
DON PEDRO, Prince of Arragon
DON JOHN, his bastard brother
CLAUDIO, a young lord of Florence
BENEDICK, a young lord of Padua
LEONATO, Governor of Messina
HERO, Leonato's daughter
BEATRICE, Leonato's niece
DOGBERRY, a constable

Critique:

One of the most brilliant of Shakespeare's plays, *Much Ado about Nothing* is nevertheless not among the favorites of most readers. The plot and the dialogue are artfully conceived and executed, but the comedy is often so near tragedy that it does not have the flavor of many of the other comedies. It was the first of his plays in which the comic and serious plots were so woven together that the outcome of one was dependent upon the other. This work was one of the last comedies Shakespeare wrote; it is thought that his awakening moral consciousness, evidenced here, forced him into the tragedies which were based so completely on themes of moral transgression and human frailty.

The Story:

Don Pedro, Prince of Arragon, arrived in Messina accompanied by his bastard brother, Don John, and his two friends, Claudio and Benedick, young Italian noblemen. Don Pedro had been successful over his brother in battle. Reconciled, the brothers planned to visit Leonato before returning to their homeland. On their arrival in Messina, young Claudio was immediately smitten by the lovely Hero, daughter of Leonato. In order to help his faithful young friend in his suit, Don Pedro assumed the guise of Claudio at a masked ball and wooed Hero in Claudio's name. Thus he gained Leonato's consent for Claudio and Hero

to marry. The bastard Don John tried to cause trouble by persuading Claudio that Don Pedro meant to betray him and keep Hero for himself, but the villain was foiled in his plot and Claudio remained faithful to Don Pedro.

Benedick, the other young follower of Don Pedro, was a confirmed and bitter bachelor who scorned all men willing to enter the married state. No less opposed to men and matrimony was Leonato's niece, Beatrice. These two were at each other constantly, each one trying to gain supremacy by insulting the other. Don Pedro, with the help of Hero, Claudio, and Leonato, undertook the seemingly impossible task of bringing Benedick and Beatrice together in matrimony in the seven days remaining before the marriage of Hero and Claudio.

Don John, thwarted in his first attempt to cause disharmony, now formed another plot. With the help of a serving-man, he arranged to make it appear that Hero was unfaithful to Claudio. The serving-man was to gain entrance to Hero's chambers when she was away. In her place would be her attendant, assuming Hero's clothes. Don John, posing as Claudio's true friend, would inform him of her unfaithfulness and lead him to Hero's window to witness her wanton disloyalty.

In the meantime Don Pedro carried out his plan to get Benedick and Beatrice to stop quarreling and fall in love with each

2481

other. When Benedick was close by, thinking himself unseen, Don Pedro, Claudio, and Leonato would talk of their great sympathy for Beatrice, who loved Benedick but was unloved by him. To each other, the three told sorrowful tales of the love letters Beatrice wrote to Benedick and then tore up. Sadly they said that Beatrice beat her breast and sobbed over her unrequited love for Benedick. Meanwhile Hero and her serving-woman would, when Beatrice was nearby but thought herself unseen, tell tales of poor Benedick, who pined and sighed for the heartless Beatrice. Thus both the unsuspecting young people decided not to let the other suffer. Each would sacrifice principles and accept the other's love.

As Benedick and Beatrice were ready to admit their love for each other, Don John was successful in his base plot to ruin Hero. He told Claudio that he had learned of Hero's duplicity and he arranged to take him and Don Pedro to her window that very night, when they might witness her unfaithfulness. Dogberry, a constable, and the watch apprehended Don John's followers and overheard the truth of the plot, but in their stupidity the petty officials could not get their story told in time to prevent Hero's disgrace. Although Don Pedro and Claudio did indeed witness the feigned betrayal, Claudio determined to let her get to the church on the next day still thinking herself beloved. There, instead of marrying her, he would shame her before all the wedding guests.

All happened as Don John had hoped. Before the priest and all the guests Claudio called Hero a wanton and forswore her love for all time. The poor girl protested her innocence, but to no avail. Claudio said that he had seen with his own eyes her foul act. Then Hero swooned and lay as if dead. Claudio and Don Pedro left her thus with Leonato, who also believed the story and wished his daughter really dead in her shame. But the priest, believing the girl guiltless, persuaded Leonato to believe in her too. The priest told Leonato to let the world believe Hero dead while they worked to prove her innocent. Benedick, also believing in her innocence, promised to help unravel the mystery. Then Beatrice told Benedick of her love for him and asked him to kill Claudio and so prove his love for her. Benedick challenged Claudio to a duel. Don John had fled the country after the successful outcome of his plot, but Benedick swore that he would find Don John and kill him as well as Claudio.

At last Dogberry and the watch got to Leonato and told their story. Claudio and Don Pedro heard it also, and Claudio wanted to die and to be with his wronged Hero. Leonato allowed the two sorrowful men to continue to think Hero dead. In fact, they all attended her funeral. Leonato said that he would be avenged if Claudio would marry his niece, a girl who much resembled Hero. Although Claudio still loved the dead Hero, he agreed to marry the other girl in order to let Leonato have the favor he had so much right to ask.

When Don Pedro and Claudio arrived at Leonato's house for the ceremony, Leonato had all the ladies masked. He brought forth one of them and told Claudio that she was to be his wife. After Claudio promised to be her husband, the girl unmasked. She was, of course, Hero. At first Claudio could not believe his senses, but after he was convinced of the truth he took her to the church immediately. Then Benedick and Beatrice finally declared their true love for each other. They too went to the church after a dance in celebration of the double nuptials to be performed. Best of all, word came that Don John had been captured and was being brought back to Messina to face his brother, Don Pedro. But his punishment must wait the morrow. Tonight all would be joy and happiness.

MURDER IN THE CATHEDRAL

Type of work: Drama
Author: T. S. Eliot (1888-   )
Type of plot: Religious chronicle
Time of plot: 1170
Locale: Canterbury, England
First presented: 1935

>   *Principal characters:*
>   ARCHBISHOP THOMAS BECKET
>   PRIESTS
>   TEMPTERS
>   KNIGHTS
>   CHORUS OF WOMEN OF CANTERBURY

Critique:

This liturgical drama dealing with the assassination of Thomas Becket is essentially an impartial representation. Eliot shows the politics, both temporal and churchly, which lay behind the murder; and he presents the archbishop as a man torn between acting and suffering. Most of the drama is in poetic form, with effective expression by the chorus. The archbishop's sermon is in prose, as are the anachronistic speeches of justification by the knights. *Murder in the Cathedral* was written for the Canterbury Festival, June, 1935.

The Story:

The women of Canterbury had been drawn to the cathedral. Instinctively, they knew that they had been drawn there by danger; there was no safety anywhere. But they had to come to bear witness. Archbishop Thomas Becket had been gone seven years. He had always been kind to his people, but he really should not return. During the periods when the king and the barons ruled alternately, the poor had suffered all kinds of oppression. Like common people everywhere, the women had tried to keep their households in order and to escape the notice of the various rulers. Now they could only wait and witness.

The priests of the cathedral were well aware of the coming struggle for power. The archbishop had been intriguing in France, where he had enlisted the aid of the pope. Henry of Anjou was a stubborn king, however, and these struggles for power would hurt someone. The priests knew that the strong rule by force, the weak by caprice; and the only law was to seize power and hold it.

A herald announced to them that the archbishop was nearing the city. They were to prepare at once for his coming. With great interest they asked if there would be peace or war, whether the archbishop and the king had been reconciled. The herald was of the opinion that there had been only a hasty compromise. He did not know that when the archbishop had parted from the king, the prelate had said that King Henry would not see him again in this life.

After the herald left, one priest expressed the pessimism felt by all. When Thomas Becket was chancellor and in temporal power, he had been flattered and fawned on by courtiers, but even then he had felt insecure. It would be better if the king were stronger or if Thomas were weaker. For a time, however, they dispelled their fears; Thomas was returning to lead them. The women thought the archbishop should return to France. He would still be their spiritual leader, and in France he would be safe. As the priests started to drive out the babbling women, the archbishop arrived and bade them remain.

Thomas Becket told his priests of the difficulties he had encountered, for rebellious bishops and the barons had sworn to have his head. They had sent spies to him and intercepted his letters. At Sandwich he had barely escaped with his life. His enemies were waiting to pounce.

The first tempter came to talk with Thomas. When he was chancellor, Thomas had known worldly pleasure and worldly success. Many had been his friends, and at that time he knew how to let friendship oversway principles. To escape his present hard fate, he needed only to relax his severity and dignity, to be friendly, to overlook disagreeable principles. Thomas had the strength to give the tempter a strong refusal.

The second tempter reminded Thomas of his temporal power as chancellor. He could be chancellor again and have lasting power. It was well known that the king only commanded, while the chancellor ruled, and ruled richly. Power was a present attribute; holiness was more useful after death. Real power had to be purchased by wise submission, and his present spiritual authority led only to death. Thomas asked about rebellious bishops whom he had excommunicated and barons whose privileges he had curtailed. The tempter was confident that these dissidents would come to heel if Thomas were chancellor with the king's power behind him. Again Thomas had the strength to say no.

The third tempter was easier to deal with. He represented a clique intent on overthrowing the throne. If Thomas would lead them, they could make the power of the Church supreme. No more would both the barons and the bishops be ruled by a king. Thomas declined the offer to lead the malcontents.

The fourth tempter was unexpected. He showed Thomas how he could have eternal glory. As plain archbishop, the time would come when men would neither respect nor hate him; he would become a fact of history. So it was with temporal power, too: king succeeds king as the wheel of time turns. Shrines are pillaged and thrones totter. But if Thomas would only continue in his present course, he would become a martyr and a saint, to dwell forevermore in the presence of God.

Thus the archbishop's dilemma came to him. No matter if he acted or suffered, he would sin against his religion.

Early on Christmas morning Thomas preached a sermon on peace. Christ left us his peace, but not peace as the world thinks of it. Spiritual peace did not necessarily mean England at peace with other countries or the barons at peace with the king.

After the Christmas time had passed, four knights came to Canterbury on urgent business. Refusing all hospitality, they began to state charges against Thomas, saying that he owed all his influence to the king. Thomas, they argued, had been ignobly born, and his eminence was due solely to King Henry's favor. The knights tried to attack Thomas, but the priests and attendants interposed themselves.

The charges were publicly amplified. Thomas had gone to France to stir up trouble in the dominion and to intrigue with the King of France and the pope. Yet in his charity King Henry had permitted Thomas to return to his see. Thomas had repaid that charity by excommunicating the bishops who had crowned the young prince; hence the legality of the coronation was in doubt. The knights then pronounced his sentence: he and his retinue must leave English soil.

Thomas answered firmly. In France he had been a beggar of foreign charity, and he would never leave England again. He had no dislike for the prince; rather, he had only carried out the pope's orders in excommunicating the bishops.

These words availed little. In the cathedral proper, the knights fell on Thomas Becket and slew him.

In turn the knights gave their reasons for the slaying. It looked like four against one, and the English believed in fair play; but before deciding, the people should know the whole story. First, the four knights would not benefit from the murder. The king, for reasons of state, would deplore the incident, and the knights would at least be banished. And really, it was hard for a good churchman to kill an archbishop.

Secondly, Thomas had been an able chancellor. The king had hoped, in elevating him to the archbishopric, to unite temporal and spiritual rule and to bring order to a troubled kingdom. But as soon as Thomas was elevated, he became more priestly than the priests and refused to follow the king's orders.

Thirdly, he had become an egotistical madman. There was evidence that before leaving France he had clearly prophesied his death in England. He was determined to suffer a martyr's fate. In the face of this provocation, the people must conclude that Thomas had committed suicide while of unsound mind.

After the knights left, the priests and populace mourned. Their only solace was that so long as men will die for faith the Church will be supreme.

MUTINY ON THE BOUNTY

Type of work: Novel
Authors: Charles Nordhoff (1887-1947) and James Norman Hall (1887-1951)
Type of plot: Adventure romance
Time of plot: Late eighteenth century
Locale: South Pacific and Tahiti
First published: 1932

> *Principal characters:*
> LIEUTENANT WILLIAM BLIGH, captain of H.M.S. *Bounty*
> ROGER BYAM, a midshipman
> FLETCHER CHRISTIAN, leader of the mutiny
> GEORGE STEWART, midshipman friend of Byam
> TEHANI, a Tahitian girl

Critique:

Written in the form of a novel and completely romantic in temper, *Mutiny on the Bounty* is a great story of adventure based upon actual fact. The story of the voyage of the *Bounty*, which sailed from England in 1787, the mutiny aboard her, the exploit of Captain Bligh in piloting a small boat across thirty-six hundred miles of open sea, the trial of the mutineers, and the final refuge of others on bleak Pitcairn Island, are all matters of record. The authors' free arrangement of their material is designed to give to factual narrative the drama and romantic atmosphere of fiction.

The Story:

In 1787 . Roger Byam accepted Lieutenant Bligh's offer of a berth as midshipman on H. M. S. *Bounty*, a ship commissioned by the English government to carry the edible breadfruit tree of Tahiti to English possessions in the West Indies, to be used there as a cheap food supply for the black slaves of English planters. Byam's special commission was to work at the task of completing a study of Tahitian dialects for the use of English seamen. After filling the ship's roster and getting favorable weather, the *Bounty* set sail, and Midshipman Byam began to learn the ways of a ship at sea. He also began to learn, when only a few days from England, of the many traits of his captain which were to lead

eventually to mutiny. Bligh's fanaticism rested on discipline, which he often enforced at the cost of justice through excessive floggings of the seamen aboard the *Bounty*. However, the principal objection the men had was their captain's exploitation of them and their rations for private graft.

When the *Bounty* arrived in Tahiti, the crew was given the freedom it deserved. Making use of the native custom, each of the men chose for himself a taio, or special friend from among the natives, who, during the sailor's stay in Tahiti, would supply him with all the delicacies the island had to offer. During the stay at Tahiti, Byam, living ashore, collected information for his language study. Most of the sailors found women with whom they lived and to whom some of them were later married. Fletcher Christian chose Maimiti, the daughter of Byam's taio. George Stewart chose a Tahitian girl named Peggy. Byam saw Tehani, later his wife, only once during his stay on the island, but from this one appearance he was highly impressed with the beauty of the princess.

Captain Bligh, on the *Bounty*, had continued to practice the cruelties which the men considered not only unfair but also illegal. One practice was the confiscation of gifts which the islanders had brought to the men on shipboard and which rightfully belonged to those men. The gifts he ordered to be put into the ship's stores. He had further placed the men on salt pork rations, amid all the plentiful fresh fruits of the island. Just before leaving Tahiti, Bligh falsely accused Christian of stealing a coconut.

Collection of the breadfruit trees was finally completed and the *Bounty* left for England, but not before four of the chagrined crewmen had attempted desertion. They were caught, returned, and flogged before the crew. This was one more incident to add to the already sullen attitude of the sailors. Feeling continued to run high against Bligh during the early part of the voyage, until that fateful night when a sudden impulse led Christian into mutiny. With his mutineering friends he gained control of the ship and subsequently set Bligh adrift in the *Bounty's* launch, in the company of as many of the loyal crewmen as that boat would hold. The launch was too small to hold all of the loyal hands and so seven had to stay behind, among them Byam and Stewart, his close friend. The mutiny left the *Bounty* manned by twenty-three men, including the seven loyal men.

With Christian in command, the *Bounty* sailed about in the South Seas, the mutineers searching for a suitable island on which to establish a permanent settlement. After several attempts, all balked by unfriendly natives, Christian returned with the crew to Tahiti. By a show of hands, the crew again split, some of the men continuing with Christian their search for a permanent home, the others, including Byam and Stewart, remaining at Tahiti. They expected eventually to be picked up by an English vessel and returned home to continue their naval careers.

After Christian and his crew had sailed to an unknown destination, Byam and his friend established homes on the island by marrying the native girls with whom they had fallen in love during the first visit to the island. Byam went to live in the home of Tehani, his wife, and there continued his language studies. During that idyllic year on the island, children were born to the wives of both Byam and Stewart. Then H. M. S. *Pandora* arrived, searching for the lost *Bounty*. Unaware that Bligh, who had miraculously reached England, had not distinguished between mutineer and loyal sailor among the men who remained on the *Bounty*, Byam and Stewart, anxious for some word of home, eagerly met the newly arrived ship. They were promptly placed in irons and imprisoned. They saw their wives only once after imprisonment, and had it not been for the ship's doctor on the *Pandora* they would have suffered greater hardship than they had experienced on the *Bounty*. The doctor made it possible for Byam to go on with his studies, a task which gave the prisoners something to do and kept them from losing their minds.

The *Pandora* sailed for England with a total of seven prisoners, four of whom were not guilty of mutiny. They suffered many unnecessary hardships, the greatest occurring during a storm in which the *Pandora* was sunk. The captain delayed releasing the men from their irons until the last possible moment, an act which cost the life of Stewart, who was unable to get clear of the sinking *Pandora* and drowned.

The survivors, gathered on a small island, were forced into a decision to try to make the voyage to Timor, in the Dutch East Indies, the nearest island of call. Their experiences in open boats, with little or no water and food, were savagely cruel because of the tropic sun, the madness from lack of water, and the foolish attempts of the *Pandora's* captain to continue to treat the prisoners as prisoners. Eventually the group reached Timor and there found passage on a Dutch ship bound for England.

Returned to England, the prisoners awaited court-martial for mutiny. The loyal men, falsely accused, were Byam, Morrison, and Muspratt. Three of the mutineers with them were Ellison, Burkitt, and Millward, sailors who were convicted of their crime and hanged. The evidence concerning the innocent men finally reached a point where the decision rested upon the testimony of Robert Tinkler, another midshipman on the *Bounty*. Tinkler was believed lost at sea, but he turned up in time to save the lives of Byam, Muspratt, and Morrison.

Byam continued his naval career and eventually he became the captain of his own ship. In 1810 he returned to Tahiti. Tehani, his wife, was dead. His daughter he found alive and the image of her mother. In a last romantic gesture, he saw that he could not make himself known to her, and he left Tahiti without telling her he was her father. To him that beautiful green island was a place filled with ghosts of younger men, and young Midshipman Byam was one of them.

MY ÁNTONIA

Type of work: Novel
Author: Willa Cather (1876-1947)
Type of plot: Regional chronicle
Time of plot: Late nineteenth and early twentieth centuries
Locale: Nebraska prairie land
First published: 1918

Principal characters:
JIM BURDEN, the narrator and Antonia's friend
ÁNTONIA SHIMERDA, a Bohemian peasant girl

Critique:

Perhaps the most beautiful aspect of this book is its disarming simplicity. There are no witty phrases, no complicated characters; indeed, there is scarcely any plot. And yet there is a quiet, probing depth in Miss Cather's writing. *My Ántonia* is the story of a Bohemian girl whose family came from the old country to settle on the open prairies of Nebraska. While she lives on her farm and tills the soil, she is a child of the prairie, almost as much a part of her setting as the waving grass and the tall corn. But Ántonia goes also to the city, and there she knows heartbreak. She finds peace and meaning in life only after her return to the land which is her heritage.

The Story:

Jim Burden's father and mother died when he was ten years old, and the boy made the long trip from Virginia to his grandparents' farm in Nebraska in the company of Jake Marpole, a hired hand who was to work for Jim's grandfather. Arriving by train late at night in the prairie town of Black Hawk, the boy noticed an immigrant family huddled on the station platform. He and Jake were met by a lanky, scar-faced cowboy named Otto Fuchs, who drove them in a jolting wagon across the empty prairie to the Burden farm.

Jim grew to love the vast expanse of land and sky. One day Jim's grandmother suggested that the family pay a visit to the Shimerdas, an immigrant family just arrived in the territory. At first the newcomers impressed Jim unfavorably. The Shimerdas were poor and lived in a dugout cut into the earth. The place was dirty. The children were ragged. Although he could not understand her speech, Jim made friends with the oldest girl, Ántonia.

Jim found himself often at the Shimerda home. He did not like Ántonia's surly brother, Ambrosch, or her grasping mother, but Ántonia, with her eager smile and great, warm eyes won an immediate place in Jim's heart. One day her father, his English dictionary tucked under his arm, cornered Jim and asked him to teach the girl English. She learned rapidly. Jim respected Ántonia's father. He was a tall, thin, sensitive man, a musician in the old country. Now he was saddened by poverty and burdened with overwork. He seldom laughed any more.

Jim and Ántonia passed many happy hours on the prairie. Then tragedy struck the Shimerdas. During a severe winter, Mr. Shimerda, broken and beaten by the prairie, shot himself. Ántonia had loved her father more than any other member of the family, and after his death she shouldered his share of the farm work. When spring came, she went with Ambrosch into the fields and plowed like a man. The harvest brought money. The Shimerdas soon had a house, and with the money left over they bought plowshares and cattle.

Because Jim's grandparents were growing too old to keep up their farm, they dismissed Jake and Otto and moved to the town of Black Hawk. There Jim longed for the open prairie land, the gruff, friendly companionship of Jake and Otto, and the warmth of Ántonia's friendship. He suffered at school and spent his idle hours roaming the barren gray streets of Black Hawk.

At Jim's suggestion, his grandmother arranged with a neighbor, Mrs. Harling, to bring Ántonia into town as her hired girl. Ántonia entered into her tasks with enthusiasm. Jim saw a change in her. She was more feminine; she laughed oftener; and though she never shirked her duties at the Harling house, she was eager for recreation and gaiety.

Almost every night she went to a dance pavilion with a group of hired girls. There, in new, handmade dresses, the immigrant girls gathered to dance with the village boys. Jim Burden went, too, and the more he saw of the hired girls, the better he liked them. Once or twice he worried about Ántonia, who was popular and trusting. When she earned a reputation for being a little too gay, she lost her position with the Harlings and went to work for a cruel moneylender, Wick Cutter, who had a licentious eye on her.

One night, Ántonia appeared at the Burdens and begged Jim to stay in her bed for the night and let her remain at the Burdens. Wick Cutter was supposed to be out of town, but Ántonia suspected that, with Mrs. Cutter also gone, he might return and harm her. Her fears proved correct, for as Jim lay awake in Ántonia's bed Wick returned and went to the bedroom where he thought Antonia was sleeping.

Ántonia returned to work for the Harlings. Jim, eager to go off to college, studied hard during the summer and passed his entrance examinations. In the fall he left for the state university and although he found there a whole new world of literature and art, he could not forget his early years under the blazing prairie sun and his friendship

with Ántonia. He heard little of Ántonia during those years. One of her friends, Lena Lingard, who had also worked as a hired girl in Black Hawk, visited him one day. He learned from her that Ántonia was engaged to be married to a man named Larry Donovan.

Jim went on to Harvard to study law, and for years heard nothing of his Nebraska friends. He assumed that Ántonia was married. When he made a trip back to Black Hawk to see his grandparents, he learned that Ántonia, deceived by Larry Donovan, had left Black Hawk in shame and returned to her family. There she worked again in the fields until her baby was born. When Jim went to see her, he found her still the same lovely girl, though her eyes were somber and she had lost her old gaiety. She welcomed him and proudly showed him her baby.

Jim thought that his visit was probably the last time he would see Ántonia. He told her how much a part of him she had become and how sorry he was to leave her again. Ántonia knew that Jim would always be with her, no matter where he went. He reminded her of her beloved father, who, though he had been dead many years, still lived nobly in her heart. She told Jim goodbye and watched him walk back toward town along the familiar road.

It was twenty years before Jim Burden saw Ántonia again. On a Western trip he found himself not far from Black Hawk, and on impulse he drove out in an open buggy to the farm where she lived. He found the place swarming with children of all ages. Small boys rushed forward to greet him, then fell back shyly. Ántonia had married well, at last. The grain was high, and the neat farmhouse seemed to be charged with an atmosphere of activity and happiness. Ántonia seemed as unchanged as she was when she and Jim used to whirl over the dance floor together in Black Hawk. Cusak, her husband, seemed to know Jim before they were introduced, for Ántonia had told all her family about Jim Burden. After a long visit with the Cuzaks, Jim left, promising that he would return the next summer and take two of the Cuzak boys hunting with him.

Waiting in Black Hawk for the train that would take him East, Jim found it hard to realize the long time that had passed since the dark night, years before, when he had seen an immigrant family standing wrapped in their shawls on the same platform. All his memories of the prairie came back to him. Whatever happened now, whatever they had missed, he and Ántonia had shared precious years between them, years that would never be forgotten.

MY LIFE AND HARD TIMES

Type of work: Autobiography
Author: James Thurber (1894-1961)
Time: Early twentieth century
Locale: Columbus, Ohio
First published: 1933

Principal personages:
JAMES THURBER
CHARLES, his father
MARY, his mother
HERMAN, and
ROY, his brothers
HIS GRANDFATHER

To say that there are two worlds—the World of Ordinary Men and another known as the World of Thurber, which orbits erratically through our atmosphere and occasionally bumps into the countryside or blunders down a city street like a low-flying blimp—is a cliché which would never be tolerated by Mr. Thurber himself, for one of the charms of his style is a scrupulous avoidance of anything resembling the trite. One suspects that among his many phobias there must exist the dread of turning a corner in a sentence without first myopically peering around to make sure there is no cliché about to waylay him. His precision of language and careful attention to detail are the qualities which give his writing its interest and charm, his ability to impose a world of fantasy on a world of reality and to achieve an inter-relationship of the external and the internal, the factual and the imaginative. Such Thurber touches are what his followers have come to expect in all his work.

In his preface to *My Life and Hard Times,* Thurber apologizes for writing an autobiography before he had reached the age of forty and for not conforming to Ford Madox Ford's dictum that one's memoirs should paint a picture of one's time. Thurber more or less admits that he has no time, that all he intends to tell is what happened to one writer. Since all that follows could happen to no one but Thurber, he thus admits, but without saying so, the existence of the Thurber world.

This world reaches beyond the boundaries of the real or the commonplace and extends into a region of fable, peopled by such figures as Emma Inch, the cook, and her asthmatic dog Feely; colored Della, who made cretonnes for the soup and whose brother worked in an incinerator where they burn refuse; Barney Haller, the hired man, whom thunder followed like a dog; and Walter Mitty, that frustrated, comic Prufrock with his impossible dreams of heroism and glory. Strange things happen in this world because James Thurber sees it that way: an old woman with a parasol is seen to walk through a truck; a cat goes rolling across the street atop a striped barrel; an admiral in full uniform rides a bicycle across the highway in the path of an oncoming car. That these things are never what they seem but fragments of the ordinary world suddenly revealed in a new light or a different perspective is the secret of Thurber's humor. It is a form of humor little concerned with the conventional or the obvious. It arises quite naturally from a recognition of the inner, emotional chaos of a sensitive, individualistic man trapped in the affairs of the practical, demanding world, with no weapon of defense but his own resistances and inferiorities.

Hence that air of the fabulous which invests Thurber's drawings as well—the meek, rotund men whose poses are those of resignation and whose faces reveal long-thwarted efforts to think and act in a positive manner; the aggressive, rather frightening women who never seem disturbed by doubts as to *their* superiority; the huge, sadly patient dogs. They belong in a world in which life has grown complicated for men and animals, from which one way of escape leads into a Cloud-Cuckoo Land where the illogical becomes the logical and the fantastic reveals the dilemma of modern man facing the psychological confusion and insecurity of his place in a world almost devoid of sense and meaning.

Nowhere does James Thurber display to better advantage his genius for uncovering the incongruous in the everyday affairs of men, the daydream escapes from personal confusion or catastrophe, than he does in the nine episodes which center (perhaps the proper word is eccenter) around Thurber's youth in Columbus, Ohio, as told in *My Life and Hard Times*.

"The Night the Bed Fell" is about the night the bed did not fall on Thurber's father while he slept in the attic where grandfather was supposed to sleep. But grandfather, who refused to believe that the Army of the Potomac was not still trying to take Richmond, had wandered off some days before; eventually he would turn up with profane criticism of the campaign, its military leaders, and the administration in Washington. Actually, James Thurber rolled out of his cot; his mother was convinced that the bed had fallen on father and he must be pulled from the wreckage; a visiting cousin poured a glass of camphor over himself, and father was sure that the house was on fire. Mother, who always called it the night on which the bed fell on father, was looking on the bright side of things when she said she was glad grandfather had not been there.

"The Car We Had to Push" is about all sorts of things, but mostly about grandfather's brother Zenas, who contracted the chestnut tree blight and died of that strange malady in 1866.

"The Day the Dam Broke" is about the day the dam did not break. Expected catastrophes have a way of not happening in the Thurber world, but the effects are very much the same. The citizens of Columbus thought it had broken and they fled in panic, hysterical at the time but hilarious in the retelling.

The police were summoned to the Thurber household on "The Night the Ghost Got In," and grandfather shot one policeman in the shoulder under the hallucinated impression that the men in blue uniforms were deserters from General Meade's army.

"More Alarms at Night" deals with brother Roy's feigned delirium; even at the best of times Roy was likely to sing "Onward, Christian Soldiers" or "Marching Through Georgia" in his sleep. He awakened father in the small hours, called him Buck, and announced that his time had come. Father, a mildly nervous man, aroused his family. Everyone assured him that he had had a bad dream. The sketch also deals with another night when James awoke poor father to get help in remembering the name of a New Jersey city, Perth Amboy. Sure that his son had gone mad, father ran from the room.

"A Sequence of Servants" deals with just what the title indicates. There were 162 of these servants, including a colored one, Vashti, who told her lover that he must never tangle with her jealous stepfather, who had married her mother just to be near Vashti. But Thurber (the writer) cannot stay away from the negative; it turns out that Vashti had invented her stepfather to pique the lover.

A memorable Airedale named Muggs is "The Dog That Bit People." When he died, after biting almost everybody in Ohio—including Lieutenant-Governor Malloy—mother wanted to bury him in the family plot under "Flights of angels sing thee to thy rest" or some equally misappropriate inscription. The family dissuaded her, however, and Muggs was interred along a lonely road beneath an epitaph of Thurber's choice: "Cave canem." Mother was always quite pleased with the classic dignity of that simple Latin phrase.

"University Days" presents Bolenciecwcz, star tackle on the Ohio State football team, whom an economics professor tried to make eligible for the Illinois game by asking him to name one means of transportation; after hints, prods, and auditory and visual demonstrations by the professor and the whole class, Bolenciecwcz mentioned a train and the day was saved. There is also an agricultural student named Haskins, who wanted to be a journalist and whose beat for campus news covered the cow barns, the horse pavilion, the sheep house, and the animal husbandry department in general.

The final sketch, "Draft Board Nights," finds Thurber being incessantly called before the board which always turned him down because of poor eyesight, and then, through some repetitive mistake, kept calling him back. He eventually drifted into service, not in the army, but as an unauthorized and undetected examiner of draftees—a pulmonary man, to be exact. What put a merciful end to it all was the Armistice.

For critics to debate the place of Thurber in contemporary literature is useless. His humor, which creates its effects according to the laws of its own logic and yet always with a savoring of common sense, is superbly his own, as his would-be imitators have discovered. His manner is nimble without being racy; it has poignance without sentimentality. His touch with words is delicate yet precise. Best of all, he illustrates his own books with his inimitable drawings which, like his prose pieces, distort the familiar into the fantastic without—again, this is Thurber's secret—losing touch with reality.

THE MYSTERIES OF PARIS

Type of work: Novel
Author: Eugène Sue (1804-1857)
Type of plot: Mystery romance
Time of plot: Mid-nineteenth century
Locale: France and Germany
First published: 1842-1843

Principal characters:
RODOLPH, Grand Duke of Gerolstein
FLEUR-DE-MARIE, his daughter by Lady Sarah Macgregor
LADY SARAH MACGREGOR, his morganatic wife
CLÉMENCE D'HARVILLE, wife of one of Rodolph's friends
LA CHOUETTE, and
SCHOOLMASTER, two Paris criminals
JACQUES FERRAND, a hypocritical and cruel lawyer
MADAME GEORGES, befriended by Rodolph
RIGOLETTE, Fleur-de-Marie's friend

Critique:

The Mysteries of Paris is a novel which was written mainly to arouse public opinion for reform of the penal system and the poor laws. The descriptions of the poor, the needy, and the afflicted among the unfortunates of Paris are many and vivid. The novel is interspersed with short tales of misfortune and comments by the author as to how many of the difficulties could be remedied by new laws and new charities. The story which allows full freedom to the expression of these ideas is an amazing one. It contains almost a hundred main characters, to say nothing of the numerous minor character studies. Almost every minor plot contains enough material for a novel, and the major plot is intricate and detailed.

The Story:

Rodolph, the Grand Duke of Gerolstein, a small German state, was a handsome young man in his thirties in 1838. Behind him lay a strange past. As a youth he had been brought up in his father's court by an evil tutor named Polidori, who had done his best to warp and confuse the young prince's mind. Polidori had been urged on by the beautiful but sinister Lady Sarah Macgregor, who had been told in her youth that she was destined some day to be a queen. Sarah had decided that Rodolph, heir to a duchy, would be the perfect husband for her, and with the aid of Polidori she had forced Rodolph into a secret morganatic marriage. In England, where she had fled, she gave birth to a daughter. Rodolph's father was furious, and he had the marriage annulled. One day, after he had threatened to kill his father, Rodolph was sent into exile. Before long Sarah lost all interest in her child and paid her Paris lawyer, Jacques Ferrand, to find a home for the girl. Ferrand gave the child into the care of some unscrupulous child-takers and after a few years falsely wrote to Sarah that the child had died. Sarah forwarded the letter to Rodolph.

Rodolph moved to Paris where he amused himself by roaming through the slums in disguise. Although he was strong, agile, and a fine fighter, the young duke was always followed by his faithful servant, Sir Walter Murphy. Together they ferreted out the secrets and mysteries of Paris streets. One night Rodolph chanced to save a young girl who was being attacked. When he had heard her story, he was so touched by it that he decided to help her. Fleur-de-Marie, as she was called, was an orphan who had been brought up by gangsters and had been in prison. Freed, she was recognized by her old tormentors and captured by them, drugged, made a prisoner, and compelled to suffer the greatest indignities. Feeling that she was really innocent of the crimes into which she had been forced, Rodolph took her to the farm of Madame Georges. The girl's beauty, her sad plight, and the fact that she was the age his dead daughter would have been, aroused his interest and pity.

Madame Georges was likewise a woman whom the duke had befriended. Her criminal husband had deserted her, taking their son with him. Rodolph had searched the streets of Paris for a clue to the whereabouts of Madame Georges' son. At the farm Fleur-de-Marie soon developed into a devout and delightful young woman.

Rodolph continued to live his double life. He attended diplomatic balls and the parties of thieves, and on both planes he found much to do to help people to live better lives. At last, in order to learn better the secrets of Paris, he took lodgings in a boarding-house in one of the poorer sections of town. There he met many needy families, and in countless ways he helped them all. One of the occupants of the house was a girl named Rigolette, who had been Fleur-de-Marie's friend in prison. Rigolette was hard-working and kind, and Rodolph learned a great deal about the people of the house from her.

One day he learned that Clémence d'Harville, the wife of one of his good friends, was involved in an intrigue with a lodger in the house. It did not take him long to discover that the person behind this affair, plotting the destruction of d'Harville and his wife, was Lady Sarah Macgregor. As soon as he could, Rodolph warned Clémence and saved her from her folly. Clémence was unfortunate in that she had been forced into marriage with d'Harville by her mother-in-law, for she did not love her husband. Because he and their daughter were subject to epileptic fits, her life was an unhappy one. D'Harville by chance learned of his wife's unhappiness, and contrived to commit suicide in such

a way that everyone thought his death accidental. By this act he saved Clémence from greater unhappiness and atoned for the evil he had committed in marrying her.

While staying at the lodging-house, Rodolph had learned of the numerous evil deeds of the hypocritical lawyer, Jacques Ferrand. When Rodolph learned that Ferrand was planning the murder of Clémence's father, he and Sir Walter Murphy succeeded in thwarting the lawyer's evil scheme. Ferrand was also responsible for the imprisonment of Rigolette's lover. In order to get to the bottom of Ferrand's plans, Rodolph remembered Cicely, a beautiful woman who had once been married to his private doctor, but who later became a depraved creature. Rodolph secured her release from prison and had her introduced into Ferrand's household, where she could spy on his activities and learn his secrets.

Meanwhile Sarah had asked Ferrand to find a young girl whom she could claim was really her child by Rodolph, for she hoped that if she could produce the dead girl she could effect a reconciliation, now that Rodolph was the reigning duke of Gerolstein. Ferrand, learning the whereabouts of Fleur-de-Marie, hired La Chouette, an ugly one-eyed woman, and a criminal called the Schoolmaster to kidnap the girl from the farm of Madame Georges. When the Schoolmaster arrived at the farm, he discovered that Madame Georges was his wife, the woman he had deserted. He did not succeed in getting Fleur-de-Marie. Instead, she was put in jail for failing to give testimony concerning a crime she had witnessed before Rodolph had saved her from the slums. By chance, Clémence found the girl while on a charitable errand. Not knowing that Fleur-de-Marie knew Rodolph, she tried to make the girl's life more pleasant in prison.

When Sarah learned that Fleur-de-Marie had been under the care of Rodolph's friends, she became jealous and made arrangements to have her killed as soon as she could be released from the prison. Ferrand, entrusted with plans for her death, had her released from prison by an accomplice who pretended to be an agent of Clémence d'Harville. On leaving the prison, Fleur-de-Marie met Rigolette and told her old friend of her fortune. Rigolette, who knew Clémence through Rodolph, was pleased. After they parted, Fleur-de-Marie was seized by Ferrand's hirelings and taken into the country, where she was thrown into the river. But some passersby saw her in the water and pulled her ashore in time to save her life.

In the meanwhile La Chouette, learning that Fleur-de-Marie was really the daughter of Rodolph and Sarah, had hurried to Sarah with her information. Sarah was shocked at the discovery. La Chouette, seeing a chance to make more money by killing Sarah and stealing her jewels, stabbed her protector. The attacker escaped with the jewels and returned to the Schoolmaster to taunt him with her success. The two got into a fight, and the Schoolmaster killed La Chouette. He was captured and put into prison.

Through Cicely, Rodolph had also learned that his daughter was not really dead. Cicely had had little difficulty in uncovering Ferrand's past. As soon as he knew what Sarah had done, Rodolph went to see her, and despite her terrible wound he accused her violently of the shameful and criminal neglect of her daughter.

On returning home, Rodolph was surprised to hear that Clémence had visited him. Clémence had had the fortune to find Fleur-de-Marie in the home where she had been cared for after her escape from drowning, and she had brought the girl to Rodolph. Clémence did not know that events had proved that Fleur-de-Marie was Rodolph's daughter, and so the reunion of father and child was not without pain as well as pleasure, for Clémence and Rodolph had long secretly known that they loved each other.

Rodolph begged Clémence to marry him and be a mother to his child. He felt sure that Sarah would die, and the way would thus be clear for their happy life together.

Rodolph remarried Sarah on her deathbed so that their daughter could be called truly legitimate. Information that Rodolph had received from Cicely also made it possible for him to free Rigolette's lover from prison, and it turned out that he was the long-lost son of Madame Georges. With these problems solved, Rodolph planned to return to Germany. First, however, he used his knowledge of Ferrand's activities to force the lawyer to establish many worthy charities. His money gone, Ferrand went into a decline and died soon afterward. Rigolette's lover became administrator for one of the charities, and after their marriage he and Rigolette lived happily with Madame Georges.

Rodolph returned to Germany with Fleur-de-Marie as his legitimate daughter and Clémence as his wife. For a time the three lived together with great happiness. Then Rodolph noticed that Fleur-de-Marie seemed to have moods of depression. One day she explained, weeping, that his goodness to her was without compare, but that the evil life that she had led before he had rescued her from the slums preyed constantly on her mind. She begged to be allowed to enter a convent. Seeing that nothing he could say would change her mind, Rodolph gave his permission.

While serving as a novice at the convent, Fleur-de-Marie's conduct was so perfect that when she was admitted to the order she immediately became the abbess. This honor was too much for her gentle soul to bear, or for her weak, sick body to withstand, and that very night she died. Rodolph, noting that the day of her death was the anniversary of the day on which he had tried to kill his father, felt that the ways of fate are strange.

THE MYSTERIES OF UDOLPHO

Type of work: Novel
Author: Mrs. Ann Radcliffe (1764-1823)
Type of plot: Gothic romance
Time of plot: Late sixteenth century
Locale: France and Italy
First published: 1794

Principal characters:
EMILY ST. AUBERT, a young French aristocrat
SIGNOR MONTONI, a villainous Italian married to Emily's aunt
VALANCOURT, Emily's sweetheart
COUNT MORANO, a Venetian nobleman in love with Emily
MADAME MONTONI, Emily's aunt

Critique:

The Mysteries of Udolpho is the most famous of the Gothic novels extremely popular at the end of the eighteenth century. The mysterious elements of the story are always explained in some natural way, for Mrs. Radcliffe was too much of an eighteenth-century rationalist to succumb completely to the supernatural. The characters in the book are stilted both in action and conversation. Mrs. Radcliffe was at her best only when describing scenery, such as the rugged Pyrenees and Apennines, or when describing an atmosphere of suspense in creating her effects of terror.

The Story:

After the death of his wife, Monsieur St. Aubert, a French aristocrat, took his daughter on a trip in the Pyrenees Mountains. High on a mountain road the St. Auberts met a young nobleman dressed in hunting clothes. He was Valancourt, the younger son of a family with which M. St. Aubert was acquainted. Joining the St. Auberts on their journey, the young man soon fell in love with eighteen-year-old Emily St. Aubert, and the girl felt that she, too, might lose her heart to him.

St. Aubert became desperately ill and died in a cottage near the Chateau-le-Blanc, ancestral seat of the noble Villeroi family. After her father's burial at the nearby convent of St. Clair, Emily returned to her home at La Vallée and promptly burned some mysterious letters which her father had requested her to destroy. With the letters she found a miniature portrait of a beautiful unknown woman. Since she had not been told to destroy the portrait, she took it with her when she left La Vallée to stay with her aunt in Toulouse.

Valancourt followed Emily to Toulouse to press his suit. After some remonstrance, the aunt gave her permission for the young couple to marry. Then, a few days before the ceremony, the aunt married Signor Montoni, a sinister Italian, who immediately forbade his new niece's nuptials. To make his refusal doubly positive, he took Emily and her aunt to his mansion in Venice.

There Emily and Madame Montoni found themselves in unhappy circumstances, for it soon became apparent that Montoni had married in order to secure for himself the estates of his new wife and her niece. When he tried to force Emily to marry a Venetian nobleman, Count Morano, Emily was in despair. Suddenly, on the night before the wedding, Montoni ordered his household to pack and leave for his castle at Udolpho, high in the Apennines.

When the party arrived at Udolpho, Montoni immediately began to repair the fortifications of the castle. Emily did not like the dark, cold, mysterious castle from which the previous owner, Lady Laurentini, had disappeared under mysterious circumstances. Superstitious servants claimed that apparitions flitted about the halls and galleries of the ancient fortress.

Soon after Montoni and his household had. settled themselves, Count Morano attempted to kidnap Emily. Foiled by Montoni, who wounded him severely in a sword fight, Morano threatened revenge.

A few days later Montoni tried to force his wife to sign over her estates to him. When she refused, he caused her to be locked up in a tower of the castle. Emily tried to visit her aunt that night. Terrified at finding fresh blood on the tower stairs, she believed her aunt murdered.

Ghostly sounds and shadows about Udolpho began to make everyone uneasy. Even Montoni, who had organized a band of marauders to terrorize and pillage the neighborhood, began to believe the castle was haunted. Emily heard that several hostages had been taken. She was sure that Valancourt was a prisoner because she had heard someone singing a song he had taught her and because one night a mysterious shadow had called her by name. Her life was made one long torment by Montoni's insistence that she sign away her estates to him, lest she suffer the same fate as her aunt.

The aunt had not been murdered, as Emily found out through her maid, but had become so ill because of harsh treatment that she had died and had been buried in the chapel of the castle.

Morano made another attempt to steal Emily away from the castle, this time with her assistance, as she was now afraid for her life. But Montoni and his men discovered the attempt in time to seize the abductors outside the castle walls. Shortly afterward Montoni sent Emily away, after forcing her to sign the papers which gave him control of her estates in France. At first she thought she was being sent to her death, but Montoni sent her to a cottage in Tuscany because he had heard that Venetian authorities were sending a small army to attack Udolpho and seize him and his bandits. His depredations had caused

alarm after the villas of several rich Venetians had been robbed.

When Emily returned to the castle, she saw evidence that there had been a terrible battle. Emily's maid and Ludovico, another servant, disclosed to Emily on her return that a prisoner who knew her was in the dungeons below. Emily immediately guessed that the prisoner was Valancourt and made arrangements to escape with him. But the prisoner turned out to be Monsieur Du Pont, an old friend of her father. Emily, Monsieur Du Pont, the girl's maid, and Ludovico made their escape and reached Leghorn safely. There they took ship for France. Then a great storm drove the ship ashore close to the Chateau-le-Blanc, near which Emily's father had been buried.

Emily and her friends were rescued by Monsieur Villefort and his family. The Villeforts had inherited the chateau and were attempting to live in it, although it was in disrepair and said to be haunted. While at the chateau Emily decided to spend several days at the convent where her father was buried. There she found a nun who closely resembled the mysteriously missing Lady Laurentini, whose portrait Emily had seen at the castle of Udolpho.

When Emily returned to the chateau she found it in a state of turmoil because of weird noises that seemed to come from the apartments of the former mistress of the chateau. Ludovico volunteered to spend a night in the apartment. Although all the windows and doors were locked, he was not in the rooms the next morning. When the old caretaker came to tell Emily this news, she noticed the miniature Emily had found at La Vallée. The miniature, said the servant, was a portrait of her former mistress, the Marquise de Villeroi. More than that, Emily closely resembled the portrait.

Meanwhile Valancourt reappeared and once again made plans to marry Emily, but Monsieur Villefort told her of gambling debts the young man had incurred and of the wild life he had led in Paris while she had been a prisoner. in Italy.

Because of that report Emily refused to marry him. She returned in distress to her home at La Vallée to learn that Montoni had been captured by the Venetian authorities. Since he had criminally secured the deeds to her lands, the court now restored them to her, and she was once again a young woman of wealth and position.

While Emily was at La Vallée, the Villefort family made a trip high into the Pyrenees to hunt. Almost captured by bandits, they were rescued by Ludovico, who had so inexplicably disappeared from the chateau. He had been kidnaped by smugglers who had used the vaults of the chateau to store their treasure, and he disclosed that the noises in the chateau had been caused by the outlaws in an effort to frighten away the rightful owners.

Informed of what had happened, Emily returned to the chateau to see her friends. While there, she again visited the convent of St. Clair. The nun whom she had seen before, and who resembled the former mistress of Udolpho, was taken mortally ill while Emily was at the convent. On her deathbed the nun confessed that she was Lady Laurentini, who had left Udolpho to go to her former lover, the Marquis de Villeroi. Finding him married to M. St. Aubert's sister, she ensnared him once more and made him an accomplice in her plot to poison his wife. When the marquis, overcome by remorse, fled to a distant country and died there, she had retired to the convent to expiate her sins.

Emily's happiness was complete when Monsieur Du Pont, who had escaped with her from Udolpho, proved that Valancourt had gambled only to secure money to aid some friends who were on the brink of misfortune. Reunited, they were married and went to La Vallée, where they lived a happy, tranquil life in contrast to the many strange adventures which had parted them for so long.

THE MYSTERIOUS ISLAND

Type of work: Novel
Author: Jules Verne (1828-1905)
Type of plot: Adventure romance
Time of plot: 1865-1869
Locale: An island in the South Pacific
First published: 1870

Principal characters:
CAPTAIN CYRUS HARDING, an engineer
NEBUCHADNEZZAR, his Negro servant
GIDEON SPILETT, a reporter
JACK PENCROFT, a sailor
HERBERT BROWN, an orphan
AYRTON, a mutineer
CAPTAIN NEMO, captain of the *Nautilus*

Critique:

The Mysterious Island is in a sense a sequel to Jules Verne's famous *Twenty Thousand Leagues Under the Sea*, for in this work Verne describes the death of Captain Nemo; but it is primarily a story of survival and a celebration of the adaptability and ingenuity of intelligent, hardworking, God-fearing man. Verne shows the great satisfaction that can be derived from personal accomplishment. The wealth of detail and description and the valid explanations of mysterious happenings create a sense of realism.

The Story:

On March 24, 1865, a balloon carrying five persons who were escaping from Richmond, capital of the Confederacy during the War Between the States, fell into the sea. Caught in a storm, the balloon had flown some seven thousand miles in five days. The five passengers were Captain Cyrus Harding, an engineer in General Grant's army; his Negro servant, Nebuchadnezzar; Gideon Spilett, a reporter; Jack Pencroft, a sailor; and Herbert Brown, the fifteen-year-old orphan son of one of Pencroft's former sea captains.

The balloon fell near an uncharted island, and Harding, together with his dog Top, was washed overboard. Its load lightened, the balloon then deposited the other travelers on the shore of the island. The next morning Nebuchadnezzar, who

was known as Neb, went to look for his master while the others explored the island.

The next day Herbert, Pencroft, and Spilett took stock of their resources, which consisted of the clothes they wore, a notebook, and a watch. They suddenly heard Top barking. The dog led them to Captain Harding who, having been unconscious, was at a loss to explain how he had arrived at a place more than a mile away from the shore.

When Harding was stronger, the group decided to consider themselves colonists rather than castaways, and they called their new home Lincoln Island. Harding found on the island samples of iron, pyrite, clay, lime, coal, and other useful minerals. The colonists made bricks which they used to construct an oven for the making of pottery. From Top's collar they were able to make two knives, which enabled them to cut bows and arrows. Eventually they were able to make iron and steel tools.

Under the brilliant direction of Harding, who seemed to know a great deal about everything, the colonists worked constantly to improve their lot. After discovering a cave within a cliff wall they planned to make this their permanent residence; they called it Granite House. They made a rope ladder up the side of the cliff to the door of the cavern, which they equipped with walls of brick, furniture, and candles made from seal fat.

One day Pencroft found washed up on the beach a large chest containing many useful items, including books, clothes, instruments, and weapons. On another occasion the colonists returned to Granite House to find that their home had been invaded by orang-utans, who suddenly became terrified at something and began to flee. The colonists killed all but one that they domesticated and called Jup.

The colony prospered. They domesticated various animals, used a stream to power an elevator to Granite House, and made glass windows. They built a boat designed by Harding and named it the *Bonadventure*. As they were sailing it they found a bottle with a message, saying that there was a castaway on nearby Tabor Island. Pencroft, Spilett, and Herbert sailed to Tabor Island, where Herbert was attacked by a strange wild man. Pencroft and Spilett succeeded in capturing the creature and they took him back to Lincoln Island, where he began to become civilized again. One day he confessed with shame that his name was Ayrton, that he had attempted mutiny on one ship, had tried to seize another, and had finally been put ashore on Tabor Island by one Captain Grant, of the *Duncan*. Ayrton, who repented his past life, was accepted by the colonists as one of them. He lived at a corral which the colonists had built some distance from Granite House.

One day the colonists sighted a pirate ship. A battle between the pirates and the colonists developed, and just when things were going badly for the colonists, the pirate ship seemed to explode. Later the colonists found the remains of a strange torpedo that had destroyed the ship.

A short time later the colonists discovered that the telegraph system which Harding had built to the corral had broken down. When they went to the corral to investigate, they were attacked by some of the pirates who had not perished with their ship, and Herbert was seriously wounded. Ayrton, moreover, was gone. While the colonists were trying desperately to keep Herbert alive, the pirates set fire to the mill and sheds close by Granite House and destroyed the plantation. By the time the colonists were able to make their way back to Granite House, Herbert had weakened seriously. The one thing needed for his recovery, sulphate of quinine, was lacking on the island, but on the crucial night, which might have been Herbert's last, the colonists found a box of quinine beside Herbert's bed, and the medicine enabled him to recover.

Finally the colonists set out to find their mysterious benefactor and to exterminate the pirates. When the expedition arrived at the corral, they found Ayrton, who had been tortured by the pirates but who was still alive. Top then discovered the corpses of all the remaining pirates, who had been killed in a mysterious way.

The colonists made plans to build a ship large enough to carry them back to civilization. When they discovered smoke rising from the crater of the volcano, they redoubled their efforts to complete the boat.

One day the colonists received a call on the telegraph telling them to go to the corral immediately. There they found a note which told them to follow the wire that had been attached to the telegraph line. They followed the wire into a hidden cove, where they found the fantastic submarine *Nautilus* and its captain, their benefactor, Captain Nemo. He told them how he had been a rich nobleman in India, how he had been defeated in his fight for the independence of his country, and how he and his followers, disgusted with the ways of man, had built a gigantic undersea craft. His followers having died, Nemo, old and alone, had taken the *Nautilus* to Lincoln Island, where he had lived for the past six years, giving aid to the colonists because he believed them to be good people. After presenting Harding with a box of jewels and pearls and making a last request that he be buried in his ship, he died. The colonists sealed the *Nautilus* with Captain Nemo's body inside and then opened the flood valves to sink the ship.

Following some advice Captain Nemo had given him, Harding investigated the caverns beneath the island and saw that, as soon as the sea water penetrated to the shaft of the volcano, the entire island would explode.

The colonists worked with all haste to complete work on the boat. By March of their fourth year on the island the hull had been built, but on the night before the launching the entire island was shattered with a tremendous roar. All that was left of Lincoln Island was a small rock formation. The colonists had all been able to reach safety there, but their ship had vanished. The colonists stayed on the rock formation for nine days.

On March 24 they sighted a ship. It was the *Duncan*, which had come to rescue Ayrton after his exile of twelve years on Tabor Island. The colonists went to America, and with the treasure Captain Nemo had given them they bought land in Iowa. They colonized it and prospered in their new home.

THE MYSTERY OF EDWIN DROOD

Type of work: Novel
Author: Charles Dickens (1812-1870)
Type of plot: Mystery romance
Time of plot: Mid-nineteenth century
Locale: England
First published: 1870

Principal characters:
EDWIN DROOD, a young engineer
JACK JASPER, Edwin's young uncle and guardian
ROSA BUD, Edwin's fiancée
NEVILLE LANDLESS, an orphaned young man
HELENA LANDLESS, Neville's sister and Rosa Bud's schoolmate
DURDLES, a stonemason and friend of Jack Jasper
MR. CRISPARKLE, Neville Landless' tutor and friend

Critique:

The Mystery of Edwin Drood was Charles Dickens' last novel, begun when the author was already sick and exhausted. It was not finished, and no notes to indicate what the solution in Dickens' mind might have been have ever been discovered. Many people have tried to hypothesize a probable ending and to write a conclusion, but no solution has been satisfactory; Dickens' secret died with him. One of the most interesting theories, however, finds Mr. Jasper the murderer and relates the death of Edwin Drood to the secret society of Thugs in India, a sect that murdered by strangulation. This novel is almost entirely a murder mystery. Although some of Dickens' earlier novels had contained elements of a mystery plot, this book is the only one to be so completely of that type. It was probably inspired by the work of Dickens' friend, Wilkie Collins, a famous author of mysteries.

The Story:

Mr. Jack Jasper was the young choirmaster of the cathedral at Cloisterham. Young as he was, he was also the guardian of his orphan nephew, Edwin Drood, who was only a few years Jasper's junior. In spite of his positions of trust, Jasper was an opium addict. Edwin Drood was an apprentice engineer who would one day become a partner in the firm that employed him, for his father had been one of the owners. Drood's profession took him all over the world, but he came back at every opportunity to Cloisterham to see his uncle and his fiancée.

Drood's fiancée, Rosa Bud, was attending a finishing school in Cloisterham. She had been there for several years, for both her parents were dead. The fathers of the two young people had been extremely close friends and each had requested in his will that the two be engaged and, at the proper time, married. As the years passed, however, the two young people realized that they were not in love and, contrary to their parents' wishes, had no desire to marry. In Rosa's last year at the finishing school they agreed that they would remain friends, but they put aside all ideas of marriage.

No one except Rosa realized that Jasper was in love with her. Rosa was very much afraid of Jasper, so afraid that she dared not tell anyone of Jasper's infatuation. But she almost gave her secret away when she ceased taking music lessons from him, lest he annoy her during the hours when they were alone.

During one of Drood's visits to Cloisterham a young couple from Ceylon, Englishmen who had been orphaned in that far-off island, came to the city. The girl, Helena Landless, who was Rosa Bud's age, entered the finishing school; the young man, who was the age of Edwin Drood, began studies under one of the

2504

minor officials at the cathedral, Mr. Crisparkle. Crisparkle, a friend of Jasper and Drood, introduced his charge, Neville Landless, to the two men in the hope that they would all become fast friends.

It turned out, however, that young Landless was very much affected by Rosa and was irritated by Drood's casual attitude toward her. The very first evening that they were together in Jasper's lodgings, the two quarreled, and Jasper realized that if he had not interceded Landless would have killed Drood in a fit of rage.

Rosa and Helena did become close friends, and Rosa confessed to Helena that she was in love with the latter's brother. Although she did not tell Jasper, he soon discovered the truth for himself and became exceedingly jealous. Jasper, who was extremely mysterious at times, and more than a little peculiar because of his addiction to opium, became acquainted with another peculiar man, Durdles, a stonemason. Durdles took Jasper about the cathedral and pointed out the various old tombs under the ancient edifice. On one of those visits, which took place in the dead of night, Durdles became very drunk. While he was asleep, Jasper took the key to an underground tomb from Durdles' pocket. What he did with it later on remained a mystery.

During the next Christmas season Mr. Crisparkle tried to patch up the quarrel between Landless and Drood. He proposed that they meet together at Jasper's lodgings and, after mutual apologies, have a congenial evening together. The two young men agreed. On Christmas morning, however, Drood was reported missing by his uncle, with whom the nephew was staying. Jasper said that late the night before the two young men had walked out of his lodgings and turned toward the river. No one had seen them afterward. When Mr. Crisparkle appeared, he reported that young Landless had left earlier that morning on a solitary walking trip. A searching party set out after him

and brought him back to Cloisterham. Young Landless was unable to convince anyone of his innocence, although there was not enough evidence to convict him of any crime. Indeed, the body of Drood was not found, although Mr. Crisparkle discovered his watch and tie pin in the river.

At first only Rosa and Helena were convinced of Landless' innocence. Soon they won Mr. Crisparkle over to their side, and he aided Landless to leave Cloisterham for a refuge in London.

Jasper vowed that he would unearth evidence that would incriminate the murderer. He also intimated that he had some evidence that Landless was the guilty person. Publicly, however, there was no indication that Edwin Drood had actually been killed.

After a few months Jasper appeared at the school and requested an interview with Rosa. As they walked in the school gardens, Jasper told of his love for her and warned her that he had sufficient evidence to send Neville Landless to the gallows. He also implied that he would use his knowledge unless Rosa returned his love. After he had gone, Rosa left the school and went to London, where she sought the protection of her guardian, Mr. Grewgious, an odd man but one who loved her because he had been in love with her mother years before. Mr. Grewgious arranged to have Rosa remain in safe lodgings in London. Mr. Crisparkle arrived the next day and began to lay plans to extricate Landless and Rosa from their troubles.

One day a white-haired stranger arrived in Cloisterham. His name, he let it be known, was Datchery, and he was looking for quiet lodgings where he could end his days in comfort and peace. Looking for a place of residence that would reflect the quaintness of the past, he took rooms across from Jasper's home in the old postern gate. Passersby would see him sitting by the hour behind his open door. Every time he heard some remark about

Jasper, he made a chalk mark, some long, some short, on the inside of his closet door.

A short time later Jasper was followed about, almost haunted, by a haggard old woman from whom he had bought opium. She had learned something about the choirmaster, apparently, and suspected a great deal more. Datchery, noting her interest in Jasper, followed her to a cheap hotel. The next morning he and the strange woman attended a service in the cathedral. When the woman told him that she knew Jasper, old Datchery returned home and added another chalk mark to those behind his closet door. . . .

(Here the story ends, for Dickens died suddenly, leaving the novel incomplete, with no notes among his papers to show how he intended to end the story.)

THE NAKED YEAR

Type of work: Novel
Author: Boris Pilnyak (Boris Andreyevich Vogau, 1894-   )
Type of plot: Regional chronicle
Time of plot: Early twentieth century
Locale: Russia
First published: 1922

Principal characters:
DONAT RATCHIN, a merchant's son, a young revolutionist
NASTIA, a chambermaid
ARKHIP, a peasant member of the party
ARKHIPOV, his father
NATALIA ORDYNIN, a young doctor
BORIS,
GLEB, and
EGOR, her brothers
CATHERINE, and
LYDIA, her sisters
ANDREY, a fugitive

Critique:

The importance of *The Naked Year* is historical. During World War I and its aftermath of revolution, Russian prose almost ceased to exist, although some types of poetry flourished. This novel is the first prose work of any stature to be published after the hiatus. Pilnyak is strongly under the influence of poetical tenets; that is, this work exalts manner over matter. Quite literally there is no plot, nor are there characters in the usual sense. Rather the author gives a series of impressions of revolution-torn Russia during one year of civil war, pestilence, blockade, and change, just before the Soviets gained firm control in 1921. The reading is irritatingly obscure at times, but effective in its blending of lyricism and realism.

The Story:

Ordynin Town was a citadel which had for years lived a normal life. That is to say, poets, artisans, and merchants dwelt there, busy with their tasks. The Ratchin family had been merchants for two hundred years, and for much of that time they had leased the salt trade. Donat, a curly-headed youth, was the youngest son. Already he counted on taking his place in the market, on buying and selling and ruling his clerks.

The monastery held an important place in the lives of the people, for its bells regulated their lives. At nine o'clock the town went to bed. Anyone up and about after that hour had to identify himself to the watch. Pranks of boys and dwarfs provided the only excitement, and the stationer's store was the intellectual center of the town.

Donat at fifteen fell in love with a chambermaid named Nastia. Every evening he went to her kitchen and read church history aloud to her. When Ivan, his autocratic father, heard of the attachment, he had both Donat and Nastia whipped; that same night Ivan sent his housekeeper to Donat's bed. Afterward Donat learned how to get out of the house at night. For a while he clambered out of a window and went to see the persecuted widow of a rich money-lender.

In 1914 war came, and in 1917 revolution. From ancient Ordynin the inhabitants were called up to learn the craft of murder, to kill and die. Donat was sent to the Carpathians. The first

THE NAKED YEAR by Boris Pilnyak. Translated by Alec Brown. By permission of the publishers, Harcourt, Brace & Co., Inc. Copyright, 1929, by Payson & Clarke.

casualty of Ordynin was Classic-Spark, a loafer who committed suicide when the vodka ran out. Because the merchants of Ordynin refused to pay a sufficient bribe to the engineers who were laying the railroad tracks, the railway station was put some distance away. Ordynin was doomed to remain in the backwash of progress and change.

The Ratchin house was requisitioned by the Red Guard, and the salt market was broken up. Donat returned from the war full of hatred for the old order. He ordered that the salt building was to be destroyed and a house for the people erected in its place.

In the monastery Olly Kuntz printed blank orders for arrest and imprisonment. Arkhip, a peasant unused to writing, was in command, and frequently he laboriously penned orders of execution. Comrade Laitis took Olly to the cinema and saw her home. Later he came back with his soldiers to arrest Andrey, a lodger, but Andrey cleverly gave them the slip and got away. The soldiers broke into Olly's room when they searched the building, and Olly wept out of sympathy for Andrey. Semyon, a bookish man interested in masonry, was much impressed by Andrey's cleverness.

Old Arkhipov, Arkhip's father, went to see the doctor. His fears were confirmed when the doctor and Natalia Ordynin, his assistant, told him he had cancer of the stomach. At the moment Arkhipov decided that he must die, Arkhip was signing an execution warrant. That evening the father asked Arkhip's advice, and on his son's suggestion he shot himself in the mouth.

After two years Gleb returned to the manor. No one could remember whether the town was named for the Ordynin family or whether the family took its name from the town. At any rate the Ordynins had been lords for a long time; now the seal of Cain was on them. In the run-down house no one greeted Gleb, but soon Egor, his brother, half-naked and dirty, came stumbling in with the serv-ant Martha. Martha had found her master in a brothel and brought him home. Egor had paid for the spree by selling his sister Natalia's coat.

Gleb learned bad news. Earlier Boris, his older brother, had locked Egor in his room and then had raped Martha. Since Egor was half in love with her, the crime seemed serious. When Boris came into Gleb's room, Boris announced gloomily that he was suffering from syphilis, a family disease. Then Gleb thought of his lunatic father, a religious fanatic in his old age, and of the brothers and sisters who had died in infancy.

Arina, the mother, sold clothes and furniture to make ends meet. Natalia, already suspected of too much fondness for Arkhip, alienated herself from the family by going to live at the hospital where she worked. Catherine, the youngest daughter, was pregnant, and Lydia, the other sister, advised her to have an abortion. To her dismay, Catherine learned that she also had syphilis, but when she ran to Lydia for comfort, her sister, under the influence of morphine, paid little attention to her.

Andrey joined a brotherhood near the Black Streams. The peasant girls called him out to their dances at night and he was happy for a time. Aganka, the gayest and hardest-working of the girls, attracted him greatly, but she died during the hot summer. Smallpox and typhus broke out and all Russia suffered from pestilence and famine and war. Andrey became Irina's betrothed, although the comrades frowned on marriage as sentimental nonsense. Donat Ratchin was the unbending leader of their anarchistic commune.

The commune ceased to be a haven when the band of strangers arrived. Armed, they killed most of the men at the instigation of Harry, their English leader, and then rode on to join an uprising in the Ukraine. Andrey was lucky to get away.

Boris was furious at first when Ivan,

president of the poverty committee, requisitioned the Ordynin manor. He had known Ivan for years and despised him as an unlettered peasant. In a spirit of bravado Boris left home on foot. A friendly peasant gave him shelter the first night, but the apprehensive peasant made him leave early the next morning. Later that day Boris found space in a refugee wagon.

The famine became worse. The old men would barter with traveling merchants because there was no money to use in buying. There were no young men left to work; they had all gone off with the Reds or the Whites. People did anything they could for bread. At Mar Junction, the railway station, the Red Guards would often requisition young women who came in on the refugee train.

The Whites occupied Ordynin, and when they left the Reds swarmed back. All over the town committees and commissions sprang up. The Moscow functionaries even reopened a mine outside the town. Although the mine was a deathtrap because of its antique equipment, men were forced to work in it.

Arkhip, busy with his many duties, felt keenly his lack of education. Natalia, the only normal Ordynin, was a doctor under the new government. Arkhip had long known Natalia, and at last, needing an educated partner and wanting children, he asked her to marry him. Natalia thought of her university days, when she had been in love. It was a painful memory. She would welcome this new kind of mating, with no love and with no pain. But in spite of her resolutions she felt herself close to Arkhip and talked of the coziness of their union.

Arkhip went home and thumbed in vain through his dictionary. He did not know the word coziness, nor could he find it.

NANA

Type of work: Novel
Author: Émile Zola (1840-1902)
Type of plot: Naturalism
Time of plot: 1860's
Locale: Paris and rural France
First published: 1880

> Principal characters:
> NANA, a beautiful courtesan
> FAUCHERY, a dramatic critic
> STEINER, a wealthy banker
> GEORGE HUGON, a student
> PHILIPPE HUGON, his brother, an officer
> FONTAN, an actor
> COUNT MUFFAT DE BEUVILLE,
> SABINE, his wife
> MARQUIS DE CHOUARD, and
> COUNT XAVIER DE VANDEUVRES, well-known figures of the Parisian
>   world of art and fashion

Critique:

Nana, one of Zola's Rougon-Macquart series of novels picturing French life and society in the period from 1852 to 1870, was written to portray a successful courtesan not sentimentally or romantically but realistically. As Zola presents her, Nana is moronic, vulgar, greedy, and cruel, and her story is a sermon warning men against a devotion to lust. The novel is a powerful indictment of the social decay which marked the reign of Napoleon III.

The Story:

M. Fauchery, theatrical reviewer for a Paris paper, was attending the première of The Blonde Venus at the Variety Theatre because he had heard rumors of Nana, Venus of the new play.

Smart Paris was well represented at the theatre that night, and Fauchery and his cousin Hector de la Faloise noted a few of the more interesting people. In the audience were Steiner, a crooked but very rich banker who was the current lover of Rose Mignon, an actress in The Blonde Venus; Mignon, who served as procurer for his own wife; Daguenet, a reckless spender reputed to be Nana's lover for the moment; Count Xavier de Vandeuvres; Count Muffat de Beuville and his wife, and several of the city's well-known courtesans.

The play, a vulgar travesty on the life of the Olympian gods, was becoming boresome when Nana finally appeared, and with beautiful golden hair floating over her shoulders walked confidently toward the footlights for her feature song. When she began to sing, she seemed such a crude amateur that murmurs and hisses were beginning to sound. But suddenly a young student exclaimed loudly that she was stunning. Every one laughed, including Nana. It was as though she frankly admitted that she had nothing except her voluptuous self to offer. But Nana knew that was sufficient for her audience. As she ended her song she retired to the back of the stage amid a roar of applause. In the last act, Nana's body was veiled only by her golden locks and a transparent gauze. The house grew quiet and tense. Nana smiled confidently, knowing that she had conquered them with her marble-like flesh.

Thus Nana, product of the streets of Paris, started her career as mistress of the city. To get money for her scrofulous little son, Louis, and for her own extravagant wants, she sold herself at varying prices to many men. She captivated Steiner, the banker, at an all-night party after her initial success as Venus. He bought her a country place, La Mignotte, a league from Les Fondettes, home of Madame Hugon, whose seventeen-year-old son George had called Nana stunning the opening night of *The Blonde Venus* and who had been enraptured with her at Nana's party. Nana, making no pretense of belonging exclusively to Steiner, invited a number of friends to visit her at La Mignotte.

Madame Hugon entertained Count Muffat, his wife Sabine, and their daughter Estelle at her home in September. George, who had been expected several times during the summer, suddenly came home. He had invited Fauchery and Daguenet for a visit. M. de Vandeuvres, who had promised for five years to come to Les Fondettes, was likewise expected. Madame Hugon was unaware of any connection between the coming of Nana to La Mignotte and the simultaneous visits of all these men to Les Fondettes.

George escaped from his doting mother and went in the rain to Nana, who found him soaking wet as she was gathering strawberries in her garden. While his clothes were drying, he dressed in some of Nana's. Despite Nana's feeling that it was wrong to give herself to such an innocent boy, she finally submitted to George's entreaties — and she was faithful to him for almost a week.

Muffat, who had lived a circumspect life for forty years, became increasingly inflamed by passion as he paid nightly visits to Nana's place, only to be rebuffed each time. He talked with Steiner, who likewise was being put off by Nana with the excuse that she was not feeling well. Meanwhile Muffat's wife attracted the attention of Fauchery, the journalist.

Eleven of Nana's Parisian friends arrived in a group at La Mignotte. George was seen with Nana and her friends by his mother, who later made him promise not to visit the actress, a promise he had no intention of keeping. His brother

Philippe, an army officer, threatened to bring him back by his ears if he had anything more to do with Nana.

Being true to George was romantically pleasing, but financially it was unwise, and Nana at last gave herself to the persistent Muffat the night before she returned to Paris to see whether she could recapture the public that had acclaimed her in *The Blonde Venus*.

Three months later Muffat, who had taken the place of castoff George, was involved in financial troubles. During a quarrel with Nana he learned that his wife Sabine and Fauchery were making a cuckold of him. Nana, by turns irritated or bored by Muffat and then sorry for him, chose this means of avenging herself on Fauchery, who had written a scurrilous article entitled *The Golden Fly*, obviously about Nana herself.

Having broken with Muffat and Steiner, Nana gave up her place in the Boulevard Haussmann and went to live with the actor Fontan. But Fontan became increasingly difficult and even vicious, beating her night after night and taking all her money. Nana returned to her old profession of streetwalking to pick up a few francs. After a close brush with the police, Nana grew more discreet. Also, she left the brutal Fontan and sought a part as a grand lady in a new play at the Variety Theatre. Given the part, she failed miserably in it; but she began to play the lady in real life in a richly decorated house which Muffat purchased for her. Despite Nana's callous treatment of him, Muffat could not stay away from her.

In her mansion in the Avenue de Villiers Nana squandered money in great sums. Finding Muffat's gifts insufficient, she added Count Xavier de Vandeuvres as a lover. She planned to get eight or ten thousand francs a month from him for pocket money. George Hugon reappeared, but he was less interesting than he had once been. When Philippe Hugon tried to extricate his young brother from Nana's net, he also was caught. Nana grew bored. From the streets one day she picked up the slut Satin, who became her vice.

In a race for the Grand Prize of Paris at Longchamps, Nana won two thousand louis on a horse named for her. But de Vandeuvres, who owned the filly Nana as well as the favorite Lusignan, lost everything through some crooked betting. He set fire to his stable and died with his horses.

Muffat found Nana in George's arms one evening in September and from that time he ceased to believe in her sworn fidelity. Yet he became more and more her abject slave, submitting meekly when Nana forced him to play woolly bear, horse, and dog with her, and then mocked his ridiculous nudity. Muffat was further degraded when he discovered Nana in bed with his father-in-law, the ancient Marquis de Chouard.

George, jealous of his brother Philippe, stabbed himself in Nana's bedroom when she refused to marry him. He died of his self-inflicted wound and Nana was briefly sorry for him. This utterly evil woman also broke Philippe. He was imprisoned for stealing army funds to spend on her.

Nana thrived on those she destroyed. It was fate which caught her at last. Visiting her dying son after a long absence and many conquests in foreign lands, she caught smallpox from him and died horribly in a Paris hospital. The once-beautiful body which had destroyed so many men lay like a rotting ruin in a deserted room as outside there sounded the French battlecry. The Franco-Prussian war of 1870 had begun.

THE NAPOLEON OF NOTTING HILL

Type of work: Novel
Author: Gilbert Keith Chesterton (1874-1936)
Type of plot: Fantasy
Time of plot: Late twentieth century
Locale: London
First published: 1904

> Principal characters:
> AUBERON QUINN, King of England
> ADAM WAYNE, Provost of Notting Hill
> MR. TURNBULL, a general
> BUCK, Provost of North Kensington

Critique:

Although *The Napoleon of Notting Hill* is at first glance an amiable fantasy and satire on staid government, its appeal to romance is a solid criticism of seriousness. In the early twentieth century, when Great Britain was at the height of a peaceful prosperity, it seemed that law and order would eventually swallow up eccentricity and puckish fun. Chesterton rebelled against orderly progress from precedent to precedent and struck a vigorous blow for human worth. As prediction his novel is undoubtedly false, but what he envisioned as desirable is far preferable to what we have in our own time.

The Story:

Although they were his friends, Barker and Lambert often considered Quinn a fool, even a dangerous man, for he persisted in seeing the ludicrous where they saw only the grave. On this particular afternoon Quinn was walking behind his two friends, and as he saw the buttons on their tail coats, he thought them very much like dragon's eyes. Forever afterward he thought of their backs as two dragons shuffling to the rear.

By the end of the twentieth century such imagination was scarcely appreciated. The whole world had become orderly. The smaller nations had disappeared, and among the larger nations Great Britain was by far the most extensive and best organized. The king was now chosen by lot instead of by heredity on the theory that anybody could be a good king. Parliament was only a memory of the days when government was a tedious process. As a reflection of the times, every one wore sober, uniform clothing. Armies and wars were almost forgotten.

During their walk Quinn and his friends were astonished to see a fine looking man in a green military uniform decorated with many insignia. The man was attracting a good deal of attention, for the people had never seen brilliant clothes before. When Lambert and Barker invited the man to dinner, they learned that he was the ex-president of Nicaragua, the last small state to be conquered. They considered the ex-president an affable, saddened man. He still believed firmly in the right of individuals and of states to be different, but he was obviously very old-fashioned in his thinking. In fact, after they argued with him and showed him the current reasoned view, he went out and committed suicide.

Quinn, later on, was as usual entertaining his friends with pointless quixotic stories. Barker and Lambert listened patiently at first, but the meaning of the vague stories always eluded them. At last, in exasperation, they told Quinn to go stand on his head. To their surprise, Quinn did so, and competently. While he was thus attracting attention from the passers-by, some policemen came up. Thinking they were to be reprimanded, all began to apologize. But the policemen brought word that Quinn had been chosen king. Barker protested loudly that

Britain had no need to choose a buffoon as king. Quinn, however, was quite willing to be a king. He immediately styled himself King Auberon.

One day the king was taking a stroll when a boy of nine in a cocked hat struck him smartly with a wooden sword. Instead of punishing the boy, Auberon gave him a coin and complimented him on his knightly bearing. The sight of the boy in his make-believe armor gave the king an idea for bringing life and joy to staid London.

As soon as he could, he appeared before a historical society with his great innovation. All the districts of London which had been cities in earlier days were to be returned to their former autonomy. North Kensington, South Kensington, Notting Hill—all were to have a provost as their chief official. The provosts were to be garbed in medieval splendor and were to be accompanied by an honorary guard armed with halberds. Although the announcement was received with incredulity at first, the people humored their fanciful king. One provost objected to the guards, however, on the grounds that when he was obliged to take a bus, often there were no seats for his henchmen.

Ten years later the plan was still in effect. One day the Provost of North Kensington, who was in private life Mr. Buck, a linen draper, came to the king with a serious and angry face. A new highway through London was being planned, and the Provost of Notting Hill refused to sell the land necessary for a right of way. Soon other provosts came in to second Mr. Buck's complaint. The Provost of Notting Hill, they complained, was taking his office much too seriously; the offer for the land was more than fair, and anyway Notting Hill was little more than a slum. The king in a puckish mood upheld the independence of Notting Hill. He was interested to hear that the stubborn provost was Adam Wayne, once a nine-year-old boy with a wooden sword.

The difficulty arose from the fact that young Wayne had never been out of London, and he thought Notting Hill the most beautiful place in the world. Imbued with chivalric ideals, he had no intention of allowing a modern highway to run through his beloved narrow streets. To get help in his fight to preserve his domain, he visited the merchants in his territory. He found them apathetic to their peril. They were interested only in making money.

The one kindred spirit he found was Mr. Turnbull, who kept a toy shop. Mr. Turnbull had a collection of lead soldiers and a brick model of Notting Hill. With the enthusiastic toy dealer, Wayne sat down to plan the defense of Notting Hill. Coöperation was the easier to get because Wayne promised to make Turnbull a high officer in the army.

Mr. Buck reasoned out that Notting Hill could muster at best only two hundred defenders. If he could lead five or six hundred men against them, it was mathematically certain that the Notting Hill stronghold could be taken and the highway would go through. At dusk, thinking to have an easy conquest, he marched his men against the district. But Wayne had shut off the gas and plunged the streets into darkness. The cunning defenders of Notting Hill then fell on the attackers with halberds and swords.

After this defeat the other provosts combined a larger force and in broad daylight attacked again. This time they could find no opposition. While they were searching everywhere for the small Notting Hill forces, Wayne again used superior strategy. Giving a half crown to all boys he could find, he ordered the urchins to hire hansom cabs and have the drivers come to the heart of Notting Hill. Then Wayne kept the horses and used the carriages to construct a barricade around the center of his district. Amply provisioned, the defenders prepared to sit out a siege.

As more attackers came to join battle, it looked at last as if Notting Hill must fall. Once again Wayne was equal to the occasion. He sent out word that if the besiegers did not withdraw at once, he would open the reservoir and flood the narrow streets.

Sullenly the men from the other districts acknowledged their defeat for the time being. Again they prepared for a fresh attack. At last all of London was ready. With banners flying and with axes and halberds held high, the soldiers closed in on Notting Hill. Wayne knew his defeat was at hand. King Auberon, admiring the resurgence of local pride, went into the thick of things as a reporter. He was knocked down and left for dead on the ground. Wayne also fell mortally wounded. And so Notting Hill was taken.

Afterward, as disembodied voices, Auberon and Wayne compared notes. The king had brought laughter to London, Wayne had brought love. They were content.·

THE NARRATIVE OF ARTHUR GORDON PYM

Type of work: Short story
Author: Edgar Allan Poe (1809-1849)
Type of plot: Adventure romance
Time of plot: Early nineteenth century
Locale: High seas
First published: 1838

Principal characters:
ARTHUR GORDON PYM, an adventurer
AUGUSTUS BARNARD, his friend
DIRK PETERS, a sailor

Critique:

Presented as the journal of Arthur Gordon Pym, this story is one of those celebrated literary hoaxes so well suited to Poe's talents and taste. The model of the story is the Gothic tale of horror, and in its effects of terror and the unbelievable it equals any other of Poe's tales. It includes such matters as the eating of human flesh and the discovery of human life in regions where the map of the world shows only sea waste. In all other respects the story illustrates the remarkable ability of the writer to simulate the truth when dealing with the unnatural or the supernatural.

The Story:

Arthur Gordon Pym was born the son of a respectable trader at Nantucket. While still young he attended an academy and there met Augustus Barnard, the son of a sea captain, and the two became close friends. One night after a party Augustus awoke Pym from his sleep and together they set off for the harbor. There, Augustus took charge of a small boat and they headed out to sea.

Before long, Pym, seeing that his companion was unconscious, realized the sad truth of the escapade. Augustus had been drunk, and now in the cold weather was lapsing into insensibility. As a result their boat was run down by a whaler and the two narrowly escaped with their lives. They were taken aboard the ship which had run them down and returned to port at Nantucket.

The two friends became even more intimate after this escapade. Captain Barnard was at that time preparing to fit out the *Grampus,* an old sailing hulk, for a voyage on which Augustus was to accompany him. Against his father's wishes, Pym planned to sail with his friend. Since Captain Barnard would not willingly allow Pym to sail without his father's permission, the two boys decided to smuggle Pym aboard and hide him in the hold until the ship should be so far at sea the captain would not turn back.

At first everything went according to schedule. Pym was hidden below in a large box with a store of water and food to last him approximately four days. Great was his consternation to discover, at the end of the fourth day, that his way to the main deck was barred. His friend Augustus did not appear to rescue him. In that terrible state he remained for several days, coming each day closer to starvation or death from thirst.

At last his dog, which had followed Pym aboard the ship, found his way to his master. Tied to the dog's body was a paper containing a strange message concerning blood and a warning to Pym to keep silent if he valued his life.

Pym was sick from hunger and fever when Augustus at last appeared. The story he had to tell was a terrible one. Shortly after the ship had put to sea the crew had mutinied, and Captain Barnard had been set adrift in a small boat. Some of the crew had been killed, and Augustus himself was a prisoner of

2516

the mutineers. Pym and Augustus located a place of comparative safety where it was agreed Pym should hide.

Pym now began to give his attention to the cargo, which seemed not to have been stowed in accordance with the rules for safety. Dirk Peters, a drunken mutineer, helped both Pym and Augustus and provided them with food.

When the ship ran into a storm, some of the mutineers were washed overboard. Augustus was once more given free run of the ship. Augustus, Pym, and Peters planned to overcome the other mutineers and take possession of the ship. To frighten the mutineers during a drunken brawl, Pym disguised himself to resemble a sailor recently killed. The three killed all of the mutineers except a sailor named Parker. Meanwhile a gale had come up, and in a few hours the vessel was reduced to a hulk by the heavy seas. Because the ship's cargo was made up of empty oil casks, there was no possibility of its sinking from the violence of the heavy seas. When the storm abated, the four survivors found themselves weak and without food or the hope of securing stores from the flooded hold. One day a vessel was sighted, but as it drew near those aboard the *Grampus* saw that it was adrift and all of its passengers were dead.

Pym tried to go below by diving, but he brought up nothing of worth. His companions were beginning to go mad from strain and hunger. Pym revived them by immersing each of them in the water for awhile. As their agony increased, a ship came near, but it veered away without coming to their rescue.

In desperation the men considered the possibility of eating one of their number. When they drew lots, Parker was chosen to be eaten. For four days the other three lived upon his flesh.

At last they made their way into the stores and secured food. Rain fell, and the supply of fresh water, together with the food, restored their hope. Augustus, who had suffered an arm injury, died. He was devoured by sharks as soon as his body was cast overboard.

A violent lurch of the ship threw Pym overboard, but he regained the ship with Peters' help just in time to be saved from sharks. The floating hulk having overturned at last, the two survivors fed upon barnacles. Finally, when they were nearly dead of thirst, a British ship came to their rescue. It was the *Jane Guy* of Liverpool, bound on a sealing and trading voyage to the South Seas and Pacific.

Peters and Pym began to recover. Within two weeks they were able to look back upon their horrible experiences with almost the same feeling with which one recollects terrible dreams.

The vessel stopped at Christmas Harbor, where some seals and sea elephants were killed for their hides. The captain was anxious to sail his vessel into Antarctica on a voyage of exploration. The weather turned cold. There was an adventure with a huge bear which Peters killed in time to save his companions. Scurvy afflicted the crew. Once the captain decided to turn northward, but later he foolishly took the advice of Pym to continue on. They sailed until they sighted land and encountered some savages whom they took aboard.

The animals on the island were strange, and the water was of some peculiar composition which Pym could not readily understand. The natives on that strange coast lived in a state of complete savagery. Bartering began. Before the landing party could depart, however, the sailors were trapped in what seemed to be an earthquake, which shut off their passage back to the shore. Only Pym and Peters escaped, to learn that the natives had caused the tremendous earth slide by pulling great boulders from the top of a towering cliff. The only white men left on the island, they were faced by the problem of evading the natives, who were now preparing to attack the ship. Unable to warn their comrades, Pym and Peters could only watch helplessly while the savages boarded the *Jane Guy* and overcame the six white men who had remained aboard. The ship was almost demolished. The savages brought about their own destruction, however, for in exploring the ship they set off the ammunition and the resulting explosion killed about a thousand of them.

In making their escape from the island Pym and Peters discovered ruins similar in form to those marking the site of Babylon. When they came upon two unguarded canoes, they took possession of one and pushed out to sea. Savages chased them but eventually gave up the pursuit. They began to grow listless and sleepy when their canoe entered a warm sea. Ashy material fell continually around and upon them. At last the boat rushed rapidly into a cataract, and a human figure, much larger than any man and as white as snow, arose in the pathway of the doomed boat. So ended the journal of Arthur Gordon Pym.

A NARRATIVE OF THE LIFE OF DAVID CROCKETT

Type of work: Autobiography
Author: David Crockett (1786-1836)
Type of plot: History and adventure
Time of plot: 1780-1834
Locale: Tennessee
First published: 1834

Principal character:
DAVID CROCKETT, the narrator

Critique:

Davy Crockett has long been a familiar figure in American history. As a hunter and frontiersman he is often likened to Daniel Boone, and his heroic death at the Alamo has stirred our imaginations. Whatever charm this autobiography may have must rest in the reader's interest in Crockett himself, for the book is almost graceless. Crockett seldom locates places, gives dates, or names people. Even his two wives are never called by name. The sections dealing with the Creek War are almost completely flat. We see Crockett as a petulant hater of Andrew Jackson and a slaughterer of bears. Yet because of the author, and the picture of frontier life he presents, the book is an important document in our American past.

The Story:

Crockett claimed that he wrote his own story because a spurious autobiography had been circulated concerning his exploits. He had never had much schooling, and the writing was likely to be ungrammatical. But Crockett had become a figure by reason of his frontier life and his election to Congress. Those people who admired a real man who was no follower of Andrew Jackson were asked to take the narrative kindly.

John Crockett was born either in Ireland or on a ship bound for America. The earlier part of his life was spent in Pennsylvania. Rebecca Hawkins was born in Maryland. After John served in the Revolutionary War, he and Rebecca settled in Tennessee, a dangerous and troubled region. John's parents were killed by the Creek Indians, one of his brothers was captured, and another was wounded.

David, son of John and Rebecca, was born on August 17, 1786. His earliest recollection was of a near tragedy. He was playing on the bank of a river with his four older brothers and a older friend of fifteen. The five bigger boys got into the Crockett canoe for a lark. All would have been well if any of the Crockett boys had been paddling, but the fifteen-year-old asserted his authority and took the paddle. David watched from the shore as the boy let the canoe drift closer to a rapids. Fortunately, a neighbor working nearby saw the danger and waded out just in time to keep the canoe out of the treacherous rapids.

The Crockett family, dirt poor in that border area, moved several times before David was twelve, each time seeking a better living. At last John established a tavern on the road to Knoxville. The customers were largely wagoners. One day a Dutchman driving a herd of cattle stopped by, and John bound David over to him. The boy made a trip of over four hundred miles on foot to help the Dutchman deliver cattle.

At the end of the trip David was paid five or six dollars. He wanted to go home then, but his master ordered him to stay. Not knowing any better, David thought himself forced to remain with the Dutchman. But the plucky boy watched his chance and told his story to some friendly wagoners. They agreed to take him home if he could escape the Dutchman. In the middle of the night David crept away, and by riding in the wagons and walking a great deal, he eventually got back home.

John thought David should get some book learning. A neighbor had opened a school nearby, and David attended classes for four days. Then he had a fight with a bigger boy and was afraid of the beating the teacher would administer. Each day he hid out in the woods when he was supposed to be in school. When John discovered what David had been doing, he took after the boy with a hickory stick. David ran away, determined to avoid a beating.

Finding work here and there, David lived somehow. For months he helped a wagoner who kept his meager pay in trust for him. When the wagoner made a trip to the neighborhood of Baltimore, David resolved to look over the city. He was enchanted by the large ships in the harbor. Screwing up his courage, he went aboard a ship and had a talk with the captain. When he was offered a place as cabin boy on a voyage to England, he accepted joyfully. But when he returned to the wagoner to quit and collect his wages, his employer kept him by force from leaving and refused to turn over the money.

After some time he got away from his brutish wagoner and started the long trip home. Obtaining employment with a kindlier wagoner, David told his woes. Sympathetic people collected a purse of three dollars, and David thought himself amply provided for. Finally after a long succession of odd jobs, he got back home. He was fifteen years old. The family was still scrimping to get along in the tavern.

David worked out for various neighbors to pay off debts contracted by his father. At the end of a year his father was free and clear, but David kept on working for wages, as his clothes were worn out. One of his employers was a Quaker with a pretty niece to whom David paid court. When she at last told him she was already engaged, David was quick to leave his job.

Next he courted a neighbor girl who seemed pleased with his advances. When David proposed to her, she accepted and set a date for the wedding. The day

before the marriage was to take place, David went part way to her house to stay overnight with another neighbor. There his intended's sister met him with the news that his fiancée had been married the day before to another man.

Nothing daunted, David with the help of friends was introduced to an Irish family with a marriageable daughter. Although at first the mother liked David, she turned against him as a son-in-law. She relented only after David prepared to take the girl away to be married at his house. With some calves, a few store articles, and his gun David settled his bride in an outlying cabin.

After the birth of his second son news came that the Creeks were on the warpath. Even though his wife objected, David left to join the militia. Soon his superior marksmanship and his knowledge of the woods made David a leader of the soldiers pursuing the Creeks. During the campaign the greatest hardship was hunger. In one engagement the militia trapped and burned to death forty-six Creeks in a log cabin. Afterward, hearing that potatoes had been stored in the cellar, David went back and rescued the supplies.

For nearly a year the whites pursued the Indians, killing all the Creeks they could find and burning their towns. At the end of the year the rebellion was crushed. Having had his fill of fighting, David returned home.

When his wife died, David was left with two sons and an infant daughter. Finding it impossible to live without a helpmate, he married a widow with two children. She had a tidy farm and David became a man of substance. In spite of his lack of education, he was successively a magistrate and a member of the legislature. He had good ability at vote getting, chiefly because he offered liquor and chewing tobacco to his constituents and told them racy stories.

By that time David had a mill and a distillery. During the spring floods his buildings were washed away. Once more a poor man, David took up new land farther west. There he gained great renown as a bear hunter, killing one hundred and five bears in a year. He was also elected to the legislature from his new territory.

David's reputation as a hunter and story-teller kept him in politics for a long time. He was shrewd enough to learn something of government by listening, and at last he passed for an able man.

After being defeated once, he was elected to Congress, where he fought valiantly for the interests of his border region. He was proudest of the fact that he voted according to his conscience only, and put foremost the interests of his beloved Tennessee. Above all, he was one man who never knuckled down to Andrew Jackson.

NATHAN THE WISE

Type of work: Drama
Author: Gotthold Ephraim Lessing (1729-1781)
Type of plot: Philosophic humanism
Time of plot: Twelfth century
Locale: Jerusalem
First published: 1779

Principal characters:
NATHAN, a Jewish merchant
RECHA, his adopted daughter
SULTAN SALADIN, son of the ruler of all the Saracens
SITTAH, his sister
CONRAD VON STAUFFEN, a Templar who was spared by the Sultan
DAJA, a Christian woman and Recha's companion

Critique:

Nathan the Wise is a fitting climax to a great career, a deeply humane verse drama expressing Lessing's philosophy of enlightenment and tolerance. The protagonist, a rich Jewish merchant, is based on and a tribute to the playwright's good friend, the humanitarian Moses Mendelssohn, grandfather of the composer. The high point of this interesting play occurs when Nathan relates the famous folk parable, found in both the *Decameron* and the *Gesta Romanorum,* of the three rings which represent the three major religious faiths. The true faith (ring) is that one which best serves mankind, Lessing suggests, thereby writing an eloquent plea for religious tolerance and freedom.

The Story:

Nathan, a wealthy Jewish merchant, had just returned to Jerusalem from Babylon when Daja, the deeply prejudiced Christian companion to the Jew's adopted daughter, a girl orphaned during the Third Crusade, told him of the dramatic rescue of his beloved Recha from their burning house. Nathan, in spite of the fact that he had suffered severely at the hands of Christians and Saracens alike, wished to reward the young man who had so courageously saved the girl's life. His benefactor proved to be a young Templar who recently had been pardoned by the sultan.

Each day, at Recha's urging, Daja had attempted to thank and reward the brave young man as he made a daily visit to Christ's tomb, but each time he rudely repulsed her. Recha, as the result of shock over her narrow escape as much as from gratitude to her benefactor, suffered hallucinations in which she believed that the young Templar was her guardian angel. Nathan thought it miraculous that Sultan Saladin should spare a Christian knight's life or that the Templar would desire to be so spared. The truth was that the Saracen's leniency had been based on the young man's resemblance to his own dead brother Assad.

Daja, told by Nathan to seek out the young man and invite him to their home, found him in a bad mood after rejecting a friar's request from King Philip that he spy on and murder Saladin, a treacherous deed he vehemently refused to consider. The knight again told Daja that he had performed his rescue of Recha through whim and therefore would accept no reward. Nathan then met with and begged the youth, a penniless stranger in a strange land, to accept aid and friendship. Boorish though the young knight was, he offered to let Nathan buy him a mantle to replace his own burned in the fire. At this suggestion the Jew shed a tear and dissolved the intolerant Templar's disdain and suspicion. On this note they shook hands, friends. Nathan learned that the young man was Conrad von Stauffen, a name somehow associated in the Jew's mind with the name Filneck, but before he could inquire further the Jew received a message demanding his presence at the sultan's palace.

The young knight, in the meantime, called on Recha. Something immediately drew them together, some mutual feeling not unlike romantic love. He hastened off, however, to avert any disaster which might befall Nathan at the hand of Saladin, who had summoned the Jew to obtain from him money to replenish the treasury so that the war against the crusaders might continue. To put the Jew somewhat at a disadvantage, Saladin asked enlightenment from this man called the Wise (which Nathan denied he was) on the paradox of the several "true" religions.

Nathan then told the story of the father who possessed a ring traditionally passed on to the favorite son who would then be lord of the house. Since he loved his three sons equally well (as the Father in heaven loves us all, said Nathan), the father made exact copies of the ring and gave one to each son. None knew which was the true ring, and after the father's death a controversy arose. But the problem of the "true" ring could be resolved no more than the argument over the "true" faith—Jewish, Christian, or Mohammedan. A judge suggested that each son act as if his were the true ring and live and rule as well as he could. Finally, generations hence, it would be decided in a higher, greater court, with religions as with the ring, which was the true one.

When Nathan returned from the palace, young Conrad von Stauffen asked for Recha's hand in marriage. Astounded, Nathan said that he could not consent without due reflection. Daja, on an amorous mission, told the Templar that Recha had been born Christian but had been reared as a Jewess, a crime punishable by death. The Templar assumed that she had been stolen from her proper parents. Dismayed by Daja's story, the knight guardedly asked counsel of the Patriarch of Jerusalem, who said that in such a case the Jew must die at the stake for holding back salvation from an innocent child. Perplexed and unhappy, the young man went to confer with the sultan.

Saladin, amazed at such accusations, refused to believe ill of Nathan and asked the Christian to exercise prudence and charity. As the young Templar left to save Nathan from the patriarch's wrath, the sultan and his sister remarked the resemblance the young man bore to their long-lost brother, believed dead.

In the meantime a friar sent to spy on Nathan revealed that eighteen years ago he, the friar, then a squire, delivered Recha to the Jew for his master, Lord Wolf von Filneck, who was later killed in battle; the child's mother, a von Stauffen, was already dead. Nathan confided that his own wife and seven sons had been killed by Christians only shortly before he adopted Recha as his own, an act which saved his sanity and restored his faith in God.

Saladin, who favored the marriage of the two young people, then learned from Nathan that Wolf von Filneck's breviary, turned over to Nathan by the friar, contained a strange story. Crusader Filneck's rightful name was Assad. The sultan's brother, having married a Christian and accepted her faith, had left his son to his deceased wife's brother, Conrad von Stauffen, after whom he was named. The boy's sister he left indirectly to Nathan. The Jewish child and the Christian child both were Mohammedans; their uncle was a sultan, and their godfather was a wise man and a Jew.

NATIVE SON

Type of work: Novel
Author: Richard Wright (1908-1960)
Type of plot: Social criticism
Time of plot: 1930's
Locale: An American city
First published: 1940

Principal characters:

BIGGER THOMAS, a young Negro
MR. DALTON, Bigger's employer
MRS. DALTON, Mr. Dalton's wife
MARY DALTON, their daughter
JAN ERLONE, Mary's sweetheart
BRITTEN, Dalton's private detective
BESSIE MEARS, Bigger's mistress
BUCKLEY, state prosecutor
BORIS A. MAX, Bigger's lawyer

Critique:

Written in simple, unadorned English, Native Son succeeds in unfolding human emotions of the most primitive and sensuous nature. Richard Wright attempts in this story to create mutual understanding between his own race and the white. Bigger Thomas is not merely one twenty-year-old boy; he is an entire race. Native Son shows that the underprivileged Negro is either the church-loyal, praying, submissive type or the embittered, criminal type. The sociological pleading of the novel is subordinate, however, to the drama of a boy who finds freedom through killing and who learns the meaning of life by facing death.

The Story:

In a one-room apartment Bigger Thomas lived with his brother, sister, and mother. Always penniless, haunted by a pathological hatred of white people, driven by an indescribable urge to make others cringe before him, Bigger had retreated into an imaginary world of fantasy.

Through the aid of a relief agency he obtained employment as a chauffeur for a wealthy family. His first assignment was to drive Mary Dalton, his employer's daughter, to the university. Mary, how-

ever, was on her way to meet Jan Erlone, her sweetheart. The three of them, Mary and Jan, white people who were crusading with the Communist Party to help the black people, and Bigger, a reluctant ally, spent the evening driving and drinking. When Bigger brought Mary home, she was too drunk to take herself to bed. With a confused medley of hatred, fear, disgust, and revenge playing within his mind, Bigger helped her to her bedroom. When Mary's blind mother entered the room, Bigger covered the girl's face with a pillow to keep her from making any sound that might arouse Mrs. Dalton's suspicions. The reek of whiskey convinced Mrs. Dalton that Mary was drunk, and she left the room. Then Bigger discovered that he had smothered Mary to death. To delay discovery of his crime, he took the body to the basement and stuffed it into the furnace.

Bigger began a weird kind of rationalization. The next morning in his mother's home he began thinking that he was separated from his family because he had killed a white girl. His plan was to involve Jan in connection with Mary's death.

When Bigger returned to the Dalton home, the family was worrying over Mary's absence. Bigger felt secure from incrimination because he had covered his activities by lying. He decided to send ransom notes to her parents, allowing them to think Mary had been kidnaped. But there were too many facts to remember, too many lies to tell. Britten, the detective whom Mr. Dalton had hired, tried to intimidate Bigger, but his methods only made Bigger more determined to frame Jan, who in his desire to protect Mary lied just enough to help Bigger's cause. When Britten brought Bigger face to face with Jan for questioning, Bigger's fear mounted. He went to Bessie, his mistress, who wrung from him a confession of murder. Bigger forced her to go with him to hide in an empty building in the slum section of the city. There he instructed her to pick up the ransom money he hoped to receive from Mr. Dalton.

Bigger was eating in the Dalton kitchen when the ransom note arrived. Jan had already been arrested. Bigger clung tenaciously to his lies. It was a cold day. Attempting to build up the fire, Bigger accidentally drew attention to the furnace. When reporters discovered Mary's bones, Bigger fled. Hiding with Bessie in the deserted building, he realized that he could not take her away with him. Afraid to leave her behind to be found and questioned by the police, he killed her and threw her body down an air shaft.

When Bigger ventured from his hideout to steal a newspaper, he learned that the city was being combed to find him. He fled from one empty building to another, constantly buying or stealing newspapers so that he could know his chances for escape. Finally he was trapped on the roof of a penthouse by a searching policeman. Bigger knocked him out with the butt of the gun he had been carrying with him. The police finally captured Bigger after a chase across the rooftops.

In jail Bigger refused to eat or speak. His mind turned inward, hating the world, but he was satisfied with himself for what he had done. Three days later

Jan Erlone came to see Bigger and promised to help him. Jan introduced Boris A. Max, a lawyer from the Communist front organization for which Jan worked.

Buckley, the prosecuting attorney, tried to persuade Bigger not to become involved with the Communists. Bigger said nothing even after the lawyer told him that Bessie's body had been found. But when Buckley began listing crimes of rape, murder, and burglary which had been charged against him, Bigger protested, vigorously denying rape and Jan's part in Mary's death. Under a steady fire of questions from Buckley, Bigger broke down and signed a confession.

The opening session of the grand jury began. First Mrs. Dalton appeared as a witness to identify one of her daughter's earrings, which had been found in the furnace. Next Jan testified, and under the slanderous anti-Communist questioning, Max rose in protest against the racial bigotry of the coroner. Max questioned Mr. Dalton about his ownership of the high-rent rat-infested tenements where Bigger's family lived. Generally, the grand jury session became a trial of the race relations which had led to Bigger's crime rather than a trial of the crime itself. As a climax to the session the coroner brought Bessie's body into the courtroom in order to produce evidence that Bigger had raped and murdered his Negro sweetheart. Bigger was returned to jail after Max had promised to visit him. Under the quiet questioning of Max, Bigger at last was able to talk about his crime, his feelings, his reasons. He had been thwarted by white people all his life, he said, until he had killed Mary Dalton; that act had released him.

At the opening session of the trial Buckley presented witnesses who attested Bigger's sanity and his ruthless character. The murder was dramatized even to the courtroom reconstruction of the furnace in which Mary's body had been burned. Max refused to call any of his own witnesses or to cross-examine, promising to act in Bigger's behalf as sole witness for the defense. The next day in a long speech Max outlined an entire social structure, its effect on an individual such as Bigger, and Bigger's particular inner compulsions when he killed Mary Dalton. Pleading for mitigation on the grounds that Bigger was not totally responsible for his crime, he argued that society was also to blame.

After another race-prejudiced attack by Buckley, the court adjourned for one hour. It reopened to sentence Bigger to death. Max's attempts to delay death by appealing to the governor were unsuccessful.

In the last hours before death Bigger realized his one hope was to communicate his feelings to Max, to try to have Max explain to him the meaning of his life and his death. Max helped him see that the men who persecuted Negroes, poor people, or others, are themselves filled with fear. Bigger could forgive them because they were suffering the same urge that he had suffered. He could forgive his enemies because they did not know the guilt of their own social crimes.